Additional Praise for
WHAT THE (BLEEP) JUST HAPPENED . . . AGAIN?

"A rip-roaring, full blast, raise-the-roof, sidesplitting account of what the (bleep) just happened over the past few years—and how we can get our country back. A literary twenty-one-gun salute to freedom."
—*Mark Levin*

"This is the book Barack Obama and his pals don't want you to read. Crowley has the guts to tell the truth about the damage they've inflicted. No sugarcoating. No political correctness. Just the facts—and they're damning. *This book is pure dynamite.*"   —*Sean Hannity*

"Monica Crowley wants to wage war against forces that would wipe out traditional America. But what's different in her book is the positive attitude she brings. You'll be happy to read her words. No (bleep)!"
—*Bill O'Reilly*

"Can this nation be saved? Monica Crowley answers with a resounding 'yes!' in this brilliant, hilarious page-turner that may well—in fact, *should*—influence the very future of America."—*Larry Kudlow*

"A brilliant and persuasive analysis of the relentless assault by the Obama administration on the principles that have made America the most exceptional nation in the world. And, a very well-developed presentation of rational optimism—*the happy warrior*—as the process for restoring American ideals."
—*Rudolph Giuliani*

WHAT THE (BLEEP) JUST HAPPENED ... AGAIN?

THE HAPPY WARRIOR'S GUIDE TO THE GREAT AMERICAN COMEBACK

MONICA CROWLEY

BROADSIDE BOOKS
An Imprint of HarperCollinsPublishers
www.broadsidebooks.net

HarperCollins books may be purchased for educational, business, or sales promotional use. For information, please e-mail the Special Markets Department at SPsales@harpercollins.com.

Broadside Books™ and the Broadside logo are trademarks of HarperCollins Publishers.

A hardcover edition of this book was published in a slightly different form as *What the (Bleep) Just Happened?* in 2012 by Broadside Books, an imprint of HarperCollins Publishers.

FIRST BROADSIDE BOOKS PAPERBACK EDITION PUBLISHED 2013

Library of Congress Cataloging-in-Publication Data has been applied for.

ISBN: 978-0-06-213130-0

13 14 15 16 17   OV/RRD   10 9 8 7 6 5 4 3 2 1

FOR MY COUNTRY

If ever the Time should come, when vain & aspiring
Men shall possess the highest Seats in Government,
our Country will stand in Need of its experienced
Patriots to prevent its Ruin.

—Samuel Adams, 1780

CONTENTS

PREFACE

Several weeks before the 2012 election, I noticed that one of my neighbors had slapped a sticker on her apartment door: OBAMA/BIDEN 2012. In order for me to get home each day, I had to walk by that sticker, which also declared that the incumbents would lead us "Forward!" This neighbor had placed a similar sticker on her door in 2008, and at that time, I had a sinking feeling that she was supporting the winning side.

Not this time, however. I had seen the polls, most of which showed either a tied race or Governor Mitt Romney and Congressman Paul Ryan slightly ahead of President Barack Obama and Vice President Joseph Biden. I had traveled to many swing states to speak at big rallies and to talk with voters. In 2008 I had hoped Senator John McCain had a chance to defeat Barack Obama but knew deep down it wasn't likely. In 2012, however, the situation felt completely different: the energy for Romney-Ryan was very real, much of the polling seemed to reflect it, and there seemed to be a stronger than even chance that the Republican ticket could really win.

That's why every time I passed her door, I nodded in the direction of the sticker and said to myself (and sometimes out loud), "Don't be so sure this time, missy . . ."

On election night, November 6, 2012, I was on the air at Fox News for a while and then joined some friends to watch the later results come in. As state after state was called for President Obama, I headed home, drowning in a sense of profound depression and utter disbelief. This couldn't really be happening, right? I—and so many others—weren't seeing things when we looked at the pre-election polling and saw the size of the Romney campaign rallies and felt the dynamism on the GOP side. How could all of that have been so misleading? How could our assumptions—and our gut feelings—have been so incorrect? How could we all have been so off?

As I passed my neighbor's door and began to put my key in my lock, I heard her whooping with joy and yelping, "Oh my God! We did it! I can't believe it! I just can't believe it!"

I couldn't believe it either. My heart sank. Tears sprung to my eyes. The race had just been called for Obama, and I knew that from that moment on, America would be a far different place.

———

It is profoundly disturbing to watch a once great power commit suicide in real time.

There have been many arguments made about why Mitt Romney (and so many other Republicans) lost that night: the Republicans ran poor campaigns; Romney played it too safe; Obama ran a more effective campaign; the Democrats' bogus "war on women" worked; Republicans failed to "talk" effectively to women and Latinos and black voters . . . and on and on. Some of the analysis and criticisms are legitimate, others less so. But they all represent secondary points compared to the tectonic shifts happening in the country.

A slight majority—but a majority—of the American people *knowingly* chose four more years (at least) of high unemployment, anemic economic growth, break-the-bank spending, unsustainable and record-breaking deficits and debt, unpopular and bankrupting socialized medicine, and record numbers of people on food stamps and living in poverty. They *knowingly* chose four more years . . . of that.

Some have attributed Obama's win more to his hypnotic hold on so many people than to his actual policies, but I think that's too simplistic a view. While Obama *is* a uniquely seductive figure, and while many still feel a deep emotional investment in the first black president, it *is* his policies that are—paradoxically—greatly responsible for his win.

When Obama came into office in January 2009, he set into full motion a grand project embraced by the Far Left for decades. It has two major parts. The first, in three subparts, is both strategic and tactical: (a) to expand government as fast and as widely as possible; (b) the ultimate objective of *that* is to expand the number of people dependent on government as fast and as widely as possible; (c) and the ultimate objective of *that* is to leverage the widespread dependency into a permanent Democrat voting majority. If you are getting a constant stream of freebies from a government promising to stick it to the "rich" guy while providing you with cradle-to-grave "security," you are less likely to vote out the guy doling out the free stuff.

Obama had a multipronged strategy to achieve those three goals, but two were particularly effective. First, he chose a path of divide and conquer to pit Americans against one another in order to make it easier to slide in his radical redistributionist agenda. He divided us by class, gender, race, and age. He turned the American motto, "E Pluribus Unum" ("Out of Many, One") upside down. It is now "Out of One, Many." The American experiment cannot go on as it once did driven by divisions and envy rather than by unitary values and common goals.

Second, Obama understood was that if you expand government and dependency on it *as quickly as possible*, you take the sting out of a bad economy. The more government aid and programs to "take care" of you during an economic crisis, the less likely you are to throw the bums out who caused—or who are prolonging—the economic crisis. Explosive government dependency means that many Americans—who would normally be bearing the brunt of this atrocious economy—do not feel the kind of acute pain they would have in the past. As recently as fifteen to twenty years ago, an incumbent presiding over this kind of disastrous economy would be thrown out on his ear (*see*: Carter, Jimmy; *see*: Bush, George H. W. Carter's economy was dismal, but Bush 41 got tossed for a much milder economic downturn than the epic disaster of the Obama economy's).

Take the big pain out of a bad economy by getting people dependent, win elections. Get that coveted permanent Democrat voting majority. Although the country is still fairly well divided, enough dependents and those who love dependency chose that path to bring us close to that permanent Democrat voting majority—if we're not already there. Normal Americans look at Obama's economic record and see destruction. Obama, his fellow leftists, and now, sadly, a slight majority of Americans, look at it and see success.

Obama strove mightily to get us to that tipping point, and he may have achieved it. Four more years and we will be well past it.

The second major part of the grand project has to do with redistribution. As I argue later in the book, Obama's grand project is so much bigger than just the transfer of wealth here at home. For Obama, the redistribution is *global* and not strictly limited to wealth. Obama and his single-minded band of leftists are in the process of redistributing *everything* American: our power, our wealth, our resources, our military and diplomatic advantages, our economic competitiveness, our leadership, our borders, and, most of all, our unique exceptionalism.

In 2008 and then again in 2012, the majority of Americans handed the keys to the kingdom to a man with a hyperambitious redistribution in mind, a globally viral form of it that would ultimately engineer the death of America as we have known it. The grand project is almost complete. And the reason it's moved so fast is not solely due to Obama's and the Far Left's single-minded focus and cold efficiency in carrying it out. It's also because for decades we have ceded control of the culture, the media, and the campus to the Left, and they have leveraged that control into the nearly omnipotent power to change the very nature of the nation. As a result, America is now by and large a country made up of immature and selfish adolescents (of all ages), a vocal contingent of Vagina Voters, a grossly corrupt media, and a growing army of takers who increasingly view socialism as the preferred political and economic system.

This is the "fundamental transformation" of the nation of which Obama spoke in 2008. After his reelection, I heard many observers argue that now, as a second-term president, he'd "move to the middle" because "he'll be concerned about his legacy." While that's true for normal presidents, it's not true for this one. Normal presidents want to be remembered as peacemakers and strong economic stewards. Obama wants to be remembered as the president who "fundamentally transformed" the nation by turning its trajectory away from individual and economic freedom and toward what he once smoothly called "collective salvation."

Meet the new Obama, same as the old Obama.

We must now navigate our way around this new America: one of ever bigger government, greater dependency, higher taxes, ever more spending and crippling debt, socialized medicine, and dwindling freedom. It's a bleak future—one that resembles more the imploding nations of Western Europe than the United States of America—but it's one that we *must*, and, more important, *can*, fight.

It may very well be that it's going to take a full-blown crisis to wake us from our torpor. We may have to be broken before we can begin to put ourselves back together again. After all, the slight majority who voted for Obama and the status quo also rejected the responsible plans of Romney and Paul Ryan to deal with the imminent crises *now, before* they blow up and consume us. But the majority has chosen to close its eyes and float along for now. At some point, however, the laws of economics *will* kick in and the reckoning *will* come. So we may have to experience a massive implosion—complete with catastrophic economic collapse and social upheaval—before we can start to fix it.

It's an ugly reality, but it may very well be the case.

The day after the election, November 7, 2012, I got an e-mail from a treasured friend. She hadn't slept all night, despondent over Obama's win and what it represented for the future of America. One line in particular struck me:

"Crazy —," she wrote. "America was the best idea the world has ever produced . . . and we just threw it away."

Powerful words, for three reasons: (1) the reminder that America is not simply a physical place but an *idea* based on individual freedom;

(2) the sense of resignation that a slim majority had voted to toss it out in favor of the bondage of statism; and (3) the use of the past tense ("was") to describe America.

Of all the messages sent to me after the election, that's the one that moved me from grief to anger and then to steely resolve. America *is* the greatest idea the world has ever produced, and we don't have to put up with the choice made by the other half of the country to discard it.

Shrug our shoulders in resignation? Commit to statism and redistribution forever? Say good-bye to American exceptionalism? "Well, the Constitution was nice while it lasted, and it had a good run, but sayonara!" I don't think so.

America is the best idea the world has ever produced. And that's why we've got to go Churchillian on this thing. We must never give up. We must never give in. We must never surrender. We must fight for this beloved country. It may be slipping beneath the waves, but it can still be rescued. This is *our* grand project.

I know it's tougher than ever to be a Happy Warrior. We're not feeling very positive, and we're exhausted from the fight. But let's take a deep breath and realize two things: America *can* be saved, and she is *worth saving.*

This is why we fight! Time to suit up again.

Let's (bleeping) roll.

Monica Crowley
December 2012

PART I

AMERICA, INTERRUPTED

What the @$%&! just happened to America? What the @$%&! happened to our strength and greatness? What the @$%&! happened to our powerful free market system? What the @$%&! happened to our traditional rocket path of growth? What the @$%&! happened to American jobs? What the @$%&! happened to our prosperity? What the @$%&! happened to the greatest health care system in the world? What the @$%&! happened to our constitutionally limited government? What the @$%&! happened to our superpower status? What the @$%&! happened to our ability to be respected and feared? What the @$%&! happened with multiple bailouts and unprecedented spending? Sixteen trillion dollars in debt?

What the @$%&! just happened?

This is the question most Americans are asking. It's the question that has been driving us bananas since November 4, 2008, when a newly elected president and Democratic Congress went full steam ahead with a radical plan to transform the United States into Absurdistan. Americans have greeted each day since with an incredulous "What now?" What epically anti-American, destructive, and weird policy, announcement or development are we going to get hit with today?

Team Obama and his determined band of leftists have played a skillful game of political whack-a-mole (or Barack-a-mole). They would pop up with one insane policy and before anyone could even begin to address it, they would pop up with another crazy initiative, and before anyone could begin to address that, up they would pop with yet another maniacal proposal. Nobody could keep up with the leftist madness, which of course was the point. Before we knew what actually hit us, most of us felt like strangers in a strange land.

The last few years have been a bizarre stroll through a surreal landscape. America hasn't been *looking* like America. It's been looking like an America painted by Salvador Dalí, all dripping landscapes, liquid clocks, and warped reality . . . like what Paul Pelosi sees when he wakes up every morning. It's as if America has fallen down the rabbit hole. It's America in *The Twilight Zone*.

More important, America hasn't been *feeling* like America. Everything we once thought we knew for sure is no longer true, and that in turn has rocked us to the very core. We used to know that if we lost our job, we would be able to find another one. Or that if we chose to, we would stay in the same home over the course of a thirty-year mortgage or longer. Or that after a recession we would have explosive comeback growth. Or that our children would have it better than we did. Or that despite downbeat times, we would return to our sunny national outlook soon enough. None of those things holds true today.

The shattering of those assumptions has shaken us. We aren't used to feeling this strange kind of prolonged uncertainty and fear. We aren't used to being off-kilter, wobbly on our feet, unable to count on our exceptional nation to buoy us.

The Tea Party grew out of this irrepressible sense that something isn't right, not because of an external threat, but because of an internal one. That's why the Tea Party went from being an incipient movement to representing mainstream America—it stood in opposition to all of the things that lent to that sense that something was wildly off: out-of-control spending, taxes and debt, bailouts, widespread government intervention in the private sector, and explosive government. Many Americans, looking at this long litany of offenses, decided to do as William F. Buckley once exhorted, and "stand athwart history, yelling, 'Stop!'" Which, incidentally, is the same directive most massage therapists utter when former vice president Al Gore disrobes.

The American ability to self-correct is one of the most elemental reasons for our nation's survival. The Declaration of Independence is famous for its high-concept principles of individual liberty and basic human dignity as well as Thomas Jefferson's lyrically beautiful prose. But the core of the document is actually the lengthy list of abuses committed by King George, which served as the rationale for the taking up of arms against England in the name of independence. We have a different kind of fight before us now, this time for the very survival of what the Founders built.

What the @$%&! just happened to their—our—country?

One day in 1984, Michael Jackson made a visit to the White House. He was at the height of his fame, with his album *Thriller* well on its way to becoming the best-selling album of all time. The Reagan White House had asked Jackson for permission to use his smash hit, "Beat It," in a campaign to combat teen drinking and driving. Jackson obliged, and he arrived at the White House to receive a public-safety award and personal thanks from the Reagans.

The now-iconic photograph of the three of them reveals much about the towering personalities and even more about America. Jackson stands between the Reagans, wearing a tamer version of his famous sequined faux-military costume. Hands clasped in front of him, he waits silently as the president finishes making a point to Mrs. Reagan and she responds. His eyes as wide as saucers as he gazes up at the president, Jackson makes obvious his legendary offstage shyness as he stands mere inches from the Leader of the Free World. The world's greatest performer had discovered himself on a stage even bigger and more profound than the ones to which he was accustomed. His awe is palpable. And Reagan, the experienced showman, looks just as dazzled to be in the presence of a young man who had set the world (and earlier, his own hair) on fire with a raw, sheer, devastating talent.

The boy from Tampico, Illinois, standing with the boy from Gary, Indiana: two children of the Midwest who went on to become among the most influential people the world has ever known. Both men had recognized and seized the uniquely American opportunity that great risks could be met with great rewards. They also understood that great risks could be met with great failure, that there were consequences to risk and chance, to decisions and gambles, to ideas and the execution of them. And still, they chose to hone their talents, work hard, sacrifice, and persevere until they had achieved their wildest dreams. Because, after all, wasn't that what America was all about in the first place? The wide-open space to succeed or fail? The land of opportunity, where government was small so individual ambitions could be big? The country in which there was no such thing as dreams too wild to pursue?

America cleared the path. Whether you succeeded or failed was up to you. The one thing this country would never prevent you from doing was trying.

During the 2008 presidential campaign, candidate Barack Obama once referred to his biracial background and itinerant childhood and said, "In no other country on earth is my story even possible." True. But then in 2009, while attending the Group of 20 (G-20) summit in Europe, he was asked if he believed in American exceptionalism. He replied haltingly, "I believe in American exceptionalism, just as I suspect that the Brits believe in British exceptionalism, and the Greeks believe in Greek exceptionalism."

Not exactly the way President Reagan would have answered, nor, for that matter, Michael Jackson.

———

The concept of American exceptionalism has been a victim of its own extraordinary success. In just over two hundred short years, the United States went from being a collection of defiant colonies subject to the rule of a distant tyrant to the world's greatest superpower; hyperdominant militarily, economically, culturally, politically, and ideologically. Plus, we have Lady Gaga. No other modern nation had been built not on the ambitions of men but on the freedom of the individual. No other nation or empire had achieved so much so fast. No other nation had achieved such greatness while exercising such profound goodness. No other nation liberated more people and defended freedom more aggressively at such great expense in lives and treasure—and asked for so little in return—as the United States of America.

That exceptionalism became such a given—both for Americans and for the rest of the world—that everyone began to take it for granted.

America might have its ups and downs, its economic booms and recessions, its strong leaders and weak ones, its periods of dominance and times of retrenchment, its *Godfather* trilogies and its *Harold and Kumar* trilogies, but the assumption was that American power would always be there: reliable, sturdy, clear and present. The idea that American power and exceptionalism might evaporate for good was unthinkable. We had always been the indispensable nation and we always would be. Wouldn't we?

What made the United States exceptional from the start was its design as a nation of laws, not of men, built on the concepts of individual liberty and equal justice before the law, with freedoms ranging from speech to worship, and rights from gun ownership to assembly. The Founding Fathers institutionalized these freedoms for the individual, so we would be safe from the suffocating burdens and capricious claims of a too-powerful state. Those freedoms would allow individuals to do as they pleased within the reasonable confines of the law and to achieve in ways big and small, the benefits of which would redound to America at large.

Even in extremely difficult times, we had never before lost the ideal—and the reality—of American exceptionalism. Faced with the darkest days of civil and foreign wars, economic depression and recessions, weak leadership at home or aggressive, hostile threats from abroad, the American people always had faith in the uniqueness of our democratic experiment, which produced the greatest engine of economic growth, the most influential culture, and the most far-reaching effects of innovation. In addition to the incandescent lightbulb, the airplane, and the iPad, America gave birth to the ShamWow. And that Chia Pet shaped like Barack Obama's head.

And yet the man who acknowledged that his story was only even possible in America is intent on destroying many of the very individual liberties and limited government that made it so. Obama has swung a wrecking ball at economic freedom out of the noxious leftist belief that greater wealth redistribution and government-directed enforcement of social and economic "justice" make a fundamentally better nation. He has also swung a wrecking ball at American primacy in the world. He is not seeking the destruction of the free market system and our super-power status for their own sakes. He seeks them as necessary steps to ultimately "remake America" as a European-style redistributive state that seizes ever more power as it cultivates ever greater dependency while it's forced to wear a dunce cap and sit humiliated in a corner of the world.

In several short years, Obama has fundamentally shifted the balance away from the individual and toward government, and has altered the national psyche from self-reliance to ever-growing reliance on government. It took Thomas Jefferson, Benjamin Franklin, John Adams, and several other Founders a few months to draft the Declaration of Independence. It took Obama even less time to draft and implement his own Declaration of Dependence.

———

Obama's reference to "British" or "Greek" exceptionalism reveals his belief that *the United States does not stand alone with a particular greatness*, but that every nation is great in its own way, and that America is simply one of many nations with something cool to offer. This kind of relativist, multicultural, "we're all unique in unique ways," "every kid must win at dodgeball" thinking is the basis for his economic and foreign policies, from his scheme to nationalize health care to his failure to consistently champion freedom for those struggling for it around the world. Unless those struggling include illegal alien abortion doctors who belong to the Teamsters Union. It is the rationale for his Vesuvian explosion of big government and the higher taxes he needs to finance it. It also explains Obama's irrepressible urge to apologize for past perceived or invented American injustices and ill-conceived foreign "meddling." In Obama's kaleidoscopic left-wing view, no nation is better than any other and we're all socialists* now.

———

* I'm not referring to "socialism" in the technical sense (government ownership of the means of production). Economic fascism (government control of industry without ownership) is a closer description of what Team Obama envisions, but I use "socialism" throughout as shorthand for government-directed redistributionism.

As dark a vision as this is, however, there is something even bigger and more sinister at work, something grander in scale and more destructive in purpose. We tend to think of Obama's redistributionist agenda as limited to what he calls "spreading the wealth around" here at home.

Obama's redistributionist scheme, however, is so much bigger than just the transfer of capital within his home country. For Obama, self-styled "president of the world," the redistribution is *global* and not strictly limited to wealth. Obama and his single-minded band of leftists are in the process of redistributing *everything* American: our power, our wealth, our resources, our military and diplomatic advantage, our economic competitiveness, our leadership, our borders, and, yes, our unique exceptionalism.

These are the very things that built American greatness. We value them. He resents them, which is why he is constantly apologizing for them. His intent is to have every element of American greatness turned over to the rest of the world so that they may be watered down and ultimately eradicated.

If his strategy were merely wealth redistribution here at home, we could roll it back with an emphatic change in leadership in 2012 and beyond. But Obama is not content to simply remake America, but to undermine her by placing redistributionism on steroids and then selling out every component of American greatness. He also knew that he had just a few years to accomplish this global dilution of everything American, so he became a Redistributionist-in-a-Hurry.

In 2008, we handed the keys to the kingdom to a man with a hyper-ambitious redistributionism in mind, a globally viral form of it that would ultimately engineer the death of America as we knew it.

Michael Jackson and Ronald Reagan came from nothing to reach the pinnacle of success. They were able to work their way to the very top because government did not stop them, shake them down, and strip them of their earned bounty. Obama told us that his story—like Reagan's and Jackson's—was not even possible except in America, but his leftist joyride is destroying the very exceptionalism that made *all* of our stories possible.

And to think: it's all by design.

The tyranny we face today does not stem from an external force, but from a far more dangerous and insidious internal one. It's a threat that moves stealthily, within the system, claiming to represent American values even as it seeks to undermine and ultimately destroy them. It comes from the darkest corners of the failed socialist ideology, but its champions hauled it out of the dustbin of history, slapped some lipstick on it, and rebranded it as "compassion" and "justice" and "fairness." Those who had tried to impose it from afar failed because Americans wouldn't tolerate the defeat of their system at the hands of another. But if the threat came from within, from messengers who looked like them, would they resist? *Could* they resist?

The precedent and pace of American exceptionalism gave us a false sense that our number one status would always be secure and that we didn't have to spend much time or energy tending to it. Our thundering victory over fascism in World War II left us with a massive industrial base, from which we rapidly built the world's biggest economy and rebuilt the economies of the rest of the newly free world. Our decisive victory over Soviet communism left us with unchallenged global political, economic, and military power. Those triumphs set in stone our own perception that our exceptional status was unshakable.

While we fought the fearsome ideologies of fascism and communism abroad, however, we turned a blind eye to an ideology that was undermining us from within. We allowed a watered-down socialism to creep in, take hold, and metastasize. We allowed it to slowly chip away at our fundamental principles until, eventually, it stood on equal ground. Once the anti-American radicals who embraced grand redistributionism saw the lack of firm resistance to their agenda, they pushed forward and increased their demands.

Their grand strategy of global redistribution is based on two overarching and interlocking beliefs: first, that *by definition*, exceptionalism is unfair and unjust, and second, that whatever "exceptionalism"

America has enjoyed has been earned at the expense of social and economic "justice." America, they believe, must be stripped of its exceptionalism if that equalizing "justice" is to be achieved, and that exceptionalism must be farmed out globally in order to weaken America's power, status, and influence. The United States must be reduced to just another country, such as Myanmar or Ecuador. Nothing special. Just another country on the United Nations roster. What the anti-American radicals were not prepared for and what came as a pleasant surprise to them was the extreme fragility of that exceptionalism.

If America were to be broken as an exceptional power and remade as a redistributive nirvana, it needed to be done at the right moment and with the right Leading Man.

In the modern center-right nation, a far-left presidential candidate could never win a general election, never mind govern from the progressive outer banks. They had tried and failed before with extremists such as Michael Dukakis, Al Gore, and John Kerry, so the Left had to recalibrate. If it were ever to seize the brass ring of the presidency and be able to leverage it into a full transformation of America, the Left needed to go beyond its previous helping of man, ideology, tank, and swift boat. It needed to find the perfect marriage of man and mission.

It took them decades, but the leftists finally found it in the strange hologram of a man named Barack Hussein Obama.

———

Who was he? Nobody really knew. But he came complete with an Etch-A-Sketch history, making him the perfect vessel for the Left. The biracial son of an absentee Kenyan communist father and an absentee Kansan communist mother who spent his youth in Indonesia and Hawaii, attended Occidental College and Columbia and Harvard universities, and who presented in an elegant way that was non-threatening to whites, Obama was almost too good to be true. America was about to meet the Fresh Prince of Chicago.

What made him even more delectable to the Left was that he was no mere pretender to the throne. Obama was an authentic heir to the radical Left movement of the 1960s, which had been mainstreamed into American politics and culture via academia, Hollywood, and the media. And perhaps even more important, as the first viable black candidate for president, he would benefit from a tsunami of white guilt. A vote for Obama would allow white America to feel they had advanced toward vanquishing racism once and for all. A vote for Obama was a chance for many in white America to give themselves a feel-good moment. Even Joe Biden pronounced him "clean and articulate" during the 2008 Democratic primaries. So many people were consumed with proving their racial tolerance: Look, everybody! No racial complexes here! Just a supremely open-minded, enlightened post-racial voter!

The emotional pull of the racial element was not to be underestimated. A long conga line of white leftists had been defeated for president. But a biracial leftist would be granted all kinds of passes, excuses, and protections. The race card, played subtly by Obama but boldly by others, would prove to be the most powerful weapon in the Obama/leftist arsenal.

Obama also had superb leftist street cred, including personal associations with such notable sixties radicals as domestic terrorists Bill Ayers and Bernardine Dohrn, who wanted to get the socialist revolution going by killing their fellow Americans, the anti-American racist preacher Reverend Jeremiah Wright, in whose pews Obama sat for nearly two decades, and the PLO sympathizer Rashid Khalidi. A true Amalgam of Awfulness. The only thing missing was Louis Farrakhan.

Obama had also apprenticed in the dark arts. And not the cool kind of dark arts they teach at Hogwarts. I mean the dark arts of Saul Alinsky community organizing, which relentlessly stoked class warfare in order to create a pre-revolutionary climate. Obama had never expressed an unadulterated love for America, only deep critiques of its racial divides, social and economic injustices, and bullying ways in the world. His detached persona mirrored a detachment from fundamental American values. The Left tried to smear his critics by saying they were trying to paint him as "Other," as something other than traditionally American. But in his actions, associations, and words, that was exactly true, and it was precisely the reason the Left knew that in him it had found its deliverance.

It helped their cause that he was cool in every way. He was cool, as in "hip," with Nas playing on his iPod and his 2008 campaign sending tweets to his followers at Kanye West concerts. But he was also cool as in "unflappable," which would come in handy as he led the leftist revolution. He was charismatic and charming, a natural salesman who delivered a spoonful of sugar to make the redistributionist medicine go down. He was also calm, self-possessed, intellectual. How could someone that seemingly rational want to radicalize the United States? Most people would not believe the truth about him and his motives—at least until it was too late.

The leftists had found their Dreamboat Date to the Big Dance, and, boy, did they get lucky.

The rest of us, meanwhile, were kidnapped, blindfolded, given roofies, tossed in the trunk, and taken on a $5 trillion bender. When we awoke, we found that our hair was mussed, our skirt was twisted, and our shirt was buttoned wrong. We had a hangover, without first having had any fun, or Bradley Cooper.

What the @$%&! just happened?

Americans are generally slow to anger. Because most of us deeply appreciate and exercise our freedom to go about our own business, we will take a lot of punches, abuse, disrespect, and challenges from our own leadership or from abroad. But at some point, even the most patient and understanding American has had enough. And it's at that point, when Americans are finally roused from their agreeable acquiescence, that our leaders had better check themselves.

Just as Thomas Jefferson cataloged a long list of abuses of the American people by the British sovereign, many Americans have compiled their own modern list of abuses suffered at the hands of Barack Obama and his congressional toadies:

We are mad as hell about a nearly trillion-dollar economic "stimulus" that stimulated government but did nothing to excite the private economy.

We are mad as hell about long-term high unemployment.

We are mad as hell about taxpayer bailouts of failing businesses and industries.

We are mad as hell that random TSA agents can now fondle us at the airport.

We are mad as hell about a president who has regularly ruled by fiat, bypassing Congress and the public by appointing unaccountable policy "czars" and issuing mandates through executive order.

We are mad as hell about telephone book–sized bills pushed through, unread, by the Democratic leadership.

We are mad as hell about the government takeover and destruction of the best health care system in the world.

We are mad as hell about the multitrillion-dollar price tag to pay for that monstrosity.

We are mad as hell about the shady, slimy, greasy backroom dirty dealing the Democrats did to cobble it together.

We are mad as hell about the legislative tricks and straight party-line vote they used to pass it.

We are mad as hell about multiple annual deficits over $1.3 trillion.

We are mad as hell about a national debt speeding toward $17 trillion.

We are mad as hell that this president's wife goes on late-night burger runs while telling us to graze in her organic garden.

We are mad as hell about the national humiliation of having our credit downgraded for the first time in U.S. history.

We are mad as hell about the steadfast refusal by most Democrats—and some Republicans—to cut spending in real and deep ways.

We are mad as hell about the Democrats' equally steadfast obsession with raising our taxes.

We are mad as hell about their weaselly cowardice in their refusal to take on the biggest sources of explosive spending: entitlement programs.

We are mad as hell that illegal aliens are still streaming into the United States.

We are mad as hell about a foreign policy that embraces our enemies and makes our friends walk the plank.

We are mad as hell about the commander in chief apologizing for American power and action.

We are mad as hell about an arrogant leadership that is bankrupting the nation while empowering itself.

Above all, we are mad as hell that American exceptionalism is deliberately being turned into unexceptionalism.

Americans will take a lot, but they will not tolerate the rape and pillage of their nation by the Orwellian forces of a sick and discredited redistributionist ideology. They will reject it even more when they believe their own leadership is hijacking American exceptionalism and deliberately diluting it in order to serve a *global* redistributionist scheme.

It's no coincidence that the movement that developed to push back found its inspiration in the Boston Tea Party of 1773. The original tea party was a seminal pre-revolutionary event. It crystallized the colonists' objections to being ruled and taxed from afar and their desire for the basic human dignity of having a voice in their own affairs. In a significant way, this was the beginning of American exceptionalism: What made these powerless subjects think they could confront the king of the most powerful empire on earth? The courage of those early Americans came when they realized they were not powerless at all. They discovered that their power came not from the barrel of a gun but from their unity around the idea that all men were created equal, endowed by their Creator with certain unalienable rights, that among these were life, liberty, and the pursuit of happiness.

We were born in revolt: revolt against oppression, revolt against taxation without representation, revolt against those who ruled by royal decree, revolt against tyranny.

The odds were stacked hugely against us. On one side there was the British army: well trained, well equipped, a professional fighting force in their crisp red coats. On the other side, a bunch of farmers with pitchforks, preachers with muskets, country lawyers with bayonets, rich and poor, fathers and sons, a ragtag bunch of men and boys. Their very unexceptional nature is what made their achievement so exceptional. In that motley collection of early patriots, we see the first American ingenuity, the first American feistiness, that uniquely American combativeness and competitive spirit.

Most important, the early Americans knew that their demands were not radical. To King George, they constituted treason. But to the patriots, and later for the whole of humanity, they were basic rights that came not from government but from God. They believed, they *felt*, that they were on the right side of history. Even then, they knew they were part of a grand political and spiritual experiment. They didn't know how it would end, but they also knew they didn't have a choice but to fight.

Several years after the Revolutionary War and the adoption of the Constitution, Benjamin Franklin wrote, "The important ends of civil government are the personal securities of life and liberty. I am a mortal enemy to arbitrary government and unlimited power. I am naturally very jealous for the rights and liberties of my country, and the least encroachment of those invaluable privileges is apt to make my blood boil."

If Franklin were to get a gander at the unlimited power seized by our current arbitrary government, his blood pressure would be off the charts.

Franklin went on to say: "Only a virtuous people are capable of freedom. As nations become corrupt and vicious, they have more need of masters. But America is too enlightened to be enslaved."

Are we still too enlightened to be enslaved? Are we still virtuous?

Obama and the Democrats have answered those questions with a resounding no, which is why they are forcibly imposing their own version of "virtuous" redistribution, like a bunch of demented Robin Hoods. The majority of Americans are answering those questions with thundering yeses, which is why they're opposing the Democrats' madness. It is as basic a conflict as was the one between the British king and the early Americans: Should the United States be a land of individual freedom, truly representative government, and free market prosperity, or should it be a land of an omnipotent state, central economic planning, and, in the words of Obama, "collective salvation"?

Obama and much of the Democratic Party have answered that pointed question with an emphatic push toward statism. That very anti-American approach has cracked every foundation upon which America has rested, and has led, in turn, to a growing sense of American defeatism, economic crisis and collapse, failed leadership, U.S. impotence abroad, and national malaise. We are watching the sequel to Jimmy Carter unfold, but this time the destruction is much more dangerous and consequential.

The United States has experienced some extraordinary seminal events: the decision to take up arms against England; the adoption of the Constitution; the Civil War and the assassination of Abraham Lincoln; the Great Depression; World Wars I and II; the cold war; the civil rights movement; September 11, 2001. Each event was profoundly jarring to the status quo. The nation was turned inside out, forced to deal with challenges it had never before imagined. And yet, in each case, America managed to find its bearings and ultimately emerge from the test with different national strengths and skills.

The current seminal moment is one of those unprecedented events. The economic meltdown, which began in late 2007—accelerated in the autumn of 2008 and continuing through today—gave rise to two levels of anxiety. The first level is immediate and urgent economic fear: Will I lose my job? Will I ever find another job? Will the bank foreclose on my home? Will I soon be homeless, living in Kenya like Barack's half brother, George Hussein Onyango Obama?

The second percolates under the first and is far more profound and transformative. *It is the feeder notion of an America in decline.* It's the fear that the very nature of America is changing—or perhaps has already been irrevocably changed. It's the fear that the America of our Founders and of days past—of limited government, individual freedom, free markets, of innocent youth and prosperous adulthood—is disappearing. It's the fear that what made America great—liberty that led to creativity, innovation, risk and reward, and natural optimism—is slipping away. Who can be optimistic when the government micromanages us all down to the lowest common denominator, from breast exams to bottled water, from sodium intake to central air? It's the fear that the once-fearless Frontier Nation is becoming regressively European in its policies and sensibilities.

It is the fear that America the Exceptional is becoming America the Ordinary. Or worse, that it's becoming America the Weak and Passé, the twenty-first-century Sick Man of the World.

The tangible effects of this era can eventually pass if we change leaders and policies. But the *intangible* effects will be more insidiously persistent because they stem from a kind of faltering faith. And that is much harder to restore than a healthy job market.

There has been a weird vibe in America for a few years. It has left, in the words of the Grateful Dead, a "smoking crater" in our individual and collective psyches. But just as we have during every other seminal moment, we will turn a crisis of confidence and fear into an opportunity for fight and renewal. And we will succeed because we are not about to be the first generation to drop the "exceptional" ball.

Fortunately, the United States is still a nation of, by, and for the people. Despite the most strenuous exertions of Obama and his dour band of leftists, the country is NOT of, by, and for the federal government. At least it isn't yet. No matter how many times Dennis Kucinich attempts to lure you into his spaceship, remember that you do not work for him. We still have time to reverse their grand statist experiment, but only if we make the right decisions going forward. No nation is guaranteed primacy. It's up to the people, who are generally far more rational and grounded than their leaders, to do the hard work of keeping us number one. To stay number one, we're going to need a president who does more than just wake up at noon and play Xbox 360 in between destroying our exceptionalism.

The United States is not yet ready for the toe tag. America is like those people who are declared dead, wheeled into the morgue, and three days later, sit bolt upright and scream, "I'm alive! What the hell? And how did Jar Jar Binks get into the White House?"

The vast majority of Americans are now sitting bolt upright. It took a while for the country to become hip to what Team Obama was up to, because nobody wanted to believe that any president, administration, or political party was capable of such deliberate destruction. What is this, a Metallica concert? The great awakening began in the summer of 2009, when polling began to show a creeping sense among the American people that the new administration's policies were veering dramatically off the usual American course. We began to notice that something just might be awry when skateboarding champion Tony Hawk was given permission to skateboard through the White House. Yes, that actually happened. Many were still willing to give Obama and his agenda the benefit of the doubt, but as he doubled down on his redistributive agenda even as it not only failed to produce results but began to make things worse, the dissatisfaction became more widespread.

Conservatives who insisted that Barack Obama is a socialist and anti-American radical have often been dismissed as cranks and conspiracists due to a lack of explicit statements on his part to this effect. Of course, Obama and his allies are smart enough not to openly declare their agenda. They don't run around wearing Carrie Bradshaw–esque nameplate necklaces that say "Redistributionist." They don't broadcast an intent to downgrade America at home and abroad by weakening her economically, militarily, and philosophically. In fact they would vociferously deny this if asked. But if you take a hard look at their actions, the choices they've made, the people Obama surrounds himself with, you can't help but conclude, as I have done, that their true objectives are not what they claim. Their words may be moderate, but everything I've seen and heard points to their truly radical intentions. Moreover, this is a conclusion that millions of other Americans have also drawn. They have awakened to the threat. And they are increasingly alarmed and indignant.

That alarm expressed itself in the Tea Party movement, the 2009 election of Republican governors in the deep blue state of New Jersey and the purple one of Virginia, the January 2010 election of a Republican to succeed leftist demigod senator Edward Kennedy in Massachusetts, and the near rout of congressional Democrats in the November 2010 midterm elections. It expressed itself in the outrage over ObamaCare in town halls across the nation. It expressed itself in the election of additional Republican governors and state legislatures who, despite the rancorous pushback from government unions and their allies, effected fiscal reforms to stave off their own states' declines. It expressed itself in plummeting job approval numbers for Obama and Congress, as well as sustained opposition to his signature legislation, from the "stimulus" to ObamaCare to the Dodd-Frank financial regulatory bill. It expressed itself in a growing backlash against his administration's war on business. And most important, it has expressed itself in a national soul-searching over what America has been, what it is, and what it should be.

Most Americans reject wholesale the notion that our best days are past, set in amber like an ancient dinosaur fibula. Weakness, uncertainty, and retrenchment are for other, lesser nations—follower nations. We do not follow. We lead, and not "from behind," either. That's why most Americans rage against the idea of U.S. decline and will do everything in their power to reverse it.

That impulse is not simply a matter of national pride. It reflects a fundamental understanding of America's unique role in the world, and that if America goes down, the wheels come off. And we certainly don't want the country to morph into a gigantic version of Charlie Sheen in his "tiger blood" days. We have a duty *not* to pack it in, retreat, give up. We are not a nation of quitters. And we are not about to quit now just because we have had a mustache-twirling radical in the White House who has tied the nation to the railroad tracks.

Anger, however, can only take a cause so far. It's largely a destructive force, which is why most leftists are always so angry. Disingenuous leftist "entertainers" such as Bill Maher, Michael Moore, and Janeane Garofalo have built a cottage industry on being pissed off. Leftists seek to destroy the existing order, which they think is a tool of oppression of whites/the "rich"/heterosexuals/The Man. They revel in chronic outrage over made-up "injustices" in the hope of provoking chaos: once chaos sets in, the established order becomes vulnerable. And that's when the Left moves in for the kill, fangs bared, going right for the jugular of economic freedom and limited government. It's the same way Michael Moore behaves at lunchtime. Anger is what drives the Left. It is its indispensable emotion.

It's also what ultimately limits the Left's freedom of action. The two main reasons most Americans routinely reject leftist ideology are that (a) its redistributionist "justice" agenda is thoroughly anti-American, which you do not have to be the smart Kardashian sister to see, and (b) it's driven by negativity, which is as anti-American as is wealth redistribution. The United States has always been a positive, can-do, fearless, upbeat nation, even in our earliest, most uncertain, and darkest times. Optimism is as much a part of our national fabric as are the Declaration of Independence and the Constitution, both of which reflect that vibe: "the pursuit of happiness," "in order to form a more perfect Union." The message has always been positive. The Left has always been on the anger wavelength, while the rest of America is on the sunny-side-up one. The Left is much more than the Grinch who wants to steal Christmas. It's the Grinch who wants to steal EVERYTHING.

The Left also failed to realize that while anger can provoke action, it has a tougher time building anew. For that, you need something to believe in, not simply something against which to rage. If the Left seeks the destruction of core American values in order to replace them with social "justice" ones, the rest of us seek their rebuilding and reinforcement: rugged individualism, personal freedom, hard work, constitutionally limited government, fiscal responsibility, free markets, and a muscular foreign policy.

The desire to reclaim America for those values may have grown out of a seething anger over their deconstruction at the hands of leftists such as Obama, Senate Majority Leader Harry Reid, former Speaker of the House Nancy Pelosi, and other zanies. But if that anger were to continue to drive the push for an American renaissance, it would never be successful. We do not play on the Left's sick battlefields. Instead, we play on ours, the American plain of optimism.

Accept American decline? Hell, no. First we got angry at the Left's sacrilege, and now we will buck up and begin to repair the damage.

We must, and will, return to our roots as a nation of Happy Warriors.

The term "Happy Warrior," which is now firmly associated with Ronald Reagan, originated in a poem written in 1806 by the English poet William Wordsworth called "Character of the Happy Warrior." Written following the death of Lord Nelson at the Battle of Trafalgar, it is an ode to the warrior who, despite battlefield defeats and painful injury, continues the fight cheerfully because he believes in the righteousness of the cause and the draw of the warm home that awaits him. The poem begins:

> *Who is the happy Warrior? Who is he*
> *That every man in arms should wish to be?*
> *—It is the generous Spirit, who, when brought*
> *Among the tasks of real life, hath wrought*
> *Upon the plan that pleased his boy thought:*
> *Whose high endeavours are an inward light*
> *That makes the path before him always bright;*

Although conceived by an Englishman, the concept of the Happy Warrior became a perfect symbol of American exceptionalism as the United States emerged as a great power. It married American optimism with American virtue. The Happy Warrior was formidable. The *American* Happy Warrior was unbeatable.

It wasn't long before politicians saw the political benefit of casting themselves as Happy Warriors. President Grover Cleveland loved the poem so much that he would often recite it unsolicited and requested that it be read at his funeral. Franklin Roosevelt nominated a far-left wealth redistributionist, Alfred E. Smith, at the 1924 Democratic National Convention by cloaking him in non-threatening "reformer" garb and calling him "a happy warrior on the political battlefield."

Roosevelt himself channeled the concept of the Happy Warrior in his jaunty carriage and frank but rallying messages to the nation during the depths of the Great Depression and World War II. Roosevelt understood the image's power, both conceptually and symbolically, and he used it to great effect as he sought to move government from a limited enterprise to an activist one.

Flashes of the Happy Warrior concept could be seen in John F. Kennedy, who, during his 1961 inaugural address, said: "Let every nation know, whether it wishes us well or ill, that we shall pay any price, bear any burden, meet any hardship, support any friend, oppose any foe, in order to assure the survival and the success of liberty." As president, Kennedy was also staunchly pro-growth, cutting marginal tax rates and reining in government spending.

Several years later, the mythology returned, when the 1968 Democratic nominee for president, Hubert Humphrey, explicitly called himself a "happy warrior" as he fought against communism and for social and economic "justice." He even called his campaign plane "The Happy Warrior."

Ronald Reagan luxuriated in the concept of the Happy Warrior as he aggressively sought to defend the United States and defeat our enemies. Those policies, paired with his natural "morning in America" demeanor, conveyed the Happy Warrior far more than any campaign plane ever could. Reagan did not need to invoke the Happy Warrior because everybody already knew him to be one.

Bill Clinton—our forty-second president and national treasure—initially presented himself as something of a Happy Warrior running against the tired, older president George H. W. Bush as a devil-may-care rascal infused with a joyful confidence. It was only later that we saw that the Happy Warrior was not happy at all, but a selfish baby boomer possessed by a malignant narcissism.

Clinton's nomination and election as president, however, revealed a fault line that began with Alfred Smith (who actually *opposed* the New Deal and campaigned against Tammany's corruption) and ran through the Democratic Party throughout the twentieth century, but has now completely ruptured.

In 1968, there were three major groups on the political scene: (a) the Great Silent Majority, led by Richard Nixon; (b) the "happy warrior" Democrats, led by Humphrey; and (c) the far-left kooks.

The kooks were made up of aging New Dealers, antiwar radicals, zonked-out hippies, free-love yippies, angry feminists, and coercive racial activists, whose common agenda was to transform America into a socialist utopia. Many of them poured into Chicago in 1968 for the Democratic National Convention, sparking riots that led to chaos and violence. Who knew that utopia involved water cannons and the Black Panthers? The spectacle of a Democratic mayor of Chicago, Richard Daley, having to use police force against a violent collection of leftists, crystallized the moment: the counterculture, led by the anti-American radicals, had taken over the Democratic Party. The year 1968 would mark the last pro-American Democratic presidential ticket in Humphrey/Muskie.

In the years after 1968, the kooks used their leverage within the party to nominate fellow kooks: George McGovern, Jimmy Carter, Walter Mondale, Michael Dukakis, Al Gore, John Kerry, and Barack Obama. The pro-American "happy warrior" Democrats were sidelined by the most radical, anti-American elements of the leftist movement. Some weren't even part of the Democratic Party at all but were avowed socialists and communists. And yet they managed the wholesale takeover of one of the nation's two major political parties and commandeered it to one electoral disaster after another.

Those political losses occurred in large part because the centrist Democrats fled what was now the party of the kooks. The old-school Democrats in the tradition of Humphrey and Kennedy and Smith—who opposed massive expansion of government power, believed in a strong foreign policy, and truly loved America—were grandfathered into the Great Silent Majority. Former left-leaning intellectuals, such as Irving Kristol, Norman Podhoretz, David Horowitz, and Jeane Kirkpatrick, led the exodus. No longer welcome in the new-left Democratic Party, they were also increasingly horrified by its rabid anti-Americanism. Many of them had been supporters of Democrats Harry Truman, John F. Kennedy, Senator Henry "Scoop" Jackson, and Humphrey. Now, however, they saw their party being eaten alive by a new virus of radicalism.

They were staunch anticommunists who believed, as did Truman, Kennedy, and Humphrey, in "bearing any burden and paying any price" to defeat that lethal ideology. Their final break with their former party took place over the Vietnam War, which the Left opposed as immoral but which they saw as a necessary exercise of U.S. power. It was an ideological divide that could not be bridged. And they— along with tens of millions of others—turned to the Republican Party, giving Richard Nixon and Ronald Reagan major victories in 1972, 1980, and 1984. Their landslides were a direct result of the abandonment of mainstream Democrats by the new lords of the Far Left.

The only blip on the leftist radar was Bill Clinton, who was a product of two developments: (a) the perceived end of the cold war and global communism, which generated a peace dividend and domestic confidence in handing over the national security controls to a Democrat; and (b) the rise of the Democratic Leadership Council, which cultivated "third way" candidates between the Republicans and the Far Left. For more than a quarter of a century, the DLC promoted centrism and championed moderate, pro–free market Democrats. Its goal was to get Democrats back to the mass-market center in which they had thrived before the kook takeover. During its zenith, the DLC boasted members such as Senators Sam Nunn, Joseph Lieberman, Evan Bayh, and Charles Robb, as well as congressmen such as Harold Ford Jr. and Democratic National Committee chairman and governor Ed Rendell.

Unfortunately, like many of the moderate Democrats it supported, the DLC met a grisly political end. After Clinton, the leftists regained control of the party and began living large again. When the kooks achieved their ultimate victory in 2008, the moderate "Blue Dog" Democrats were whipped into submission by Obama, Pelosi, and Reid, who made sure they voted their way on their highly unpopular, big-government programs, such as ObamaCare and "stimulus" spending. In November 2010, those moderate Democrats were routed.

Almost half of the Blue Dog coalition lost reelection, and the DLC found that it no longer had a vibrant Democratic middle to serve. It shuttered in February 2011. Democratic centrism had been rendered irrelevant once and for all. The DLC went extinct because it had no place in Obama's America.

———

The time is now ripe for a new brand of Happy Warrior. The new model will turn on its head the concept the Democrats used for decades. The new Happy Warrior will retain the pro-Americanism but discard the impulse toward social and economic "justice." Instead, the new Happy Warrior will cheerfully fight for constitutionally based first principles and will steer us away from a kook-driven decline that will produce what former ambassador John Bolton has called "a post-American world." In this "post-American world," we'll all speak Arabic, spend Chinese currency, and get abortions at the 7-Eleven. There is no nationalism in the post-American world, only worldism. When the American *people* become Happy Warriors, the country thrives; when they hibernate, the kooks run wild, putting radicals on the Supreme Court, whacking Granny with universal health care, and importing al-Qaeda terrorists from Gitmo to participate in a poetry slam with Attorney General Eric Holder.

So we must reinvent the Great Silent Majority as Happy Warriors once again. Make no mistake: we are in a war for the nation's future. Barry and the kooks (not to be confused with Bennie and the Jets) are preoccupied with the destruction of the existing order of economic and personal freedom and redistributing our power and wealth globally in order to punctuate the end of America.

Their efforts have already led to one kind of profound change: events that were once unthinkable are now everyday occurrences. It was once unthinkable that the United States would ever have a national debt careening toward $17 trillion, that our debt would ever be downgraded, that socialized medicine would ever become law, that 8 percent–plus unemployment would be the "new normal," that terrorist regimes would proceed unimpeded toward nuclear weapons, that tin-pot tyrants would thumb their noses at the United States, that we would spurn our closest allies, that people in one nation fighting against violent oppression would be assisted by Washington while others were abandoned.

The kooks have made American impotence acceptable, and that in turn has made it acceptable to dis, confront, challenge, and downgrade America in ways that would have been inconceivable before the kook takeover. They have converted the United States from the king of the global jungle into a paper tiger, whom very few respect or fear any longer. Everyone from credit ratings agencies to third-rate tyrants now feels free to take a swipe at the American piñata. (And with this piñata, you don't want to be around when it bursts, because when it does, you'll be covered in millions of illegal aliens.) The kooks have taught others how to treat us and, indeed, their anti-American behavior has changed others' behavior toward us.

This is, perhaps, the most dangerous development to emerge from the kooks' global redistributionism. Whenever America has been perceived as weak, history's darkest chapters of chaos and destruction occurred. When everyone from big-time foreign enemies to small-time domestic thugs believe they can hit the United States with impunity, America shrivels up, much like George Costanza's unfortunate "shrinkage" incident after leaving the pool on a classic episode of *Seinfeld*.

The leftists, however, did not bank on the rise of the Happy Warrior. The Happy Warrior is the antithesis of the kook. The Happy Warrior takes pride in the very essence of America and seeks to protect it and advance it, as the kooks assault it as immoral, counterproductive, and evil. Two and a half years before they orchestrated Occupy Wall Street, the kooks Occupied the White House. They may have been running the show, but now they have met their match.

Happy Warriordom is about a new positive national attitude, new leadership, and new policy environment that will make the American rebound possible. The United States is, by its very nature, a forward-looking, frontier-driving, dynamic nation. We are instinctively a nation of Happy Warriors. We just have to tap into it again. As Thomas Paine told his fellow Americans when General George Washington's men were freezing in the snow at Valley Forge: "We have it in our power to begin the world over again."

The conventional wisdom is that the Founding Fathers gave us three branches of government. Not true. They gave us four: the executive, the legislative, the judiciary . . . and the American people. As Thomas Jefferson once said, "Should things go wrong at any time, the people will set them to rights by the peaceable exercise of their elective rights." The Founders vested us with the power to change our government and the direction of the nation because they feared that one day the three other branches would be in the crapper. That day has arrived: the presidency is held by a radical redistributionist, the Congress cannot stop itself from spending us into oblivion, and the courts are legislating left-wing insanity from the bench. All three branches are engaged in social engineering in every part of American life. It is now up to the Founders' stealth fourth branch to stop it.

A few years ago, I got to know the brilliant former *Saturday Night Live* player Darrell Hammond, whose masterful impression of Bill Clinton remains one of my all-time favorite comedy bits. One day, our conversation turned to the Islamic terror attacks of September 11, 2001. I spoke glowingly of President Bush's handling of the chaos of that day. Darrell nodded a few times, and then, after a long moment, he looked straight at me and said, "He got out of the chair."

I blinked at him, puzzled.

He asked me to imagine that I was the president of the United States. One minute, he said, you are sitting in a classroom in Florida, surrounded by a sea of small, innocent faces. You are reading them a story and speaking about education policy. One minute, it's a normal day. The very next minute, you are told that a shadowy terrorist group has attacked civilian sites such as New York's World Trade Center using commercial aircraft. All you know is that two planes have hit their targets. You do not know how many more are still in the air. You do not know how many more Americans will die before the day is over. You just know that you are responsible for the safety of three hundred million of them. You also know that no other president has ever experienced anything like this, so there is no one to whom to truly turn. The nation's security rests with you and, in your heavy responsibility, you are completely alone.

"The burden must have been excruciating as he sat in that classroom," Darrell continued. "A lesser person would have been paralyzed under the weight of it. But after only eight seconds, President Bush *got out of the chair.*"

American exceptionalism is not just a vague, dreamy abstraction. It is a reality based on our extraordinary beginnings, our stunning history, and our unique foundational principles. Part of that exceptionalism has always been a government small enough and agile enough to manage whatever curveball history threw our way. The explosive growth of government and debt has taken that advantage away. But just as we have done in the past, we can restore the nation. We do not lack confidence in America. We lack confidence in our government's policies. We did not create this economic disaster. Our government's policies did. We do not have to meekly stand by while they tell us to get used to "the new normal," to live with less, to accept that our children will inherit a weaker America, that we must atone for our past "excesses," to forget the impossible dream of America. When they shrug with resignation over America's decline, they overlook one critical thing: us.

In the age of Obama, if we don't laugh, we cry. And there's no crying in a book by Monica Crowley. America: it's time to rediscover our inner Happy Warriors! And it's time to march forward with our Happy Warrior's battle cry to make America *America* again.

This is our challenge. This is *our* "shovel-ready job."

Here's what the @$%&! just happened . . . and how we get our groove back. Because when the unthinkable happens, we get out of the chair.

PART II

THE SKINNY SOCIALIST
IS A BIG FAT LIAR

We're the ones we've been waiting for.

—*Barack Obama, 2008*

The greatest snake charmer that ever existed.

—*Fidel Castro on Obama, 2010*

There's a lot about him we don't know.

—*Tom Brokaw to Charlie Rose,
shortly after Election Day, 2008*

Why can't I just eat my waffle?

—*Barack Obama, in response
to a foreign policy question asked at
a Pennsylvania diner, April 2008*

LeBron, Baby

In midsummer 2004, Democrats prepared to nominate the junior senator from Massachusetts and kept woman, John Kerry, for president of the United States. North Carolina senator and professional girlie-man John Edwards had run unsuccessfully for the nomination and jumped at the chance to be Kerry's running mate. Early in the primary race, Edwards had enjoyed some traction, in large part because of the "two Americas" class warfare theme he had repeated endlessly. "We still live in a country where there are two different Americas," he said. "One, for all of those people who have lived the American dream and don't have to worry, and another for most Americans, everybody else who struggles to make ends meet every single day." Edwards's chief political strategist at the time had also recommended use of the divisive "two classes" rhetoric three years earlier, when he served as an adviser to the losing New York City mayoral campaign of Fernando Ferrer. Ferrer spent much of his campaign bemoaning the "two New Yorks." The mastermind who came up with that particular class warfare language? David Axelrod.

At the same time that Axelrod, whose face looks like the one on a Rollie Fingers baseball card, was guiding Edwards's unsuccessful 2004 run for the presidency, he was also advising someone else, a young man for whom the idea of America as unjust, immoral, and inherently bad was a more natural fit than it ever was for Edwards.

Axelrod saw something in this fresh political character beyond his obvious smarts and charisma. He saw someone marinated in the redistributive ideology, who believed in it deeply, and who was trying to bring about that change to his Chicago precincts. This man was living and breathing the "two Americas" concept; his biracial background symbolized it in ways no amount of rhetoric from a pampered white candidate like Edwards ever could. The redistributionist language rolled off his tongue with ease as he stoked class and racial and ethnic grievances through his work with "community organizations" such as Project Vote and ACORN (the Association of Community Organizations for Reform Now). And yet, the most compelling activity on his résumé was a onetime appearance in 2001 on the Chicago public broadcasting program *Check, Please,* in which his great Harvard-educated mind reviewed restaurants like Dixie Kitchen & Bait Shop.

In this man, Axelrod and the kook brigade (which sounds like a fantastic bar-band) had finally found the perfect vessel for the radical transformation of America, from "two Americas" to one, remade in the European socialist model. They had discovered the staff-wielding figure who would deliver them the promised land, and it helped their cause immensely that he did not appear to be a kook at all. He cloaked his radicalism with intellectual elegance, an electric smile, and a smooth, high-end Generation X hipness. Back in his college days, that radicalism was also draped in the coolness of weed smoke, hemp necklaces, and Panama hats. What other future politician was cool enough to have taken his future wife to Spike Lee's *Do the Right Thing* on their first date?

As the 2004 Democratic National Convention drew closer, the organizers went in search of a keynote speaker. Both political parties usually try to name a young up-and-comer whom they can showcase and promote as a new party star. Axelrod suggested the vibrant young man whose U.S. Senate campaign he was then advising. The organizers took one look at Barack Obama and gave him the floor. On July 27, Obama addressed the nation for the first time. His speech was a softer and more unifying version of the "two Americas/two New Yorks" theme Axelrod had been crafting for other candidates for years. "There's not a liberal America and a conservative America—there's the *United States* of America," he said to rapturous applause. He might as well have said, "There's not a Burger King America and a McDonald's America; there's not a Nike America and a Reebok America; there's not a Tupac America and a Biggie Smalls America." It didn't matter *what* he said; it was *how* he said it.

He also debuted themes that would become familiar to Americans over the next few years: "In no other country on Earth is my story even possible," he said, as he stressed "hope" as fundamentally American, even for "a skinny kid with a funny name who believes that America has a place for him too." He concluded by using a phrase that would later become the title of his presidential campaign book: the "audacity of hope," he said, is "God's greatest gift," allowing him to believe that the lives of average Americans can be improved with the "right" governmental policies.

This was not a keynote address. This was Obama's first presidential campaign speech. The audience, despite having no clue who this wispy Illinois state senator was, nonetheless went bananas during and after his speech, chanting his name and waving flags wildly. The reaction was a little *too* passionate, a little *too* over-the-top, for an unknown character. Alas: the mighty wheels of the Obama machine, led by David Axelrod, were already moving. If more people—from the Clintons to the Republicans—had been paying closer attention in 2004, they would have seen the beginnings of a well-planned, precise, and systematic campaign to elect for president a stealth kook who would radicalize the nation in ways no one could yet imagine. No matter what it took to get this man in the White House, the Axelrod apparatus was prepared to do it. From Ben & Jerry's "Yes, Pecan" ice cream to unofficial Barack Obama urinal cakes, nothing was too low-rent for the Obama Chicago Mafia to get a vote.

After that 2004 speech, Obama was poised to become the Big Kookuna, and he relished the role. His self-regard and self-confidence in his ability to grab the brass ring were boundless. Moments before striding out onstage, the then-obscure community organizer looked out at the crowd and told *Chicago Tribune* reporter David Mendell, "I'm LeBron, baby," referring to NBA superstar LeBron James. "I can play at this level. I've got game."

From that moment on, Obama was on a single-minded mission to take the presidency in order to, in his words, "fundamentally transform" America. And in order to effect the transformation, he didn't need merely the votes of Americans. He needed their hearts. He needed their souls. He needed their money, and a lot of it. And so, beginning with that 2004 speech, he, Axelrod, and several others launched a campaign built on a Dear Leader–esque cult of personality. It was Barack As LeBron: smooth, precise, charismatic, cool—a leader who would persuade with the full force of his talents, the liquid silk of his words, his worldly manner. He would not simply get voters to *think* about him. He would get voters to *feel* him. He would *seduce* them.

Bill Clinton was a master of voter seduction (and *actual* seduction), but he had projected a constant, cloying neediness. Clinton was a garden-variety narcissist; he needed to seduce everyone in the room in order to feel adored and validated. His favorite "seduction du jour" was the use of two words: "kiss it." Obama is a much more sophisticated kind of narcissist; he views himself as entirely superior to everyone around him and therefore doesn't much care what you think—except in terms of how it might affect his ambitions. Obama is the antithesis of needy. He would seduce not by begging people to love him but by convincing people that if they *didn't* love him, they were excluding themselves from a life-changing experience.

No one who runs for president suffers from a small ego. But Obama brought something far beyond an outsized ego. His was the Death Star of all political egos. Obama's ego was (and is) so big that it's like an ego planet all to itself, with smaller egos orbiting it like the moons of Jupiter. He brought an unparalleled arrogance, self-assurance, and sense of his own transcendence that he worked hard to hide. But every once in a while, he would let slip just how totally awesome he thought he was. As president, he once "joked" at an Alfred E. Smith dinner that he was like Superman, sent from Krypton by his father Jor-El to "save the Planet Earth." Later in his presidency, he told *60 Minutes*, "I would put our legislative and foreign policy accomplishments in our first two years against any president—with the possible exceptions of Johnson, F.D.R., and Lincoln—just in terms of what we've gotten done in modern history." With that comment, Obama put George Washington, John Adams, Thomas Jefferson, and Ronald Reagan on notice that they were now chopped liver. Even his wife, Michelle, occasionally rolled her eyes at his breathtaking hubris. While watching the masses drooling over him at his swearing-in to the U.S. Senate, Michelle Obama said, "Maybe one day, he'll do something to merit all this attention."

Actual achievement was for lesser mortals. In 2008, he told a group of congressional Democrats, "I have become a symbol of the possibility of America returning to our best traditions." Humility was for losers.

Becoming that "symbol of possibility" was not merely a happy coincidence. It was a well-crafted, orchestrated plan perfectly executed by Obama, Axelrod, and the few other members of Obama's hermetic inner circle to send Americans into an irresistible political spell.

The Obama cult of personality was built primarily on five things: the dynamism of the man, the power of his personal story, the change he represented (generational, political, racial), the emotional draw of white guilt, and the call on the American heart for idealism. I won't dwell on the lesser-known sixth pillar, which involves a miniature bust of Barry's head, constructed out of Marshmallow Peeps. Obama brought a sense of newness to the national scene. The Clintons, quickly cast out as the old brand, were replaced by the new Obama brand that promised a different kind of politics. Different for sure: out with the dress stains and in with the Constitution stains! He would not be merely a politician or even merely a president but something more. Obama would be a transcendent figure. He would transcend business as usual, bitter partisanship, and dirty backroom dealings. He would sit above base politicking and direct things from a nobler perch. He would restore honor and camaraderie to government. The emotional pull of all of these elements combined made for an unstoppable force. Neither the once-omnipotent Clinton machine nor the opposing political party could turn back the tsunami forces marshaled and directed by Obama and his tight cabal.

The myth-making actually began in 1995, when Obama published

Dreams from My Father when he was only thirty-four years old. (By the way, who pens their memoirs before the age of thirty-five, besides former child stars like Drew Barrymore?) The book was not merely an inspiring tale of one man's personal journey. It served a much more profound purpose: it was a preemptive autobiographical strike. When he later entered public life, Obama pointed anyone with questions about his murky past to the memoir, so that what he had written would be taken at face value. No need for investigative journalists to dig into his past when it was all there in black and white, presented by the man himself!

The book was rereleased after his raise-the-roof speech at the 2004 Democratic National Convention in order to reinforce the idea that he was some sort of prodigy: a young genius with a sixth sense. He wrote boldly about his early radical associations, though he was careful to tone down their true beliefs and influences on him. His father, Barack Obama Sr. (dear God, can you believe there was actually *another* one?), was a committed communist who, while serving as a finance minister for the Kenyan government, urged the "redistribution" of income through higher taxes, even at a "100 percent" tax rate, in order to deliver maximum services to the people, and he chronically demonized corporations. His mother, Stanley Ann Dunham, was a communist sympathizer who practiced critical theory with heavy strains of Marxism and attended a leftist church nicknamed "the little red church" because of its communist leanings. Obama's grandfather introduced him to poet and communist Frank Marshall Davis, to whom he refers in *Dreams from My Father* as "Frank." Davis became a mentor and father figure to the young Barack, schooling him early in the ways of radical redistributionism. Davis was a labor movement activist who worked—along with Vernon Jarrett, the father of William Jarrett, ex-husband of one of Obama's closest confidantes, Valerie Jarrett—in the Communist Party–dominated group Citizens' Committee to Aid Packing-House Workers. As Obama himself recalled in *Dreams from My Father*, "It made me smile, thinking back on Frank and his old Black Power, dashiki self. In some ways he was as incurable as my mother, as certain in his faith, living in the same sixties time warp that Hawaii had created."

Thanks in large part to the influence of his parents and Davis, Obama admitted that as a student, he sought out Marxist professors. In April 1983, while a senior at Columbia University, Obama attended a "Socialist Scholars Conference" at Cooper Union, a confab touted as a tribute to Karl Marx. He was so taken by the socialist ideology that he attended the 1984 conference as well. According to Stanley Kurtz's *Radical-in-Chief*, the archived files of the Democratic Socialists of America (DSA) show Obama's name on a conference registration list. Actually, it said Steven Quincy Urkel . . . but we knew who it really was. At the 1983 socialist hoedown, attendees included radical redistributionist and ACORN adviser Frances Fox Piven and community-organizing "theorist" Peter Dreier, who later served as an adviser to Obama's 2008 presidential campaign. As his radicalism fully flowered, Obama grew close to an even fuller array of influential kooks, including but not limited to his twenty-year-long association with the racist, anti-Semitic, anti-American radical Jeremiah Wright, in whose pews Obama sat silently for two decades, never uttering a peep of protest, and who claims American whites invented AIDS to kill blacks. Obama also had a fifteen-year-long friendship with William Ayers, the cofounder of the Weather Underground domestic terrorism group, which described itself as a communist revolutionary organization. (It was in Ayers's living room that Obama launched his political career in 1995.) Obama struck up a shady business relationship with the criminal Tony Rezko and had possible ties to Khalid Abdullah Tariq al-Mansour, the former Black Panther turned Muslim adviser to the Saudi royal family whom the late Manhattan borough president Percy Sutton claimed asked him to write a letter of recommendation to Harvard Law on Obama's behalf—an allegation Obama denied. Obama also enjoys a continuing relationship with PLO sympathizer Rashid Khalidi. Obama was fed radical Marxist literature, anticolonial propaganda, and revolutionary poetry as they all sang Leninist show tunes.

None of these associations were coincidental, nor were they one-way. The older kooks steered their willing pupil toward ever-greater anti-American radicalism. Obama, through his actions and words, increasingly indicated his affinity for the ideas of wealth redistribution and class warfare and his problem with the exercise of U.S. power around the world. The kooks could not believe their good fortune in cultivating such a dreamy vessel for their ideas. They were in love with Obama, and he was in love with them. After all, the "dreams" to which he referred in the title of his book were his father's dreams of radical redistributionist transformation.

<hr>

Obama was clearly a young man on a quest to establish "social and economic justice" by leveraging the existing political tools and opportunities available to him. Community organizing, the hyper-localized method of mobilization to effect socialist change developed by Saul Alinsky, was his preferred route.

Published in 1971, Alinsky's leftist revolutionary how-to, *Rules for Radicals* (which he dedicated to Lucifer), quickly became a kook bible. It is a comprehensive step-by-step manual for how the redistributionists could deconstruct America; first the existing order must be destroyed systematically, locally, block by block, then state by state, and ultimately nationally. The strategy was to work *within* the system until enough power had been accumulated to destroy it. It was what the leftists called "boring from within." (In modern times, the term "boring from within" is reserved exclusively for Obama's State of the Union addresses.) The former radical David Horowitz once described his old fellow kooks as "termites," setting "about to eat away at the foundations of the building in expectation that one day they would cause it to collapse." Once the existing capitalist order was taken down, full-on redistributionism could be maneuvered in its place.

Throughout the twentieth century, there had been various incarnations of the revolution. As Bill Ayers put it as his group bombed the Pentagon, "Kill all the rich people," he ordered. "Break up their cars and apartments. Bring the revolution home, kill your parents, that's where it's really at." Decades later, the old revolutionary was still at it, invoking themes of income inequality as he instructed the useful idiots of Occupy Wall Street on how best to overthrow American capitalism.

Alinsky, his contemporaries, and their radical successors knew that, given Americans' fierce rejection of these fundamentally anti-American views and policies, it would help to have a crisis as a pretext. If a natural crisis did not exist, one could be created through the radical grass roots. This is one of the reasons why he founded the Industrial Areas Foundation (IAF) in 1940 "to train people to reorganize" and which he used to infiltrate traditional organizations such as churches. After Alinsky's death in 1972, IAF morphed into successor groups, including ACORN, Citizen Action, National People's Action, and the Gamaliel Foundation. The Gamaliel Foundation describes its vision as "shared abundance for all," which is a polite way of characterizing wealth redistribution. In the summer of 1985, newly minted community organizer Barack Obama joined Gamaliel, where his work was paid for by the Woods Fund. Later, from 1993 to 2002, Obama would serve on the board of the Woods Fund with . . . guess who? . . . the terrorist and self-described "socialism advocate" Bill Ayers.

If the existing capitalist system were to be destroyed from within, those invested in the system could be expected to put up a fight to try to stop it. In order to marginalize them, Alinsky recommended neutralizing the opposition through humiliation, mockery, questioning of motives, smears, outright lies, and ultimately aggression if necessary: "Pick the target, freeze it, personalize it, and polarize it."

Alinsky preached polarization, not negotiation. Alinskyite organizers are taught to be tough when confronting what they call "the enemy" but to paint every move not as ideological but pragmatic. Hence Obama's constant refrain that he's a neutral pragmatist, the "adult in the room," just trying to get results. "Look Ma! No ideology!" The first rule of Alinsky's "power tactics"? "Power is not only what you have but what the enemy *thinks* you have." Demonize the opposition, remind them of the power you hold, and leverage it to stir chaos, divisions, and destruction, all while casting yourself as the reasonable broker.

Team Obama internalized these lessons well. After college, Obama moved to Chicago to be trained in community organizing by Gerald Kellman, an Alinsky protégé, who schooled Obama in the Alinskyite "power tactics," including hiding their true goals by any means necessary. Obama himself went on to teach those Alinsky tactics at the University of Chicago. In 1990, he wrote an article called "Why Organize? Problems and Promise in the Inner City," which was published in that hot periodical *Illinois Issues* and as a chapter in *After Alinsky: Community Organizing in Illinois*.

On page xix of *Rules for Radicals*, Alinsky writes, "As an organizer I start from where the world is, as it is, not as I would like it to be. That we accept the world as it is does not in any sense weaken our desire to change it into what we believe it should be—it is necessary to begin where the world is if we are going to change it to what we think it should be. That means working in the system."

In chapter 2 of *Rules for Radicals*, Alinsky emphasizes the objective: "The means-and-ends moralists, constantly obsessed with the ethics of the means used by the *Have-Nots against the Haves*, should search themselves as to their real political position. In fact, they are passive—but real—allies of the Haves. . . . The most unethical of all means is the non-use of any means. . . . The standards of judgment must be rooted in the whys and wherefores of life as it is lived, *the world as it is*, not our wished-for fantasy of *the world as it should be*." (Emphasis added.)

It must have been a mere coincidence that Michelle Obama quoted from this passage during her speech at the Democratic National Convention. Referring to a visit her husband had made to a Chicago neighborhood, she said, "Barack stood up that day and spoke words that have stayed with me ever since. He talked about 'the *world as it is*' and '*the world as it should be*.'" She continued, "All of us driven by a simple belief that the world as it is just won't do—that we have an obligation to fight for *the world as it should be*." If only America would follow Barack through the back of the magical Marxist wardrobe. She had used the radicals' phrase "fighting for the world as it should be" before, so her invocation of Alinsky at the convention should not have come as a surprise to anybody paying attention. Most Americans heard that phrase—"fighting for the world as it should be"—as a siren call to idealism, a summons to a noble mission of improving the nation and world. But what the Obamas *meant* by "fighting for the world as it should be" and what most Americans understood that to mean were two very different things. Their "world as it should be" was one built on "social and economic justice" in which the have-nots would *seize* power, money, and resources from the haves. The "two Americas" would be jammed into one in which the playing field was forcibly leveled.

Although Obama was leading the kook parade, his chief political strategist, David Axelrod, had his own revolutionary street cred. Before he got to Obama, Axelrod was mentored by Chicago journalist and political activist Donald C. Rose, who was a member of the Communist Party front, the Alliance to End Repression. Axelrod met Rose while a student at the University of Chicago, and Rose took him under his wing. They worked together over the course of several years, with Rose and another communist-linked mentor, David Canter, showing Axelrod the ropes of community organizing and mobilization through the 1982 Chicago mayoral campaign of Harold Washington and the 1992 U.S. Senate race of Carol Moseley Braun. The group with whom they worked also helped to elect Obama to Braun's Senate seat and ultimately to the presidency.

Obama took the Alinsky techniques national beginning in 2004, playing the role of the "reasonable" liberal intellectual, even as he planned the ultimate redistributionist takeover. Alinsky's dream—of destroying the existing capitalist system and replacing it with a redistributionist one—was about to be realized, beyond ol' Saul's wildest dreams. In fact, on August 31, 2008, the *Boston Globe* published a letter to the editor from Alinsky's son, L. David Alinsky. He cheered Obama for having mobilized the masses at the Democratic National Convention "Saul Alinsky style." "Obama learned his lesson well," he wrote. "I am proud to see that my father's model for organizing is being applied successfully."

On Super Tuesday 2008, Obama proclaimed that the radicals' dream was within reach: "This is it! We are the ones we've been waiting for!

We are the change we seek!" Precisely. And ever since that day, Obama has carried around a makeup compact, and during quiet moments alone he pulls it out, peers down into its tiny mirror, and whispers, "We love you."

———

Obama never made a deep secret of his beliefs or intentions. He wrote extensively about his mission to bring "social and economic justice" to America in both of his books and spoke often about his redistributive beliefs. He voted that way too. He was so into redistribution that he even had a "tramp stamp" of Mao Zedong tattooed onto the small of his back. Oh wait: that was former White House communications director Anita Dunn. In 1995, the same year he published *Dreams from My Father*, Obama said this: " . . . working on issues of crime and education and employment and seeing that in some ways certain portions of the African American community are doing as bad if not worse, and recognizing that my fate remains tied up with their fates, that my individual salvation is not going to come about without a *collective salvation for the country*. Unfortunately, I think that recognition *requires that we make sacrifices and this country has not always been willing to make the sacrifices that are necessary to bring about a new day and a new age*." (Emphasis added.)

Two points are evident here: (a) Obama believes that the "collective" is superior to the "individual" and that "collective salvation" must take precedence over individual action or freedom; and (b) it's our fault that the country hasn't reached that vaunted "collective salvation" yet because we've been selfish, capitalist pigs, but he was going to move our consciousness to a higher, less greedy plane.

In 2001, as an Illinois state senator, he gave an interview to WBEZ radio and advocated wealth redistribution as reparations for slavery and other injustices toward "previously dispossessed peoples." He said, "But the Supreme Court never ventured into the issues of *redistribution of wealth* and sort of more basic issues of *political and economic justice* in this society. And to that extent as radical as people tried to characterize the Warren court, it wasn't that radical."

And then Obama made one of the most revealing statements of his political life: "[The Warren court] *didn't break free from the essential constraints that were placed by the Founding Fathers in the Constitution*, at least as it's been interpreted, and the Warren court interpreted it in the same way that generally the Constitution is a charter of negative liberties."

Consider his explosive words: "break free from the essential constraints that were placed by the Founding Fathers in the Constitution." This is a revolutionary sentiment. Obama is calling for *actively* charging against what the Founders intended and enshrined in the Constitution. His comments go further than simple leftist arguments about the "living Constitution" in which the document conceptually passively evolves. He is calling for a *concerted and deliberate* effort to shatter the very constraints the Founders put in place—to prevent abuses of the kind he's advocating! This is the very essence of Obama's redistributive radicalism: it's all about "breaking free" from the Founders' constraints to build a wholly different kind of America. His entire kook philosophy is summed up in that one sentence.

He continued: "It says what the states can't do to you, it says what the federal government can't do to you, *but it doesn't say what the federal government or the state government must do on your behalf.* And that hasn't shifted. One of the I think tragedies of the civil rights movement was because the civil rights movement became so court focused, I think that there was a tendency to lose track of the political and *community organizing* and activities on the ground that are able to put together the *actual coalitions of power* through which you bring about *redistributed change* and in some ways we still suffer from that." (Emphasis added.) In fact, the Constitution explicitly *limits* the powers of the government because the Founders feared wild-eyed activist power hogs like Obama. But it is those same limits from which Obama would like us to "break free." No wonder he'll take any opportunity to get the words "Constitution" and "negative" in the same sentence.

There was, however, one phrase in the Constitution Obama found particularly useful to his mission. As he began running for president in earnest, he and his inner circle, Axelrod, Iranian-born Chicago crony Valerie Jarrett, strategist David Plouffe, and wife, Michelle, kept the focus squarely on the carefully crafted image of Barack as Symbol. He understood the necessity of keeping himself as ambiguous as possible, saying in his second book, *The Audacity of Hope*, "I am a blank screen, on which people of vastly different political stripes project their own views." He knew the power intrinsic in the ability to be both a blank screen and a chameleon, and he exploited it brilliantly. He hit every emotional button precisely when it needed to be hit: "change" after eight years of President Bush and wearying wars, "yes, we can" optimism when the nation was down in the dumps, and, most important, "hope" that "things could be better." Plus, let's be honest: liberals in this country just *love* getting "free" crap, and he promised it to them.

———

Herein lies the brilliance of the Obama deception. Obama took the historical, traditional, and natural American impulse for a "more perfect union" and turned it on its head. And he accomplished this feat of constitutional perversion with very few people noticing.

Starting in 1995 with the publication of *Dreams from My Father*, Obama has seized the phrase and the meaning of "a more perfect union" and co-opted it for the redistributionist cause. The phrase "a more perfect union" means different things to different people. To most Americans, it means the constant vigilance needed to ensure maximum individual liberty, as the Founders intended.

When Obama invokes "a more perfect union," however, he means one that "spreads the wealth around" while diluting American exceptionalism until it's nonexistent. Getting America to *that* version of "a more perfect union" is the ultimate mission of the leftists, who loathe America and everything for which she stands, from individual freedom to global dominance.

When he spoke about creating a "more perfect union," he believed that he was the only one who *could*—or *should*—be doing the perfecting. When he made his garishly ostentatious statement, "We're the ones we've been waiting for," he was really saying, "*I'm* the one who will at last change the very nature of America. *I* will judge when you've made enough money and who should get it instead. *I* will judge what health care you should receive. *I* will decide that the country must atone for its past sins and *I* will lead its penance."

In the spring of 2008, Obama's campaign was rocked by revelations that he had sat in the pews of Trinity United Church of Christ for over twenty years, listening to, absorbing, and apparently agreeing with the anti-American rantings of Pastor Jeremiah Wright. Audiotapes and videotapes surfaced of Wright pounding the church podium as he spewed anti-American invective.

That Obama sat in Wright's church for over twenty years, never registering a protest against any of Wright's inflammatory statements, threatened to define Obama as the anti-American radical some already suspected him to be. The controversy needed to be nipped in the bud quickly if his campaign were to survive.

On March 18, he gave a speech on his relationship with Wright, which he announced he was ending, and then spun his comments into a broader thought piece on race and American ideals.

Obama's address about Wright became known as the "more perfect union" speech. He began, "'We the people, in order to form a more *perfect* union.' This was one of the tasks we set forth at the beginning of this campaign—to continue the long march of those who came before us, a march for a *more just, more equal*, more free, more caring and more prosperous America. I chose to run for the presidency at this moment in history because I believe deeply that we cannot solve the challenges of our time unless we solve them together—unless we *perfect* our union by understanding that we may have different stories, but we hold common hopes. . . . It is not enough to give health care to the sick, or jobs to the jobless, or education to our children," Obama said. "But *it is where we start*. It is where our union grows stronger. And as so many generations have come to realize over the course of the two hundred and twenty-one years since a band of patriots signed that document in Philadelphia, that is where the *perfection* begins."

Despite throwing both Wright and his white grandma under the bus in order to save his presidential campaign, Obama received wide praise for the speech, which was considered by many to be the best of his political career. But while most people were focused on his perfectly orchestrated message of racial "unity" and "healing"—epitomized by the man himself—he had embedded a much more powerful message. The union must be "perfected," *not* in the way most Americans understand that constitutional concept, *but as the kooks intend it.*

He has peppered other speeches with the phrase "a more perfect union," and each time he has used it in service to the redistributionists' ideal of "remaking America." On August 6, 2009, he got word that the Senate voted to confirm his Supreme Court nominee, Judge Sonia Sotomayor, self-described "wise Latina," to the nation's highest bench. He gave a statement that sounded much like his 2004 convention speech, saying that the Bronx-born Latina exemplified "the very ideals that have made Judge Sotomayor's own uniquely American journey possible." And then he added that "the Senate has upheld today in breaking yet another barrier and moving us yet another step closer to a more *perfect* union" by confirming someone who would help to carry out Obama's dream of "breaking us free from the essential constraints that were placed by the Founding Fathers in the Constitution."

Most Americans heard one thing when he spoke of "perfecting the union" whereas he intended something completely different, just as they had when he and Michelle spoke of "fighting for the world as it should be." In fact, throughout the 2008 campaign, Obama let people fill in the blanks of his "blank screen" with whatever assumptions they wished, and he never disabused them of their own fantasies.

Obama allowed white voters to assume that a "more perfect union" meant closing the door on slavery and racism once and for all. He allowed black voters to see racial triumph. He allowed college kids and other young voters to see a youthful, hip guy who liked the same hip-hop music they did and who would pave the way for a brighter future for them. He allowed the wealthy to alleviate rich guilt by appealing to a sense of "justice" as he asked them to pay more of "their fair share." He allowed the poor to think that his support for big-government programs meant that they would always be taken care of by the state. He allowed women to swoon and men to feel like he was a hoop-shooting, ESPN-loving, brackets-picking best buddy. He was the perfect political Rorschach test.

The money shot on his Rorschach strategy came five days before the election when a voter in Sarasota, Florida, named Peggy Joseph attended an Obama campaign rally. Asked by an interviewer what she saw in Obama that drew her to vote for him, she replied, "I never thought this day would ever happen. I won't have to worry about putting gas in my car; I won't have to worry about paying my mortgage. You know, if I help him, he's gonna help me."

There it is. Not only did Joseph tell us what she and countless other Obama voters saw in him—a nonstop big-government goodie giveaway—but she unwittingly revealed the leftists' grand strategy of moving America away from individual self-reliance and global excep-tionalism and toward "collective salvation" and global inconsequence. Joseph was down with that; she just wanted to be on board, hand ex-tended, palm up. With her few exclamatory statements, Joseph summed up the Obama Kook Crusade.

If voters were still unclear about Obama's intentions, an episode on the 2008 campaign trail should have taken away all doubt. On October 12, an employee of a plumbing contractor, Joe Wurzelbacher, was playing football with his son in his front yard in Holland, Ohio, when Obama came campaigning through town. Obama stopped, perhaps expecting the fawning adulation he received elsewhere. From Joe the Plumber, however, he got a direct question about his tax plan, which Wurzelbacher correctly suspected was a nasty bit of class warfare: "I'm getting ready to buy a company that makes two hundred fifty to two hundred eighty thousand dollars a year. Your new tax plan's going to tax me more, isn't it?"

Obama responded with a gassy answer about how his plan would affect small businesses and admitted that for individuals and busi-nesses with revenue over $250,000 per year, the marginal tax rate would go up.

And then Obama revealed his ultimate objective: "It's not that I want to *punish your success. I just want to make sure that everybody who is behind you, that they've got a chance at success, too. . . . I think when you spread the wealth around, it's good for everybody.*" (Emphasis added.)

Classic kook.

That exchange between Obama and Joe the Plumber became a seminal moment of the campaign, but for the wrong reason. Most observers focused on Joe as a symbol of middle-class working Americans and how they were being squeezed by taxes and regulations. But the more revelatory moment was Obama's "spread the wealth around" remark. He spent so much time during the campaign projecting an image of moderate reasonableness, but if voters were truly focused on what he was actually telling them, they would have seen the truth. Obama was no reasonable moderate. He could not get to the presidency fast enough in order to "spread the wealth around."

Of course he wants to "punish your success." This reminds me of the old, reliable breakup line: "It's not you, it's me." Of course it's you, which is why they're breaking up with you! I quote the great George Costanza, who once said, "You're giving me the 'it's not you, it's me' routine? I INVENTED 'it's not you, it's me.' So NOBODY tells me it's not me, it's them. If it's anybody—IT'S ME!"

In April 2010, Obama gave a speech in Illinois about financial reform. In his prepared remarks, he was supposed to say this: "Now, we're not doing this to punish these firms or begrudge success that's fairly earned. We don't want to stop them from fulfilling their responsibility to help grow our economy." Instead, he went off teleprompter and supplied his own thoughts on the matter of making money: "We're not trying to push financial reform because we begrudge success that's fairly earned. *I do think that at a certain point, you've made enough money. But you know, part of the American way is, you can just keep on making it* if you're providing a good product." (Emphasis added.)

The idea that you can "keep on making money" that Obama cannot touch is abhorrent to him. He was essentially saying that you can just go make that money again in order to justify his taking it from you the first time around. But the point is that he never intends to *stop* confiscating it from you. After all, his ravenous beast of government needs constant care and feeding.

In 2011, Obama spoke at one of his taxpayer-subsidized "green jobs" boondoggles during which he portrayed "the rich" as lazy Thurston Howell III types on the perpetual three-hour tour. "I believe," he said, "that we can't ask everybody to sacrifice and then tell the wealthiest among us, well, you can just relax and go count your money, and don't worry about it. We're not going to ask anything of you." No; instead, Obama planned on taking the SS *Minnow* out of port in order to crash the ship onto the rocky shoals of redistributionism.

Obama speaks with such disgust about the "rich," as if the "rich" became rich by sitting around, doing nothing, relaxing. If sitting around, doing nothing, and relaxing are the gauge of wealth, then he's got to be more loaded than Richard Branson. As if the country "doesn't ask anything" of the "rich," when they carry the vast majority of the tax burden. As if the "rich" spend all day eating bonbons, "counting their money," and watching *Kourtney & Kim Take New York*. (Okay, they may do that last one, but only because, I mean, who can resist?) Understand: he doesn't want the Olsen twins' money or Bill Gates's or Tiger Woods's or Harvey Weinstein's money. Obama's friends can keep *their* wealth. Instead, he wants to confiscate the wealth of the small businessman. He wants the property of the oil worker, the local dry cleaner, and the insurance salesman. Regular Americans are his targets.

In fact, in mid-2011, Obama's acting solicitor general, Neal Katyal, went before the Sixth Circuit Court of Appeals to argue in defense of ObamaCare's "individual mandate." He told the court that if somebody didn't like the mandate, they could just earn less money. After all, as Obama said in the fall of 2011 while criticizing the banks, "You don't have some inherent right just to—you know, get a certain amount of profit." He'll see to that.

Less than a week before the 2008 election, Obama could sense full kookdom was in reach, saying, "We are five days away from fundamentally transforming the United States of America."

Note his deliberate and continual use of the words "remake" and "fundamentally transform." When he said he sought a "more perfect union" to "remake this great nation" and that he was psyched about "fundamentally transforming" the nation, many of us chose to believe he meant the election of the first black president or being free of the last president or improving the economy. And that's how he wanted it.

Obama and his advisers knew their agenda would scare the pants off the American people if they came at them full-frontal, like a *Playgirl* magazine with Barry on the cover that no one wanted to buy. The people needed to be buttered up with lies about the real agenda so they were content and sedated before the kook ax came down. The leftists kept their ideas close to the vest and their inner circle very closed, lest someone from the outside gain entry and full view of the real agenda. Obama, wife Michelle, Axelrod, and Jarrett made up the core. They were the Un-Fantastic Four! All of them came from Chicago. None had political executive experience. None had global leadership experience. There was not a single older, wiser adviser close to them to offer advice based on his or her own deep experience. Many folks scratched their heads, wondering why Obama didn't have a Henry Kissinger or James Baker around, or why he wheeled out economic and business leaders like Paul Volcker and Warren Buffett but didn't listen to them. Keeping the inner team limited and cloistered was by design. The more people close to the inner sanctum, the more people who might risk exposing the true kook agenda.

In fact, when Rahm Emanuel left the chief of staff job to run for mayor of Chicago, Obama replaced him with Bill Daley from—you guessed it—Chicago. Unlike his brother Richard—the retired Chicago mayor—Bill Daley had business experience, and Obama used him to try to reassure the private sector that his policies weren't fanatically antibusiness, which, of course, they were. Daley not only couldn't carry the lie that the administration was business friendly. He couldn't penetrate the Kook Inner Sanctum. Because of their need to protect the Big Kookuna and the agenda, they kept him perpetually on the outside. Daley lasted just a few months in the job before being shunted aside. Soon enough, it was back to the original barbershop quartet of radicalism. With all four working to reshape America in the image they harmonized to, every tone, every melody, and every lyric was used to push their master plan. There were many other advisers and strategists on the periphery, of course, but the tight-knit group kept a lid on the extent of the kookdom.

In order to make it work, they needed to do two things. First, they needed Obama to be a Candidate Zelig. Leonard Zelig is the character portrayed by Woody Allen in the film *Zelig*. Zelig is an enigma, a curiously nondescript man who has a mysterious ability to transform himself to resemble those who surround him. In the movie, Zelig gains fame as a "human chameleon."

Obama needed to transform himself before he could transform America. In order to disguise his radicalism, he became whomever he was around. To folks like Peggy Joseph, for example, he was Santa Claus. If he were a Marvel Comics character, he'd definitely be the archvillain Chameleon, who did such dastardly deeds as disguising himself as Captain America in order to gain the trust of Captain America's fellow Avenger, Iron Man. With each person Obama sat down with, from Rick Warren to Oprah Winfrey, he would put on a different face, tailor-made for that particular audience. Underlying every incarnation, however, was one theme: he would be their savior. As he indicated many times, he believes in "collective salvation," by which he means salvation delivered by the state. But he made sure that when people looked at him, they saw only the concept of "salvation," hence his deliberate use of Jesus/messiah imagery.

The second thing the Obama inner circle needed to do was amp up the cult of personality begun in 1995 with the publication of *Dreams from My Father* and stoked in 2004 with his convention speech. If many Americans could be swept up in the carefully crafted Orwellian projection of the man, they would be less inclined to focus on what he actually intended to do. They needed to make each person feel as if their vote for Obama were their own personal success. The voters needed to be caressed and cuddled, told how enlightened and beautiful they were, taken dancing, and given endless cheap wine in the back of a limo. As Candidate Zelig charmed each audience, he dripped with charisma and flashed a 100-watt smile. He glided through crowds, getting people to lean in to try to shake his hand or touch him, like the sick woman who was healed simply by touching Jesus's garment. He spoke in carefully modulated tones, often using hypnotic techniques such as repetition ("Yes, we can! Yes, we can! Yes, we can!") and the "yes set," which is an exchange that is intentionally set up to get a positive answer. For example, during the campaign he would ask the crowd if they were ready for "change," and they would yell "yes!" Then he would ask them if they were ready for "hope," and they would shriek "yes!" And then he would button it up by asking if they were ready to "fundamentally transform America," and once again, they'd howl "yes!" He had them so hysterically riled up that nobody stopped to think. Do you want higher taxes? (Yes!) Do you want illegal aliens to vote? (Yes!) Do you want me to use the sauna alone with Hugo Chávez? (Yes!)

Obama was also an adept "grievance identifier." Merely by identifying your grievance, he'd suggest he'd fix it. To Peggy Joseph, who either didn't want to or couldn't pay her mortgage, he'd pay it for her. Your 401(k) down? No problem! Obama was going to take hold of the economy. Can't afford a new car? No worries! Obama would take care of that. Jobs to the jobless! Health care to the sick! Apologies to the world! Free government-issued tighty whities, featuring Obama's face sewn on the inside!

Obama was ingenious at laying out the nation's grievances, and soon enough he had millions of people nodding in agreement: "Yes, that's right." "Yes, I have that problem, and that one, and that one too!" Pretty soon, you were agreeing to problems you didn't even know you or the nation had. This was one of the key essences of the redistributionists' strategy: convince you of a set of problems and then tell you that only government can solve them. Why fix something yourself when there's someone in front of you—Barack Obama—who is offering to fix it for you? In short order, Obama was riding the "hope and change" tsunami. If Bill Clinton had indulged the Elvis cult, Obama ratcheted up a level and indulged the Jesus cult. In fact, the Obama campaign even trained volunteers to "testify" about how they "came to Obama" the way one would testify about how they "came to Jesus." These would be the same Obama campaign staffers who often referred to him as a "black Jesus." John Lennon had provoked a public outcry in 1966 when he claimed that the Beatles were "more popular than Jesus." Forty-two years later, Obama laid claim to the same proposition and was adored for it.

———

The mainstream media fell into the Obama trance as well, although they needed even less of the hypnotic induction than most people. Since the vast majority of reporters and editors in print and television media are left-wing, they had a built-in ideological affinity for Obama. They were predisposed to love him and he them, like two juvenile delinquents at a warehouse rave party taking Ecstasy and playing with glow sticks. In the past, however, although many so-called journalists would openly support the Democratic candidates, they didn't necessarily fall in love with them. Until Barack. Many in the left-wing media either remembered or idealized the Kennedy years, with a young, handsome Democrat in the White House, surrounded by a glamorous wife and young children. Obama updated Camelot for the twenty-first century, and the media lapped it up like parched puppies. They would do their part to re-create the Kennedy mystique around this dynamic black couple, help him get elected, and maintain the mythology.

The press took their cheerleading to absurd levels. The then *Newsweek* editor Evan Thomas took the "black Jesus" metaphor literally when he gushed, "I mean in a way Obama's standing above the country, above—above the world, he's sort of God." MSNBC host Chris Matthews spoke of the homoerotic charge he got while listening to Obama speak: "I have to tell you, you know, it's part of reporting this case, this election, the feeling most people get when they hear Barack Obama's speech. My, I felt this thrill going up my leg."

In June 2008 the Associated Press went out of its way to tell us that Obama is a "great man." In a piece of ostensibly straight reporting, the AP gushed: "Indonesians were rooting for the man they consider to be a hometown hero. Obama lived in the predominantly Muslim nation from age 6 to 10 with his mother and Indonesian stepfather and was fondly remembered by former teachers and classmates." The AP then helpfully quoted from some "regular" admirers:

"He was an average student, but very active," said Widianto Hendro Cahyono, forty-eight, who was in the same third-grade class as Obama at SDN Menteng elementary school in Jakarta. "He would play ball during recess until he was dripping with sweat. I never imagined he would become a great man." Away from the reporter and missed by the AP, the man then added, "But as I remember, the great man still has a terrible jump shot." Just kidding.

Shortly after Obama had clinched his party's nomination, the AP ran another piece suggesting that if you don't vote for Obama, you might be a racist. They posed two questions about the candidates:

"Will [Senator John] McCain be able to overcome the country's intense desire for change by separating himself from the unpopular Bush while sticking close on issues of war and taxes?" And, "Will Obama be able to overcome the country's unsavory history of slavery and lingering bigotry that deeply divides the public to be elected the first black president?"

In other words, if you don't vote for McCain, you're anti-Bush. Yay! But if you don't vote for Obama, you're a racist. And you hate America.

The AP's work here is done. I could go on with a gazillion other examples of the mainstream media drooling over Obama, but then this book would be the size of the ObamaCare bill.

A particularly egregious example of the media's pro-Obama activism was the attempt by some of them to bury the Jeremiah Wright scandal. As tapes of Obama's longtime pastor spewing vicious anti-American rhetoric flooded the airwaves, the left-wing media tried to ignore the story until they couldn't anymore, and that's when they panicked. They needed to figure out a way to defend Obama against the allegations that by sitting in Wright's church for twenty years, he agreed with Wright's brutally anti-American and racist views. Obama's candidacy was in peril. Bill and Hillary Clinton were licking their chops, as were the Republicans. Obama needed his chestnuts pulled out of the fire, and the left-wing media obliged.

As the *Daily Caller* originally reported, members of JournoList, a listserv made up of hundreds of left-wing journalists from media organizations such as *Time*, Politico.com, the *Baltimore Sun*, the *Guardian*, *The Nation*, Salon.com, and *The New Republic* were outraged that George Stephanopoulos of ABC News had asked Obama why it had taken him so long to dissociate himself from Wright's comments. The left-wing journalists jumped into action, with Thomas Schaller of the *Baltimore Sun* suggesting, "Why don't we use the power of this list to do something about the debate?" and writing a "smart statement expressing disgust" at the questions Stephanopoulos had asked Obama.

At one point, Chris Hayes of *The Nation* tipped his kook hand: "Our nation disappears people," he wrote on JournoList. "It tortures people. It has the blood of as many as one million Iraqi civilians—men, women, children, the infirmed—on its hands. You'll forgive me if I just can't quite dredge up the requisite amount of outrage over Barack Obama's pastor."

There it was: kookdom in all of its anti-Americanism. No wonder so many in the left-wing media sought to protect and advance Obama. The media honestly believed in the man and his mission and they would do whatever they could to make his presidency a reality. No rigorous probing into his background. No demands that he release the most basic life records that they demand of other candidates, such as college and law school records, Selective Service registration, medical records, law practice client list, or Illinois state senate records. We demanded answers. How long has he had a subscription to *Good Housekeeping*, *Teen Vogue*, and *Hustler*? How many speeding tickets does he have? How often does he rent *House Party 2* from Netflix? These are all records we'd like to see, but the press just checked out. No tough questions. Just polite requests to touch his garments and sepia-toned hagiographies.

Once he became president, he used the full force of the White House to create an Orwellian landscape, in which media organizations and reporters that didn't play the Obama propaganda game were intimidated and punished. During Obama's hard sell of ObamaCare in August 2009, the White House appointed health care "czar" Nancy-Ann DeParle and former ABC News correspondent Linda Douglass to lead the effort to monitor the blogs and "casual conversations" of ObamaCare opponents and then report them to the president. The *Boston Herald* got slammed by the White House for having the audacity to run an op-ed by the former Massachusetts governor and GOP presidential contender Mitt Romney. The *San Francisco Chronicle* was punished by Team Obama because a print pool reporter recorded anti-Obama protesters at a Bay Area fund-raiser. A local Texas reporter at WFAA TV was criticized by the president himself for interrupting him. CBS News investigative reporter Sharyl Attkisson was "screamed at" by White House flunky Eric Schultz for probing the Fast and Furious gunwalking scandal. The Obama 2012 reelection team launched "Attack Watch," which, as they put it, was "a new way to track and respond to attacks against President Obama." And the White House orchestrated a war on an entire news network, Fox News. If media organizations did not toe the line, fall in, and gush over Obama and his agenda with the appropriate enthusiasm, they were called out, dressed down, and punished.

Every crusader needs protectors, and the left-wing media became Obama's Knights Templar.

While many Americans took leave of their senses and unplugged their brains, Obama continued his march.

On August 28, 2008, Obama strode onstage in Denver at the Democratic National Convention to accept his party's nomination for president. All around him were towering, fake Greek columns. Eighty-four thousand swooning fans hung on his every word. And once again, he dropped obvious clues about his intentions: "It's time for us to *change America*," he said. And "America, now is not the time for small plans." And in his inaugural address on January 20, 2009, the day when the kooks finally seized the brass ring, Obama again stated his objective: "Starting today, we must pick ourselves up, dust ourselves off, and begin again the work of *remaking* America."

The inaugural extravaganza, during which Obama sat by the Lincoln Memorial as Beyoncé and Bono crooned to him and awaited his Caesarian thumbs-up or thumbs-down, was the moment the Obama Hypnosis finally jumped the shark. In another moment that perfectly encapsulated the height of the Obama hysteria, college student Julio Osegueda attended an Obama town hall in Fort Myers, Florida, just weeks after Obama was sworn in, and he had a breathless freak-out: "Oh, it is such a blessing to see you, Mr. President! Thank you for taking time out of your day! OH, GRACIOUS GOD, THANK YOU SO MUCH!!!!!" Julio needed to get shot with a tranquilizer dart and buy a new set of undies after Obama was done with him.

Once he was sworn in as president, however, the American people took a backseat to Obama's redistributionist agenda. After all, the people weren't critical to his plans. In fact, we were an impediment to them, something to be massaged, finessed, lied to, and manipulated. As Jon Stewart aptly noted in *Rolling Stone* in the fall of 2011, "I think he was already kind of over us by the time he got into office."

To Obama, any public disapproval of his plans needed to be removed or crushed. Campaigning as a unifying transcendent figure and governing as a redistributionist involved two different skill sets. Once he became president, the unifying, amber-lit guy disappeared and was replaced by Big Daddy.

Every president assumes a somewhat paternalistic role as he leads the nation. He's the guy in charge, shaping the country, leading us in war, making or keeping the peace, herding Congress, and presiding over 300 million citizens who look to him for protection, reassurance, and guidance. Obama, however, has taken the daddy role and supersized it. Let's face it. Obama is the worst national daddy EVER. He's like Alec Baldwin, Michael Lohan, and David Hasselhoff, rolled up into one giant dysfunctional, un-paternal narcissistic nightmare.

In his inaugural address, Obama returned to a phrase that he had used before as he admonished us to "put away childish things." In framing it that way, he subliminally put each listener—each American—in the position of *being* a child. And of course, the nanny state he is building makes children out of *all* of us as the government—with him sitting at the top—strips your freedom and makes you a dependent. But don't worry—Big Daddy will ensure that you have the care you need. Everyone gets a bib, a high chair, and a sippy cup with a smiling Barry on the front.

By virtue of his super-paternalistic role, Obama elevated himself over Congress as well as the American people. Two days after he was sworn in as president, Obama invited top congressional leaders to the White House to discuss plans for economic "stimulus." When Republican senator Jon Kyl challenged him over the package's massive spending and tax "cut" to people who do not pay income taxes, Obama shot back: "I won."

Two months later, the House Democratic Caucus met with Obama to discuss his budget proposal. When the president spotted Democratic representative Peter DeFazio, who had voted against the "stimulus," Obama leaned in to him and said, "Don't think we're not keeping score, brother."

This was the presidency, done Sopranos-style. But it was also designed to remind Congress of who was Boss. Big Daddy was now on the scene, and that coequal branch of government thing? Forget it. In fact, Obama took to routinely lecturing Congress about this or that policy, repeatedly summoning congressional leaders to the White House on whims, convening numerous joint sessions to make them show up and applaud his latest kook proposal for health care or jobs. During the 2011 debt debate, Obama even instructed members of Congress to "eat their peas" and get a deal in front of him. "Hey, you kids! Stop fighting and play nice!" This was Big Daddy on steroids, presiding over his rapidly growing welfare state in which all of us are infantilized and, like dutiful children, silenced.

The Planet of the Kooks

The United States has had forty-four presidents. Some of them have been brilliant; some of them have been less swift. Some have been effective chief executives; others couldn't manage their way out of a paper bag. Some got it on with interns; others farmed peanuts and hated Israel. Some have been intellectuals; others have been populists. Some left in disgrace; others *should* have left in disgrace. Some have only earned one term; others ran their wives in an effort to co-opt a third term. Some were visionary; others couldn't see past tomorrow. Some were great, articulate communicators; others needed the English edition of *Rosetta Stone*.

We've had all kinds in the presidency, but Obama represents a first. All previous presidents had guiding political philosophies, which they all bent—to some degree or another—when it became too difficult politically to stick to them or when the American people resoundingly rejected what they were doing. Some of them pressed on anyway, but all of them at least acknowledged the American people and registered their discontent. All previous presidents had at least some degree of responsiveness to the people they led. Not Obama. This president is driven by such a devout and fervent ideology that nothing—not big majorities of the American people, not the Constitution—can stop him. We've seen other transformative presidents—Lincoln, FDR, Reagan—but none of them attempted to transform the nation into something wholly unrecognizable as America—until this one.

Over the decades, the redistributionists had realized that whenever they went full frontal with their ideas and policies, the American people rejected them out of hand as anti-American and destructive. If, however, they painted those same ideas with a brush of emotionalism, the ideas would become more palatable. After all, who among us doesn't want children to be educated? Who doesn't want clean drinking water? Who wants to see the poor go without health care or the elderly to have to subsist on cat food? Of course, no rational, caring person wants to see any of those things, particularly in the wealthiest country on earth. Social safety nets were created to ensure that no one in America went without the basic necessities of food, shelter, and medical care. But that wasn't enough for the kooks. Once they took over, Maslow's hierarchy of needs was expanded to include free DirecTV, Ferragamo dress shoes, and contraception. A bit of a stretch from food and shelter.

This was the essence of Obama's Declaration of Dependence. Instead of treating them as temporary helping hands to only those in need, the redistributionists saw the programs as gleaming opportunities for the massive expansion of government power as well as leverage to build a permanent Democratic majority. If they could maneuver the programs into ever-growing entities that covered ever-growing numbers of people, those same people would become ever dependent on government and, therefore, ever grateful to the party and ideology that made that assistance available to them.

The leftists were also ingenious at casting those who opposed their plan to metastasize government as cold jerks who wanted to throw Grandma in the snow and the homeless back into the street. Their emotional extortion allowed them great leeway to build the redistributionist state they sought with limited resistance, even from many conservatives. The kooks had managed to make kookdom desirable, even expected.

The redistributionists use spending blowouts not as mere vehicles to "take care of people" or to secure their own reelection. They use big spending for a much more sinister purpose. Health care "reform" is not about health care. Environmental "protection" is not about the environment. Medicare is not about medical services for the elderly. Medicaid is not about medical services for the poor. Social Security is not about protecting senior citizens. None of these programs is about their superficial purpose. Their real purpose is to take wealth and assets from one group and redistribute it to another in order to build an increasingly redistributionist system, one that tightened its vise grip on you before you knew it.

Obama took the ball and not only ran with it but broke world land-race records. Team Obama has executed a near-perfect application of

Alinsky's *Rules for Radicals*. Any other American president would have been flipping his lid over stubbornly high unemployment, perhaps the most politically toxic element in any bad economy. Obama never broke a sweat. He would roll out the occasional "jobs plan" and propose ever more government spending, but he never seemed all that disturbed by 9 to 10 percent unemployment, zero job creation, or anemic economic growth. He has never been ashamed of his spending binge. He has never run from it or defensively defended it. To the contrary, he has been proud of his massive spending, calling it "necessary" and constantly proposing *more* spending.

The question is: For *what* is his unprecedented spending "necessary"? The reason Obama has never broken a sweat over the bankrupting spending and the collapsing economy is that it is all *intentional*. The reason Obama has always proposed more government spending and never got serious about deficit and debt reduction is that *he does not think we have a spending and debt problem*. In his view, there is *never* enough money because the government should *always* be doing more.

Obama's Declaration of Dependence rests on economic upheaval because it serves the greater goal. The objective all along was to use and prolong the economic chaos to expand government as well as the number of people dependent on it. And ever-greater numbers of people dependent on government means ever-greater *need* for ever-bigger government. That, in turn, would ultimately result in a permanent Democratic voting majority. Indeed, in 2011 the Obama administration, through the U.S. Department of Agriculture, launched a multimillion-dollar initiative to recruit more food stamp recipients even though the food stamp rolls had already reached record levels. In September 2011, Oregon bragged that it had received a $5 million "performance bonus" for ensuring that people eligible for food assistance receive it and for "its swift processing of applications." That bonus was in addition to a separate $1.5 million award from Team Obama for making "accurate payments of food stamp benefits to clients." Note their use of the word "clients" to describe welfare recipients.

The redistributionists have always kept their eyes on the prize. They have played the long game. And they have carefully cloaked another truth: since the balance between government power and liberty is zero-sum, the more power the government amasses, the less liberty there is for the individual. Their massive spending is deliberate: it is a coldly calculated move to destroy the fiscal health of the country in order to justify a constantly metastasizing state. It's like the classic 1958 horror/sci-fi flick *The Blob*. The Blob starts out as a tiny jellylike substance. But it quickly grows and grows, until its mass is enormous and completely uncontrollable, consuming everything in its path of destruction.

In a real sense, Barack Obama sees himself as a modern-day Robin Hood. But the concept of "taking from the rich and giving to the poor" is an oversimplification of the Robin Hood story, and a false analogy to boot. Robin Hood, in fact, would never have existed without an authoritarian regime levying higher taxes, confiscating wealth and property, and suppressing liberty. Robin Hood was a leader of a rebellion, standing up for the rights of the individual versus the burden of the state. He was a champion for people from whom things had *already* been *taken*, . . . not a champion for those who started out with nothing. Obama wants a world in which wealth is stolen from the wealthy and given to those who never earned it and never will. Barack Obama is no Robin Hood. He's Prince John.

As we all learn by age three when we drop our ice-cream cone and Mom and Dad say no to another, life isn't fair. That basic rule of life's road has never been accepted by the delusional Left, which continues to believe that with massive government activism, life in America can be a nonstop Woodstock: blissful communal living in which everything is shared and no one has an advantage over another. Just imagine a White House lawn that's been transformed into a giant muddy mess, where Joe Biden, Valerie Jarrett, and Jay Carney play Typhoon Lagoon in the filth while Crosby, Stills, Nash, and Young and Santana serenade them for Three Days of Peace, Love, and Liberal Garbage.

This is the kooks' dream. All American resources are to be freed up in service of it.

For the leftists, ideology trumps everything. It trumps politics, retaining congressional majorities, even reelection. The kind of clear shot to "remake America" that Obama and the kooks got after the 2008 election was rare. The shot would probably not happen again for a long time, if ever.

So the mission needed to be executed with dispatch. Obama didn't even wait to be sworn in before he began installing his powerful shadow cabinet. The *Washington Post* reported that Obama transition director John Podesta said that "Obama *deliberately* was building a strong, centralized White House organization." (Emphasis added.) It would be made up of a vast number of unaccountable "czars" who reported only to Obama. These czars were like something out of a wiseguy movie. They could operate with impunity, do all of President Obama's dirty work, and, at the end of a typical workday, White House chief of staff Rahm Emanuel would hand each of them a sweaty wad of untraceable bills.

Other presidents had appointed individual czars to deal with specific issues, but none had built such a massive czar apparatus to bypass Congress and work behind the scenes in a coordinated, systematic way. To be fair, Barack didn't come up with the idea to beef up the number of czars right away. It was only after he caught an airing of *Batman Begins* on basic cable while campaigning and was inspired by Liam Neeson's character in the League of Shadows, a vigilante ninja crime syndicate that operates out of the confines of regular society. Obama created his *own* League of Shadows. Their mission was to get the leftist agenda done by implementing Obama's executive orders and by bureaucratic fiat. After all, he couldn't "remake America" by himself.

Obama's initial group of czars was a delightful collection of communists, socialists, and other sundry radicals. In fact, he met them all at socialist summer camp, where together they would make arts and crafts projects like a hammer and sickle constructed out of boondoggle, pinecones, and Popsicle sticks. After a long day of nature hikes up the Ho Chi Minh Trail and skinny-dipping with Madeleine Albright, they would roast Marxist marshmallows and tell scary stories about capitalism around the campfire.

Among those he appointed were:

Carol Browner, energy and environment czar. As recently as December 2008, she was listed as a commissioner in Socialist International, a global organization of socialist and labor parties that chronically condemns U.S. policies. Browner was one of fourteen official leaders of the socialist group's Commission for a Sustainable World Society. That's a particularly shadowy group whose objective is to establish a world government to control the world's wealthiest economies by using the pretext of global climate change.

Cass Sunstein, regulatory czar. In his book *The Second Bill of Rights: FDR's Unfinished Revolution and Why We Need It More Than Ever*, Sunstein waxes rhapsodic about socialism and the need for ever-bigger government: "In brief, the second bill attempts to protect both opportunity and security, by creating rights to employment, adequate food and clothing, decent shelter, education, recreation, and medical care." Socialized medicine and free Ho-Hos for everyone! No wonder there's no Cass without "ass."

In an op-ed for the *Chicago Tribune*, Sunstein argued more directly for a socialist revolution as he lectured us to celebrate paying taxes: "In what sense is the money in our pockets and bank accounts fully 'ours'? . . . Without taxes, there would be no liberty. Without taxes there would be no property. Without taxes, few of us would have any assets worth defending." And then came the killer kook concept: "There is no liberty without dependency."

That's the very essence of kookdom, right there, in Sunstein's neat little phrase. For Obama, Sunstein's efficient approach to redistributionism made him perfect to oversee all existing regulations and create new, more economy-killing ones.

Van Jones, green jobs czar. Born Anthony Kapel Jones, he decided to go by the nickname Van, probably to sound more interesting and hard-core. Let's face it: Would *you* take anyone named Tony Jones seriously? How many Marxists named Tony Jones do you know? Without his "Van," he'd merely be a bespectacled dork named Tony Jones.

In his early career as a radical activist, Van was a leading member of Standing Together to Organize a Revolutionary Movement (STORM), a San Francisco–area Marxist-Maoist group. He was arrested in 1993 during the Rodney King riots and again in 1999 during the Seattle protests against the World Trade Organization. By that time, Jones was a fully committed Marxist-Leninist-Maoist who hated capitalism for its alleged exploitation of minorities worldwide. He made it his mission to undercut and ultimately destroy the global capitalist system by mobilizing leftist mobs and by seeking to remake entire sectors of the economy, primarily the energy industry, by leveraging the phony concept of green jobs. As he said, "This movement is deeper than solar panels! . . . We're gonna change the whole system! . . . We want a new system!" In the fall of 2009, after just a few months on the job, Jones was forced to resign his czar post after Glenn Beck first reported on his communist ties. Jones moved into the George Soros–supported Center for American Progress, the leftist receptacle for radicals needing to move further below the radar. You've got to give it to Van: he doesn't even bother to disguise the fact that he's a raving communist maniac.

Ron Bloom, car czar. He was responsible for the forced closure of thousands of Chrysler and GM dealerships around the country that resulted in the loss of up to two hundred thousand jobs. His only experience with automobiles involved sitting on his couch watching *The Dukes of Hazzard*. His leftist kookdom was revealed in all of its glory in a February 2008 speech, in which he said, "Generally speaking, we get the joke. We know that the free market is nonsense. . . . We know this is largely about power, that it's an adults-only no-limit game. We kind of agree with Mao that political power comes largely from the barrel of a gun." Memo to Obama's first communications director, Anita Dunn: you weren't the only Mao-lover in the White House.

Vivek Kundra, information czar. Also known as: Who the Heck Is Vivek? Obama appointed him the nation's chief technology officer, in charge of a $71 billion budget, even though Kundra pleaded guilty to shoplifting $134 worth of stuff from JC Penney in 1997. Just days after his appointment, Kundra was placed on administrative leave after his former office was raided by the FBI. He would have been Obama's point man in reading your e-mails. "Hi Vivek! OMG. LOL. ☺ "

John Holdren, science czar, who looks like he probably auditioned for the lead role in *The Shaggy Dog*, but don't let the cuddly look fool you. Holdren is a particularly nasty piece of leftist work. He has called America "the meanest of wealthy countries" and has endorsed one-world government in a "surrender of sovereignty" to "a comprehensive planetary regime" that would control and dispense all global resources, redistribute the confiscated wealth, draft a world army, direct a "de-development" of the West, and limit the growth of the world's population through compulsory abortion. Babies, schmabies! Who needs 'em?

Nancy-Ann DeParle, health care czar. A strong proponent of health care rationing. While we're aborting babies, let's kill Grandma too!

Ed Montgomery, car recovery czar. A former ACORN board member who serves on the academic advisory committee for the Soros-funded Center for American Progress.

Alan Bersin, border czar. An advocate of open borders, because after all, sovereignty is overrated.

Obama, with the assistance of the radical czars and his wingmen in Congress, got the leftist rampage rolling. In the first hundred days alone, Obama pushed through the nearly $1 trillion "stimulus"; got a half-trillion-dollar omnibus spending bill; offered up a measly $100 million in "cuts" in a nearly $4 trillion initial proposed budget, all while claiming he wanted "fiscal responsibility"; nationalized much of the U.S. auto industry; screwed General Motors' bondholders; pledged transparency while stonewalling disclosure of where the TARP (Trouble Asset Relief Program) money went; nominated five tax cheats to his cabinet; began to launch Adventures in Socialized Medicine; oversaw a Department of Homeland Security report that called our returning veterans "security risks"; politicized the 2010 Census by moving it into the White House; announced the closure of Guantánamo Bay without a plan to actually do so; released top-secret Central Intelligence Agency interrogation memos; opened the door to prosecutions of CIA officials who had engaged in enhanced interrogations of terrorist suspects; failed to respond to a North Korean nuclear missile test launch; was all smiles for longtime U.S. enemies Hugo Chávez, Fidel Castro, and Daniel Ortega; bowed to Saudi king Abdullah; began his Apology Tour to offer his regret for past American injustice; and insulted our closest ally, Great Britain, not once but twice, first by returning a bust of Winston Churchill that had been a special gift, and second, by giving Her Majesty Queen Elizabeth II an iPod loaded with his speeches (because, after all, Obama speeches are like Lay's Potato Chips: you can't have just one).

The kooks knew that their redistributionist omelet could not be made without breaking a few eggs and that they might lose a few bodies along the way. Indeed, as time passed, the Obama Hypnosis began to wear off and the redistributionists' agenda ripened. Pretty soon, "stimulus," omnibus spending, bailouts, ObamaCare, Dodd-Frank financial regulation, and suffocating Environmental Protection Agency and National Labor Relations Board regulations were no longer the dynamic new policies of the hip new president but the destructive policies of a president bent on deconstructing America. Despite his assurances that his policies would produce glowing economic results, they instead wreaked a tornadic path of economic terror.

Within a few months of their takeover, the Democratic casualties began to pile up. There were more dead carcasses on the ground than in the final scene of *Reservoir Dogs*. In November 2009, voters in deep blue New Jersey and purple Virginia elected Republican governors, Chris Christie and Robert McDonnell, respectively. In January 2010, voters in deep blue Massachusetts elected a Republican senator, Scott Brown, to replace Edward Kennedy. In November 2010, voters across the country swept Republicans into control of the House and closer control of the Senate, while the GOP took eleven governorships from Democrats in states such as Ohio, Michigan, Pennsylvania, and Iowa, as well as one governorship previously held by an independent in Florida. In September 2011, two Republicans won special congressional elections in Nevada and in a New York district that had been represented by such left-wing icons as Geraldine Ferraro, Chuck Schumer, and Anthony Weiner. There were a few Democratic wins during this time in special elections in upstate New York and California, but the overall trend was overwhelmingly Republican. Being a Democrat was like being a leper, as they watched their precious limbs rot away and fall off, one after another.

And yet Obama shrugged off these losses as transactional costs in the "fundamental transformation of America." In perhaps the most telling example of Obama's Alinskyite view that the radical ends justified even steep political losses, one of the last remaining Democratic moderates in the Senate, Arkansas senator Blanche Lincoln, begged Obama to abandon kookdom. Increasingly nervous about how Obama's radicalism would affect her reelection chances in 2010, Lincoln tried to get Obama to repudiate "extreme" liberals such as then-House Speaker Nancy Pelosi and move toward the center. During a February 3, 2010, meeting Obama held with Senate Democrats about Obama-Care, Lincoln pleaded with him to moderate his far-left agenda because, she said, it was sowing job-destroying "uncertainty" in the business community. She asked him point-blank: "Are we willing as Democrats to push back on our own party?"

Obama's reply? Sorry, Blanche: you're crud out of luck.

"If the price of certainty," he shot back, "is essentially for us to adopt the exact same proposals that were in place for eight years leading up to the biggest economic crisis since the Great Depression—we don't tinker with health care, let the insurance companies do what they want, we don't put in place any insurance reforms, we don't mess with the banks, let them keep on doing what they're doing now because we don't want to stir up Wall Street—the result is going to be the same." Obama's words made clear that he had no intention of "moderating" his agenda or "triangulating" Bill Clinton–style. His own personal political survival—as well as the political careers of his fellow Democrats—placed a distant second to the implementation of the kook agenda. In fact, Obama occasionally indicated that his fate may be a single term as president. In January 2010, he told ABC News that he would "rather be a really good one-term president than a mediocre two-term president." And in June 2011, he told NBC News, "I'm sure there are days where I say one term is enough."

To Obama, if he could slam the entire redistributionist agenda into one term, he'd gladly check out after four years, even if that meant a reelection loss. "My work here is done, America. Socialism 4-ever! Peace out!"

There was, however, another critical element to the kooks' strategy, one that was even more important than the cult of personality opiate they kept mainlining to the masses. America had been hit with heroin, morphine, codeine, and finally Baracksycontin. And still, things were about to get worse. When it came time to discuss major policies, from the "stimulus" to ObamaCare to the budget and spending to the debt ceiling, the redistributionists made the Republicans and everyone else believe that they were engaged on the same playing field when, in reality, the kooks were on a different one entirely.

Time and again, the Republicans took Obama at his word that he wanted real fiscal responsibility, deficit reduction, spending cuts, cost-containing health care reform, job creation, and economic growth. Time and again, they believed him when he said he was interested in their ideas and was willing to listen to them. And each time, the Republicans would ready their alternative market- and individual-based proposals, present them to Obama, and eagerly await his promised "conversation" about them, only to be met with a rolled-up newspaper slapped across their noses. The congressional Republicans received worse attention, harsher treatment, and less face time than Obama's dog Bo. In fact, at one point Bo decided he was going to relieve himself inside the White House. Upon discovery, the president blamed the mess on Eric Cantor.

The perfect symbol of the disconnect between what the kooks were actually doing and the Republicans' naive belief that they were to be included in policy making was Representative Paul Ryan's budget presentation in the spring of 2011. When the GOP took control of the House in January 2011, they began work on a budget. Ryan, the chairman of the House Budget Committee, had been working on budgetary issues for years and labored tirelessly on a major reform document that proposed serious spending cuts and structural changes to Medicare, Medicaid, and other entitlement programs in order to rescue them from the jaws of insolvency. Ryan, all boyish good looks and earnest demeanor, released the Republican budget and prepared for brutal political attacks but also at least serious engagement from the White House on the issues. He accepted Obama's invitation to attend a major address by the president on spending and the deficit.

Ryan was seated front and center, perhaps expecting to hear the president announce that he was finally ready to meet the GOP and him halfway in order to restore fiscal order. Instead, Ryan and his plan were met by a relentless barrage of partisan insults, policy attacks, and Obama's own budget proposal that was so ludicrously budget-busting that it was later unanimously defeated in the Senate 97 to 0. Representative Ryan should have known something was amiss when he was seated in the "naughty chair" and forced to wear a KICK ME sign while Joe Biden tied Ryan's shoelaces together. Ryan was by far the more thoughtful and mature of the two men in the room that day and the only one with a serious budget plan, but Obama assumed the Big Daddy persona and cast Ryan as the naive schoolboy who needed to be taught a lesson.

Regardless of the issue, the president would blow a dog whistle and Republicans would eagerly come running to the table with their own ideas and proposals, only to be blown off in the most disrespectful and cavalier ways by Obama and the leftists. Obama never had any intention of reining in government, cutting spending, reducing the deficit, considering market-based ideas for health care reform, carrying out tax reform, or engaging in serious entitlement reform (see his immediate blow-off of his own deficit reduction commission, Simpson-Bowles). While he was busy "perfecting America" on one playing field, the Republicans were operating obliviously on another one. And the Republicans didn't even realize they were being played.

The GOP was Obama's booty call. The Republicans were willing to be "friends with benefits" in the hope that a relationship would form. Meanwhile, Barry was just looking for a casual hookup in order to get what he wanted. Indeed, he already had a longtime girlfriend named Karla Marxism . . . so for him, it was simply "Wham, Bam, No Thank You, John Boehner."

His True Stripes

I believe all the choices we've made have been the right ones.

—*Barack Obama, October 2011*

Barack Obama sold himself as the One who was going to bring us all together. He campaigned as the guy who, because of his biracial makeup and cool-cat demeanor, was the *only* one who could unite the nation and erase divisions based on politics, race, gender, and religion. The one area he deliberately left out was class divisions. He would need those in order to accomplish his redistributive mission. But he promised that under his leadership, other splits that have long riven America would be healed. He was unique. Special. A one-of-a-kind man for the moment.

Instead of making good on his Rodney King–esque "can't we all get along" promise, however, Mr. "I'm a uniter, not a divider 2.0" managed to divide the nation in ways unimaginable before his presidency. We are more polarized politically, economically, racially, and culturally than ever.

And yet, notice that Obama hasn't moved to fix these deepening divides. He hasn't done any of the "healing" he promised because he never had any intention of healing anything. Like a dutiful Alinskyite, he never let a crisis go to waste, and he created them when necessary. If everyone were getting along and the economy were a job-creating dynamo, there would be no crisis atmosphere to justify his massive, unprecedented expansion of government.

He *needs* the economic situation to stay dire. He *needs* spending to continue to spiral upward. He *needs* the debt to reach unprecedented levels. He *needs* unemployment to stay high. He *needs* the classes pitted against each other. He *needs* a growing pauper class to keep the class conflict going. He *needs* a wealthy class constantly under assault. He *needs* government-sector unions strong and growing. He *needs* union thugs on the march. He *needs* conflict between the public and private sectors. He *needs* a southern border out of control. He *needs* a world thrown into disarray by retrenching American leadership. He *needs* to have the latest iPad before everyone else.

Obama and his fellow redistributionists have inflamed all of these crises as pretexts to sink the tentacles of state power into every part of our lives, from our checkbooks to our Chevy Tahoes to our hot dogs to our tonsillectomies. Obama has so consolidated power in his own hands and in the hands of the very few unelected kooks around him that freedom as we've always known it is slipping away.

Chaos and control: the very elements of George Orwell's *1984* are the exact underpinnings of the Obama presidency.

And sitting atop it all is the one person we hire to look out for us: the president. He has always been a Trojan horse who said all of the right things, who whispered empty, sweet nothings like "hope" and "change" and "healing" and "perfecting," but who—once he had gotten us to say "yes, we can"—sank the knife into our backs, à la Michael Corleone. "We knew it was you, Barry. You broke our heart. You broke our heart!"

The writer Maya Angelou once said, "When somebody shows you who they are, *believe them . . . the first time.*"

Obama's beliefs and policies were so extreme and destructive that many Americans tried to explain or justify them away, by claiming to themselves and others that he was "really not that bad" or that "his

critics find any reason to attack him." The defensive crouch sometimes expressed itself in a benign way ("he's in over his head") and
sometimes in a much darker way ("his critics are racist"). As time
went on, other excuses were offered: he was "trying to do too much,"
"naive," "incompetent." When he continued to present the same big-
government, big-spending policies and refused to moderate his positions, some people invoked Albert Einstein's famous definition of
insanity as doing the same thing over and over again, expecting a
different result. The *New York Times* even prepared a piece that suggested Obama suffered from clinical depression. Color me naive, but
I have a hard time believing that a man who spends so many of his
waking hours planning the latest celebrity visit to the White House is
secretly the next Sylvia Plath.

He is not naive, incompetent, insane, or depressed. And the longer
we've danced around, trying to explain his commitment to redistributionism with every pop psychological diagnosis in the book, the longer
we've given him to methodically effect his agenda.

Every once in a while, a kook will forget the left-wing code of
omertà and blurt out exactly what the organized crime syndicate
known as the Far Left is up to. Ladies and gentlemen: give it up for
the Reverend Al Sharpton, who on March 21, 2010, gave some smell-
ing salts to a hypnotized nation. "First of all, then we have to say the
American public overwhelmingly voted for socialism when they
elected President Obama," Sharpton said. "Let's not act as though the
president didn't tell the American people—the president offered the
American people health reform when he ran. He was overwhelmingly
elected running on that and he has delivered what he promised." Duh.

The self-proclaimed "blank screen" was not a messiah but he was
messianic. Just days after Barack Obama was elected president, NBC
News patriarch and prominent liberal Tom Brokaw gave an interview
to PBS's Charlie Rose. Here is part of their incredible exchange:

ROSE: I don't know what Barack Obama's worldview is.

BROKAW: No, I don't either.

ROSE: I don't know how he really sees where China is.

BROKAW: We don't know a lot about Barack Obama and the universe of his thinking about foreign policy.

ROSE: I don't really know. And do we know anything about the people who are advising him?

BROKAW: You know that's an interesting question.

ROSE: He is principally known through his autobiography and through very aspirational [sic] speeches, two of them.

BROKAW: I don't know what books he's read.

ROSE: What do we know about the heroes of Barack Obama?

BROKAW: There's a lot about him we don't know.

The left-wing press—of which Brokaw and Rose are major parts—knew Sarah Palin's dress size and how Michelle Obama got her smokin' biceps, but when it came to the candidate they had promoted so vigorously, some of the nation's biggest "journalists" were thunderstruck but how little they knew about him—by their own choice.

We blindly and willingly gave the keys to the kingdom to a stranger who then blindfolded us and took us on a socialist joyride. What a long, strange trip it's been—and not in the good Grateful Dead way. As all of the Obama weirdness and destruction unfolded, most Americans began to feel like the coed at the frat party who drinks too much wine out of a box, goes home with the guy she thinks is Ryan Reynolds, only to wake up instead with the Situation.

What the @$%&! just happened? A bad case of beer goggles.

But unlike our fictional coed, in our drunken political stupor we actually married the guy. And the divorce is going to be really, really expensive.

PART III

SIZE MATTERS

The nine most terrifying words in the English language are: "I'm from the government, and I'm here to help."

—*Ronald Reagan, July 28, 1988*

Government can help.

—*Barack Obama, August 16, 2011*

The Keynesian Coma

In 1934, the *Chicago Tribune* printed a scathing political cartoon that struck at the heart of Franklin Roosevelt's massive expansion of government known as the New Deal. At the top of the cartoon are the words "Planned Economy or Planned Destruction?" Underneath is a drawing of a horse-drawn wagon, filled with Roosevelt's economic advisers, such as Vice President Henry Wallace, Interior Secretary Harold Ickes, Director of the National Recovery Administration Donald Richberg, and chief intellectual architect of the New Deal, Rexford Tugwell, who is pictured driving the out-of-control, speeding wagon. As they pass around a bottle labeled POWER, they laugh with glee as bags of money fly off the wagon. They are identified as the "Young Pinkies from Columbia and Harvard" and the "Brains Trust." A sign hangs off the back of the wagon that says they are DEPLETING THE RESOURCES OF THE SOUNDEST GOVERNMENT IN THE WORLD. At the bottom of the cartoon are two communist titans. In the lower right corner stands Joseph Stalin, who is seen saying, "How red the sunrise is getting." In the lower left corner sits Vladimir Lenin writing a sign of his own: PLAN OF ACTION FOR U.S. SPEND! SPEND! SPEND! UNDER THE GUISE OF RECOVERY—BUST THE GOVERNMENT—BLAME THE CAPITALISTS FOR THE FAILURE—JUNK THE CONSTITUTION AND DECLARE A DICTATORSHIP. His final thought: "It worked in Russia!"

Published just one year into Roosevelt's first term, the cartoon proved prophetic. Roosevelt and his merry band of leftist intellectuals took the nation on a socialist joyride in the name of dealing with the economic catastrophe of the Great Depression. Eighty years later, a White House chief of staff went on national television and resurrected the sacred leftist mantra. "You never want a serious crisis to go to waste," Rahm Emanuel intoned. "And what I mean by that is an opportunity to do things you think you could not do before." That 1934 cartoon proved to be a red warning flag not just for Roosevelt's unprecedented spending and growth of government but for many of the Democratic presidents and some of the Republican ones who followed him. In fact, on November 24, 2008, *Time* magazine actually published a cover image of Obama as FDR, titled "The New New Deal."

The multiple economic catastrophes we face today did not develop overnight. They were the result of decades of gross fiscal mismanagement, either done in service of an ideological agenda (the Left) or out of a misguided desire to appear "compassionate" (the Republicans). Either way, we have seen explosive deficit spending to fuel an ever-ravenous government.

The cartoon from 1934 reveals something else. For years, leftists have spun the big lie that while they embrace big government, their approach is not that different from the Republicans' approach. It's just a question of scale, you see. All politicians spend. The Left just wants to spend a bit more to make sure that the most vulnerable people are cared for and the system "works for everybody." The Left has effectively peddled this drivel for years, even as leftist administrations and Congresses chronically outspent Republican ones by staggering amounts. In fact, they've spent so much more money than Republicans that if you visit the U.S. Mint, there's literally a Socialist Walk of Fame. But unlike in Hollywood, where you can see celebrity hands in cement, here, molded in cement, are the ass-prints of FDR, LBJ, and Obama, where they sat on their derrieres as president, laughing as trillions of dollars rolled off the printing presses.

This is why the 1934 cartoon is so profoundly terrifying: it reveals a much darker motivation on the part of the leftists than merely a desire to maintain a reasonable social safety net. It shows that the kooks are driven by a pathological desire to deliberately spend like mad as a means to seize ever-greater power and ultimately to undermine the constitutional form of government. That cartoon predicted Roosevelt's big-government, big-spending orgy, and it was eerily predictive of a young twenty-first-century president and his wrecking crew taking it to a whole new level. The current "Young Pinkies from Columbia and Harvard," drunk on their own "Power," have taken us headlong into "Planned Destruction."

The preamble to the Constitution refers to promoting the general welfare, a concept that the kooks have hijacked and morphed into promoting the welfare *state*. From the time that cartoon was published in 1934, the Left has sought to establish a massive voting bloc of dependents who would guarantee perpetual Democratic control, allow the constant empowering of the state, and reduce us to a nation of needy subjects. The welfare state they have built is entirely incompatible with the rest of the Constitution, particularly the phrase "and secure the blessings of liberty to ourselves and our posterity." Dependents are not free.

To make their dark grand strategy work, however, the kooks needed the veneer of intellectual legitimacy. They found it in the macroeconomic work of John Maynard Keynes. Prior to the rise of Keynes in the 1930s, American economics had been guided by the "invisible hand" principle of the free market as first explained in 1776 by Adam Smith. Keynes's work gave the kooks an alternative approach, which they have subsequently used—and abused—to an appalling extent.

Put simply, Keynes saw government spending as an indispensable but *temporary* tool to be used judiciously to correct certain perceived imbalances in the economy. Since there was no entity as large and flush as the central government and since government was the only entity that could print money, government was the biggest and best source of economic stimulus. The Keynesian assumption is that government spending has a big positive effect on growth, particularly when the economy is faltering. Keynes was also opposed to higher taxes in a recessionary or depressionary period.

A critical part of Keynesian theory is the "multiplier effect," first introduced by British economist and Keynes protégé Richard Kahn in the 1930s. It essentially argued that when the government injected spending into the economy, it created cycles of spending that increased employment and prosperity regardless of the form of the spending. Here's how the multiplier is supposed to work: a $100 million government infrastructure project might cost $50 million in labor. The workers then take that $50 million and, minus the average saving rate, spend it on various goods and services. Those businesses then use that money to hire more people to make more products, leading to another round of spending. This idea was central to the New Deal and the growth of the Left's redistributionist state.

The great free market economist and Nobel Laureate in Economics Milton Friedman, among others, showed that the Keynesian multiplier was both incorrectly formulated and fundamentally flawed, in that it ignores how governments finance spending—through either taxation or debt. Raising taxes takes the same or more out of the economy than saving; raising money by bonds causes the government to go into debt. Growing debt then incentivizes the government to raise taxes or inflate the currency to pay it off, which in turn decreases the value of each dollar that the workers are earning. The Keynesians also ignore the fact that saving and investing have a multiplier effect at least equal to that of deficit spending, without the drag of debt.

Keynes turned the commonsense laws of economics upside down: that debts need to be repaid, that demand curves slope downward, that higher taxes mean less growth and less of whatever it is being taxed. The FDR Keynesians' defiance of the basic rules of economics led to such absurdities as the New Deal decision to pay farmers to burn their crops and slaughter their livestock to maintain high food prices. It's Mad Hatter economics, based on the leftist assumption that the government can spend your money better than you can. The reality is that in this Wonderland, Alice is no longer at the Hatter's Tea Party. Instead, she's in a soup line, waiting to get a hot bowl of gruel, the ingredients of which now include the March Hare and the Dormouse.

Today's Keynesian cultists have so abused Keynesian theory that Keynes himself might not even recognize it. The kooks have taken the central aspect of his comprehensive economic thinking—massive infusions of government spending—and *institutionalized* it in order to make it *permanent*. Of course, eventually all of that spending must be paid for, through either higher taxes or perpetual borrowing, both of which have eventual net negative impacts on the overall economy. It's a nasty economic death spiral, but today's Keynesian cultists refuse to acknowledge this basic flaw in their logic. They also tend to disregard the free market and the individuals who make it up: the entrepreneur, the risk taker, the innovator. They are peripheral, if they exist at all in today's Keynesian kookdom. The only entity that matters is the all-powerful state.

While Democratic presidents from Roosevelt to Johnson massively expanded the size of government and put us into a Keynesian slumber, Obama has spent us into a Keynesian coma.

Roosevelt kicked off the modern government spending spree with the New Deal programs and Social Security, and the activist government template he put in place—in terms of both discretionary spending and entitlement spending—began to grow and spread like a horror movie virus. Lyndon Johnson seized the Rooseveltian model and supersized it. He began huge welfare programs in public housing and food stamps that quickly took on lives of their own. And most significantly, he introduced health care as a government entitlement. In 1965, Johnson launched Medicare, the program for the elderly, and Medicaid, the program for the poor. In retrospect, early projections of their future costs are hilariously absurd. Medicare was projected to cost $12 billion by 1990 but instead rang in at $110 billion. Today, Medicare's future unfunded obligations come in at a mind-blowing $40 *trillion*. For its part, Medicaid cost $3 billion in inflation-adjusted dollars in 1966, $41 billion in 1986, and a whopping $243 billion in 2010.

Social Security had been manageable until 1972, when Democrats increased benefits by 20 percent, added an annual cost-of-living adjustment, and tacked on built-in additional benefits that would rise along with wages instead of inflation. Incredibly these entitlement enhancements were added to the 1972 *debt-ceiling* bill.

FDR had originally designed Social Security to be a national retirement program for workers beginning at age sixty-five—at a time when life expectancy was less than that. Today life expectancy is eighty years old and climbing. In 1960, five workers supported a retiree. Today, a mere 1.75 workers do. The retirement age has not kept pace with the aging and growing population; the system is increasingly top-heavy and projections are that it will be completely drained by 2037, if not earlier.

Furthermore, none of the benefits that were added over time were required to undergo annual budget reviews, resulting in costs mounting faster than Lindsay Lohan's jail sentences. And given the population growth and the expansion of coverage to increasing numbers of people, it's no wonder that entitlement costs are astronomical: according to 2011 government information, today approximately 50.5 million Americans are on Medicaid, 46.5 million are on Medicare, 52 million receive Social Security, 5 million get Supplemental Security Income, 8 million are on unemployment insurance, 48 million receive food stamps, and 24 million benefit from the earned-income tax credit. You can also add in the 9 million people who get free Brazilian waxes, the 7 million people who get a lifetime supply of Mentos, and, finally, the 750 people who receive free rides on Ruth Bader Ginsburg's Jet Ski, all covered by the American taxpayer. In 1965, when Johnson began the new wave of government expansion, these types of payments made up 28 percent of the federal budget. Today they are 66 percent of it. They are costing us over $2.1 trillion per year, and that's *before* the widespread retirement of the baby boomers and the true fiscal onset of ObamaCare, both of which will set TNT under the budget and blow it up, Wile E. Coyote–style. Combined, these redistributionist programs have unfunded liabilities totaling an eye-popping $117 trillion. That total is more than all the registered wealth in the world.

Since the Democrats took control of Congress in 2007, more Americans are more dependent on government for their income than at any point since 1929.

Luxuriating in the dirty trough of big-government spending, however, was not restricted to the Democrats. Under President George W. Bush, for example, Republicans should have cut domestic discretionary and entitlement spending to bring the budget under control in wartime. Instead, they went on a spending binge, blowing hundreds of billions of dollars on a new Medicare prescription drug benefit, education including No Child Left Behind, expensive transportation legislation, and home ownership assistance that helped to lead to the housing bubble and ultimately the 2008 financial meltdown. This was the net result of "compassionate conservatism," a concept even more sinister than outright leftism because of its deceptive characterization. It was neither "compassionate" nor "conservative."

There is big government, however, and then there is *really* big government. What we have experienced from the Obama administration has been government on the scale of the alien mother ship in *Independence Day*. In a February 2009 cover piece that seemed to invoke that 1934 cartoon, *Newsweek* proclaimed, "We're All Socialists Now." The then editors Jon Meacham and Evan Thomas wrote, "Whether we want to admit it or not . . . the America of 2009 is moving toward a modern European state." And: "As entitlement spending rises over the next decade, we will become even more French." Would this be the same Europe that has suffered from weak economic growth, high unemployment, ever-higher taxes, growing uncompetitiveness, and crippling debt crises, thanks to decades of economic redistributionism? Would this be the same Europe that is experiencing economic chaos, riots, and strikes as a result of socialist economic policies? Oh yes, by all means, let's become more European. Despite both the hard sell of Democrats over the decades and the soft sell of Obama in particular, the majority of Americans today reject this approach. In late

2010, Gallup released poll results showing that most Americans do not, in fact, believe that we are all socialists now. Every fall since 2001, Gallup has polled on a series of questions related to the size and activism of government. The 2010 results showed widespread and deep disapproval of large-scale government intervention in the private economy. Given the economic upheaval since 2008, it's striking that Americans are more likely to say there is too much intervention, spending, and regulation, particularly when Obama and the Democrats have been selling those big-spending policies as critically necessary to prevent an economic death march. As Gallup put it, "The average American is *less* appreciative of increased government control over business during the past year, rather than more so."

More important, Gallup found a sharp increase in the number of Americans critical of the overall size of government. They noted, "This sentiment stretches to 59 percent of Americans now believing the federal government has too much power, up eight percentage points from a year ago."

Gallup concluded: "An expanded proportion of Americans in 2010 believe *the government has overstepped its bounds—growing too intrusive and too powerful. Also, nearly half now consider the government a threat to individual liberty.*" (Emphasis added.)

We're all socialists now? Not so much.

———

The central question of our time—upon which the future of America hangs—is this: What is the proper size, scope, and role of government? How we resolve it will determine what kind of country we will be going forward. The debate fiercely rages in Washington, state capitals, and local communities. The debate refers to the size of everything: the size of government, the size of government spending, the size of the debt, the size of entitlements, the size of taxes, the size of the bills passed against the will of the people, the size of the political egos making the decisions. This fight will also determine the size of the Republican Party's cojones, and whether it has the ability to stand up to a tenacious redistributionist with a God complex who has the media in his pocket.

Americans see that this is not just about merely big government. If the 2006 and 2008 elections were a repudiation of the Republicans' brand of big government, then the 2010 election was a repudiation of Obama's brand of *really* big government.

Most Americans want to get back to what the Founders gifted to us: a limited federal government, restricted to certain enumerated powers, with all others reserved to the states, governed by fiscal responsibility and staying largely out of the way of the free market and the individuals operating in it. We want to awake from the Keynesian coma. After all, the fight over the size of government is really a fight about individual liberty and opportunity. And right now, liberty is losing.

Size matters.

Does This Spending Make Me Look Fat?

In December 2010, a printing press problem forced the federal government to shut down the production of the new $100 bills and quarantine more than one billion of them—more than 10 percent of all existing cash—in a vault in Fort Worth, Texas. The new hundreds were apparently so Jetsons futuristic that the presses could not actually print them properly. Many of the bills creased, leaving a blank space, making them look like Monopoly money (which, after all of this printing, is probably worth more than our *actual* money). Because the correctly printed bills were mixed in with the flawed ones, all one billion bills needed to be sorted. The Treasury Department reported that if this were to be done by hand, it would take twenty to thirty years to complete. Imagine how many jobs could have been created over those two decades! Clearly Team Obama dropped the Keynesian ball on this one because they turned it over to an automated system that took just over a year to do it. The flawed bills, which cost us

$120 million to print, were burned. The only way the leftists can deal with their insane deficits is by printing money, and their beloved government can't even do that right.

If you are looking for a metaphor that sums up perfectly the Obama era, complete with its Lucy Ricardo Take-a-Bad-Situation-and-Make-It-Worse approach to the economic crisis, that one takes the cake. It's too bad that those flawed bills had to be destroyed. They could have come in handy during Obama's unprecedented spending blowout. U.S. dollars are growing increasingly worthless. The numbers associated with Obama's spending orgy are so big as to be tragicomic. In 2000, the entire federal budget rang in at $1.8 trillion. Spending under Obama in fiscal 2011 hit a new high of $3.7 trillion, up $141 billion from 2010. That is an increase from the previous record in 2009 of $3.5 trillion. Obama has increased federal spending 30 percent above the normal modern level. During the sixty years prior to his presidency, spending averaged approximately 19 percent of gross domestic product. Under Obama, it has ballooned to nearly 25 percent, and that's before the Mother of All Entitlements, ObamaCare, fully kicks in. Forty-three cents of every dollar the federal government spends is now borrowed.

The roughly $3.8 trillion in annual spending is made up of three categories: discretionary spending, mandatory spending for entitlements and welfare programs, and net interest on the debt. The three biggest budget monsters drive the mandatory spending: Social Security at an annual $727 billion, Medicare at $491 billion, and Medicaid at $275 billion. They eat up about 70 percent of total mandatory spending, 40 percent of the entire budget, 67 percent of tax revenue, and 10 percent of GDP. When other mandatory spending such as welfare, food stamps, unemployment insurance, child nutrition programs, and Supplemental Security Income are factored in, it amounts to 14 percent of GDP. Throw in the cost of Michelle Obama's secret burger runs and the cases of Nicorette that Barry orders online and you've got yourself a serious fiscal crisis.

Since the beginning of Johnson's Great Society War on Poverty, government has spent $15.9 trillion (in inflation-adjusted 2008 dollars) on these social welfare programs. By comparison, the cost of all military wars in U.S. history comes in at $6.4 trillion (in inflation-adjusted 2008 dollars). Despite the massive amounts of money already earmarked for them, Obama called for the largest increases in welfare-related programs in U.S. history.

In 2007, the year before the financial crisis, the government took in $2.568 trillion in revenues and spent $2.728 trillion, leaving a $160 billion deficit. In 2011, the government took in roughly $2.230 trillion and spent $3.629 trillion, leaving a deficit of $1.399 trillion.

The nearly trillion dollars in additional spending did not all come from entitlements, although spending there went up as well. Obama has increased *discretionary* spending by a whopping 84 percent. That discretionary spending would only be at 80 percent, but the extra 4 percent went toward a White House investment in Just for Men Touch of Gray, so the president can maintain the urbane Cornel West look that he so admires.

In the first few months of the Obama administration, he breezed the following big-ticket items through his compliant Democratic Congress: the $862 billion "stimulus"; $3 billion for Cash for Clunkers; hundreds of billions of dollars in additional omnibus spending and for bailouts of the financial, automobile, mortgage, and insurance industries; and even $12.1 billion in new funds for the Internal Revenue Service. He also proposed a $3.5 trillion initial budget. Not bad for a few months' work.

As soon as he entered office, Obama instructed congressional Democrats to come up with a bill that would "stimulate" the economy and jump-start job creation. Left-wing economists such as the *New York Times*'s Paul Krugman and others argued for a massive Keynesian spending spree, and when the Democrats produced their nearly $1 trillion package, Krugman and other kooks argued that it was too small and wouldn't have the desired economic impact. Go really big or go home, they said. As designed, the "stimulus" was meant to first buy off Democratic political constituencies, such as government-sector unions, by making transfer payments to state and local governments to prevent public-sector layoffs. If new jobs were created as well, then that would have been an added benefit. They proclaimed the "stimulus" an immediate spur for millions of "shovel-ready jobs," but after most of the money had been dispersed, only 6 percent went for supposedly "shovel-ready" infrastructure. That guaranteed that Team Obama and the Democrats could constantly ask for more money for infrastructure, since so little of it was ever finding its way to those projects.

As economic writer John Crudele has repeatedly pointed out, if a project were truly "shovel-ready"—meaning, on the verge of hiring workers—it would have already been funded. So federal money from the "stimulus" would have only replaced funds already allocated by the states for projects. That means there would be no net gain in jobs, just a movement of money from state to federal budgets and vice versa—which is what happened, hence the lack of real job creation. What was always ironic about Obama's claims of shovel-ready jobs was that the man pushing them looks like the most Unhandy-man with a toolbox in all of America. How can you be Mr. Fix-It when you're really Mr. Break-It? If Obama were ever asked to *get* shovel-ready and actually dig a ditch, there's a pretty good chance he'd have no idea on which end of the shovel the handle was located.

Before it passed in mid-February 2009 with no Republican votes in the House and just three GOP votes in the Senate, the then House Minority Leader John Boehner referred to the "stimulus" as a "trillion-dollar crap sandwich." Even at that early date, the American people agreed. A Gallup poll published on February 3, 2009, showed that only 38 percent of Americans believed that Obama's "stimulus" bill should be passed "as Obama proposed it," while another 37 percent believed it should have undergone "major changes." Seventeen percent believed the bill should have been "rejected outright." A separate Associated Press–GfK poll in September 2009 showed that half of those surveyed said deficit reduction should be the priority over increased spending on health care, education, or alternative energy. Nearly six in ten Americans said they were not confident that the $862 billion "stimulus" would do any good.

Did Team Obama, Team Reid, and Team Pelosi listen to the clear wishes of the American people? No. They passed the Spending Bill That Ate Tokyo and wheeled out White House economics adviser Christina Romer to proclaim that their glorious spending achievement would keep unemployment at or below 8 percent. We were also promised $1.50 or even up to $3.00 of economic benefit from every $1.00 the government spent. This was supposed to be the "Keynesian multiplier" in full bloom. Never mind that for the government to spend $1.00, it needs to take that dollar out of the private economy that is supposed to create jobs. Furthermore, the leftists hamstrung the states by attaching all kinds of strings to the "stimulus" money, including what they could spend it on, what they were prohibited from cutting, and a requirement to keep "stimulus" projects going once the "stimulus" money ran out, which most cash-strapped states could not do. This was redistributionism with Corleone muscle.

The kooks also were wholly unembarrassed that their ginormous "stimulus" contained ludicrous porktastic spending items such as:

- $200,000 for gang tattoo removal in Los Angeles
- $1.2 million to study the breeding habits of the woodchuck
- $2 million to construct an ancient Hawaiian canoe
- $6 million to upgrade the two-block-long Senate subway
- $350,000 to renovate the House Beauty Salon
- $250,000 to study TV lighting in the Senate meeting rooms
- $3.1 million to convert a ferryboat into a crab restaurant in Baltimore
- $50 to convince Barbara Mikulski to jump off the ferryboat
- $6.4 million for a Bavarian ski resort in Kellogg, Idaho
- $11 million for a private pleasure boat harbor in Cleveland
- $500 billion to paint Bill Clinton's face on the side of the pleasure boat
- $320,000 to purchase President McKinley's mother-in-law's house
- $500,000 to build a replica of the Great Pyramid of Egypt in Indiana

- $33 million to pump sand onto the private beaches of Miami hotels.
- $150,000 to study the Hatfield-McCoy feud
- $84,000 to find out why people fall in love
- $85,000 to find out why people hate this list
- $1 million to study why people don't ride bikes to work
- $2 million to study why people don't ride unicycles to work
- $19 million to examine gas emissions from cow flatulence.
- $144,000 to see if pigeons follow human economic laws
- $219,000 to teach college students how to watch television
- $100,000 to study how to avoid falling spacecraft
- $16,000 to study the operation of the komungo, a Korean stringed instrument
- $1 million to preserve a sewer in Trenton, New Jersey, as a historic monument
- $6,000 for a document on Worcestershire sauce

Mmmmm . . . bacon! Pass that Worcestershire!

The results of the "stimulus" were dismal; for each "job" it supposedly "created or saved," it cost us $430,000. The "stimulus" was always meant to be a political act, not an economic one, which is why it was a mountain that produced a mouse.

But the kooks remained unembarrassed about the bill's failure to generate any significant job creation or economic growth. In fact, the failures of "stimulus" grants reinforced that the entire exercise was an epic waste of taxpayer money. A "stimulus" grant of nearly $500,000 to grow trees in Nevada (thanks, Harry Reid!) created a whopping 1.72 jobs, according to the administration's own website, Recovery.gov. According to the *Wall Street Journal*, that's quadruple the cost of creating a job in a nonsubsidized private farm. Massachusetts-based Evergreen Solar got millions in "stimulus" cash in addition to $58 million in state aid, only to lay off eight hundred workers in March 2011 and file for bankruptcy. A Seattle-based "green energy" company used its $20 million in "stimulus" funds to create fourteen jobs, weatherize all of three homes to the tune of $6.66 million per home, and then declare bankruptcy. And let's not forget the $75 million that went into genetic research to determine whether Kathy Griffin and Andy Dick are really the same person.

Perhaps the greatest example of Obama cronyism coupled with epic "stimulus" failure is Solyndra. Solyndra was a Fremont, California–based solar panels company that received a stunning $535 million in "stimulus" low-cost loans and loan guarantees from the Department of Energy. Two years later, in August 2011, it laid off 1,100 employees, declared bankruptcy, and was raided by the Federal Bureau of Investigation. How did a single company manage to get its hands on over a half billion dollars in taxpayer money? It turns out that one of Solyndra's primary investors, Tulsa billionaire George Kaiser, was a key Obama backer, and he and other Solyndra board members and executives donated a total of $87,050 to his 2008 campaign. Kaiser made several visits to the White House and appeared at White House events with administration officials. Within ten days of Obama's own Office of Management and Budget saying, "This deal is not ready for prime time"—echoing warnings from the Bush administration not to proceed with the massive infusion of taxpayer dough—Solyndra scored the loan.

Immediately after the loan went through, Biden appeared via satellite at the groundbreaking for a new Solyndra facility, and Obama touted it as being on the cutting edge of his vaunted "green jobs" agenda. As the scandal unfolded, the White House invoked executive privilege to avoid having to turn over some e-mails involving sensitive internal discussions about Solyndra, which one official referred to as a "(bleep) mess." So much for Obama's promise of see-through "transparency." Perhaps once that official was done looking at the Solyndra debacle, he should have surveyed the entire Obama agenda and asked, "What the (bleep) just happened?"

It also turns out that the Solyndra loan was restructured so that in the event of a default, the American taxpayers would be moved to the back of the line, behind private investors such as Obama supporter Kaiser. Amazingly, just days before the bankruptcy was announced, the Obama administration was considering a taxpayer-funded bailout for the company. When that didn't materialize, Team Obama began spinning faster than a circus clown with a bunch of plates. On the day the bankruptcy was announced, a spokesman for Obama's Department of Energy said, "The project we supported succeeded." In the corrupt, crony-driven world of the Obama redistributionism, the mega-waste of $535 million of taxpayers' money, a bankruptcy, and the layoffs of over one thousand people are a "success" and in the words of Obama himself, "a good bet."

But what about "green job" creation? Surely all of those hundreds of billions of dollars created countless "clean energy jobs," right? The Energy Department loan guarantee program from which Solyndra and other bankrupt or shaky companies benefited created ONE new permanent job for every $5.5 million spent. If a private company had been loaned $535 million, it would have created hundreds, perhaps thousands, of jobs. But in Solyndra's case, the government didn't just choose winners and losers, it took a loser and tried to make it a winner. And the taxpayer was left holding the half-billion-dollar bag. Furthermore, in the fall of 2011, the Department of Energy's Office of Inspector General announced over one hundred investigations into how "stimulus" money was spent. And Peter Schweitzer of the Hoover Institution reported that 80 percent of all green energy "stimulus" recipients were Obama campaign donors. Solyndra was just the tip of the bogus melting iceberg.

To add more corruption to injury, thousands of other companies that got countless billions of dollars in taxpayer "stimulus" funds owed the government millions of dollars in unpaid taxes. According to the Government Accountability Office, at least 3,700 government contractors and nonprofit organizations that got more than $24 billion from the "stimulus" owed $757 million in back taxes as of September 30, 2009. An engineering firm that received $100,000 in a "stimulus" contract owed $6 million in taxes. The Internal Revenue Service called it "an extreme case of noncompliance." I'll say. A social services nonprofit that got more than $1 million in "stimulus" funds owed taxes of $2 million. And a security firm that owed $9 million got more than $100,000 in funds. For Team Obama, no taxes, no problem!

Perhaps the most spectacular example of Obama "stimulus" crony-ism and abuse of power was his abrupt firing of an inspector general who was investigating Kevin Johnson, a former NBA star and Obama supporter, for misusing taxpayer money. Gerald Walpin found that an $850,000 AmeriCorps grant to Johnson's Sacramento nonprofit was being redirected toward bumping up staff salaries, meddling in a local school election, and having AmeriCorps members perform personal services, such as washing Johnson's car. Walpin recommended that Johnson, an aide, and the nonprofit itself be "suspended" from receiving future federal funds.

In November 2008, however, Johnson was elected mayor of Sacramento, and his suspension might have barred the city from receiving "stimulus" money. In April 2009 Walpin received a phone call from the White House telling him he had one hour to submit his resignation and clear out his desk. It would seem that if you're a former point guard for the Phoenix Suns, you get preferential treatment from the Hoop Dreams President. But if you're an honest old man and a good public servant doing your job, then you get fired and humiliated by the Obama White House. There was one problem, however: in 2008 Congress had passed the Inspector General Reform Act, sponsored by none other than Senator Obama. It required the president to give thirty days' notice and a reason before terminating an inspector general. So Team Obama had to stand down on the Walpin firing for one month, during which they tried to smear him for "inappropriate conduct" and for being "disoriented and confused." This was economic stimulus, the Chicago way.

With such a massive trillion-dollar waste, it's no wonder Team Obama could so easily indulge in Orwellian proclamations of jobs "created or saved" by the "stimulus," a measurement they created out of thin air. No one could prove the negative: that without the "stimulus," X number of jobs would have been lost. So they just made up the number X. When the "stimulus" was passed, Team Obama claimed that it would "create or save 3.5 million jobs." The deceptive language of "jobs created or saved" is much like that of "spending cuts," which are not actual cuts but reductions in fantasized budget projections. It's all hand shadows dancing on the wall. This "jobs created or saved" garbage is like trumpeting your diet when you failed to gain another twenty pounds by forgoing a second Whopper for lunch. Either way, you're still fat and sloppy.

When jobs hemorrhaged to the point that the unemployment figure sailed to 10.2 percent in October 2009, Team Obama was forced to back off from making up how many jobs were "created or saved." By December 2009, they were shamed into abandoning their Alice in Wonderland formula, sending out a spokesman from the very FDR-sounding "Recovery Board" to put the final nail in the coffin: "Since the Office of Management and Budget is not going to use 'jobs created or saved' anymore, we're not going to use it either." And by the fall of 2011, Team Obama had bailed on the entire charade, referring only to "jobs supported."

The leftists sold the "stimulus" as a way to generate confidence that the government was large and in charge, and that, in turn, was supposed to spark economic confidence and growth. In reality, the "stimulus" was meant to be a nearly trillion-dollar redistribution of income. In practice, it was a redistributive mess. Job creation, when any jobs were created at all, fell far short of what is required just to absorb new entrants into the job market alone, and unemployment mostly stayed in the 9 percent range for the next two years.

GDP growth has also remained anemic, with quarterly growth either paltry or nonexistent. By comparison, during the tax cut–driven Reagan recovery of 1983–1984, quarterly growth rates soared to 7 and 8 percent, while on average between 300,000 and 500,000 new jobs were created each month. During the three summer months of 1983, 1.7 million new jobs were created and the unemployment rate fell a full percentage point. That was a real Recovery Summer!, unlike the bogus Recovery Summers! Team Obama kept telling us to expect (note the emphatic exclamation point, also put to good use by the '80s pop duo Wham!). Indeed, Recovery Summer! was akin to a slasher flick in which nobody survives. The proof is in the payout pudding:

the "stimulus" was signed on February 17, 2009. Through August 5, 2011, $668 billion of the "stimulus" money was paid out. That equates to $743 million spent per day and $30 million spent per hour. On nothing, for nothing, except to fulfill the kooks' redistributionist fantasy. On that score, it succeeded wildly.

As a huge political slush fund, the "stimulus" followed in the grand tradition of the bailouts. Bailouts are perhaps the most odious concept in capitalism. The free market guarantees opportunity. It does not guarantee outcomes. According to the kooks, that's capitalism's fatal flaw. Government should be in the business of guaranteeing outcomes in order to enforce "fairness" and "equality." For the banks, the kooks—when they're not regulating them to death—are good for business. Banks do well with big-government spending because they get major fees in debt issuance, so they're inclined to work with the kooks. Bigger government spending, bigger fees for them.

When the financial crisis hit in the autumn of 2008, the panic was so widespread and the problems so grave that even the Bush administration agreed to TARP, a $700 billion fund approved by Congress, to stabilize the shaky banks and unfreeze lending, which had seized up. Half of the designated amount, $350 billion, went out under President Bush. That first half was pushed onto Congress by Bush's Treasury secretary, Henry Paulson, a humanoid who resembles the tall, thin alien at the end of *Close Encounters of the Third Kind*. Individual members of Congress still have panic attacks and nightmares about Paulson's powers of mind persuasion, which he used to get their TARP vote. Some have even claimed that Paulson took them up into his mother ship and gave them an anal probe. Having his own misgivings about the bailout, Bush reserved the balance for use at the new president's discretion. Obama then released the remainder. On February 5, 2009, the new Treasury secretary, Timothy Geithner, reminded the bankers that they were now wards of the state. "Public assistance," he pointedly told them, "is a privilege, not a right."

They joined the insurance giant American International Group (AIG) and Fannie Mae and Freddie Mac, the government-sponsored enterprises (GSEs) largely responsible for the housing collapse, and other financial institutions of all sizes, in government welfare-dom. In 2008 alone there were over 740 separate bailouts totaling hundreds of billions of taxpayer dollars.

There were dozens of other bailouts that took place after September 2009, and many of the banks and other financial entities that took or were forced to take bailout money repaid it with interest. At the time, the argument prevailed that only the government was big enough and flush enough to pump enough capital into the banks, many of which were designated "too big to fail." In other words, if those financial institutions were allowed to collapse, much of the financial system as well as those around the world would also collapse, creating a global economic catastrophe. But the banks were given money through TARP to lend and instead sat on it. The Federal Reserve paid them interest to hold the money, thus defeating the purpose of the capital infusion to unfreeze lending.

Despite that stated rationale of preventing an economic Armageddon, many Americans viewed as corrupt the bailouts of banks that had made risky bets. The countervailing argument was that if market forces were allowed to play out, the faltering banks would have gone under and the pain associated with their collapse would have been acute. But the market would have shaken out the failures, the toxic assets, and the bad loans, the system would have flushed through, and in the end the financial sector would have been healthier. This was the same argument against massive government intervention in the housing sector, which has also prevented that market from clearing itself out. Government intervention prevents sharp pain in the near term but ends up prolonging the pain over a longer period of time. It staves off the inevitable but never fully avoids it.

For the kooks, the bailouts served another purpose: to get the financial institutions under the wing of the government, from which it would be exceedingly difficult to extricate themselves. As Geithner told them, the banks (as well as every other industry that either needed or was forced to take federal money) were turned into welfare children. And the leftists' objective was to keep them so for as long as possible. On September 14, 2009, one year after the initial financial panic, the *New York Times* ran a piece titled "U.S. Is Finding Its Role in Business Hard to Unwind," in which they wrote, "Mr. Obama plans to argue, his aides say, that these government intrusions will be temporary. At the same time, however, he will push hard for an increased government role in overseeing the financial system to prevent a repeat of the excesses that caused the crises." And so he did: when TARP ran its course, the Obama administration sought and got a major financial regulatory overhaul, the twenty-three-hundred-page Wall Street Reform and Consumer Protection Act, also known as Dodd-Frank (named for those two paragons of congressional financial oversight, Senator Christopher Dodd and Representative Barney Frank), which enshrined in law the concept of "too big to fail" and, with it, the rationale for a perpetual government presence. One form of dependency ended and was replaced by another. Like a drug addict looking for a higher thrill, eventually marijuana just doesn't do it, and you have to move on to the harder stuff like cocaine and heroin. By the look of the Hill staff who wrote the Dodd-Frank bill, they must have been sampling the product.

Joining the banks in Bailoutville were General Motors and Chrysler, which became poster children for why government should not inject itself in the private sector. In the autumn of 2009, the two automobile companies faced a collapse that would assuredly lead to their ultimate end as viable businesses and the loss of tens of thousands of jobs. Lost in the chaos was the fact that a third American car company, Ford, had seen the difficulties approaching, realigned its business operations, made cars that consumers actually wanted to buy, and did not require or ask for taxpayer money. That's what companies are supposed to do in a market system. Sadly, most of the government's and media's attention was focused on the companies that had failed to adapt to the market—and got rewarded for it.

President Bush began the auto bailout ball rolling, and Obama picked it up with relish. Obama saw not only an opportunity to partially nationalize the auto industry but a chance to pay back some of his most devoted supporters. The auto bailouts were a systematic redistribution of great amounts of ownership from existing shareholders and creditors to the auto unions. Like the "stimulus," the auto bailouts were a political act, not an economic one. If GM and Chrysler had been allowed to go into standard bankruptcy without the government bailout, restructuring would have taken place, an individual or company (U.S. or foreign) would have come in and paid the value, and the companies would have moved on. The unions, however, would not have fared as well. Thus, the Obama intervention.

An estimated $80 billion in taxpayer dollars were poured into GM and Chrysler. In the bailouts, GM gave the United Auto Workers (UAW) union 17.5 percent of its common stock, $6.5 billion of preferred shares, and a $2.5 billion note to fund a trust that will take over retiree health care costs. In the Chrysler bankruptcy, the UAW owned 55 percent of the stock in the restructured company. Here's the deal. If GM and Chrysler want to be Government Motors, that's fine. But from now on, I want all cars that come from those two companies to say so. I want them covered in images of the Obama administration, just like the advertisers covering NASCAR vehicles. I want side view mirrors shaped like Obama's ears, I want the front bumper to resemble Janet Napolitano's triple chin and I want a tailpipe shaped like Biden's finger. Those sweetheart union deals pale in comparison to another one the UAW got in, of all places, ObamaCare. Bloomberg News uncovered an even bigger bailout to the UAW buried deep in the health care "reform" bill, which included $10 billion to pay for some of the most expensive medical costs for millions of autoworkers, steelworkers, teachers, and other early retirees with coverage. This move helped to offset health care concessions made by the UAW as part of the taxpayer rescue of GM and Chrysler. In other words, the union ended up giving up nothing. This was a classic case of Barry Three-Card Monte, where the chief confidence man in the White House makes a mark out of the taxpayers by taking sweet UAW deals out of one bill and dropping them into another. It's simple: create a fake UAW stooge willing to make concessions who says he's on the side of the American people, while he's really on the same side as the card dealer the whole time.

Meanwhile, GM's bondholders got screwed. GM had $27.2 billion in unsecured bonds owned by the public. These were owned by mutual funds, pension funds, hedge funds, and retail investors who bought them directly through their brokers. Under the restructuring deal, they were forced to exchange their $27.2 billion in bonds for 10 percent of the stock of the new GM. This amounted to less than five cents on the dollar. If you were one of the bondholders, too bad for you. Your wealth just got redistributed to the unions.

GM was quickly reminded that Obama literally owned it. In an extraordinary and unprecedented exercise of power, the chief executive of the United States forced the resignation of the chief executive officer of a major American company. One day, Rick Wagoner was the CEO of GM. The next, he was escorted out of his position by the president, who also demanded that the companies close hundreds of dealerships. Obama repeatedly said, "I have no interest in running the car companies," and yet he seemed to be relishing doing exactly that.

Since it was your money GM accepted, you might want to know how the company has spent some of it: tens of millions of taxpayer dollars went into weatherization projects in Maine and to "offset its carbon footprint."

Most hilariously, GM was working on a reality television show about their electric flop, the Chevy Volt. It was to feature all ten people in America who actually own one, four of whom needed loaner cars after their Volts burst into flames.

Meanwhile, after the big transfusion of taxpayer money into Chrysler, over 58 percent of that American icon went to an Italian company, Fiat. Another rousing bailout success.

Did, however, the $80 billion "save" American jobs? According to Paul Gregory, research fellow at the Hoover Institution, on the day it filed for its taxpayer-funded bailout, GM had 92,000 employees. After bankruptcy, it had 77,000 workers, a 16 percent loss. Gregory projects that had GM gone through a regular bankruptcy, it would have experienced roughly the same job loss—and the taxpayers would not have been on the hook. The bailouts did not save "millions" of jobs, as Obama, Biden, and the leftist gang promised. In fact, they probably only saved about 4,000.

And the cost to taxpayers? Obama's own Treasury Department estimates that you and I will take it on the chin by $23.6 billion, despite GM turning a big profit. But hey, at least Obama took care of one of his biggest political constituencies and forced Detroit to make drivable toaster ovens.

———

No worries, though. All of this spending was being done in the name of economic "justice." What could go wrong?

In January 2011, after having presented two $3.5 trillion–plus budgets and while preparing a new $3.8 trillion one, Obama made a big show in his State of the Union address of proposing a five-year budget "freeze" of nondefense discretionary spending. How meaningless and destructive was it? Let us count the ways.

First, when it comes to actually shrinking government, Obama is just not that into it. When Senator John McCain proposed exactly this kind of budget freeze during the 2008 campaign, Obama dismissed the idea out of hand, calling it a budgetary "hatchet" when what was needed was a "scalpel."

Second, Obama spent his first two years *increasing* budgetary outlays by almost 25 percent. That means that the current baseline—at which he wants to freeze—is nearly 25 percent *higher* than it was when McCain originally proposed the idea. No wonder Obama didn't mind suggesting a freeze. (He would continue spiking the spending baseline.)

Third, the so-called freeze did *not* apply to the big budget busters: Social Security, Medicare, and Medicaid, nor did it include things like the interest payments on the national debt. In fact, his "freeze" only covered about one-seventh of the budget. The other six-sevenths of the budget would continue to explode out of control.

Fourth, suggesting a "freeze" at such steeply high levels was insulting to our intelligence and destructive to our dire fiscal situation. Annual deficits are over $1 trillion, the national debt is careening toward $17 trillion, and Obama suggested grabbing more cookies out of the cookie jar. The jar is empty, and he's still grasping.

Finally, most Americans have indicated repeatedly and emphatically that they want the federal government not to freeze astronomical spending levels, but to *cut* spending—drastically. Obama simply wouldn't—couldn't—do it. If anyone were wondering if Obama would moderate after the 2010 election, his disingenuous spending freeze should have erased all uncertainty. He blew a few kisses in the direction of so-called centrism, but where it counted—on the size, scope, and spending of government—he showed us that he hadn't changed one iota. His circumstances had changed; he had to deal with a Republican House. But he has not had a change of ideological heart, nor has he moved to the much-ballyhooed center. He had to pretend he liked Republicans and was willing to embrace some of their ideas. In reality, he loathes those ideas and the GOP majority pushing them. And he loathes having to compromise, which is why he always does so little of it.

His appeasement fake-out didn't work. Nobody was buying the "freeze" even as he was proposing it, for in that same speech, he also proposed *boosting* spending by an additional $20 billion, which he proudly claimed was $50 billion less than the additional spending he proposed in his 2010 State of the Union.

From that point on, Obama went for broke—quite literally. His next budget was so huge—$3.8 trillion—that it was rejected unanimously by the Senate, 97–0. Not even one kook senator could muster the political courage to back it.

Did that stop the Obama Spendthrift Express? No. In August 2011, he proposed $109 billion more for a new infrastructure bank and hundreds of billions of dollars more in government loans and loan guarantees for union-exclusive construction and green jobs boondoggles. Obama's desire to spend other people's money hit a crescendo of madness when he surprise-attacked John Boehner in the congressional cafeteria so he could steal his cigarettes and lunch money.

Even a few Democrats were taken aback by Obama's full-steam-ahead spending approach. After his party got creamed in November 2010, House Minority Whip Steny Hoyer said, "Now that we're at $14 trillion in debt, I think the answer is—responsibly—we're not going to get there [a balanced budget] in ten years, but we have to be on a very considered path to get there. . . . We've dug such a deep hole."

Pardon me? Where was Hoyer during the bailouts, the "stimulus," and the ObamaCare debate? He supported every spending proposal. If we ran our households the way the Democrats ran the national budget, we would be in jail for writing bad checks and fraud, sharing a cell with Bernie Madoff and making license plates.

Not that the early budgetary deals of this new age were any great shakes. The first real fiscal test came several months after the Republican congressional near sweep in November 2010. In April 2011, it dawned on members on both sides that their last temporary Band-Aid on the budget, a continuing resolution, was about to expire. Democrats and Republicans ran around with their hair on fire, trying to get a new spending deal in place to carry the nation through the beginning of the next fiscal year, starting October 1, 2011. Apocalyptic visions of national park closures and other unthinkable events associated with a government shutdown were unfurled. Members rushed to the microphones to assure the American people that a shutdown would be avoided at all costs. After all, who among them wanted to be blamed for denying little Sally and Jimmy a chance to visit the Lincoln Memorial?

Republicans, in particular, fell victim to the stalking shadow of the 1995 government shutdown. That year, Republicans shut down the government over disputes with Clinton and the Democrats over spending. The media and the Democrats attacked the GOP for its "heartless" ways and failure to carry on "good government." The myth spun out of that shutdown was that as a result, Republicans got creamed in 1996 at the polls. The reality, however, was far different: House Republicans lost only nine seats that year. In fact, nationally, the House GOP ran even with the Democrats, scoring 47.8 percent of the vote to the Democrats' 48.1 percent. And in the Senate, Republicans actually picked up two seats. Contrary to the myth, the 1995 government shutdown did not damage the Republicans and forced the Democrats to work toward balancing the budget and reforming welfare.

In 2011, however, the Republicans were spooked by the media's and the kooks' constant invocations of 1995. So once again, the Republicans caved and agreed to another stink bomb of a budget deal. For perspective, the federal government under Obama has been spending about $11 billion *per day*. Under the April 2011 agreement, the sides agreed to "cut" $38 billion, which times out to under *four days' worth* of federal spending.

The agreement had two big outcomes that put Republicans on the losing side. First, the Democrats successfully termed $38 billion in reductions as "cuts." By calling them "cuts," they could scream about how the GOP wanted to throw Grandma in the snow (a rhetorical absurdity usually reserved for battles over Social Security), make Grandpa eat cat food (another lefty oldie but goodie), and "kill women" (a new kook hit uttered gleefully by Democratic congresswoman Louise Slaughter). They could then appear to reluctantly go along with these "cuts" and get credit from a public desperate to see fiscal restraint and government shrunk.

These "cuts" were no such thing. The $38 billion number was an amount being denied to an *imaginary budget never adopted*. This deal came after two previous years in which Obama so increased baseline spending that he had everyone working from incredibly elevated levels. If you spend $50, then you spend $100, and then you propose to spend $150, and someone asks you to cut your budget, so you slash $10, and now you are spending $140. Is anybody buying that that's a true "cut"? The April 2011 budget deal actually ended up costing $3.2 billion *more* in the short term, according to the Congressional Budget Office, and federal spending actually increased that year by 5 percent. So much for "cuts." In an act of rebellion against a country and Congress that didn't buy his sincerity in budget cutting, Barry broke out the Uncle Sam MasterCard and went online to order a Hoodie-Footie Pajamagram to cheer himself up.

Adding new entitlement to injury, the deal didn't even address stopping or at least slowing funding for ObamaCare, the Biggest of All Redistributionist Programs and the promise of defunding and repeal of which got many Republicans elected in the first place. In their first opportunity to really take it on, the GOP whiffed.

The Republican leadership, in getting totally maneuvered, gave away its major weapon in the fight, a weapon given to them by the Tea Party and the American people through their big 2010 election victories: the leverage they had in holding out the possibility of a government shutdown. House Speaker John Boehner actually said, "We'll never shut down the government." Never? What a Junior League mistake. This is Politics 101, and frankly War 101: you never tell the enemy what you will do, and you never tell them what you will not do. And the GOP disarmed itself, both for that battle and for the budget and debt battles to come. From that point on, the Democrats knew that not only would the GOP not fight for serious budget cuts, they would cave at the first threat of a possible shutdown. Nobody on the Republican side was running grand strategy. The Democrats are ruthless street fighters, and Republicans always succumb to the false attack that *they* are the thugs. If this were professional sports or the military, John Boehner would have found himself on a bus back to the minor leagues or doing push-ups in front of a drill sergeant. You never telegraph your moves to an angry mob of loopy Bolshevik nuts.

The Democrats got their budget, almost fully intact given the elevated baseline, and they saw the GOP run away like Bill Clinton from a jealous husband.

Moreover, Obama and the kooks got the benefit of hilarious spin saying the GOP "won." They knew the GOP didn't win, and that's why they were happy to let them have their little Charlie Sheen "duh, winning" headlines.

For years prior to this deal, Republicans assured us that they "got it" about spending and the seriousness of the deficit problem. In April 2011, they got together with the spendaholics on the other side and decided that the crisis they have been telling us about isn't really serious enough to deal with seriously. It's the status quo all the way, baby!

And of course, their weaselly cowardice on that first big budget deal after they took control of Congress set the stage for further wimpiness over the debt ceiling and later budget fights. Republicans always seem to be the last group of people on earth to discover that liberals will lie, cheat, steal, or feign ignorance to get whatever they want.

There was, however, a conservative game-changer. Representative Paul Ryan, the chairman of the House Budget Committee, has shown enormous courage in trying to move his party and the nation back to fiscal responsibility. In April 2011, the same month his party agreed to the hot mess of a budget deal, Ryan introduced the Path to Prosperity. The plan was both dynamically pro-growth and adamantly reformist. Put simply, it argued for $6.2 trillion in spending cuts over ten years by bringing spending to below 2008 levels and a reduction in marginal tax rates, eliminating income taxes on capital gains, dividends, and interest, as well as the corporate tax rate, the death tax, and the alternative minimum tax. It proposed reforming the entitlements by moving Medicare to a premium-support model, in which Medicare would pay a lump sum to the plan chosen by the beneficiary, subsidizing its cost, and changing Medicaid so the states would receive block grants to give them flexibility in handling their individual Medicaid needs, particularly once the labyrinthine new mandates of ObamaCare kick in. (Ryan stuck to his guns and proposed a similar reformist budget for FY2013.)

Ryan's budget sought to empower individuals through increased choice and less government involvement. It also aimed to save those very entitlement programs from extinction. In fact, Rick Foster, the chief actuary of Medicare, endorsed the Ryan plan as the best way to save Medicare from insolvency.

The Democrats reacted in typical Drama Queen fashion. "Hands off my Medicare!" shrieked former Speaker of the House Nancy Pelosi as she led the charge against the Ryan plan. "Dead on arrival" was another one of her clever retorts. The problem is that Ryan and his plan's supporters are operating on the level of logic, reality, and American values, while the kooks are operating on the level of thug redistributionism. If any of their redistributive pillars were dismantled and turned into empowerment vehicles for the individual rather than the government, a major part of their socialist superstructure would collapse. They could not allow it.

On April 15, 2011, the House passed the Ryan budget 235 to 193. No Democrats voted for it, and only four Republicans voted against it. One month later, Democratic Majority Leader Harry Reid saw to it that it died in the Senate by a vote of 57 to 40.

Republicans have been a bit politically schizophrenic as they deal with the new fiscal austerity demands from the people. While they went along with the weak 2011 budget deal and punted on the debt-ceiling deal, they also voted resoundingly for the Ryan plan, which would have dealt responsibly with both immediate and longer-term budget challenges by encouraging growth and restructuring existing programs in order to salvage them. Many Republicans argue that they require majorities in the Congress as well as control of the White House in order to advance these reforms. That's a fair argument. But it would have been nice to have seen a greater consistency from them as they fought the early battles for real spending cuts, when the Tea Party wind at their backs was at its strongest.

Because they didn't hold the line early, Obama moved even more shamelessly to ratchet up spending. In early September 2011, just five weeks after agreeing to some minuscule cuts and restraints on spending as part of the debt-ceiling deal and presiding over the first humiliating downgrade of the nation's debt, Obama summoned a joint session of Congress to call for *another* half trillion dollars for redistribution under the guise of a "jobs bill." Two weeks prior to Obama's announcement, Democratic representative Maxine Waters had expressed her desire for a $1 trillion spending package. Obama must have welcomed that statement because it made his call for half a trillion dollars seem reasonable.

Obama then began to claim that his latest spending extravaganzas would "be paid for," but by that he meant with nearly $2 trillion in tax hikes. The logistics of deficit and debt reduction would be conveniently punted to a deficit "supercommittee," which didn't even make it to the usual last-minute, hair-on-fire phase of congressional panic. It just petered out, after Republicans indicated a willingness to give on revenue increases but Democrats refused to give an inch on their pledge to raise taxes by over $1 trillion. Meanwhile, the Obama Spending Bus rolled on, with Obama proposing yet another $3.8 trillion budget for 2013 with no restraint in sight.

Obama did not make a series of rookie mistakes when he demanded ever more spending. His objective has always been clear: to spend as much money as possible in order to "remake America" by essentially bankrupting her, driving down her currency, and stoking class envy as a way to generate social upheaval. An economically weakened America would more easily fold into redistributive policies. An economically crippled America would be less likely to exert hard power on the world stage, thereby allowing a redirection of necessary funds to the domestic redistributionist dream—and to the global redistributionist dream as well.

In a spasm of leftist honesty, Obama once said, "At some point, you've made enough money." By that, he meant that the leftists, as the vanguards of social and economic "justice," will determine which of your assets, income, and property shall be yours and which shall be turned over to the state for redistributive purposes. This is exactly the kind of capriciousness of an all-powerful state against which the Founders built protections. But the leftists have found ways around those defenses because the Founders never anticipated the rise of this particular brand of kook.

There always was a clear method to Obama's spending madness. The staggering spending was designed not to help the economy but to rapidly expand the welfare state so that it would be extraordinarily difficult to ever roll it back. The Mad Hatter in the White House is not mad at all, but a quite sane and ruthless operative who knows exactly what he is doing.

I See Debt People

Blessed are the young, for they shall inherit the national debt.

—*Herbert Hoover, January 16, 1936*

When President Hoover made that statement, the gross national debt was $34 billion. Today the federal government spends that amount in three days.

The United States National Debt Clock, located on the Web at www.USDebtClock.org, should come with a warning sign like the kind you see before you board the Space Mountain roller coaster at Disney World: WARNING! FOR SAFETY, YOU SHOULD BE IN GOOD HEALTH AND FREE FROM HIGH BLOOD PRESSURE, HEART, BACK OR NECK PROBLEMS, MOTION SICKNESS OR OTHER CONDITIONS THAT COULD BE AGGRAVATED BY THIS ADVENTURE. EXPECTANT MOTHERS SHOULD NOT RIDE. The faint of heart should not look at the National Debt Clock. Every other American should look at it daily. The speed with which the debt numbers fly upward is both fascinating and horrifying: fascinating that any government could spend so much money and accrue such staggering debt so fast, and horrifying because it's *our* government spinning those numbers ever higher.

It used to be that the word "trillion" was used only in astronomy, and even there, it was used only sparingly. When the late astronomer Carl Sagan wanted to invoke enormity, as in countless stars or light-years in distance, he would use the ambiguous term "billions and billions," and it sounded so huge. Today, our national debt is hurtling though time and space toward $17 trillion, or 17,000 billions. One trillion seconds ago, much of North America was still deeply buried in the Ice Age. Today Sagan's phrase—"billions and billions"—sounds positively quaint.

On June 9, 2009, just a few months after Obama's inauguration, the Associated Press ran an article that unwittingly revealed the new president's attitude, strategy, and objective regarding massive new spending and the inevitably huge new debt. The headline: "Obama: It's OK to Borrow to Pay for Health Care." The tagline of the story: "Obama—proposed budget rules allow deficits to swell to pay for health care plan." The piece then laid out Obama's position. "President Barack Obama . . . proposed budget rules that would allow Congress *to borrow tens of billions of dollars and put the nation deeper in debt* to jumpstart the administration's emerging health care overhaul. . . . It would carve out about $2.5 *trillion worth of exemptions for Obama's priorities* over the next decade. His health care reform plan also would get *a green light to run big deficits* in its early years." (Emphasis added.)

All of the bank-breaking spending was designed to undercut the nation's economic strength and its global exceptionalism. If the United States had both a crippled economy and a crippling debt, it could no longer retain its status as the global number one. And the kooks intend to do the takedown, mainly by spending us past Debt Purgatory and into Debt Hell. And once we reach Debt Hell, Obama intends to do two things during his trip to damnation. The first is to give a high five to his old buddy, Saul Alinsky. The second is to shake down Lucifer for all of his extra cash, so that Barry can spend Beelzebub's life savings too.

For years, the leftists registered phony "concern" about the deficit and debt to mask their true intentions: How else to explain Obama's decision to empanel by executive order a "deficit commission" only to blow off their entire set of recommendations? Or his repeated claims to want to get the deficit spending under control, only to follow them with demands for ever more spending? Or his failure to bat an eye when Standard & Poor's downgraded U.S. debt based primarily on an unwillingness to restrain government spending?

Obama constantly put on the mask of fiscal discipline as he pretended to offer support for things that would actually reduce the long-term debt crisis, such as entitlement reform and meaningful spending cuts. But as soon as the Republicans became encouraged that he might actually mean it, he backed away from Medicare, Medicaid, and Social Security reform faster than Snooki from a pair of sensible shoes.

At first, Team Obama and the kooks were able to get away with the huge deficit spending and exploding debt because they couched their policies in terms of temporary crisis intervention, and because it took people a while to realize that this was no run-of-the-mill Democratic administration. Because Obama sang a melodious tune of moderation during the 2008 campaign, many people, including those on Wall Street, assumed that he would behave much as Bill Clinton had in office.

Of course, the death of HillaryCare and the Republican control of Congress helped check the wild spending impulses of Clinton and the kooks on his left. And let's face it: all of the naked intern mambo Bill was doing in the White House kept him from focusing on too many left-wing pet projects at one time (HillaryCare was his wife's idea).

For Clinton, the deficit was to be reduced. For Obama, the deficit is to serve as proof that his radical redistributionist regime is under way. It took the United States over 190 years from the start of constitutional government to amass $1 trillion in debt. Today we add $1 trillion about every nine months. In 1941, our public debt was about $43 billion, which averaged about $370 per citizen. Today, with a population that has about tripled, each American's share is roughly $50,000. And the cost per taxpayer is about $140,000 and climbing. You might want to work a little harder.

When Bush left office, he was rightly assailed by fiscal conservatives for spending too much, as he had signed into law a huge new entitlement in Medicare Part D and new federal education guidelines in No Child Left Behind. He left behind a 2008 budget deficit of $450 billion, in large part due to the initial $350 billion TARP payout—a onetime "extraordinary" budget item. In 2008, that deficit was about 3 percent of GDP. Obama blew up the annual deficit to about $1.5 trillion, or 11 percent of GDP.

When Obama took office, the total national debt was $10.6 trillion. In his first 945 days, Obama increased it by $4.247 trillion, the fastest increase under any president ever. Under President Bush, the nation's debt increased $4.9 trillion, but it took him 2,648 days to do it.

The *total* national debt, which includes the debt held by the public as well as intragovernmental debt (that is, what one part of the government owes to another part), was an acute 69 percent of GDP at the end of the Bush years. Obama's profligate spending has now pushed that level over 100 percent. (According to the Congressional Budget Office, the public debt–to–GDP ratio could reach 200 percent by 2037, assuming that the entire economy doesn't collapse first.) The last time U.S. debt topped the size of the entire economy was in 1947 following the complete economic mobilization of World War II. At least then we had the salvation of the free world to show for it. By 1981, the debt-to-GDP ratio had dropped to 32.5 percent. And now, we've sailed back over the 100 percent of GDP mark with just a few recalled Chevy Volts and shrimp on a treadmill to show for it.

In just the first nine months of fiscal year 2011, the United States had already paid more to service its debt ($385 billion) than some 195 countries had in total annual economic output, including Nigeria, Sweden, the Philippines, Austria, and Switzerland.

Before Obama became president, the kooks controlling Congress were running wild. From January 2007, when they took control of the House, until January 2010, when the Republicans took over, the Democrats increased the national debt by $5.343 trillion. Under Speaker Nancy Pelosi, $3.66 billion *per day* was added to the debt. She was the sixtieth Speaker of the House. During her tenure, she amassed more debt than the first fifty-seven speakers combined. Recall with fondness her epic lie upon entering the Speakership in January 2007 that there would be "no new deficit spending. Our new America will provide unlimited opportunity for future generations, not burden them with mountains of debt."

Since Obama assumed power, the national debt is growing by roughly $6.6 billion per day, a few billion more per day than the debt Pelosi was amassing. Kooks always try to outdo each other.

Events such as wars and the financial crisis are extraordinary events that usually necessitate deficit spending; when the event is over, we know that we should address the debt increase, as we did after World War II. The kooks of today, however, have hijacked deficit spending and now use emergencies both real and made up to justify making the debt crisis worse.

As our debt has exploded, unfriendly nations have seen an opportunity to buy up our debt both as a relatively safe investment and as a point of leverage with Washington. We are now at the mercy of the Chinese loan shark. China is our top foreign creditor, holding nearly $2 trillion. If the Chinese keep buying our debt, in a few years the interest we pay them will fund their entire military, which will in turn be in a position to challenge us more aggressively. This is a different form of the Saudi equation: we buy Saudi oil, and the Saudis take our cash and plow some of it into terrorism and Islamic infiltration projects. The Chinese are not interested in violence, at least not yet. However, if they reach a point when our interest payments on the debt have financed their military amply enough to where they no longer fear us, then we should prepare for the Chicom version of the Trojan Horse to be used against us. But in this circumstance, instead of a horse left as a gift, we may find that a giant fortune cookie has washed ashore on the West Coast, and if one of those blunt-smoking munchies-lovin' surfers bites into it, the Communist army could come pouring out.

The Chinese are keenly interested in gaining as much economic leverage over the United States as possible as they grow their own economy. And we are helping them do it by paying them about $1 billion a week in interest. The International Monetary Fund predicts that the Chinese economy will overtake the American economy as the world's biggest by 2016. Its state-managed capitalism, currency manipulation, and favorable trade balance give China major economic advantages, but its huge U.S. debt holdings means it increasingly has us by the cojones.

Not to be outdone by its former cold war frenemy, Russia has gotten in on the U.S. debt game, holding about $110 billion of our debt, which it also sees as an opportunity to squeeze us on various geostrategic and economic issues. By 2020, all foreign official holdings of

U.S. Treasury securities will be a whopping 19 percent of the GDP of the rest of the world. It's all seemingly stable now, but by 2020, will the rest of the world want to sink one-fifth of its GDP into America? Will we still be such an attractive deal? Unlikely. The only thing that might save us is that many other nations are in worse shape. Still, today the United States is increasingly the dependent beggar, a hulking, limping version of a Dickensian street moppet.

If Obama's Debt Dance of the Seven Veils were to be successful, however, he needed to at least pretend he was interested in debt reduction. He needed a big, splashy show, something that would distract the American people from the reality of his blowout spending and ginormous debt. So he did what he usually does when he is surrounded inescapably by the truth: he punted responsibility to other people. In early 2010, Obama commissioned a bipartisan group of eighteen former public officials and experts to examine ways to get the national debt down to about 3 percent of GDP by 2015. Chaired by former Republican senator Alan Simpson and Clinton White House chief of staff Erskine Bowles, the National Commission on Fiscal Responsibility and Reform spent months wrangling with spending and entitlement issues, and in November 2010 they issued their draft report, backed by only eleven of the eighteen members, short of the fourteen-member supermajority it needed for full endorsement.

Put simply, the group proposed capping federal spending at 21 percent of GDP, down from Obama's new high baseline of 25 percent, but up from the historical average of 18 to 19 percent. It suggested lowering all marginal tax rates in exchange for eliminating most loopholes and deductions (including on mortgage interest), imposing a gas tax, raising the retirement age for Social Security, cutting Medicare and Medicaid costs, and slashing farm subsidies and spending on everything from defense to the government travel budget. And like Jimmy Carter's put-on-a-sweater proposal of the late 1970s, Simpson-Bowles recommended that all members of Congress shave off all of their head and body hair to make a giant blanket to keep Americans warm in the winter. I know it wasn't exactly lambs' wool, but the Bowles crowd thought it could help lower heating costs.

Predictably, almost everybody in Washington freaked out. Conservatives would not abide nearly $1 trillion in new taxes, and the leftists would not go for massive restructuring of their beloved redistributionist programs. The only person in the nation's capital without an opinion? The president, from whom we got crickets and tumbleweeds. He thanked the commission members for their service and then promptly blew off their recommendations. He barreled forth with new spending proposals, including those now-infamous 2012 and 2013 budgets that clocked in at $3.8 trillion each. His cavalier disregard of his own commission's proposals reinforced once again that he was the Chief Kook, leading his band of leftists on their mission to TNT the federal balance sheet. When Obama flipped the bird to the Simpson-Bowles recommendations, it was like a guy being told to change his diet because of high cholesterol who promptly leaves the doctor's office and goes out to eat two pizzas, four cheeseburgers, a bucket of KFC, eight packs of bacon, six tacos, and a block of Velveeta and washes it all down with the grease left over from cooking it all.

On the heels of the pointless exercise of Bowles-Simpson came yet another battle over spending and the debt that once again set everyone in Washington running around with their hair aflame. In late 2010 it was clear that the national debt was flying headlong into the previously set debt ceiling of $14.3 trillion. While they still controlled big majorities in the lame-duck congressional session, the Democrats easily could have given Obama the clean debt-ceiling hike he requested. Senate Majority Leader Harry Reid, however, had other political plans: he wanted to wait on the debt-ceiling issue until after the Republicans gained control of the House in January 2011, so they would be forced to have some ownership over any debt-ceiling increase.

Obama, meanwhile, seemed to suffer from self-afflicted debt-ceiling amnesia. In 2006, then senator Obama condemned the debt-ceiling increase Bush had requested in an operatic display of self-righteousness: "The fact that we are here today," he intoned, "is a sign that the U.S. government can't pay its own bills. It is a sign that we now depend on ongoing financial assistance from foreign countries to finance our government's reckless fiscal policies. . . . *Increasing America's debt weakens us domestically and internationally.* . . . America has a debt problem and a failure of leadership. Americans deserve better." (Emphasis added.)

Savor the irony: Senator Obama was urging Congress not to vote for an increase that would have raised the debt limit to $9 trillion, while he has presided over a debt extravaganza that forced a new debt ceiling of $16.7 trillion. In 2007 and 2008, when the Senate voted to hike the limit by $850 billion and $800 billion, respectively, Obama didn't even bother to vote. Of course, he voted in a flash for TARP, which added $700 billion to the debt. In 2011, he was asking for a clean hike pushing the debt limit to nearly $17 trillion with no conditions and no questions asked.

"Failure of leadership," "reckless fiscal policies," "Americans deserve better." These words were spoken by a man who complained about Bush-era spending levels and then quadrupled them, who expressed grave concern about the Bush-level national debt and then blew it up by over $5 trillion. He told us that he worried about "the burden of debt" and then created a monstrous new health care entitlement that will add trillions to that debt. This is a man who scored political points by bashing Bush's "failure of leadership" but whose own spending explosion is sold as a necessary "investment."

When asked in 2011 about his 2006 vote against raising the debt ceiling, Obama took sanctimony to a new level: "I think that it's important to understand the vantage point of a senator versus the vantage point of a . . . president. . . . As president, you start realizing, 'You know what? We—we can't play around with this stuff. This is the full faith and credit of the United States.' And so that was just an example of a new senator, you know, making what is a political vote as opposed to doing what was important for the country. And I'm the first one to acknowledge that."

Isn't that special? He made a "political" vote just to stick it to Bush in 2006. It's also gratifying to see that he makes a distinction between being president and being a senator. As a senator, he could hide behind ninety-nine others. As president, the buck is supposed to stop with him, although one would never know it, given how much blame shifting he has done over the years.

Meanwhile, during this period of political air hockey, the major credit agencies, such as Standard & Poor's, Moody's, and Fitch, were warning that if the United States didn't move to begin reducing deficit spending, a credit downgrade of the nation's debt might occur. This set off a furious debate over whether the ceiling should be raised yet again to accommodate even more destructive spending and, if so, by how much. As the negotiations with the House GOP leadership grew contentious, Obama alternated between paternalistic condescension, telling the debt negotiators to "eat their peas," and petulant childishness, as he warned House Majority Leader Eric Cantor not to "call his bluff." He threatened to take his case to the American people, which he did repeatedly to no avail. Most polling showed that the majority of Americans didn't want the debt ceiling lifted, and certainly not without deep accompanying spending cuts.

Obama and his troops flashed the impending doom card, predicting "catastrophe" and "default" if the ceiling were not raised, despite the fact that the government had more than enough revenue coming in every month to cover debt service as well as essential services such as defense. Obama took the lies to a despicable new level when he said that he could not "guarantee that [Social Security] checks go out." He knew that under law, Social Security payments must be made and that the government had enough money every month to cover them. Of course, the truth has never slowed down the kooks, so onward they went, screaming about possible "default" and scaring Grandma even as they knew that default was never a possibility.

While the Democrats were drumming up drama over the debt ceiling, House Republicans were actually doing something proactive to bring the debt down. They proposed and passed legislation known as Cut, Cap, and Balance, which would have cut federal spending dramatically, capped spending at roughly 18 percent of GDP, and added a requirement that all future budgets be balanced via a balanced-budget amendment (BBA) to the Constitution. When it got to the Senate, Reid immediately tabled it, refusing even to allow it an up or down vote. However, instead of fighting for Cut, Cap, and Balance—the only plan that would have dealt effectively with spending and debt and probably satisfied the ratings agencies about their seriousness of purpose—the Republicans caved and agreed to go back to the drawing board.

The GOP is particularly sensitive to calls from the leftist "elites" to "compromise." The assumption is that compromise for the sake of compromise is an inherently good thing. The truth is that compromise usually leads to a bad deal with unintended and disastrous consequences.

When the Democrats controlled the White House and both houses of Congress from January 2009 to January 2011, they not only refused to compromise with Republicans, they mocked the very idea of compromise by barring the GOP from meetings, debate, and offering amendments to key legislation. They railroaded Republicans every which way but loose. Their idea of "compromise" was no compromise at all.

When it came time to do the debt-ceiling deal, the Republicans should have pressed the idea that it was now the Democrats' turn to compromise. During the negotiations, Obama and the Democrats masterfully spun their position as a compromise between tax hikes and spending cuts. I'll give you spending cuts, they offered, if you give me tax increases. That was exactly the *wrong* formulation, and the GOP should have turned it around and demanded a *real* compromise: in exchange for giving the Democrats the debt-ceiling increase they wanted, the Republicans should have demanded passage of Cut, Cap, and Balance. Period.

It should not have been an exchange about spending cuts versus tax increases. It should have been a debt level hike in exchange for policies that would have prevented the country from getting into the same crisis again in less than a year. The Democrats would have recoiled from that compromise because they wanted to be able to continue to put the gun to our heads. Every year or so, we will have another debt-ceiling crisis, and every year or so the GOP will have to cave in on tax hikes and illusory spending "cuts." It's about time that the Republicans reach down into the black pit that is Nonna Nancy Patricia D'Alesandro Pelosi's purse and pull their gonads out, so they can strap them back on and tell that Baltimore street woman, "No, *grazie!*"

Cut, Cap, and Balance would have put an end to that cycle of Democratic extortion, which is why Reid torpedoed it while calling it "the worst piece of legislation" in history. The Republicans made a huge strategic mistake by going wobbly. Is anyone running strategy for the Republicans? Anyone? Bueller?

The resulting debt-ceiling agreement was yet another budgetary hot mess. In exchange for the largest debt increase in history—$2.5 trillion—Congress agreed to cut spending by a measly $6.67 billion in 2012. Since the government spends $3 million *per minute*, it blew through that amount of "savings" in the first thirty-seven hours of the new borrowing authority. Most of the Boehner "savings" were back-loaded in the out-years, meaning that they, like the caps on discretionary spending worth roughly $900 billion over ten years, were meaningless because they'd likely disappear down the road. The deal boosted the debt ceiling over fourteen months but the spending "cuts" were to be phased in over ten years. At one point, Obama dramatically threatened to veto over the "cuts," which was amusing since the deal truly cut just about nothing. The debt deal put us on a trajectory to incur $7.8 trillion in more debt over ten years, even given the unrealistic projections of economic growth and revenue. The negotiators also did what they always do: they punted the tougher additional spending-cut decisions to the congressional "supercommittee." Even Simpson and Bowles, the chairs of Obama's defunct deficit commission, called it "a crisis merely postponed." In fact, the debt crisis ended up being postponed by a mere three months; by the last week of 2011, Obama was back to request *another $1.2 trillion* debt hike.

Boehner tried to put lipstick on the debt deal pig by making two pronouncements. First, since the GOP only controlled one-half of one-third of the government, this was the best deal they could get at the moment. Second, he made a contradictory statement. He chirped that he had gotten "98 percent" of what he had wanted. That statement, of course, undermined the first; if you only control an itty-bitty portion of the government, how then could you say that you got 98 percent of what you had wanted? Again: Bueller? Besides, didn't John Boehner used to work in a blue-collar bar? Isn't that part of his Horatio Alger story? If so, then why doesn't he stop crying in front of cameras and start doing shots of Crown Royal, throwing bar stools, and kicking some liberal ass?

After all of the debt deal machinations, the unthinkable happened anyway.

———

"Mr. President! Your country just got downgraded! What are you going to do next?"

"I'm going to two reelection fund-raisers!"

Obama's version of Disney World.

On August 5, 2011, Standard & Poor's did what they had threatened for months and downgraded U.S. debt from its sterling AAA credit rating to AA+. For the first time in American history, our creditworthiness took a humiliating blow. The United States—the greatest superpower the world had ever known—was instantly cut down with a Backwaterville credit rating.

What the @$%&! just happened?

The kooks had seized control of the nation's wallet.

In the spring of 2011, Treasury secretary Timothy Geithner was asked point-blank what level of risk existed for a possible debt downgrade. He answered, "No risk." He went even further, saying, "Things are better than they've been if you want to think about the prospects for improving our long-term fiscal position." That prediction was right up there with those giddy administration predictions for Recovery Summers! I and II.

This is how fundamentally unserious Obama was about pursuing real debt reduction: six months before the downgrade, he offered a budget that *increased* spending and the debt so preposterously that after ten years, annual deficits would have still been running over $1 trillion. Four months before the downgrade, he delivered a budget speech full of absurd gimmicks and degrading insults to House Budget chairman Paul Ryan's budget plan, which had courageously offered a meaningful proposal to reduce spending and bring down the debt. In April 2011, White House press secretary Jay Carney announced that Obama wanted a clean debt-ceiling increase with no spending restraints at all. Seven days later, Standard & Poor's issued a negative outlook to our AAA rating, something Obama Treasury officials tried to prevent by privately urging S&P to reconsider because the "debt was manageable." Obama also refused to put ObamaCare on the table, despite a $1 trillion price tag over the first few years with its projected costs growing faster in its out-years. In large part, it was Obama's repeated unwillingness to deal with the debt crisis in a serious way that provoked the downgrade.

As Standard & Poor's put it: "We view President Obama's and Congressman Ryan's proposals as the starting point of a process aimed at broader engagement, which could result in substantial and lasting U.S. government fiscal consolidation. *That said, we see the path to agreement as challenging because the gap between the parties remains wide.*" (Emphasis added.)

The president's open hostility to a mature debt-reduction plan while offering no mature plan of his own was the final straw for Standard & Poor's. Of course, Team Obama immediately set about to shoot the messenger, claiming the ratings agency's numbers were off and that they could not be trusted because they had missed the big blowups at Fannie Mae, Freddie Mac, Enron, and WorldCom. Furthermore, just days after the downgrade, the Holder Justice Department leaked to the *New York Times* that it was conducting an investigation into whether Standard & Poor's improperly rated scores of mortgage-backed securities in the years before the financial crisis. The *Times* story took pains to say that the investigation had been begun before the credit downgrade, but the leak came almost immediately afterward. The Department of Justice tossed Moody's into the investigation as well, for good measure.

The problem with the downgrade, however, wasn't the messenger but the message: it's the spending, stupid! Unsustainable entitlement programs have grown over many decades and across many presidents and Congresses. But the biggest chance to begin correcting the problem was during the 2011 debt-ceiling debate, and both sides ran for the hills. This downgrade should make everyone feel a bit impotent. It's like going to bed with Ralph Fiennes and waking up the next morning with former Labor secretary Robert Reich . . . that is, if you can actually locate him under the covers. One minute, you're getting frisky with the hot star of *The English Patient*, and the next, you find yourself drowning in Munchkinland. Now, THAT'S a downgrade.

Right on cue, some of our largest foreign creditors scolded our fiscal irresponsibility. Russian prime minister Vladimir Putin called the United States a "parasite," saying, "They are living beyond their means and shifting a part of the weight of their problems to the world economy." The Chinese government chimed in as well, using the official Xinhua news service to say that Beijing had "every right" to demand that Washington safeguard Chinese dollar assets and to call for the United States to "come to terms with the painful fact that the good old days when it could just borrow its way out of messes of its own making are finally gone. . . . To cure its addiction to debt, the United States has to re-establish the common sense principle that one should live within its means." Savor the irony: the Chinese communists and the Russian pseudo-communists are lecturing us about our spending and debt levels, and the commies are right.

Immediately following the commie pile-on, the Euro-schoolmarms at the World Economic Forum gave the United States a second downgrade. They dropped America further down their global ranking of the world's most competitive economies. We are now number five, behind Switzerland, Singapore, Sweden, and Finland. While praising us for our productivity, highly sophisticated and innovative companies, and flexible labor market, the forum called us out for "a number of escalating weaknesses" such as astronomical government debt.

The commies get it. The Euro-socialists get it. But Obama and the kooks? Oh, they get it, all right. I thought there was only a finite number of ways to describe Obama as a leftist, but what do you call a guy who's sitting to the left of the Communist Chinese and the socialist governments of Europe?

The Government in Your Eyeball, Ear Canal, Toe Fungus, and Places Where the Sun Don't Shine, a.k.a. ObamaCare

CHRISTMAS EVE, 2009
WASHINGTON, DC

'Twas the night before Christmas, when all through the House
Not a Democrat was stirring, not even Nancy Pelosi, the louse.
The health care bill was hung by the chimney with care,
In hopes that Senate Democrats soon would be there.
The American people were nestled all snug in their beds,
While visions of defeating ObamaCare danced in their heads.
But Pelosi in her kerchief, and Harry Reid in his cap,
Hoped their caucus wouldn't bolt home for a long winter's nap.
When out on the Hill there arose such a clatter,
Reid sprang from his bed to see what was the matter.
Away to his office he flew like a flash,
And threw himself on the bill, which was done slapdash.
All 2,000 pages looked like the new-fallen snow.
"What's really in the bill? No one will ever know!"
When, his wondering eyes filled with mist
At the eye-rolling sight of eight tiny extortionists,
Reid jumped up, so lively and quick,
He knew in a moment their payoffs must click.
More rapid than eagles his bribers they came,
And he whistled, and shouted, and called them by name!
"Now Landrieu! Now Lincoln! Now Lieberman and Nelson!
On Dodd! On Feingold! On Sanders and Levin!
Here's your payoff! Now go do the deed!
And vote for this sucker in our hour of need!"

He told them that his back was to the wall,
And he told them, "Now go! And dash away all!"
So back to their states the extortionists flew,
With their hundreds of millions, and other goodies, too.
And then, in a twinkling, Reid heard on the roof
Pollsters showing him the extent of his goof.
As he drew in his head, and was turning around,
Down the chimney President Obama came with a bound.
Having done no heavy lifting, he looked rested and ready
To sign this monstrous bill, even without Teddy.
A bundle of political threats he had flung on his back,
And he looked so smug, the thug, as he opened his pack.
His eyes, how they twinkled! His dimples, how merry!
His cheeks were like roses, his nose like a cherry!
His droll little mouth was drawn up like a bow,
He knew his fellow Dems; he knew how it'd go.
He was thin and skinny, not at all a jolly elf,
And Reid laughed when he saw him, in spite of himself!
A wink of his eye and a twist of his head
Soon told Reid he had nothing to dread.
Obama spoke not a word, which was unusual for him,
Ready to sign a bill that will make health care more grim.
"Higher premiums! Fewer doctors! Higher taxes and fees!
And this bill's just the beginning—oh, what a tease!"
He sprang to his feet and bid Reid good-bye,
And went back to the White House in the bat of an eye.
But Reid heard him exclaim, and it sounded like a prayer:
"Happy Christmas to all, and to all ruined health care!"

(With my apologies to Clement Clarke Moore)

On December 24, 2009, Senate Democrats gave the American people the political equivalent of a fruitcake. As the Democratic Grinches prepared to vote on their version of the widely despised, destructive, and chaotic health care bill, they tried to spice up their fruitcake with distortions, distractions, and flat-out lies. With over

60 percent of the American people opposing their incoherent mess of a plan, the Democrats tried desperately to convince us that we would love this particular fruitcake. Unlike other fruitcakes, however, the health care fruitcake could not be regifted to someone else.

The Democrats reveled in their Heat Miser health care politics, oblivious to the reality that they were melting themselves out of majority control of the House and a filibuster-proof majority in the Senate. Had you been naughty or nice? It didn't matter, because the Democrats were going to stick you with a new multitrillion-dollar assault on your freedoms anyway. Nothing says "Merry Christmas" like the government mugging you and leaving you broke, beaten, and bloodied on the street. But no worries! ObamaCare covers government beat-downs.

According to Obama's Declaration of Dependence, "We hold these truths to be self-evident, that all men are created equal, that they are endowed by their Creator with certain unalienable Rights, that among these are Life, Liberty and the pursuit of Happiness . . . and oh yeah, government-run health care." That last part must have slipped Thomas Jefferson's mind. Nurse Barry couldn't wait to slap on some rubber gloves and get his feel for all of our body parts. He couldn't wait to dig, prod, and poke at our humanity while he humiliated us. Prostate check! Here comes Nurse Barry! Hysterectomy! Here comes Nurse Barry! So you think you have a hernia? Turn your head and cough for Nurse Barry!

———

The crown jewel of the kooks' redistributive state has always been socialized medicine, for one simple reason: if the government controls your health care, the government controls you. And if the best health care system in the world were disassembled and then made to resemble so many other atrocious health care systems, yet another part of America's greatness would be diluted down to unexceptionalism. This is why Obama and the kooks spent their first year and a half hysterically dashing through the health care weeds when most Americans were crying out for jobs and economic growth. In fact, the kooks quickly passed the $862 billion "stimulus," declared their work on the economy done, and turned immediately to the most important item on their socialist checklist. They moved fast and with near-complete disregard for public opinion. And they made sure that their redistributive superstructure was built on a direct infringement of your personal liberty: an unprecedented legal mandate to buy a good or service as a basic condition of living in the United States. The "individual mandate" to purchase health insurance or face an IRS-enforced fine is so constitutionally dubious that it made its way to the Supreme Court. The kooks, however, knew exactly what they were doing: launching the Mother of All Redistributionist Programs that would fundamentally change the very character of America while reducing America itself.

Health care "reform," as they called it, was about neither reform nor health care.

For decades, leftists had tried to get it done, from Theodore Roosevelt through Hillary Clinton, but they failed each time for a variety of reasons. They were able to get more limited redistributive programs through that dealt with certain aspects of health care, such as Medicare and Medicaid. But they had been unable to get a massive overhaul of health care in place for *every* American—until Obama and the kooks took control. They realized they had a short window of opportunity to achieve this most ambitious "spread the wealth around" plan at last, and they didn't waste a second. Nurse Barry was in a rush and didn't have time to either debate the merits of the bill or change the nation's bedpan. His plan was to impose socialist medicine as fast as possible, while he dumped that bedpan on our heads.

The health care engineers never lost sight of what ObamaCare was *really* all about: government power and control. It was an epic seizure of freedom from the individual that was then concentrated in the hands of the state. On the most personal, intimate questions of your body and health, faceless government bureaucrats armed with slide rules would be making those decisions for you. Never mind that in every industrialized nation in which socialized medicine has been implemented, from Great Britain to Canada, horror stories abound of bankrupting costs, patient neglect, life-threatening waiting times, and rationing and above-average mortality rates. To the kooks, it was never about actually delivering better, more cost-efficient health care. It was always about seizing the ultimate power over you while maneuvering the health care system into one that served "social and economic justice." Consider a revealing kook inconsistency: for decades, pro-abortion leftists have used the battle cry, "Get government out of women's wombs!" Now, however, they want government to be in your womb, nasal cavity, and large intestine. Before you could say, "Holy British health care system, Batman!," Nancy Pelosi would be taking your pulse while Harry Reid ran your blood work.

The redistributionists are also keenly aware of the addictive power of entitlements, which are the political equivalent of heroin. When people are given a hit of the entitlement drug, they become dependent on it. And with ever more people dependent, the kooks could then enjoy a built-in justification for growing the program, the spending, and the government to support it. This is how entitlements become self-perpetuating. People start out as normal, mild-mannered citizens . . . like Bruce Banner. Give those same people entitlements, and watch what happens when you try to take them away. They each turn into the Incredible Socialist Hulk, as they crash through walls, throw cars, and watch Fox News in a fit of rage. The kooks rammed through the ObamaCare entitlement in order to get you to go from your first hit to mainlining ObamaCare in no time flat.

The kooks' ideal vision was a single-payer system, in which the government essentially runs every aspect of health care. In the past, political realities had made it impossible to achieve single payer, but the leftists never gave up hope. In 2003, then Illinois state senator Barack Obama laid out his deepest health care wish: "I happen to be a proponent of a single payer universal health care program. . . . But as all of you know, we may not get there immediately. Because first we have to take back the White House, we have to take back the Senate, and we have to take back the House."

Alas: the kooks' purest ambitions laid bare. They may have dressed them up or even disguised them occasionally, but they never made them much of a mystery. In reality, however, single payer proved a bridge too far even for some Democrats, whose resistance was based less on ideological opposition than political fear; most Americans rejected the very idea of a socialist-style single-payer system, and Democrats facing reelection in 2010 and 2012 did not want to have to vote for one. So even though the Democrats controlled big congressional majorities and the White House, getting to single payer was not to be, at least not immediately.

The redistributionists then changed their game plan. They designed a health care scheme that was as close to single payer as was politically possible, and they stacked the deck so single payer would ultimately be the end result.

A parade of leftists lined up to broadcast that very fact. When ObamaCare was passed in its final form in late March 2010, Senator Tom Harkin said, "I think of this bill as a starter home. It's not the mansion of our dreams, but it has a solid foundation." He also added, "By passing this legislation, we will achieve a progressive prize that has eluded Congresses and presidents going back to Teddy Roosevelt." The then-Speaker Nancy Pelosi also chimed in, "Once we kick through this door, there'll be more legislation to follow." Obama himself said to Democratic representative Dennis Kucinich, "We've gotta start somewhere." In other words, "Patience, my fellow kooks! We've just nationalized health care. Savor the moment."

From the start, the Democrats were united on the objective if not always on process. They could never utter aloud the true objective of ObamaCare, so they stuck to a script that would sound palatable to the general public. They attempted to sell socialized medicine as the policy equivalent of Superman: It will contain and lower costs! It will bring down premiums! It will be deficit neutral! It will eventually even save the government money! It will get us to universal coverage! It will improve quality of and access to care! If you like your current health insurance, you can keep it! It is not a government takeover! It will leap over tall buildings in a single bound! The truth: pick which grandparent you like most, because the other one has to go!

Perhaps they even believed this fantasyland drivel. But they also knew that with their big congressional majorities and the Big Kookuna in the White House, they didn't really need a public buy-in to pass the plan. If the American people came around to support it, great. If they didn't, well, tough.

Obama was obsessed with getting it done but not as obsessed with micromanaging *how* it got done. He was no Lyndon Johnson, who relished getting in the faces of members of Congress until they gave him what he wanted. Obama preferred a more absentee-father approach. Instead of pounding members every minute of the day over the intricacies of ObamaCare, Big Daddy would let them sort it all out while he hit the links or shot some hoops. Get it done, and call me when it's ready, kids!

With Obama taking a "hoop dreams" strategy to health care, the heavy lifting of the actual bill-writing was left to congressional Democrats, who then allowed kook special interests to run wild with influence over the bill. Groups such as the George Soros–funded Center for American Progress and MoveOn.org, ACORN, the Tides Foundation and its associated Apollo Alliance, and big labor unions such as the AFL-CIO (American Federation of Labor and Congress of Industrial Organizations) and SEIU (Service Employees International Union) teed up their laundry lists of demands, which the leftists happily included in the final product.

Furthermore, Team Obama worked all kinds of clandestine payoff deals with hospital groups, pharmaceutical companies, the AARP (American Association of Retired People), and unions, among others, to get them on board. The details of those deals were kept under wraps, lest the public see the billions of dollars in giveaways and promises as well as the corruption of this support-buying scheme. Before long, all of the kook interest groups and the bought-off unions and industries were singing from the same ObamaCare hymnal.

At that point, they became like the woman in a famous story about Winston Churchill. At a dinner party one night, a drunk Churchill asked an attractive lady whether she would sleep with him for a million pounds. "Maybe," she said coyly. Churchill then said, "Would you sleep with me for one pound?" "Of course not!" the woman replied indignantly. "What kind of woman do you think I am?" "Madam, we've already established what kind of woman you are," said Churchill. "Now we're just negotiating the price."

Pelosi and Reid also barred the minority Republicans from much of their corrupt process, prohibiting them from participating in closed-door sessions, debate, and adding amendments to the bill. This was the Democrats' idea of "compromise" when they held big majorities in Congress. Republicans, like children, were to be seen but not heard. Along with the GOP, the leftists also dissed the opinions of the American people, who were growing increasingly infuriated with the content of the legislation and the perverse process the Democrats were using to get it done.

In August 2009, thousands of Americans packed the town hall meetings of members of Congress, demanding answers: If I have health insurance now, will I be able to keep it? How is this going to affect my relationship with my doctor? Will government bureaucrats be making my health care decisions based on cost? Why is Chuck Schumer now performing circumcisions at my local hospital? Can I opt out? What do you mean there is an individual mandate requiring me to carry insurance? What if I want to choose not to have insurance? Then I'll have the IRS on my tail, enforcing a fine? What? When I'm close to kicking the bucket, are you going to kick it for me? Barbara Boxer is not a real boxer, so why is she speed-bag training with my colostomy bag? How is the country going to pay for this? Isn't this stripping away more of my freedom to choose my own doctor/hospital/treatment? This is what they have in socialized countries, isn't it? Why are you destroying the best health care system on earth? By the way, why is Al Franken now my wife's ob-gyn?

Rather than answer these pointed questions, many Democrats either ducked them or canceled their scheduled town hall meetings altogether. When some of them did confront their constituents, they never revealed their true motive to build a Euro-style health care system. Obama gave scores of speeches in defense of his plan, including one before a joint session of Congress in September 2009 during which he made the preposterous claims that it was "not a government takeover," that "no government bureaucrat would come between you and your doctor," and that it would be "deficit neutral." All ludicrous lies, and he knew it.

At one point, Obama even turned the most routine ailments into wildly disingenuous examples of rampant greed among doctors. "You come in and you've got a bad sore throat, or your child has a bad sore throat or has repeated sore throats," he said in July 2009. "The doctor may look at the reimbursement system and say to himself, 'You know what? I make a lot more money if I take this kid's tonsils out.'"

A few days later, he ramped up his attack on doctors by insinuating that many of them are amputating limbs willy-nilly in the dogged pursuit of money: "Let's take the example of diabetes," he said. "If a family care physician works with his or her patient to help them lose weight, modify diet, monitors whether they're taking their medications in a timely fashion, they might get reimbursed a pittance. But if that same diabetic ends up getting their foot amputated, that's thirty thousand, forty thousand, fifty thousand dollars immediately that the surgeon is reimbursed." Here comes Dr. McDreamy to take your blood pressure. Whoops! There goes your arm!

———

In trying to argue that warped pay incentives might encourage some physicians to order unnecessary tests and procedures, especially in Medicare—a legitimate point—Obama clumsily insulted doctors by suggesting that many are greedy pigs performing unneeded surgeries to rob their patients blind. The hyperbole and lies were part of the orchestrated campaign, if not to win public opinion for their vision of "reform," to at least reduce the public's resistance to it.

One Republican representative could not contain his outrage at being lied to yet again about ObamaCare. During Obama's September 2009 address to Congress, Joe Wilson of South Carolina shouted, "You lie!" after Obama stated that illegal immigrants would not receive free coverage under his plan. On the substance, Wilson was right; the bill mandated that businesses provide health insurance to all employees, with no exemptions or provisions to screen out illegals, many of whom obtain jobs by using false identities. The practical effect is that millions of illegals would be covered under the law. Obama and Pelosi knew this too, but feigned outrage when Wilson inartfully pointed it out. The thing that scared Obama and Pelosi the most was the possibility of Joe Wilson's shout heard 'round the world becoming a trend because, if that started, from then on, you'd have two or three hundred congressmen and senators screaming "Liar!" for the duration of every speech Obama would deliver for the rest of his presidency.

Furthermore, in mid-2011, Obama's Department of Health and Human Services announced it was transferring $28.8 million in ObamaCare funds to sixty-seven community health centers. Of that amount, "approximately $8.5 million will be used . . . to target migrant and seasonal farm workers," and grant recipients will not be required to check the immigration status of people seeking health services. "You lie," indeed!

Obama and the leftists also lied about the most fundamental elements of the bill. Its projected costs were manipulated through accounting gimmicks such as double counting, directing taxpayer funds to ObamaCare while shielding that same money for Medicare, Social Security, and other programs. If you tried using the same $100 bill twice for different things, you might be measured for an orange jumpsuit. But when they used such fraudulent techniques to make ObamaCare seem fiscally reasonable, those lies were simply considered the necessary means to an end. The Congressional Budget Office issued ten-year cost projections that varied from close to a trillion dollars to over a trillion dollars, but it could only process whatever numbers were handed to them. Junk numbers in, junk numbers out. By mid-2011, even Obama's chief health care kook, Health and Human Services secretary Kathleen Sebelius, was forced to admit to the fraudulent double counting. And neither she nor anyone else responsible for ObamaCare could or would tell us if the more than $500 billion in proposed Medicare cuts to help pay for it would ever materialize, or if the "doctor fix"—a hike in Medicare reimbursement rates—which was dropped to game the CBO score, would be restored. The truth is that nobody knows for sure how much ObamaCare will actually cost, although ten-year estimates now range from about $2 trillion to over

$5 trillion. Given the explosive costs of government-run health care programs such as Medicare and Medicaid, it's safe to assume that the higher-end estimates are more accurate. As the European examples have proven for decades, socialized medicine neither contains costs nor improves quality of care, but it transfers wealth really well.

As public opposition to the bill grew more heated and the cost projections jumped all over the map, the leftists tried to leverage the emotional component of health care by spinning tall tales about "health insurance victims," the most famous of whom was Obama's own mother. Obama often cited the example of Stanley Ann Dunham as he made the case for his government takeover. Tightly gripping the podium in front of him, he would make the case for a ban on preexisting exclusions by insurers by recalling his mother's deathbed fight with her insurer. "There's something fundamentally wrong about that," he'd say.

What was "fundamentally wrong" was Obama's version of events. In a biography of Mrs. Dunham Obama Soetoro, author Janny Scott revealed that her health insurer *had* in fact reimbursed her medical costs without incident. The actual dispute took place over a separate disability-insurance policy. This example proves that Obama is a particularly adept liar. You start with a political agenda, you fabricate a story to fit your message, and then you make sure the person in question isn't around to dispute the tale. Obama made up his mother's health coverage story, as well as numerous others, in order to get people *feeling* his health care "reform" rather than *thinking* about it.

When the fabricated sob stories failed to move public opinion, Obama tried more Kafkaesque absurdity. During his autumn 2009 speech before the joint session, he claimed that if they did not pass his plan, "people will die." And as the cliff-hanger vote on it approached in the Senate, Obama ludicrously claimed that if Congress failed to act, the federal government "will go bankrupt." Let's review the logic: we needed to spend an estimated $2.5 to $5 trillion on a government takeover of health care, or the country will go bust?

Other players in the theater of the absurd chimed in with hilarious attempts of their own to justify their Frankenstein bill in what turned out to be some classic kook moments. In the first classic kook moment, when asked under what constitutional authority the individual mandate was permissible, Democratic congressman John Conyers replied, "Under several clauses, the good and welfare clause, and a couple others." Of course! The "good and welfare" clause. Article I, Section Nonexistent. Somewhere, the Founding Fathers are slapping their foreheads. John Adams is turning to Thomas Jefferson, saying, "You big dummy! How could we have left out the 'good and welfare' clause?" Perhaps the Founders did not include a "good and welfare" clause because they were too busy providing for the common defense. Or because they knew that such an open-ended phrase would be used by kooks like Conyers to justify unconstitutional stuff like socialized medicine.

In a second classic kook moment, as Christmas Eve 2009 approached, the bill's Senate passage looked a bit uncertain. Democrats began desperately invoking the name of the recently deceased senator Edward Kennedy, a longtime champion of government-run health care. "Win one for Ted!" they cried. With public opposition running high and Republican opposition unanimous, Democrats resorted to propping up a dead Kennedy like a scene in *Weekend at Bernie's*.

They also laughably tried to blame the Republicans for the closeness of the vote. Democrats controlled the White House, a filibuster-proof majority in the Senate, and a huge majority in the House, and they were still whipping their votes until the last minute. Some Democrats were unsure, not because they weren't part of the kook brigade—all of them proved to be—but because they were worried about their own political skins. In the end, of course, there proved to be no such thing as "moderate Democrats" as they all fell in line.

The third classic kook moment came when Pelosi stood before a legislative group and the American people and said, "We have to pass the bill so you can find out what's in it, away from the fog of controversy." Very few, if any, of the Democrats supporting the bill took the time to read it, including the Speaker. It didn't matter to them what was actually *in* the bill, as long as there *was* a bill that razed the existing health care system and replaced it with a "spread the wealth around" one. Who needed to read the bill? Details, schmetails!

Meanwhile, back in the part of the country where the Constitution was still relevant, Republicans and others recognized the need for genuine reform of a system in which costs were spiraling out of control, and they had advanced a number of health care reform ideas that would have addressed the cost issue without nationalizing one-sixth of the economy. They included permitting insurance to be sold across state lines to encourage competition and thus reduce costs, allowing easier access to and formulation of health savings accounts, instituting tort reform, equalizing the tax laws so that employer-provided health insurance and individually owned insurance had the same tax benefits, repealing government mandates on what insurance companies were required to cover, enacting sweeping Medicare reform, and encouraging cost transparency so consumers would know what treatments cost.

They were all commonsense ideas that had broad support among business owners and the public at large, and yet—with the exception of tort reform, to which Obama tossed rhetorical kisses but was too intimate with trial lawyers to actually carry out—none of them were considered. Not applicable under the "good and welfare" clause, apparently.

As with the debates over spending and debt, the Republicans were coming at it in good faith, full of pro-American, pro-growth solutions, and the kooks were on a different playing field entirely. If they had allowed any of the market-based proposals, the entire redistributionist mission would have been undermined. They could not permit it.

The final 2,500-page bill was a socialist's wet dream, with thousands of onerous new regulations on doctors, hospitals, and other health care providers; over $570 billion in dozens of new taxes; hundreds of new bureaucracies; provisions for cost-based rationing, including the euphemistically termed "end of life counseling" (otherwise known as "death panels," the accurate term first used by former governor Sarah Palin); the establishment of a fifteen-member Independent Patient Advisory Board (IPAB, not to be confused with your iPad), which will be accountable to no one as it metes out treatment decisions (again, "death panels," anyone?); massive new fines for noncompliance; and a vesting of enforcement with the Internal Revenue Service. Obama packed and stacked the legislation like a juicehead who's constantly at GNC, buying powders, pills, and supplements to grow larger and larger until he looks like the Stay Puft Marshmallow Man.

On March 23, 2010, the Orwellian maze hilariously known as the Patient Protection and Affordable Care Act became law—without a single Republican vote. Before its final passage in the House, a group of Democrats led by Speaker Pelosi made a dramatic entrance into the Capitol. Pelosi wielded the cartoonishly big gavel used to pound another massive redistributionist program, Medicare, into law. As they carried out their macabre procession, they were confronted by thousands of Americans, whom the kooks tried to smear as "racist" Tea Partiers but who were, in fact, regular citizens terrified about the rights and freedoms they were about to lose. We actually haven't seen that giant gavel since that day. Rumor has it Pelosi sleeps in bed with it when her husband, Paul, is out of town. I wonder if Nancy knows that this gavel doesn't require batteries.

Here's a tip-off that ObamaCare was a world-class socialist disaster of tyrannical proportions. On the day it became law, Obama received congratulations from Saudi king Abdullah, who funnels money to terrorists who use it to attack and infiltrate our country; United Nations secretary-general Ban Ki-moon, whose institution is so anti-American that it's trying to undermine us in some way every day; and Cuban dictator Fidel Castro, who took a break from his busy decades-long schedule of hating us to endorse ObamaCare. Up next, valentines for ObamaCare from Iran's Mahmoud Ahmadinejad, North Korea's Kim Jong-un, Venezuela's Hugo Chávez, and Russia's Vladimir Putin! The tyrants of the world love ObamaCare because it's the biggest single destroyer yet of American exceptionalism.

A massive tangle of spending, taxing, redistributing, and general leftist weirdness, ObamaCare was an explosion of long-pent-up kook ambitions. Perhaps even the kooks were stunned by the magnitude of their achievement.

Five days after it was rammed through, Senator Charles Schumer appeared on *Meet the Press* and said, "As people learn what's actually in the bill, that six months from now, by election time, this is going to be a plus because the parade of horribles, particularly the worry that the average middle class person has that this is going to affect them negatively, will have vanished and they'll see that it'll affect them positively in many ways."

Six months later, Democrats lost their majority in the House and their filibuster-proof advantage in the Senate, in large part because of the "parade of horribles" that became more evident every day. For starters, Pelosi had stated that ObamaCare would "create 4 million jobs, 400,000 jobs almost immediately." The reality, however, was much different.

The hundreds of billions of dollars in new taxes, the Byzantine new regulations, and the incalculable costs associated with implementing ObamaCare immediately formed a dark cloud of uncertainty over businesses of all sizes. Why would a company hire someone today when it had no idea what it was going to cost it to have that employee on its books tomorrow?

That uncertainty choked off hiring and killed in the cradle the nascent economic recovery. In the summer of 2011, the Heritage Foundation released a report comparing the rate of net job growth before and after the bill's passage. January 2009 was the low point of the recession, as 841,000 jobs were shed in that one month alone. Over the next fifteen months, however, employers began hiring again, peaking in April 2010 when 229,000 new jobs were added. ObamaCare was passed in late March, and from that moment job creation came to a screeching halt. In fact, pre-ObamaCare, employers were hiring at an average rate of 67,000 (net of layoffs), but post-ObamaCare, that number dropped to a mere 6,500. There were many economic factors contributing to anemic job growth, but the adoption of ObamaCare was a major reason for the stalled recovery.

———

Obama and his ilk told us repeatedly that the law would bring down health care costs and save us money. The opposite has been true. In addition to the huge grab bag of new taxes on everything from medical devices to indoor tanning (which set off *Jersey Shore*'s Snooki), premiums have skyrocketed. Medicare's own actuary, Richard Foster, told the House Budget Committee in January 2011 that it probably would *not* hold costs down. He also laid bare one of Obama's favorite lies, that if you like your current insurance, you will be able to keep it. That, he said, would be "not true in all cases."

Related to Foster's statement about loss of coverage, several large benefits consultants, such as McKinsey and Company and Towers Watson, estimated that between 10 percent and 50 percent of employers might do cost-benefit analyses and decide it was cheaper for them to eliminate coverage, pay a fine, and push their employees off onto a government-run program.

This is what Harkin meant when he said that ObamaCare was a "starter home." The kooks *want* employers to drop private coverage and move more and more Americans into government plans. Ultimately that's how they will achieve their cherished single-payer system. Indeed, in 2011 the SEIU, which had helped to draft the bill and supported it enthusiastically, dropped health insurance coverage for 6,000 *children*. Rationing has already kicked in as well, including: new Food and Drug Administration recommendations limiting the use of the expensive late-stage breast cancer drug Avastin; new government recommendations through the U.S. Preventive Services Task Force that women get Pap tests every three years instead of every year and healthy men forgo routine prostate exams; the reduction in Medicare payments to hospitals where too many patients are readmitted after treatment for heart attacks, heart failure, or pneumonia; and states sharply limiting hospital stays under Medicaid. The Democrats gutted Medicare by over $500 billion to help pay for ObamaCare, so the cuts have begun there as well, hitting frontline hospitals and some of the sickest patients first. If the IPAB judges Grandma's heart treatment to be too expensive, she is @$%&! outta luck. Ironic, isn't it, after decades of hearing Democrats lie about Republicans wanting to "throw Grandma in the snow"? Today, Democrats actually want to help Grandma meet her maker in order to get their tax-greedy hands on her estate.

As for the rest of us: two ovaries, two testicles, two lungs . . . pick one! Who says ObamaCare isn't about choice?

ObamaCare cheerleaders also told us that it would fix the uninsured problem by getting us close to "universal coverage." In fact, after the law was passed, they announced—surprise!—that it would still leave roughly 30 million Americans without coverage. Moreover, they said that with more people covered, hospital emergency rooms would be less burdened, and yet according to the *New York Times* in May 2011, there are "fewer emergency rooms available as need rises." Unsurprisingly, ObamaCare did little to change the rate of emergency room visits. In fact, as doctors drop out of the medical profession out of frustration with the labyrinthine new regulations and as the existing physician shortage grows more acute, access to doctors will become tighter and emergency room visits will likely increase. But of course, ObamaCare was never about getting the uninsured covered.

At the state level, cash-strapped governments have warned that they cannot carry the new cost burdens of the expanded Medicaid coverage—namely ObamaCare's expansion to cover up to 133 percent of the federal poverty level—without busting their budgets.

In the longer term, ObamaCare has begun stripping out the significant financial rewards of going into medicine, thereby disincentivizing talented people from choosing it as a profession. Ultimately the most gifted people will be less likely to choose the expensive, long-haul process of becoming doctors, increasing the chances that your future heart bypass may be performed by a yahoo.

Meanwhile, when major companies such as Deere, Caterpillar, Verizon, and AT&T dared to speak out about the costs and financial burdens of the new law, they were slammed by the White House, which then supported Democratic representative Henry Waxman's attempt to drag them into a Congress Inquisition. Waxman, the son of Torquemada and Miss Piggy, attacked any company that raised a peep about ObamaCare's problems.

So corrupt was the Democrats' accounting on ObamaCare that the administration itself was forced to jettison a cherished part of it. In October 2011, Sebelius announced that the administration was bagging the Community Living Assistance Services and Supports (CLASS) Act, a program to provide long-term care and one of Ted Kennedy's dearest redistributionist dreams. Pronouncing the program fiscally unsustainable, Sebelius acknowledged that Team Obama "[did] not see a viable path forward for CLASS implementation at this time." As the Heritage Foundation reported, CLASS advocates in the administration and Congress pushed for its inclusion in ObamaCare despite warnings that it was so flawed and expensive that it would require either a major taxpayer bailout or another insurance mandate to keep it afloat. In the end, even the most creative Health and Human Services accountants couldn't make the math work and the *New York Times* was forced to admit, "It didn't add up." Down the tubes it went, the first but certainly not the last of the unsustainable ObamaCare provisions to bite the dust.

Given the long *actual* "parade of horribles," Schumer's prediction of growing public support for ObamaCare has become an absurd joke rather than reality. From the day of its passage, many polls consistently have shown full repeal favored by nearly 60 percent of the American people.

In its first act in January 2011, the new House Republican majority began the process of getting the nation out from under this economy-crushing albatross. They voted on the amusingly and correctly titled "Repealing the Job-Killing Health Care Law Act." It passed resoundingly but failed in the Senate, amid much Democratic anxiety. They knew the majority of Americans hated ObamaCare and wanted it gone. They saw big numbers of their Democratic brethren lose their political careers in large part over it in November 2010. They were running scared.

They also knew there was no real defense of ObamaCare, beyond its true purpose of redistributing wealth and health care. So they reached for another daft defense by claiming that the GOP was "obsessed" with health care when the American people wanted them focused on jobs. Let's get this straight. While they were busy "obsessing" over their redistributive health care dream, Democrats claimed that it was critical to the economy, would be deficit neutral, and would create jobs. When Republicans advanced repeal, suddenly Democrats claimed that health care had *nothing* to do with the economy and that the GOP was off in the weeds when (a) the *Democrats* had been off in the health care weeds for two years, and (b) *they* had argued it was central to the economy. When the kooks said that, they meant that it was central to their plan to create a command economy. When the Republicans said it was central, they meant that, given its costs and uncertainty, repealing it would help the economic recovery. If ObamaCare were really about improving health care, why then did Team Obama grant so many waivers for unions, businesses, and even entire states to get out of it? Why did they fulfill Bill Clinton's request for exemptions for Victoria's Secret models, Hooters girls, professional mud wrestlers, and all the members of the Lingerie Football League?

The practical economic effects of ObamaCare were so job- and business-killing that even Obama had to face the gruesome facts and give some lucky folks get-out-of-ObamaCare-free cards. The law actually does not grant any statutory authority to waive any part of it. Team Obama just made one up. They claim that the Health and Human Services secretary is authorized to issue temporary waivers to companies or insurers, freeing them from rules mandating minimum standards of health coverage. Other waivers, which Team Obama euphemistically calls "adjustments," let states ask the HHS secretary to free up requirements that insurers spend a certain percentage of premiums on medical care. And a third waiver, available in 2017, will allow states to effect their own health reforms, but only if they are consistent with ObamaCare's regulations and objectives. Within moments of the bill's passage, unions and companies began lining up to take advantage of the waiver "outs." When McDonald's, an American icon that offered full "minimed" health insurance to its 30,000 employees, said it may have to drop all coverage, Team Obama sensed a potential political disaster. It then began dispensing waivers like Pez candy.

Because there was no statutory authority to issue waivers in the first place, there were no corresponding criteria with which to decide who got waivers and who did not. It was a subjective White House determination based on politics, money, and cronyism. McDonald's, which was the subject of a front-page *Wall Street Journal* story detailing its distress over the new law, got a waiver. White Castle, a similarly iconic business, did not. Perhaps White Castle's big sin was going public *itself* with its ObamaCare problems, rather than having an outside journalist do it. The company said that a single provision in the law would eat up roughly 55 percent of its yearly income after it goes fully into effect in 2014, making it difficult to maintain its 421 restaurants and hire new workers, never mind keep up the health coverage they already provided. White Castle was no rogue health insurance evader. It had been providing health coverage to its employees since 1924 and had been paying between 70 and 90 percent of health care costs for those employees. But with ObamaCare punishing its good behavior, White Castle said it was considering dropping its employee-based coverage and dumping those employees in government-run exchanges. To the kooks, this means a job well done. Hence, no waiver for White Castle. But REI, a Seattle-based company whose CEO was an Obama campaign donor and loud advocate for ObamaCare, obtained a waiver for its 2,000 employees. Perhaps White Castle's biggest mistake was not using actor Kal Penn as its personal negotiator. Penn, a.k.a. Kumar from *Harold & Kumar Go to White Castle*, was already working in the Obama administration's executive branch as something called the associate director in the White House Office of Public Engagement . . . whatever the hell that is.

Unions, however, were the prime beneficiaries of ObamaCare's crony socialism. As a major source of financial and political support for the Democrats generally and Obama in particular, unions of all stripes formed a conga line to request ObamaCare waivers. Most of them had enthusiastically contributed self-serving ideas as the policy was being drafted, and all cheered when it passed. And yet, when it came time to implement it, many unions—from the SEIU and the Teamsters to the International Brotherhood of Electrical Workers and the Communications Workers of America—sought, and got, shelter in the protective arms of the waiver.

In fact, half of all the approximately 1,800 ObamaCare waivers granted by the administration were doled out to unions, and in six months alone, from June 2011 to January 2012, labor unions representing over half a million workers were exempted from the health care fiasco. Without the exemptions, these unions would have been forced to drop low-cost coverage for seasonal, part-time, and low-wage workers due to skyrocketing premiums. The only way they were able to keep their health care is by pleading with the White House to spare them from ObamaCare. So they made the quintessential crony deals: you rub my back, I'll rub yours. ObamaCare was for suckers, and the unions would certainly not be played for suckers.

Also not game for the ObamaCare sucker punch: former House Speaker Nancy Pelosi and Senate Majority Leader Harry Reid, two of ObamaCare's biggest political enforcers. In April 2011 alone, Pelosi's San Francisco district received thirty-eight waivers, including for high-end hotels and restaurants that could presumably afford to provide their employees with ObamaCare's minimum insurance coverage. But when they started complaining about the law's onerous costs and rules, Pelosi saw to it that they got waived out, later proclaiming them "emancipated." And after winning reelection in November 2010, Reid made sure that his *entire state* got a waiver from certain requirements of the new law because—get this—forcing them through, the department [of Health and Human Services] found, "may lead to the destabilization of the individual market." Duh!

Nevada joined Florida, Ohio, Tennessee, and New Jersey in getting statewide waivers; other states lined up with waiver requests as well, but unless your state was critical to Obama's 2012 reelection, you could forget it. If you were a Catholic, you could also forget it. In February 2012, Obama's Department of Health and Human Services issued a mandate requiring religious institutions, such as Catholic hospitals, schools, and clinics—which serve people of all faiths—to provide insurance covering contraception, sterilization, and abortion-inducing drugs, all of which violate the Church's deeply held beliefs on these matters. Many people of all faiths criticized the move, calling it a direct assault on religious freedom and yet another example of the statist coercion of ObamaCare, but Team Obama was unmoved. The kooks made sure that they and their cronies slipped the leash of ObamaCare. They know full well how destructive it is to business and the overall economy. But they also believe that the horrendous consequences should be suffered by you, not by them. After all, they're on a higher mission to transform the country.

In 2010, the American people were crossing the street, minding our own business, when the kooks came speeding down the road in a souped-up jalopy. They turned the corner on two wheels and plowed right into us. After they mowed us down, they fled the scene of the accident in an egregious hit-and-run. What the @$%&! just happened?

A twenty-five-hundred-page Rube Goldberg of government power, control, and spending. Redistributing America's top-flight health care system had to require degrading it, making it look like other failed nationalized health care services, and, through higher taxes, fees, and regulations, moving vast amounts of money from the haves to the have-nots.

Most Americans understand that in addition to being a grotesque assault on our individual freedom of choice, an unaffordable expansion of government, and a redistributive pig-out, ObamaCare is something even darker. The Founders intentionally built a small, nonintrusive federal government to guarantee individual liberty. Central to that concept is the right to private property, which the Founders protected against illegal search, seizure, and confiscation by an all-powerful state. The operative word for the Founders was "private." They ensured that every American had the right to property that couldn't be touched by government, forced into a government-run collective, or deemed by some future federal government as "excessive."

When the Founders guaranteed private property, they meant *private* in every sense of the word.

There is nothing more private than your body and your health. And the first thing the leftists set out to do in early 2009 was to seize them in an Orwellian grab of your body and health and, most important, your money. All of those once private pieces of your property are now controlled by the government and are very public indeed. And that, all along, was the true ObamaCare endgame.

Death and Taxes (But I Repeat Myself)

When I was sixteen, I took my first paying job in the real world. I was excited about entering the wonderful world of work (as I said, I was sixteen) and earning some meaningful money for the first time. I had big plans for that dough: most of it would be set aside for college and expenses, but I also had dreams of buying my first car. I pictured myself in it, driving with the top down à la Christie Brinkley in National Lampoon's *Vacation*. I couldn't afford that red Ferrari, but I'd still be fierce in my new-to-me car. The world (or at least New Jersey) would never be the same.

I blissfully worked for the first two weeks, awaiting the arrival of that first paycheck and what it represented, the beginnings of the American Dream. It arrived in a manila envelope, my name peeking through the cellophane window. I ripped it open, visions of the hot little sports car dancing in my head.

Dude! Where's my money? When I saw that government at all levels had taken nearly 50 percent of it and there was nothing I could do about it (lest the long arm of the IRS escort me to prison), I literally almost keeled over. Forget the Ferrari. Forget even the Dodge I was considering. The most I could hope for was a Flintstone rockmobile (which ironically, years later, Obama would force Detroit to build). I wouldn't be driving a Cadillac SRX. Instead, I'd be popping wheelies on a Schwinn BMX.

That's the soul-crushing and economy-destroying effect of high taxes. And yet, the Democrats are committed in a Norman Bates–with-his-mother kind of way to ever-higher taxes. Old-school liberals used to be known as "tax and spend" lefties. They'd tax like crazy and then spend whatever money the taxes brought in. Today's kooks are spending *first*—and at such unprecedented levels—that they need ever-higher taxes to pay for it. Their love affair with higher taxes is pure *Rain Man*: "Tax hikes! Definitely tax hikes!"

In mid-July 2011, Obama said two things that sum up his real objective in seeking ever-increasing taxes. In a press conference in which he expressed his frustration over the debt talks, he told the nation that he "would rather be talking about stuff that *everybody welcomes, like new programs . . .*" He also said, "I do not want, and I will not accept, a deal in which I am asked to do nothing. In fact, I'm able to keep hundreds of thousands of dollars in additional income that *I don't need*." (Emphasis added.)

There it is: the essence of the kooks' redistributionist agenda. Obama laid out the assumption that since *everybody* welcomes new government programs, you've got to smack the highest earners in the wallet to pay for them because, after all, they're parasites just lounging around "counting their money," which is also apparently just lying around, getting moldy. Of course, the Big Kookuna Obama will be the judge of how much money you need or don't need. After all, he told us that he's got a couple of hundred grand sitting around that *he* doesn't need, so you must not need much of your dough either. After all, "collective salvation" doesn't come cheap.

Higher taxes are the lifeblood of redistributionism, since they seize from the haves to give to the have-nots. The kooks are entitled to your money and assets, you see, because they are on a morally superior mission: while you might want your money for a better home or car or college tuition for your kids, the leftists want your money for their noble plan to reengineer the economy. You think they want you to have a family vacation? They don't; they want more abortion clinics. You think they want you to build your own new swimming pool? They don't; they want your money to rehabilitate a heroin junkie. You think they want you to have a bigger SUV to haul the soccer team? They don't; they want a brand-new collection of sheer shirts named for Barney Frank.

For decades, they have cleverly cloaked their true mission in various ways. They have cast it in emotional terms to which it's been difficult to object, using words such as the ubiquitous "fairness" and "doing what's right" to protect "public servants" such as teachers, police officers, and firefighters. While trying to sell the nearly $500 billion "jobs" bill in October 2011, Biden suggested that if the bill weren't passed, the number of violent crimes, including rape, would increase. Fear and guilt: these are the standard weapons in the Left's rhetorical arsenal. In February 2010, while Harry Reid pushed for a $15 billion jobs bill, he suggested that without its passage, out-of-work men were more likely to beat their wives. Apparently, as the jobs bills get bigger and more expensive, so too does the heinous nature of the crimes that will be committed if they aren't passed.

Leftists are fond of using the word "invest" as a euphemism for spending, but "investing" is not the role of government, except perhaps in building infrastructure. Obama has consistently invoked the word "invest" to make it sound like he's confiscating your money for business-savvy purposes. How can you oppose higher taxes when he's talking about the "investments" that need to be made in infrastructure, education, and job training? The word "invest" makes it sound like he's treating your money as a true investment manager would. In the real world, however, if this government were a hedge fund, the "investment managers" would have been fired a long time ago. After all, wouldn't you run for your life if you walked into a Wells Fargo bank and were greeted by Barack Obama holding a clipboard and pen? Jon Corzine, the leftist former senator and governor of New Jersey and top Obama fund-raiser, presided over an epic collapse of his securities firm, MF Global. Over $1.2 billion of client funds went missing, prompting the FBI to move in. Big-spending leftists know how to lose and waste money, not "invest" it.

Most Americans wouldn't have a problem paying a reasonable tax rate—*if* government were a good steward of our money. There are certain collective goods and services that only government can provide—such as military defense, bridges and roads, and, locally, police forces and public schools. But over the years, government has blown through so much money on things it shouldn't be involved in— from a Department of Homeland Security roundtable on "Deceptive Dating Tactics" in January 2012 to a $76 per person lunch at a 2011 Department of Justice conference—that it's now broke and cannot afford the things it's supposed to do. I mean, a $76 lunch? Really? Do people also leave the DOJ with a sweet swag bag, like they've just been to the *Vanity Fair* Academy Awards after-party? We know Attorney General Eric Holder wishes he were P. Diddy, but he's more like Raj from *What's Happening!!*

During a 2008 primary debate, ABC News' Charlie Gibson asked Obama if he'd raise the capital gains tax rate *even if he knew that cutting it would generate more revenue for the government*, as it did when Clinton had cut it. Obama responded that raising the tax, even if doing so would *reduce* revenue, might be warranted out of "fairness."

What he was really saying was that to the kooks, raising taxes is not just about raising *revenue*, although they always need more of that. It's really about raising *rates* in order to sock it to the wealthy. The redistributors are less concerned with how they bring in money to the Treasury than making sure they zap the "rich" no matter what. To the leftists, in the battle of rates versus revenue, hiking rates will win every time, despite the mountains of evidence that show that they could get more money into the government to fund their kook agenda from lower rates. It makes no logical or economic sense, but the leftists are driven by neither logic nor sense. Nobody ever got a job from a poor man. The leftists—particularly the Obama cabinet, which didn't have a single member with private-sector experience—will not see that economic truth. They're so ideologically blinded by their obsession with ever-higher taxes that not even Dr. Phil could talk them out of their addiction to other people's money. The kooks love higher tax rates because they're their most effective brute weapon of class warfare. Paint devil's horns on the "rich," then take them for everything they've got. And do it by force, by changing the tax code, enlarging existing redistributionist programs, and, whenever possible, creating new ones. While the leftists like to paint themselves as compassionate and empathetic and the Right as cold and greedy, the exact opposite is true: the Left is implacably greedy for everybody's money. The United States of America has become the United States of Grand Larceny, with leftists prodding the bodies of every American in an attempt to determine whether we've devised some new biological way of hiding nickels and dimes from them. (Hence, ObamaCare.)

———

During the 2008 campaign, Obama toned down the class warfare rhetoric. Despite his years working in the class warfare trenches as a community organizer, where his job was to drive class divisions and resentment, Obama downplayed that part of his agenda. Instead, he cast himself as a unifying leader of the rich, poor, and middle classes. He glossed over the fact that the divisions he claimed he'd heal were the precise divisions he needed to engage in his redistributionist extravaganza. In 2008, most of the American people bought his "Mr. Unity" routine because they weren't particularly focused on taxes or class divisions. That year, voters were less concerned about taxes than they had been in previous elections because they had enjoyed a fifteen-year-long respite from tax hikes. From Bill Clinton's 1993 tax increase to Obama's 2009 tax hike on cigarettes, Americans had not experienced a major federal tax increase. President George W. Bush's two waves of cuts in marginal rates in 2001 and 2003 reduced taxes for everyone and also cut 13 million people on the lower end of the income scale from paying any federal income tax. If you're paying less or no federal income taxes, you're not particularly worried about them. Because more Americans across the entire economic spectrum could keep more of their own money, the poor man could feed his family better and the rich man could give the poor man a raise. That is, until Obama became president and empowered the poor man to rob the rich man. Pretty soon, the rich man will *be* the poor man, and we'll *all* be sitting in one big crappy boat together.

Once president, Obama dispensed with the unifying rhetoric and began to wage full-frontal class warfare. At the outset, he hit out only at the "fat cat bankers on Wall Street" while waging a softer-sell class warfare on the rest of us. Higher taxes, he said, are "neighborly." He invoked the biblical verse about being "our brother's keeper," which dovetailed with his earlier comment advocating "collective salvation."

But this has never been about being your "brother's keeper." It's always been about *keeping* your brother's wealth. It has been about envy and about coveting what someone else once had. Obama even pretended to oppose higher taxes in the summer of 2009, when he said, "The last thing you want to do is to raise taxes in the middle of a recession because that would just suck up—take more demand out of the economy and put businesses in a further hole." Amen! Oh wait. He didn't mean it.

He went on to say, "These are tax cuts and changes in the tax credit system that are going to spur job creation and economic growth, and I'm proud that Democrats and Republicans worked with each other to get it done." This was his way of forcing the GOP to share ownership of the bad economy: if the extension of the Bush tax rates succeeded in improving the economy, he would take the credit. But if they failed to do so, he'd be able to say, "See? We tried the lower rates the Republicans wanted and there's been no discernible improvement in the economy." Of course, a two-year temporary extension didn't grant the kind of certainty businesses need to expand and hire. A short extension was better than a rate increase, but it would only lead to a continuation of the status quo. That, however, was an irrelevant point to Obama.

In that same press conference in which he croaked out that half-hearted praise for extending the Bush tax rates, Obama couldn't help but hit his redistributionist default button. He alluded to the government-union clash in Wisconsin and said those union workers should not be "denigrated" or "vilified." He continued: "I believe that . . . the concept of shared sacrifice should prevail. If all the pain is borne by only one group—whether it's workers or seniors or the poor—while the wealthiest among us get to keep or get more tax breaks, we're not doing the right thing."

The class warrior in him burst out. He couldn't wait to raise income taxes again so he could grow government even more—so much so that as soon as he had the opening again in 2011, he cheered their impending expiration at the end of 2012 and pushed for higher rates on those earning over $1 million per year. And in a vivid illustration of his pathology, it never occurred to him that the Bush tax rates had now become the *Obama* tax rates.

On August 4, 2011, Obama turned fifty years old. The usual birthday cards arrived from perennial favorites like Barbra Streisand, Kim Jong Il, Jay-Z, and Robert Mugabe. The day before, he celebrated by attending three reelection fund-raisers in Chicago. He had just come off an agreement with Congress to raise the debt ceiling by up to $2.4 trillion (More spending! Happy birthday, Barry!) and had begun to pound "millionaires and billionaires" for failing to "pay their fair share." That night, he met separately with one hundred of his highest-roller donors, each of whom paid $35,800 per person for some face time with him. The package also included a chance to walk the Obama family dog, Bo, a pair of Barry's sweaty gym socks, and a bag of dirty turnips from Michelle Obama's organic garden. Obama, who had added $3,938,093,118,800 to the national debt as of that fiftieth birthday, told his wealthy pals that the government needed to spend more on everything from "wind turbine and electric cars" to "cures for cancer."

Without missing a beat, he proceeded to hit those dastardly rich folk who needed to get with the "shared sacrifice" agenda. He struck out against "big money flooding the airwaves and slash-and-burn politics" as he stood in front of all that "big money" with his palm open, ready to accept their "big money" so he could "flood" those airwaves with ads pounding them. Remember when Obama pledged in 2008 to accept only public financing for his campaign? That lasted about five minutes before he threw those rules out the window and raked in unlimited amounts of money from sources big, small, and questionable. He made a similar about-face in early 2012 when he decided to embrace super PACs after spending nearly two years attacking them as "phony front groups" undermining our democracy. The man who rails constantly against the "rich" gushes over them when it's time to campaign. After all, class warfare needs a steady bankroll.

It used to be that old-school class warriors would at least fake being "men of the people." Today's class warriors don't even try to put on the act. Obama takes time out of his busy schedule of slamming those mustache-twirling "millionaires and billionaires" to hang with them on Martha's Vineyard or the Costa del Sol. New York City mayor Michael Bloomberg warns about possible economic riots as he examines his $18 billion bank account. Director Michael Moore fans the flames of class warfare as he counts his latest multimillion-dollar movie receipts. Actress Roseanne Barr calls for bankers to be limited to $100 million in personal wealth, forced into "reeducation camps," and possibly even "beheaded" in between cashing her multimillion-dollar checks from the syndication of *Roseanne*. She finds the time to do all of this while dressed up like Hitler in her kitchen as she bakes Gingerbread Jew Men in the oven (yes, she actually did this). The new class warriors are class war provocateurs rather than actual combatants. It's so dirty in the trenches! That's for the union thugs. We'll fight the class wars up here, from the pristine perches of the White House or our private jets or our rambling thirty-room mansions. To paraphrase Mel Brooks, you guys go fight the class wars. We'll wash up.

The new class warriors are made up of two essential groups: those wanting ever-greater government help and those plagued with enough "rich guilt" to want to dole it out. So, how do you spot the ones plagued by rich guilt? Those class warriors drink white wine, wear houndstooth jackets, trade aromatherapy oils, and fantasize about Leon Trotsky naked on their Facebook pages. The new class warfare is designed to enforce socialist economic policies that would have zero chance of being adopted without the trumped-up class divisions.

Today's class wars are not about grinding poverty and basic survival. Typical welfare recipients in America now generally receive a cell phone courtesy of the taxpayer lest they be caught in a food stamp emergency without the means to dial 911. Instead of economic deprivation, the modern class wars are about envy: demanding something that someone else has, regardless of how they earned it. America today is *not* run by an economic upper crust that pays no taxes and preys on the poor. In fact, the exact opposite is true: government spending on the less fortunate has never been higher, and the wealthy pay the vast majority of the taxes to support it. And yet, Obama and the kooks have invoked Alinsky rules to form class warfare battle lines like a demented version of the epic fight scene in *Braveheart*. Obama out in front, his face painted not blue but Maoist red and his army consisting of union brutes, former ACORN employees, members of the Nation of Islam, college kids, tofu-eaters, and Colin Powell. Gone was the softer rhetoric about how paying higher taxes was "neighborly" and "patriotic." In its place was more authentic kook language about how the "rich" need to shoulder more of the burden of funding "economic justice."

Obama escalated his hits on everybody on the leftist checklist of "rich" bogeymen, including most prominently "millionaires and billionaires," by whom he means those making as little as $200,000 per year or more. In a high-cost state like New York, $200,000 per year could be made by a married veteran teacher and police officer, hardly the Bill Gateses of the world. And there is quite a difference between someone making $1 million and someone making $1 billion. Obama's not exactly a Mathlete. In fact, when Obama first swept into office, fellow redistributionist senator Max Baucus, chairman of the Senate Finance Committee, which has jurisdiction over federal tax law, introduced a bill that would have increased the income tax rates on some Americans who earn as little as $104,425 per year. He proposed to raise the top *two* income brackets to 36 percent and 39.6 percent, respectively. Fortunately, the Baucus bill bit the dust, but it reveals just how much the leftists are constantly dying to raise taxes not just on the "rich" but on the middle class as well.

To his caricatured "millionaires and billionaires" Obama added the omnipresent leftist villains "corporations," "corporate jet owners," and "Big Oil" to his list of dastardly "rich" folk who needed to hand over more of their assets. Never mind that the U.S. corporate tax rate—

35 percent—is now the highest in the world, which has induced countless U.S. companies to move their operations abroad and park trillions of dollars overseas in an effort to avoid that prohibitive tax. If the corporate tax rate were lowered substantially, those companies would likely bring that money back to invest and hire. In fact, a 2011 study by the National Bureau of Economic Research published in the *American Economic Journal* found that the higher the corporate tax rate, the more companies seek to avoid it, resulting in less economic growth.

Obama also hit out at corporate jet owners regardless of the fact that scrapping the corporate jet tax break would raise just $3 billion over ten years, a mere spit in the ocean of government spending. Even his bromantic partner in all things taxes, billionaire investor Warren Buffett, refused to endorse his corporate jet tax increase, probably because Buffett's firm, Berkshire Hathaway, owns private business jet charter company NetJets. Obama also failed to mention that his own "stimulus" plan actually created a subsidy for the private jets he was demonizing. What a clustermess. Every night when Obama's head hits his Tempur-Pedic pillow, he dreams he's Samuel L. Jackson in *Snakes on a Plane*. But in Barry's fantasy, instead of fighting giant cobras, he's on a Gulfstream IV corporate jet, trying to throw bankers and floor traders from the emergency exit.

Over the past few decades, empirical evidence has shown that keeping tax rates permanently low incentivizes economic growth and job creation as it creates economic certainty, which allows for longer-term planning and puts more money in the pockets of individuals, businesses, and other risk takers who grow the economy. The dramatically lower marginal tax rates put in place by President Reagan—with a top rate of 28 percent—led to the strongest two and a half decades of economic growth in American history.

In fact, the data show that the federal income tax actually brought in *less* revenue as a percent of GDP when the highest rate was 70 percent to 90 percent than it did when the highest rate was 28 percent.

As Alan Reynolds of the Cato Institute has pointed out, when the top rates were approaching the astronomical 92 percent, total revenue was only 7.7 percent of GDP. When President John F. Kennedy lowered the top rate to 70 percent (and moved the lowest rate down to 14 percent), revenues rose to 8 percent of GDP. When President Reagan cut rates across the board and made the highest rate 50 percent and the lowest 11 percent, revenues rose again, to 8.3 percent of GDP. After Reagan oversaw the 1986 tax reform that slashed the top rate to 28 percent, revenues dropped only slightly, to 8.1 percent. Lowering top marginal tax rates paid for itself regardless of what happened to the economy or to GDP performance in any given year. Reductions in top rates under Presidents Kennedy and Reagan as well as reductions in capital gains tax rates under Presidents Clinton and George W. Bush covered their own "costs" and generated more revenue than when rates were higher. The result was consistently strong economic expansion.

The converse is also true: higher rates mean poorer economic performance. As economist Arthur Laffer has argued, as tax rates increase, the number of people paying taxes declines, leading to a shrinking tax base. That, in turn, can lead to rates that are so high to make up for fewer taxpayers that they become prohibitive. Revenue then falls dramatically and leads to further economic harm. History shows that government revenues increase when there is economic growth and more taxpayers in the workforce.

If you calculate the current top tax rate, 35 percent (scheduled to shoot up to 39.6 percent in 2013), plus state income taxes, payroll taxes for Social Security and Medicare, as well as the new 0.9 percent increase in payroll taxes to fund ObamaCare, many Americans could be looking at total tax bills of 58 percent to 70 percent of their incomes, depending on their income and the state income tax rates where they live. Only a devout kook would think this is a good idea. It's about as brilliant an idea as sticking your hand into a bowl full of mosquitoes or letting Gary Busey babysit your kids. The kooks love to point to the supposed glory days of drastically higher tax rates and pine for their reinstatement. Leftist economists like former Clinton

Labor secretary Robert Reich have argued for a return to the 70 percent top marginal rate, cheered on by the academic left and some Democrats in Congress. Reich prefers a slower, more agrarian culture, like his native homeland called The Shire, located in the Northwest part of Middle Earth.

The redistributionists, however, ignore some inconvenient truths about those high tax rates. First, there was no limit on deductible expenses, including taxes paid, installment interest on credit cards, personal borrowing, and even medical expenses, not to mention lunch with the boys. There also existed no punitive Alternative Minimum Tax, which today hits so many middle-class taxpayers that each year Congress has to exempt millions from it. As a result of the atmospheric tax rates, tax shelters sprang up everywhere and were used by nearly every investor. The end result was that the 70 percent top rate with which Reich and the Left are so in love actually wasn't that high, given all the deductions and maneuverings that were allowed. Today, a 70 percent rate would be much closer to an actual 70 percent rate and would wreak movie-monster havoc on the economy. It would have us living like Bob Cratchit in *A Christmas Carol*, dressed in hand-me-down rags, eating one terrible meal a day by candlelight with no heat in the house. To paraphrase Tiny Tim, "Goddamn Marxists, everyone." I think I got that right.

The leftists also blow off the historical evidence that lower capital gains and dividends tax rates raise more tax revenue. When the capital gains tax rate is lower, more taxpayers are willing to sell assets and fork over the tax money, so the feds get more revenue, mainly because the number and frequency of taxable transactions increase. When the capital gains tax rate gets prohibitively high, they're less likely to sell their assets and thus the revenue level drops.

The redistributionists ignore these facts; they care more about punishing the successful than filling the Treasury, although they do "heart" your money.

To be clear: neither Obama nor any of his fellow class warrior kooks ever say they want to raise taxes on YOU. They always say they want to raise taxes on your big, rich, meanie boss and those capitalist pig companies that sell you your car, the gas that goes in it, your clothes, electricity, cigarettes, and indoor tan. They never tell you that those higher taxes get passed on to you in the form of higher consumer prices. Instead, it's always about sticking it to "the man" while pretending to protect the middle class as they go about their noble government work. People forget that you don't have a right to be employed, so if "the man" takes a hit, you just might find yourself at home, broke, watching *The Steve Wilkos Show*.

At one point during the 2011 debt negotiations, Speaker John Boehner criticized the Obama White House for its intransigence over tax hikes. "Dealing with them the last couple months has been like dealing with Jell-O," Boehner said. "Some days it's firmer than others. Sometimes it's like they've left it out overnight. . . . The only thing they've been firm on is these damn tax increases."

President Jell-O was all over the map in the debt negotiations except when it came to raising taxes. Then he became President Krazy Glue. Obama referred to his desire for higher taxes as a commitment to a "balanced approach," in which "cuts" may be made (though not really) and taxes are increased to better achieve that "shared sacrifice."

The inconvenient truth is that in 2009, 51 percent of tax filers paid no federal income taxes at all. While it's true that they pay other taxes, including Social Security taxes, when it comes to federal income taxes, half of all Americans are now on a collective free ride. More outrageously, 30 percent of tax filers had a *negative* tax liability in 2009, meaning they actually made money off the tax system from refundable tax credits such as the Earned Income Tax Credit. When Democrats speak of "shared sacrifice," they demand that the wealthiest as well as jobs-generating small businesses pay even more, but they're okay with half the country not contributing anything at all. This nonpaying group is also known as a core Democratic constituency.

Into this insane mess of kook class warfare, enter Warren Buffett. For years, Buffett has been whining that his tax liability just isn't high enough, that as a gazillionaire, he should be paying much more in taxes, that his secretary is paying a higher rate than he is, and oh the humanity! As early as 2007, Obama referred to Buffett's self-imposed predicament by saying that "a secretary shouldn't pay more taxes than a billionaire." Until she showed up at Obama's 2012 State of the Union address, Buffett's secretary, Debbie Bosanek, was an elusive creature around whom we were debating national tax policy.

Here's how Buffett's tax buffet has warped the conversation. First, Buffett has claimed that he pays just 17 percent of his income to the government. Buffett usually gives himself an annual salary of $100,000, which is taxed at that rate. The bulk of his annual income, however, comes in the form of investment income, which is generally taxed at a lower rate than wages. The current top capital gains tax rate is 15 percent, hence the discrepancy with his secretary, who could be taxed at the top income tax rate of 35 percent rate, depending on her salary.

What Buffett doesn't say is that much of his capital gains and dividends income is already taxed at 35 percent (via the corporate income tax) by the time he gets to it, so in effect, taxes are being paid twice on the same earnings. After both taxes kick in, Buffett's effective tax rate would be over 40 percent by the time the feds are done with him, and that doesn't include state and local taxes. He has argued that passive capital gains should be taxed at a higher rate. But income tax and capital gains tax rates are apples and oranges, and Buffett has been making a fruit smoothie with them for years. Obama has been mixing his taxes up deliberately as well, and he's never let the disingenuousness of the comparison stop him. If Buffett is so enthralled with the idea of paying more in taxes, nothing is stopping him from writing a check to the Treasury for whatever amount he thinks might alleviate his anguish. The same is true for former Google executive Doug Edwards, who attended an Obama fund-raiser in the fall of 2011 and told him he was so rich that he was unemployed "by choice," and then begged him to raise his taxes. Edwards's hand must have carpal tunnel syndrome because he has yet to write an additional check to the government either. Funny how that works: the super-rich complain publicly about their light tax load but never pay a dime above what their accountants tell them they owe. They never want to be the only sucker paying more. Instead, they are asking *everyone* in that upper bracket to be *forced* to pay more under penalty of jail.

Further, if Buffett had real confidence in the government's ability to "invest" taxpayer money wisely, he'd not only voluntarily pay more to the Treasury. He'd also be bequeathing his massive fortune to the state upon his death. Instead, he has already committed much of his personal wealth to a private charity, the Bill and Melinda Gates Foundation. By doing so, he, like many others, reduces his estate tax exposure while also receiving the benefits of charitable deductions while he's still alive. To be clear, charitable giving is most often a noble act. It should not, however, escape notice that through the deduction, the taxpayers are in essence contributing to Buffett's charitable giving. (That is, for every dollar that Buffett gives to charity, a certain percentage would have otherwise gone to the government in the form of taxes.) This is his prerogative, of course, but while he lectures the rest of his super-rich friends to cough up more money to the feds, he minimizes how much the feds get from him every chance he gets.

While we're on the subject of tax hypocrisy, let's check out the Obamas' 2010 tax return. The first family's adjusted gross income for that year was $1.728 million. Their taxable income after deductions was $1.34 million. This means that they saved nearly $400,000 through deductions—such as $78,269 for state and local taxes and $49,945 for mortgage interest on their home in Chicago as well as charitable deductions. They also received a $12,334 tax refund from the federal government that year. So while Obama has been telling us that paying more taxes is the "neighborly" thing to do, he's been minimizing his tax bill as much as possible. If Obama really believes that "rich guys like him" should pay more in taxes, then why doesn't he pay more himself? Why does he take every possible deduction? And why didn't he sign over that $12,000 refund back to the U.S. Treasury? Here's why: so he can afford more Blu-ray discs of the movies that have been adapted from Nicholas Sparks novels, like *Dear John* and *The Notebook*. It's a romantic tradition that every Friday night, Rahm Emanuel flies in from Chicago and they watch one alone, just the two of them, wrapped in a single, oversized Snuggie.

In September 2011, Obama proposed that Congress impose the "Buffett Rule," which he described as "asking the wealthiest Americans to pay more taxes." Ask? The power of the IRS to toss your buns in prison isn't the same as a polite request.

Here's the illogic: if the tax rate were raised by 13 percent on the 237,000 individual filers reporting income over $1 million, as Obama wants, it would generate only another $26 billion or so. And that assumes that the tax increase didn't kill jobs and suffocate the economy further, which would be likely. In a universe of nearly $4 trillion budgets with trillion-dollar-plus deficits, $26 billion is a drop in the ocean. Obama needs to start the "millionaires and billionaires" clock ticking at the $200,000 mark because that's where the real dough is. In 2009, those 237,000 filers who reported $1 million or more in income paid $178 billion in taxes. But only 8,274 filers reported income of $10 million or more, and they paid $54 billion in taxes. But lower the bar to $200,000, and you hit the jackpot: 3.92 million people reported income above that level in 2009, and they forked over a whopping $434 billion in taxes. This means that 90 percent of the tax filers who would pay much more under Obama's "Buffett Rule" wouldn't be millionaires at all, and 99.99 percent wouldn't come close to being billionaires. In a world in which various taxes can eat up nearly 50 percent of a salary, $200,000 is hardly a solid measurement of "wealth." The "Buffett Rule" would hit the middle class disproportionately, despite Obama's hyper-emphasis on the Big Rich.

There may be some individual millionaires who pay taxes at lower rates than middle-income folks. According to the IRS, in 2009 there were 1,470 households that filed tax returns with incomes above $1 million but paid no federal income tax. But that's less than 1 percent of the 237,000 returns showing incomes over $1 million.

Our system appropriately has the wealthy paying more than the less fortunate. But they're not just paying more. They're paying a lot more. The richest 0.1 percent of taxpayers already pay 16.4 percent of the total tax burden—and the top 1 percent pays 39 percent of all federal income taxes. The wealthiest 10 percent are carrying 70 percent of the federal tax burden already, while nearly half at the bottom pay nothing at all. How's that for "fair"? When you hit the very bottom of that group, you'll find the quintessential Obama voters. Picture a dorm room, filled with the haze of pot smoke, crushed beer cans on the floor, empty pizza boxes, and *The Daily Show* playing in the background, while two idiots in Che Guevara T-shirts try to set their flatulence ablaze. Let's hope they're too stoned to know when Election Day is.

In fact, the top 5 percent of earners account for 37 percent of all consumer spending, about as much as the entire bottom 80 percent. Those making over $200,000 give 36 percent of all charitable contributions. This is, in essence, the crux of the leftists' ideological failure: raising taxes on the job creators, who spend, invest, hire, and donate hurts the middle and lower class, not the rich. The leftists believe they are punishing the "rich" but they are actually punishing the middle and working classes, whose livelihoods depend heavily on the fiscal health of the "rich" and the businesses and charities they power. It's a trickle-down whoopin'.

───

The real fiscal issue isn't revenue demands; it's out-of-control government spending, particularly on entitlements. As the late great economist Milton Friedman pointed out, the true burden on taxpayers is government spending because government borrowing demands future interest payments out of future taxes. The more the government spends, the heavier the burden on the taxpayer. House Budget chairman Paul Ryan put it this way: "Even if tax revenue as a share of the economy were to grow in excess of its historical average, tax increases simply cannot match the spending commitments of the federal government in the years ahead. Based on Congressional Budget Office projections of their likely policy trajectory, government spending is on pace to double within a generation." When Paul Ryan makes a statement like this, people stare at him like he's an alien, and there's a reason for that. You see, as government spending doubles within a generation, the intelligence quotient of big-spending members of

Congress divides in half. If Ryan stays in Congress another ten years, the Democrats in his audience may very well be lobotomized vegetables.

In the fall of 2011, Obama announced a new wave of class warfare that tracked perfectly with his previous policy and rhetoric. A big tip-off that it was, in fact, class warfare? Obama pointedly said it wasn't: "This isn't class warfare," he said. "It's math." And further: "The money is going to have to come from someplace." Just not from any of his big-government programs, of course. He proposed $1.5 trillion in real tax hikes along with illusory "savings" such as $1 trillion in war "savings" over ten years from wars in Iraq and Afghanistan that we will no longer be fighting. While he distracted people with his right hand by proposing another *temporary* tax cut (the payroll tax holiday), he karate-chopped the rest of us with his left hand by proposing *permanent* tax *hikes*. Sure, Barry. And as soon as we're done fighting the War of 1812, the Civil War, and Vietnam, we'll collect even more imaginary savings when we bring home all those invisible troops who aren't fighting.

Team Obama believed that thanks in large part to the nearly $1 trillion "stimulus," the economy would have been moving along enough by 2011 that they could proceed with their beloved tax hikes. When that didn't happen, they proposed temporary tax incentives and cuts such as the payroll tax holiday to get the economy going and get them to their tax hikes faster. Now they believe that the economy will be sailing along sufficiently in 2013 so they'll finally be able to enjoy their tax hike fiesta. Their goal is to get the economy to *appear* to be getting healthier in order to secure Obama's reelection, after which the massive tax hikes will kick in and the economic damage will be severe.

In the summer of 2011, riots broke out in London, Athens, and other parts of western Europe. The violence and chaos in Great Britain were particularly shocking. The British enjoy a wealthy society. There is a poor underclass and a rich upper class, but like every Western democracy, Great Britain has a large and prosperous middle class. With the exception of Margaret Thatcher, who liberated the British from the shackles of statism, over the decades British leaders succumbed to the socialist impulse that ran rampant in western Europe. As a result, the nation is teetering, thanks to a huge, unsustainable nanny state: nationalized health care, massive social welfare programs, "free" child care and education.

And yet, despite having essentially cradle-to-grave state security, they riot. They protest. They demand *more*. They *never* have enough. No matter how big the welfare state is, no matter how many programs and giveaways and freebies there are, no matter how many subsidies, no matter how much hand holding by the state—it's *never* enough.

And no matter how much you tax and confiscate from the wealthy, it's never enough. It will never *be* enough.

These rioting fools are part of a wider movement to destabilize capitalist societies, but they're the laziest people in Western civilization. For them, it's easier to throw rocks at cops than it is to train at the police academy. It's easier to scream at evil bankers than it is to open a savings account and accumulate interest. And it's easier to bitch and moan about free education than it is to actually open up a book and discover that the cult leaders of Marxist doctrines are actually an assortment of mass murderers: Stalin, Mao, Kim Il Sung, Castro . . . pick your commie, pick your poison.

On the heels of the riots in western Europe, a full mobilization began in America of what Vladimir Lenin once supposedly termed "useful idiots," those blind supporters and apologists for the communist cause. The "useful idiots" served as helpful propaganda and political tools for the Soviet Union in the Western democracies as our enemy chipped away at our system from within.

A new wave of "useful idiots" appeared on the scene in September 2011, as thousands of protesters gathered in New York, Chicago, Los Angeles, Seattle, and elsewhere, ostensibly to "occupy Wall Street." Many of the demonstrators claimed that they were protesting "capitalism" as they munched on Munchkins from Dunkin' Donuts, sipped lattes from Starbucks, and tweeted revolution from their iPhones. Most of them were either hippies aging badly or aspiring hippies. When asked what they'd like to replace capitalism with, most went deer-in-the-headlights; that is, when they weren't hurling obscenities at unnamed "fat cats," defecating on police cars, stealing from and raping their fellow protesters, tripping on all kinds of illegal drugs, committing all manner of violent crimes, getting arrested by the hundreds, and screaming anti-Semitic slurs at "the Jews running the banks and the Fed."

They often carried out their vulgar and criminal activities to the musical stylings of their resident bongo drummers, because no leftist protest is complete without sundry drum circles. They yelped about everything from corporate greed to food modification but only slowly and reluctantly mentioned their ultimate goal. I guess they were instructed by the men behind the curtain not to mention socialism early on. Have you ever heard a barista at Starbucks wax poetic about fair-trade coffee? That's these idiots. Have you ever tripped over a body lying in the aisle floor of a Barnes & Noble? That's these idiots. Have you ever gone to a concert and been asked by someone with a bone through their nose to purchase them a beer? That's these idiots. The kids at Occupy Wall Street look like they shop at Urban Outfitters. There, and at Furthur concerts.

It turns out that the Occupy Wall Street protests of useful idiot troops were created and coordinated by Kook Generals with one mission in mind: *to provide the Obama reelection effort with the handy theme of income inequality.* According to Glenn Beck and his team, who've done pathbreaking investigative work on the global socialist movement, SEIU was helping to plan Occupy Wall Street months before the protests actually materialized. Beck also unearthed a Craigslist ad posted by the Working Families Party, offering to pay community organizers $350 to $650 per week to attend the protests. I have a strange feeling that that Craigslist posting was actually found under the "missed connections: men seeking men" section. The WFP, which was established in the 1990s by prominent members of the

American socialist movement, played a key role in mobilizing and running the demonstrations, as did ACORN and the New Party, which was founded in 1992 as a socialist coalition including members of the Democratic Socialists of America. (Obama attended a New Party event in 1995 and received their political endorsement.) In 1994, a New Party newspaper listed some one hundred activists "who are building the NP," including known radicals such as Noam Chomsky, Frances Fox Piven, and ACORN's Wade Rathke.

In addition to SEIU, some of the nation's biggest unions also helped to create and direct the protests, including the AFL-CIO and the United Federation of Teachers. Financial support came indirectly from the radical leftist billionaire George Soros. When Soros isn't sleeping in his Transylvanian crypt fighting Van Helsing and dining on the blood of virgins, he's the world's biggest Marxist project financier. Furthermore, Reuters reported Soros's connection to *Adbusters*, the magazine that is reported to have come up with the Occupy Wall Street idea after the Arab "Spring" protests brought down governments in Egypt, Libya, and Tunisia. *Adbusters* is funded by the Tides Center, which collects and disseminates a huge number of donations to a slew of leftist groups. Soros's Open Society Foundations (formerly called Open Society Institute) is a major Tides Center donor, giving the group $3.5 million between 2007 and 2009. Occupy Wall Street was hardly an organic, spontaneous uprising. It was about as carefully planned and executed as a corporate shareholders' meeting.

Despite their desperate attempts to refer to themselves as "the Left's Tea Party," the comparison is about as ludicrous as one protester's sign: THE RICH WILL KILL US ALL. The Tea Party is about basic American principles of constitutionally limited government, fiscal responsibility, and free markets. It's about *preserving* America by getting back to its original values and driving forces. The Alinskyites of Occupy Wall Street are about *destroying* those very principles and replacing them with the wholly anti-American concept of enforced socialist "equality." The Tea Party pursues its goals within the system by demonstrating peacefully and respectfully. Those attending Tea

Parties sang patriotic songs, helped each other out, and picked up their litter. The Tea Party uses deodorant; Occupy Wall Street doesn't. The Tea Party helps old ladies cross the street; Occupy Wall Street throws old ladies down the stairs. The Tea Party says, "Don't tread on me"; Occupy Wall Street says, "Workers of the world unite." The Tea Party likes watching football; Occupy Wall Street likes watching rape. Nonetheless, the Tea Party got smeared by the Left as a mostly lily-white group of racist bigots who engaged in threatening or aggressive acts, when it was Occupy Wall Street that was, in fact, guilty of those things.

The Occupy Wall Street orgy was about manufacturing a nasty bit of class warfare to keep the redistributionist train rolling. While the Tea Party wants less government confiscation, the Occupy Wall Streeters want what others have and are demanding that the government take it from them by force. But this is what you get when you attempt an economic revolution in which the members of said revolution majored in poetry, women's studies, or graphic design. You get an army of economic illiterates, mad at the Wall Street day traders to whom they have to serve french fries and chicken nuggets.

The riots and demonstrations happening in the United States and in western Europe are all following the same script, written and executed by the international Left, whose objective is to roil the world, upset the existing order, and ultimately overthrow it. This is Saul Alinsky on a worldwide scale; it's global community organizing. It is the very essence and objective of the Obama agenda.

Of course, what would a radical anticapitalist protest be without Obama's old domestic terrorist pal Bill Ayers? One of the original agitators behind Occupy Wall Street, Ayers launched tutorial sessions for the kids in the streets. He inspired them with the same words he had used in the early 1970s: "Action creates facts, and facts are essential," he blogged to OWS. "The silenced majority, the 99 percent, has finally been pushed so far that it is pushing back. Every movement is improbable until it happens; after the fact it so clearly was inevitable." Billy Ayers, master of wagging the dog.

Within a day of Ayers posting his first blog on Occupy Wall Street, his old friend and the man on whose behalf all of this was being done weighed in.

Obama first said of the protests, "I think it expresses the frustrations that the American people feel."

This was followed by a series of comments in which Obama ramped up his support for the leftist movement, including saying point-blank: "We are on their side." Of course he's on their side. He IS them. They are him. They were sent into the streets to frame his 2012 campaign message of "income inequality" and to renew his platform of "economic justice."

Many observers wondered why the protesters didn't seem to have a coherent message. This was not a mystery to the Obama White House. In order to get reelected, Obama needs a fired-up base of leftist activists, just as he did in 2008. So the SEIU and other kooks set about to get the kids, hippies, socialists, commies, and rank-and-file union members riled up. It didn't matter what the message or the cause was, at least not early on. The point was to get the leftist mob acting *first*. Let the protest form and be disorderly and unreadable, because the Kook Generals would then later supply its objectives. Having invested so much in acting, the mob would then be quick to accept any justification the leftist masters supplied.

This is exactly what happened. At first, very few of the protesters could articulate why they were there. As time went on, they became a bit clearer: Anti-capitalism? Sure! Hate the banks? Me too! The wealthy should pay more! Right on! Collectivism. Fairness. Justice. More important, they would carry that energy into protesting, organizing, campaigning, and, yes, voting in 2012. That is, if they can actually find their way to the polling station. And if they're not behind bars by then. Although, from the Democrats' perspective, being in jail would not necessarily impede their ability to vote. Nor would being dead.

The Occupy Wall Street protests were a perfectly executed bit of leftist psychology: organize leftists, identify and amplify grievances, pit group against group, stoke class warfare by hitting the rich and telling others they are entitled to more of what has been robbed from them, manufacture bedlam, and then seize it to advance their agenda. This has been Obama's shtick from his earliest days in Chicago to the White House.

And yet, Obama has missed—or is deliberately disregarding—a profound flaw in his economic logic. Apart from its crass and offensive objective of dividing Americans, class warfare has always had limited utility in American politics. In the past, populists who have played that card have gained some traction by pitting the rich against everyone else, by inspiring people to haul out their metaphorical pitchforks and storm the lairs of the rich and powerful. But the key reason class warfare has had less success here than in western Europe and elsewhere is that America is an aspirational society. Built on the notions of merit, ambition, hard work, and risk and reward, the United States enshrines the promise of achievement regardless of class or status. Attacks on the rich ultimately backfire because many Americans desire to *be* rich. And they know that in America, diligence, creativity, innovation, and commitment can pay off in big ways, including amassing incredible wealth. The goal of the leftists is to kill that dream, to shatter personal goals, and to ensure that the potential of accumulating wealth is severely diminished. In Obama's world, we'll all live in cardboard boxes and eat every meal at a soup kitchen, where we'll be served leather boots boiled in water by Debbie Wasserman Schultz.

The leftists are tearing at the quintessentially American notion of success because neither they nor their agenda can thrive as long as most Americans are willing to fight for one simple truth: that maximum economic freedom leads to the most individual success—and *that* is the best and most efficient way to "spread the wealth around."

Labor Pains I: That "Three-Letter Word: JOBS"

On the afternoon of August 10, 2011, the Dow Jones Industrial Average was tanking by about 400 points. That month, as we learned later, was particularly catastrophic for jobs: zero net new jobs were created. But at lunchtime that day, the president decided to take a gaggle of young campaign volunteers who had won an essay contest about "organizing" out for a bite.

He took them to a Washington establishment called Ted's Bulletin, which is famous for—wait for it—its Great Depression–era theme. Apparently the White House image makers and communications folks were too busy playing shirtless beer pong to stop this before it could become a metaphor for unemployment in the Obama era.

— — —

The full force of the financial crisis hit in September 2008, when Lehman Brothers collapsed.

As the contagion spread and a crisis that had been limited to the financial sector morphed into a broader recession, the layoffs began. In December 2007, the nation's unemployment rate stood at 5.0 percent. By January 2009, it was 7.8 percent. The rapidly escalating unemployment situation was dire and getting worse; it was in that environment that the 2008 election would take place. It was also a situation that represented a rich political opportunity for the Obama campaign. Obama quickly and deftly positioned himself as the Only One who could "fix" the economy, with the help of some Wise Minds to advise him.

A few weeks before the election, vice presidential nominee and part-time rodeo clown Joe Biden ran to the microphones to second the notion that they were *the* ticket for economic restoration and job creation. After accusing the Republican nominee, Senator John Mc-Cain, of failing to appreciate the seriousness of the jobs picture, Biden demonstrated that he should spend more time watching *Sesame*

Street: "Look, John's last-minute economic plan does nothing to tackle the number one job facing the middle class, and it happens to be, as Barack says, a three-letter word: jobs. J-O-B-S." Well, at least he got the "B-S" part right.

Once they entered office, Team Obama did a hit-and-run on jobs in the form of the "stimulus" and then turned its attention to everything *but* the unemployment crisis: ObamaCare, cap and trade, financial regulation, raiding Gibson Guitars over its use of allegedly illegally imported wood, running guns to Mexican drug cartels, holding sit 'n' spin policy sessions at the White House, drawing devil's horns on the Republicans, smearing the Tea Party, going after California's pot dispensaries, suing Arizona over its illegal immigration law, and playing the back nine.

The "stimulus" was rushed through at warp speed for two reasons. First, they needed to *look like* they were "doing something" to create jobs. Stubbornly high unemployment is the single biggest driver of political discontent. Americans will tolerate bad jobs news if they believe that the jobs environment is improving. In 1984, President Reagan ran for reelection with an unemployment rate of 7.2 percent. But Reagan had put pro-growth policies in place, such as deep tax cuts, sound money, and deregulation, that had unemployment falling precipitously and GDP growing between 6 percent and 9 percent. By the time of the 1984 election, the U.S. economy was smokin', and he won reelection in an historic landslide.

Team Obama sold its "stimulus" as a way to at least stop the employment hemorrhaging and get the government-created job party started. They wheeled out Obama's chief economist, Christina Romer, to predict that it would create "millions of jobs" and keep the unemployment rate at or below 8 percent. Romer and fellow Obama economist Jared Bernstein argued that without the "stimulus," unemployment might rise all the way . . . to 9 percent! It subsequently climbed through the 9 percent range, sailed over 10 percent in October 2009, and then settled back into the 8 to 9 percent range for much of the rest of Obama's term. "Where are the jobs, Mr. President?" So whined the then-Speaker Nancy Pelosi in August 2003, when the July unemployment stood at—wait for it—6.2 percent. Obama's advisers Romer and Bernstein probably would also like to erase their other prediction: that by mid-2012 unemployment would be below 6 percent, with that number dropping like a cement shoe in the Hudson River.

The second reason Team Obama needed the jobs situation out of the headlines is that they were moving on to much more important things. The "stimulus" was their first shot across the redistributionist bow, but the bigger, juicier, longer-term redistributionist goals awaited. They rushed through the "stimulus" and then sped toward the crown jewels of their "more perfect union." None of that could be accomplished if they were focused solely on jobs. Unemployment? No biggie. The "stimulus" would work its redistributive magic, the economy would soon be chugging along in eternal Keynesian bliss, and government or government-supported jobs would be flowering across the land.

In the summer of 2011, Obama gassed around with his Potemkin Council on Jobs and Competitiveness, whose head, General Electric CEO Jeffrey Immelt, spends much of his time shipping major GE divisions, infrastructure, and jobs to China while paying $0 in corporate taxes on billions of dollars in profit. He also spends a good deal of time partying with Mika Brzezinski, taking showers with Chris Matthews's tingling leg, arm-wrestling Rachel Maddow, and admiring Chuck Todd's ginger beard. But just because Immelt is paying no corporate taxes and is creating jobs abroad instead of in the United States doesn't mean he can't put on a good show. As Immelt and the other "jobs council" puppets surrounded Obama, there was no discussion of the fact that Obama's own policies were smothering the economy and preventing job creation. Instead, they were more interested in yuks. At one point, Obama was asked about the epic waste of nearly $1 trillion of our money on the failed "stimulus." He smirked: "Shovel-ready was not as . . . uh . . . shovel-ready as we expected," he replied, chuckling as Immelt and "job council" advisers— including Eastman Kodak's CEO, Antonio Perez, whose company later went bankrupt—joined in the laugh. Ha ha. The joke's on you, America.

On February 24, 2009, Obama sold his "stimulus" by saying: "Over the next two years, this plan will save or create 3.5 million jobs. More than 90 percent of these jobs will be in the private sector—jobs rebuilding our roads and bridges; constructing wind turbines and solar panels; laying broadband and expanding mass transit." Hello, Solyndra! And hello, unions!

"Because of this plan," he continued, "there are teachers who can now keep their jobs and educate our kids. Health care professionals can continue caring for our sick." Hello, teachers' unions! And gangway for ObamaCare!

And month after month, year after year, Obama repeated the same song, claiming the "saving or creating" of "millions" of jobs, demanding tens of billions of dollars more for unions and green jobs boondoggles, and offering shiny justifications for ever-greater government intervention in the private sector. High unemployment is part of the price of admission to the redistributionists' theme park. That, along with the fact that it's the only amusement park where you have to pay upon entry *and* exit. My favorite ride is called "It's a Soviet World After All," where you get to work in a sweatshop while you starve to death. Because everyone knows that the only refreshments at Redistributionland are the ones you have to bring with you and distribute to the other park-goers.

During the Obama years, median income has fallen by an astounding 10 percent. Long-term unemployment has been by far the highest since the Great Depression. Job growth during the first three years of the economic recovery after a severe recession has been the slowest since the end of World War II. Unemployment has stayed above 9 percent for most of the Obama term, and when the rate did drop, it was largely because record numbers of people simply gave up looking for work altogether, shrinking the labor force to its lowest in decades. More than one in four jobs added to the economy were temporary. Total unemployment—counting all those unemployed, those working part-time who would like full-time work, and those who have simply given up looking for jobs—has been at or above 16 percent. Roughly 6 million people have exhausted ninety-nine weeks of unemployment benefits. Black unemployment has been consistently over 16 percent. Unemployment among Hispanics has been over 11 percent. The unemployment rate among the young has been close to 20 percent.

There have, however, been some sectors of the economy experiencing a boom. We've seen 100 percent employment of union skullcrackers, tenured Bolshevik college professors with hairy upper lips, Ganja grocers at medical marijuana dispensaries, and, of course, the guys running the money printing presses.

Democrats argued for extending unemployment benefits to ninety-nine weeks and beyond to help soften the blow of joblessness, and many Republicans supported it, partly because the jobs crisis is so acute and partly out of fear of being painted as heartless boobs who didn't care about the jobless. The problem is that while longer benefit terms sound humane and unobjectionable, several studies have shown that about one-third of those receiving unemployment benefits get a job immediately after those benefits run out. In 2009, when the recession was at its height, 13 million Americans were out of work but 3 million jobs went unfilled, either because the jobless didn't seek them out or they weren't trained or qualified for them.

The result has been elevated levels of unemployment for a longer period of time and an ever-growing dependency on government. As the kooks say: Bingo! In this scenario, the federal government becomes America's chief drug dealer. But instead of slinging heroin or meth, they deal unemployment benefits. The longer you take the drug, the longer you're addicted and the possibility of getting clean diminishes. Imagine if we all had to take a urine test designed to detect big-government socialism. Who would pass it in the Obama era? Would you?

Directly related to the unemployment problem, the home ownership rate has been the lowest since 1965, and foreclosures have been at their highest levels since the Depression. The decline in housing values and the banking crisis precipitated by the housing price slide have meant that even those Americans with jobs are poorer than they were just several years ago because their homes are worth on average 25 percent to 50 percent less. For most Americans, their homes are their biggest asset. When their home value collapsed, so did their financial security.

As a result of high unemployment, the housing crash, and the broader economic stasis, the poverty rate has hit an historic high; it's over 15 percent, with one out of ten children living in poverty. The official poverty level is an annual income of $22,314 for a family of four. From 2007 to 2010, the poverty rate has risen faster than in any three-year period since the recession of the early 1980s. The number of food stamp recipients has also hit record highs, with over 48 million people receiving food benefits. In fact, all government-provided benefits, including Social Security, unemployment insurance, food stamps, and other social welfare programs, rose to record highs during the Obama years.

At the same time, wages from private businesses shrank to their smallest share of personal income in U.S. history. *A record-low 40 percent of the nation's personal income came from private wages and salaries for much of Obama's term. Meanwhile, individuals got about 18 percent of their income from government programs.* This represented a major shift in the source of personal income *away* from private wages and *to* government programs.

This was the Declaration of Dependence in full action. We hold these truths to be self-evident, that all men are created equal, except people making over $250,000 per year. Those people are endowed by Obama with the responsibility to give all of their earnings to those making less. The redistributionists have created a culture in which the poor depend on them to be fed and clothed, while the rich are doing everything in their power to be free of the Iron Fist of government. Never before has a Declaration attempted so brazenly to promote "fairness" by instituting the most unfair practices imaginable.

The problem, of course, is the unsustainability of this rapid dependence on the government. The federal government relies on private wages to generate income taxes to pay for its ever-growing and ever more expensive programs. Government-generated income is taxed at much lower levels or not at all; for example, food stamps and Medicaid are not taxable income. So the more people dependent on the government, the more tax revenue is needed to support them and the more per private-sector employee is required, hence the assault on the "rich" and ultimately on the middle class. The upside-down pyramid gets heavier and heavier until it threatens to collapse. The risky game of the redistributionists is to expand the number of people at the top of the pyramid, those dependent on those carrying the load, the earners, makers, and risk takers, without totally collapsing the structure. The western European socialist democracies pushed the upside-down pyramid too far, and the whole thing imploded. The American redistributionists are playing with fire, and they know it— and most of them *want* the implosion.

Meanwhile, Team Obama constantly tried to distract us from the brutal economic reality created and sustained by its radical course. In mid-2010, Treasury Secretary Timothy Geithner wheeled out "Recovery Summer!"

On August 3, 2010, Geithner penned an op-ed for the *New York Times* titled, "Welcome to the Recovery," in which he argued that "the American economy shows that we are on a path back to growth. . . . The actions we took . . . helped arrest the freefall, preventing an even deeper collapse and putting the economy on the road to recovery. . . . We suffered a terrible blow, but we are coming back."

Not quite. Instead of changing course and trying some pro-growth policies, Team Obama went back to the exclamation points. The administration fired up "Recovery Summer, Part Deux!" in 2011, and that didn't fly either. Anemic economic growth and little to no real job creation had a way of trampling the good times. At some point, even Obama's daily economic briefings petered out. In fact, other than Tim Geithner, his entire economic team has fled faster than O.J. in the white Bronco. Larry Summers, Christina Romer, and Peter Orszag: they're all gone.

Who has replaced them? Does anybody even know? Word on the street is that they're all filming the new *Three Stooges* movie, while the real Moe, Larry, and Curly now work in the West Wing and have been placed in charge of the nonexistent economic briefings.

By the fall of 2011 the unemployment crisis had been so bad for so long that Obama had to propose a second "jobs plan," the American Jobs Act. Released after his annual sun-splashed August Martha's Vineyard vacation, the plan called for—surprise!—$447 billion in new spending.

Interestingly, it was a few Senate Democrats who put the kibosh on it. They didn't want to have to take a vote, lest its costs come back to haunt them, or against it, lest the liberal base get furious. Reid offered a 5.6 percent millionaires' surtax as a way to pay for whatever survived in the bill. "I'm comfortable" with that, replied Obama. Meanwhile, the full "jobs" bill met a grisly death in the Senate, where it couldn't even pass a procedural hurdle. Reid subsequently broke it into parts, many of which went down in defeat as well.

As the unemployment crisis grew, Obama lapsed into preposterous explanations for why the economy sucked. Over the course of several months in 2011, he blamed President Bush, a dysfunctional Washington, millionaires and billionaires, ATMs, the Japanese tsunami, the European debt crisis, and Bigfoot. Okay, I made up Bigfoot. But his kitchen-sink approach to blaming others and outside events for the poor economy rather than his own destructive policies took on a desperate air. Obama made it clear (for example, through his comments that ATMs destroyed bank teller positions) that he believes that certain private-sector innovation kills jobs. *He* wants to be able to direct innovation and technology in certain areas of the economy, particularly government, health care, and energy. By pouring taxpayer money into kook-approved industries, he intends to kill off more traditional, private-sector industries in these areas. Using Obama's logic, ATMs should be extinct right now, since Obama's handling of American funds dried the country up like a watering hole in a spaghetti Western.

In fact, in their successful attempt to "remake" many sectors of the economy, the kooks also have embarked on a wildly overzealous application of job-killing regulations. Done through legislation, bureaucratic mandate, or executive order, the onslaught of regulations has been a creative way Obama and the kooks have kept unemployment at painfully high levels. Every federal bureaucracy—from the EPA to the National Labor Relations Board to Health and Human Services—has been on a regulatory joyride, crushing countless jobs along the way. In the 1950s, the Federal Register's Code of Regulations ran about 11,000 pages. Today, it's over 80,000 pages. At one point in the fall of 2011, federal agencies were working on 4,200 rules, 845 of which directly affected small businesses. Over 100 of them were major rules, with an estimated economic cost of more than $100 million *each*. With the wave of new regulations came a wave of new government employees, as the administration sought to redistribute employment from the private to the public sector. Since Obama took office, employment at federal regulatory agencies is up 13 percent and their budgets have spiked by 16 percent. And that's before some of the biggest regulatory overhauls, such as ObamaCare and Dodd-Frank financial "reform," are fully implemented. Federal regulations drive up costs for businesses and job creators, who must stop hiring, lay people off, or pass along the increased costs to consumers. The result of the regulatory pile-on is a cloud of stifling uncertainty that stifles economic growth.

Among the worst, most job-killing of the new regulations: the Obama-appointed, pro-union, and anti-business National Labor Relations Board, which attempted to restrict where a private-sector company could locate and create jobs in America—a fundamentally anti-American premise—and they did it with the support of the president. On April 20, 2011, the NLRB issued an outrageous ruling against the Boeing Company—the nation's top exporter—for proposing the construction of a new, $1 billion facility in South Carolina, a right-to-work state.

As Boeing made clear, not a single union employee in their Washington State facility would lose his or her job as a result of the proposed new plant, but the NLRB still sided with the union, which has repeatedly carried out strikes against Boeing in recent years. By the end of 2011, the International Association of Machinists approved a new contract with Boeing in which the company agreed to build its 737 Max jet in Washington State. The NLRB then dropped its lawsuit. The whole episode was an example of union and political extortion. Nobody should be surprised if other companies, having seen this spectacle of brass-knuckles intimidation, ship their jobs abroad out of the reach of the NLRB.

On the health care front, ObamaCare is loaded with thousands of new rules and regulations, but some of the first to come on the scene directly violated Obama's pledge that "if you like your current insurance plan, you can keep it." A 2011 Kaiser Family Foundation survey found that just 56 percent of current employees' current plans are preserved by ObamaCare's "grandfathered protection." The reason the percentage was so low? Firms reported that the new regulations made being grandfathered too difficult or limited the company's flexibility in the future.

The Dodd-Frank financial regulatory bill is another regulatory monstrosity. The financial crisis was a direct result of radical social engineering in the economy. Leftists designed the Community Reinvestment Act in 1977 to promote home ownership to minority and low-income groups who had generally been shut out of the American dream of owning a home. Jimmy Carter signed the law, which Bill Clinton then expanded and broadened in the 1990s. The CRA put a legal gun to the heads of banks and other financial institutions to make loans to people who could not afford them. Community organizations such as ACORN and other shakedown artists turned home ownership into a civil right, which then made the banks the bad guys if they resisted that new "right" or the good guys if they made the loans. The process became so perverse that a *bad* credit score became a way to get *favorable* lending treatment.

The banks, then saddled with these incredibly risky loans, sought ways to bundle and sell them and otherwise spread out their risk. The house of cards grew shakier every day, particularly as the Federal Reserve's monetary pumping in the early 2000s kept interest rates low, money easy, and home prices climbing artificially. Dodd, as chairman of the Senate Committee on Banking, Housing and Urban Affairs, and Frank, as the then chairman of the House Committee on Financial Services, had oversight over the banks and the government's big mortgage giants, Fannie Mae and Freddie Mac. Instead of sounding the alarm about the banks' and GSEs' rapidly deteriorating condition and pushing reform, Dodd and Frank covered for them, actively blocked the Bush administration's attempts at reform, and, in Frank's case, even promoted them as sound just months before the subprime crisis blew up.

Instead of rotting in jail, Frank and Dodd—who got his own sweetheart mortgage deal through Countrywide Financial—wrote a "reform" bill that focused mainly on the parts of the industry that hadn't screwed up. It institutionalized "too big to fail" while pounding the financial sector with a vast array of new regulations.

Perhaps Dodd-Frank's biggest horror was its creation of a major new bureaucracy within the Federal Reserve System to "monitor" consumer loan products. The Consumer Financial Protection Bureau operates under the direction of a single "czar" who serves a five-year term, oversees a $500 million budget that is not subject to congressional or other oversight, and cannot be fired, even by the president, except under extraordinary circumstances. The first of the CFPB czars, Richard Cordray, was appointed by Obama in an early 2012 recess appointment when the Senate wasn't in recess. This regulatory monstrosity created twenty-one new rules in its first six months alone. The CFPB is a dictatorial fiefdom that is making things such as credit and debit cards, checking and savings accounts, and consumer loans tougher to get and more expensive to use, has virtually no checks on its unlimited power, and will do nothing to prevent a future financial crisis.

Of all the ghastly job-killing regulations slammed on American businesses by Team Obama, however, some of the most comprehensive and expensive are the ones flowing endlessly out of the Environmental Protection Agency. Obama chose to use the EPA as a bureaucratic sledgehammer to accomplish by diktat what he could not accomplish legislatively: a fundamental transformation of the energy sector. During the 2008 campaign, Obama made it clear what his intentions were when it came to remaking the American energy industry. "If someone wants to build a coal-fired power plant, they can," he said. "It's just that it will bankrupt them." Shortly after he was inaugurated, Obama made his point even more firmly, stating that "under my cap and trade system, electricity rates would necessarily skyrocket." Like using your refrigerator, television, air conditioner, heater, and blow dryer? It'll cost you . . . a lot more.

Obama fully intended to "bankrupt" the coal industry in order to make way for the Left's "green energy" agenda. Largely born out of the kooks' obsession with the man-made global warming scheme, "green energy" was an ideal vehicle for redistributionism. For followers of the Church of Gore, man-made global warming, later rebranded as global climate change, was built on the idea that our carbon emissions were being trapped in the atmosphere (possibly stuck in a gas bubble resulting from one of Al's late-night Taco Bell runs), causing the earth's temperature to rise rapidly and thus endangering everything from Florida's beaches to the Arctic polar bears. If humanity were to be protected from this scourge of industry, industry must fall on its knees, beg for forgiveness, agree to a slew of new government mandates, and, oh yeah, fork over gazillions of dollars more as part of its penance.

By 2010, however, the fall of the Church of Gore began. The revelation of the Climategate e-mails and other evidence that global warming alarmist scientists conspired to manipulate data, suppress conflicting information, extrapolate from weak or unsupported evidence (such as the UN's Intergovernmental Panel on Climate Change's claim that the Himalayan Glacier would melt in 2035, which was based on one group's claim that it would melt in 2350) severely damaged the credibility of the man-made warming scaremongers. Serious questions were raised about whether they were willing to abuse science to serve the greater redistributionist goal. As a result, there has been ever-growing pressure on the redistributionists to force policy changes in energy since the "consensus" they had built around scientifically dubious "evidence" is falling apart.

Even with the aggressive push from the Gore cultists, green technology had been relatively slow to develop, in large part because there wasn't a market for it. Traditional fossil fuels dominate, providing us with 98 percent of our energy, and without a massive government push to destroy the traditional energy sector, it would take far too long for "green" to gain traction. They couldn't wait for free enterprise to sort it out. What couldn't compete in the marketplace needed—and got—a huge helping hand from Big Daddy.

Cap and trade came first. The leftists sought to create a new cap on emissions and then enforce it with a series of hugely expensive mandates. The costs, of course, would get passed on to the consumer, hence those "necessarily skyrocketing" electricity prices. Because everything requires energy—from development to production to transport—cap and trade would have been tantamount to the largest tax increase in the history of the world. And by its very nature, it would have been highly regressive, hitting the poor and middle-income households harder, since they spend more of their income directly on energy, such as gas to get to work or home heating. The point was to begin to destroy the coal industry to make way for the leftists' beloved "green energy" while giving the federal government an entirely new—and massive—revenue source.

The legislation passed the Democrat-controlled House but died in the Senate, despite the Democrats' filibuster-proof majority, because a number of Democrats from coal-producing states such as West Virginia and Pennsylvania didn't take kindly to Obama's attempt to kill their leading industry.

With cap and trade dead legislatively, Obama and the kooks began making end runs around Congress to achieve their energy objectives without having to deal with Congress. Enter the EPA.

Obama empowered his EPA administrator, Lisa Jackson, to use the Clean Air Act as a rationale to impose new regulations like fairy dust (which will be regulated next) on everything from industrial boilers to farm dust, cement, greenhouse gases, and mountaintop coal removal, which a federal judge overturned. Most of these regulations have already led to plant closures, massive job losses, and higher prices for consumers. In late November 2011, Jackson admitted that objective in an interview with *Energy NOW News*, in which she was asked about the coal-fired plant closures as a result of the EPA regulatory spree. "What EPA's role is to do is to *level the playing field* so that pollution costs are not exported to the population but rather companies have to look at the pollution potential of any fuel or any process or any plant or any utility when they're making their investment decisions." At the core of any centrally planned economy is the state's forcible leveling of the playing field. Burden some industries with so many costs that they can no longer operate and replace them with state-sanctioned ones. An added benefit: the new rules will bring in tons of cash from the fines levied on companies that cannot comply with them.

Under the cumulative weight of all of the new Obama EPA regulations, the National Economic Research Associates—using the federal government's own data—projects that they would cost America over 180,000 jobs per year between 2013 and 2020.

Amid falling poll numbers and a bleak economy, Obama decided to pull back on one major new proposed regulation—but only because he didn't want to take on the political fight at that moment. In September 2011, he ordered EPA administrator Jackson to withdraw the new proposed "ozone rule," which, according to Republican senator Jim Inhofe, would have destroyed seven million jobs. Jackson was reportedly so furious at Obama's request that she considered resigning. Sadly, she stayed to hyper-regulate another day.

Obama has been methodically destroying the traditional energy industry as he goes, in order to smash the existing structure and replace it with the kooks' "green dream" (in which Gore appears on a polar bear, wearing only his Florida recount beard). As Senator James Inhofe put it, "All of this killing of our energy supply is not by accident. It's on purpose."

At the same time, Obama launched a broadside against another key part of the U.S. energy sector: the oil and natural gas industry. After the cap and trade bill failed, Obama stated a willingness to approve some limited oil exploration. In March 2010, he announced some half-measures that would allow drilling along the Atlantic coastline, the eastern Gulf of Mexico, and the north coast of Alaska, but he continued to prohibit exploration in the Arctic National Wildlife Refuge (ANWR) and Bristol Bay. He also indicated that he'd allow large tracts in the Chukchi Sea and Beaufort Sea in the Arctic Ocean north of Alaska—nearly 130 million acres—to be eligible for exploration and drilling after extensive studies, which meant they'd be ready for exploration on the twelfth of Never.

Just weeks later, on April 20, 2010, a wellhead blowout occurred on the Deepwater Horizon oil rig, which was operating on the British Petroleum Macondo Prospect in the Gulf of Mexico. The initial explosion killed eleven workers and injured seventeen others, and millions of barrels of crude oil began flowing into the waters. It became the largest accidental oceanic spill in history. And it also became a perfect metaphor for the Obama presidency: an uncontrollable poison spewing into a pristine environment unless mankind could stop it. Meanwhile, as the cloud of petroleum endangered new species, our fearless leader was focused on another animal: a Beatle, in fact. Obama took an entire evening in June 2010 to honor Sir Paul McCartney with the Gershwin Prize while the pop icon serenaded Obama in the White House as the Gulf Coast drowned in black death.

Obama, the supposed Competence Man, was caught flat-footed by the disaster. The administration claimed to be in charge while also insisting that BP take the lead. It was slow to move federal resources such as oil-absorbing booms and sand berms to deal with the leak. It was also slow to coordinate efforts among the impacted states; other Big Oil companies, who had offered equipment, manpower, and expertise; and foreign countries, such as Saudi Arabia, which had also offered technology and information it had developed as a result of spills in that other gulf. Ultimately, some foreign nations, such as

Norway, the Netherlands, and Canada, did send ships with skimming and other cleanup capabilities. Meanwhile, Obama blew a gasket of frustration because his usual management style of ordering everyone around—Congress, BP, the media, the American people—wasn't working this time. "Plug the damn hole!" he snapped.

The BP oil leak did give Obama the ideal pretext to halt permits for offshore drilling. The Interior Department's permitting review recommended a moratorium and implied that that recommendation had been peer-reviewed by a panel of drilling experts it had consulted during the review. Those experts then went public, saying that in fact they had neither been consulted on the moratorium recommendation nor agreed to it. Interior secretary Ken Salazar went ahead with the moratorium order covering all drilling in depths of 500 feet or more, leading some deepwater drilling companies to file lawsuits against the government.

On June 22, U.S. District Judge Martin Feldman issued an injunction and an order that Interior *not* enforce the moratorium because he found it, in the standard legal term, "arbitrary and capricious." The department stopped enforcement, until Salazar said publicly that he intended to reimpose the moratorium, and all drilling permits were again halted. Interior appealed Feldman's injunction to the United States Court of Appeals for the Fifth Circuit and in July lost that appeal.

Four days later, the department issued a new moratorium nearly identical to the first. In October, Interior ostensibly lifted the moratorium but no new deepwater drilling permits were issued for months, and subsequent permits were slow-walked. That same month, an Interior Department inspector general's report showed that the original review had been manipulated to mislead the public. In February 2011, a furious Judge Feldman found Obama's Interior Department in civil contempt for violating his original order dissolving the administration's offshore drilling moratorium—and the mainstream media all but ignored the story. They also largely ignored the fact that many Gulf-state Democrats like Louisiana senator Mary Landrieu opposed the moratorium. In Louisiana alone, more than 320,000 folks depend on the oil and gas industry for work. At least ten oil rigs pulled up stakes from the Gulf and moved to more lucrative areas off the coasts of South America and Africa, costing even more jobs. In 2011, the House Committee on Oversight and Government Reform reported that Obama's systematic blocking of domestic energy production in the Gulf has led to the loss of over $9 billion in capital investment in 2011 alone and tens of thousands of jobs.

In the spring of 2011, Obama's EPA went a step further and forced Shell Oil to shut down its massive exploration project in the Arctic Ocean. Shell had spent five years and $4 billion ($2.2 billion in leases alone to the federal government) to develop the area for domestic drilling. According to the U.S. Geological Survey, there are 27 billion barrels of oil in the Arctic Ocean, which Obama's EPA put off-limits. I hope the Russians enjoy!

In late 2009 the Export-Import Bank approved a $2 billion loan to Brazil's state-owned oil company, Petrobras, to finance exploration of a huge offshore discovery near Rio de Janeiro. One of Petrobras's key investors? Kook billionaire and Obama supporter George Soros. It turns out that Obama loves oil exploration and drilling in other countries, just not here at home, where it could create American jobs and lower gas prices.

The capstone to Obama's assault on the oil and gas industry came in late 2011 when his administration refused to grant permission to TransCanada to build the Keystone XL pipeline, which would have put tens of thousands of Americans to work immediately and facilitated the domestic movement of crude from a central storage hub in Oklahoma to large refineries on the Gulf Coast. Once Obama's decision was made public, the company fled into the arms of the Chinese, to whom they will sell the oil and who will export it in tankers. Without the pipeline extension, our own oil imports will necessarily increase, which means more price volatility, more dependency, more tankers coming into U.S. waters, and the likelihood of a greater environmental impact because pipelines are the most efficient and cleanest way to transport big volumes of oil.

Big Oil is, of course, one of the ol' reliable bogeymen for the leftists, who, when they're not blocking exploration, drilling, and pipelines, seek to stick it to the major oil companies through higher taxes while undermining their entire industry. The reality is that the oil and gas industry paid more taxes in 2010 than any other industry. It pays an effective tax rate of 41.1 percent, compared with 26.5 percent for the rest of the Standard & Poor's Industrials. Furthermore, the "subsidies for Big Oil" about which the Left is always screaming aren't subsidies at all. Some of the things the Left incorrectly terms "subsidies" for Big Oil include the ability to recover some exploration and manufacturing costs; Big Oil can recoup some of those costs but at a lower rate than most other eligible companies. There are other deductions from which Big Oil is blocked altogether, such as the percentage depletion deduction.

The federal government does, in fact, issue actual subsidies to things like ethanol, solar and wind energy projects (hello, Solyndra), and other wasteful items and programs as a way to take care of political constituencies and for ideological reasons. These subsidies generally support industries that probably could not survive in the open market. They should be eliminated. But to suggest that Big Oil is somehow receiving special treatment for using tax credits available to them—the way every other industry does—is dishonest.

For the leftists, their adventures in remaking the energy sector are driven by two main goals. The first is to prop up "alternative energies" out of a desire to move the country toward "clean energy" and away from foreign dependency. These good intentions are shared by many conservatives and others, but the leftists' full-frontal assault on our domestic energy producers as well as their economic engineering in energy warps the noble mission of getting us to cleaner domestic production.

The other part of the Left's mission is more sinister. It's to redistribute wealth—in this case, profits from Big Oil—and plow it into those alternative energies, which can only meet a tiny fraction of the energy demand in America. But the kooks want their money and they'll whip the market into submission to get it—even if it means much higher gas prices.

The irony is that the Left loves accusing the Right of wanting to take America backward. Yet they spend so much of their time focused on crushing the industries that are responsible for our own Industrial Revolution. The leftist obsession with windmills and waterwheels is a surefire way to bring America back to the days of *Little House on the Prairie.* Ask yourself: Would the landing craft on D-day have worked without fossil fuels? Would Buzz Aldrin and Neil Armstrong have been able to plant the American flag on the moon without fossil fuels? Would the police, firefighters, and rescue workers on 9/11 have been able to get to the scene and help the victims without fossil fuels?

———

Obama knows perfectly well how a properly regulated free market works. He just rejects it. He actually wants you to believe that being unemployed and getting paid for even *more* months to sit on your ass are boons to the American economy. The more chaos in the economy, the more customers the leftists have for all of their beloved redistributionist programs. Under their direction, the old Depression-era line, "Brother, can you spare a dime?" has now become, "Uncle Sam, cough up a bigger unemployment/food stamp/Medicare/Medicaid payment!" As a practical matter, then, Obama and the kooks need the economy down, unemployment up, and growth weak to keep their redistributionist gravy train rolling.

The leftists also knew they couldn't just rely on the beauty of their neo-socialist ideas to power their "fundamental transformation" of America. They also needed some muscle. Cue the unions.

Labor Pains II: Public Parts

President Obama! This is your army! We are ready to march! Let's take these son of bitches out and give America back to an America where we belong!

—*Jimmy Hoffa, general president, International Brotherhood of Teamsters, September 5, 2011*

In the mid-1990s, the Whole Foods supermarket franchise was under constant attack by the United Food and Commercial Workers International Union. Speaking to a reporter, Whole Foods' CEO, John Mackey, let loose with a particularly colorful description of the union damaging his business: "The union is like having herpes. It doesn't kill you, but it's unpleasant and inconvenient, and it stops a lot of people from becoming your lover."

Thug tactics? No problem. Economic extortion? Yes, we can. Arm twisting? All in a day's work. But being compared to a case of herpes? Over the line! The union protested, picketed, and boycotted (more than usual) after Mackey's comment, but ultimately neither the UFCW nor any other union could stem the decades-long move away from unions in the private sector.

In response, the kooks have worked relentlessly to alter the balance between the private and government sectors by rapidly growing government, its unions, and its unions' funds and power. They became huge and fearsome. Not even a bad case of herpes could stop them. But to tell you the truth, having herpes seems like a better deal than waking up every day and having to look to Obama, Reid, and Pelosi for leadership.

The unions had a tight, unquestioned grasp on power through their corrupt stranglehold on the Democratic Party, particularly at the state level—until a young cheesehead arrived on the scene.

It was a cold day in mid-February 2011 when the leftists watched stunned as the padlock got thrown on the door of one of their favorite redistributionist candy stores. The new Republican governor of Wisconsin, Scott Walker, proposed a budget repair bill to begin to bring his state's finances under control. Facing a huge budget deficit, Walker decided to tackle the very source of the fiscal nightmare—and a potentially lethal political third rail: government-sector unions and the state's unsustainable benefit and pension obligations. In order to close the candy store in which the corrupt unions and Democrats pigged out, Walker needed to eliminate most collective bargaining privileges for state workers—a gutsy move in a state known as the birthplace of both "progressivism" and union collective bargaining in state government.

By restructuring the relationship between government and the government-sector unions, Walker sought to do the one thing that governors of both parties had previously failed to do: protect the taxpayer. In the past, governors had negotiated huge and fiscally unsustainable pension and benefits packages and then would tell everybody the blatant lie that it was all doable. Walker decided to put an end to this nefarious, bankrupting, and vote-buying scheme. The governor was also counting on history: it wasn't just progressivism that was invented in Wisconsin. It was also the birthplace of the Republican Party.

The centerpiece of the bill was the elimination of most collective bargaining privileges for government workers, except for police and firefighters, whom Walker cited as critical for public safety. For all other government workers, the bill put everything on the table except for wages. It required additional contributions by state and local government workers to their health care plans and pensions, amounting to about an 8 percent decrease in take-home pay. Walker argued that asking employees to pay half the national average for health care benefits was reasonable, given that workers in the private sector must pay far more for their own benefits—which were, in many cases, less lavish than the ones enjoyed by government employees. Unions were barred from seeking pay increases for government workers above the

rate of inflation unless approved by the voters. Most devastating to
the government unions, the bill directed them to hold annual votes to
continue representing government workers and ended their ability to
automatically deduct union dues from government workers' pay-
checks. The practice of the government essentially wielding its tax
power on behalf of the unions made it a tool of those unions. This was
an incredibly corrupt arrangement fiercely guarded by the government unions. When Walker moved to end the state's role in dues collection, the government unions realized they were losing their
enforcer. These Wisconsin union shops were being run like Satriale's
Pork Store on *The Sopranos*. In the past, government protected and
even assisted with the thug union enforcement, so if an intransigent
Republican politician popped up, he would end up lunch for the
union. Troublemakers would be brought in through the back door
while gourmet deli meats would go out the front.

The unions predictably went berserk, claiming that Walker sought
to bust the unions. Walker calmly explained that during the campaign he said he would use all available means to bring fiscal sanity
back and that, contrary to busting the unions, he was making sure
that government employees retained protections under the civil service laws. More important, Walker reminded the unions that without
the bill, thousands of those same employees would have to be laid off.
He was trying to save their jobs, not destroy them.

Walker's reforms hit at the heart of the perverse love-in enjoyed for
decades by Democrats and their union sugar daddies. Democrats funneled ever-increasing amounts of money into the government unions
in an endless spiral of wage, benefits, and pension increases. In turn,
the unions poured massive amounts of money into Democratic campaign coffers (and a few Republicans' campaigns too). Meanwhile, the
taxpayer was forced to fork over more and more of his own money to
finance this corrupt merry-go-round. But for the Democrats and the
government unions, their incestuous relationship needed to be protected at all costs.

Walker promptly put an end to the government union/Democratic
hookup, and all Hades broke loose. It looked like the table-throwing

episode of *The Real Housewives of New Jersey*, minus the leopard coats.

Unions from across the country mobilized thousands of the usual left-wing suspects to storm the state capitol, where they remained camped out for weeks, vandalizing the capitol building, screaming about their comfy "rights," and comparing Walker to Hitler (sooooo 2004). The Reverend Jesse Jackson alighted on the scene, because what's a leftist accident scene without their Number One Ambulance Chaser? Michael Moore also descended into Madison for the free corn dogs and to bellow, "America ain't broke!" Meanwhile, in a scene out of *Escape from Alcatraz*, all fourteen Democratic state senators took a powder. Knowing that the bill would pass if they stayed since Republicans controlled their chamber, the state Democratic senators tried to deny the governor the vote by fleeing into the neighboring People's Republic of Illinois. There they checked into a no-tell motel, ordered up pay-per-view, and set about washing their underwear in the motel sink. At one point, a few of them grabbed a bag of pork rinds and a bottle of Mad Dog 20/20. Then they got real nutty and threw some pocket change into the vibrating bed.

Meanwhile, as the Wisconsin state senate Democrats made their break for the border, one state assembly Democrat indulged his inner Hugh Grant. During the budget circus, Democratic state representative Gordon Hintz received a municipal citation connected to—wait for it—prostitution. Hintz apparently enjoyed visits to a "massage parlor" that provided happy endings. This was the same Representative Hintz who told a female Republican state representative that she was "(bleeping) dead" for supporting the budget repair bill. I'm surprised Mack Daddy Hintz didn't try to keep it real by throwing Jay-Z's "Big Pimpin'" on and then attempting to beat the woman with his shoe.

So while the Republican governor was trying to fix the state's fiscal mess, the state's Democrats were running around like Charlie Sheen, complete with the hookers, being AWOL from their jobs and the manic profanity. The only thing missing for the Wisconsin Democrats? The briefcase full of blow.

Ultimately, the Democratic fugitives returned, the bill passed, and the government unions went on another rampage. They tried to overturn the law through the courts, but the state supreme court upheld it. They then tried to defeat a conservative state supreme court judge, but he survived the challenge. Then they launched recall elections against six GOP state senators, four of whom survived to retain the GOP majority. Union spending on the legislative recalls rang in at about $28 million, not exactly a good return on investment. Not ones to accept defeat gracefully (or at all), the government unions also moved to recall Walker himself. Organizing for America, Obama's state-level campaign operation, helped to coordinate the senate and Walker recall efforts by connecting the unions, local Democrats, and recall volunteers. This is how the leftists roll: what they cannot win at the ballot box they'll try to score through liberal judges and short-circuiting recalls.

But any Republican too noodle-kneed to take on the government unions should pay close attention to what happened in the Badger State: when the Wisconsin Republicans held the line on economic and government union reform, Wisconsin voters then held the line for them. In Ohio, however, where Governor John Kasich went even further and moved to eliminate collective bargaining privileges for most government-sector employees, including police and firefighters, the unions were ready. They poured big money into a repeal effort, which succeeded. But the lesson of both Wisconsin and Ohio ought to be that national and state Republicans must be fearless like Governor Walker—and New Jersey governor Chris Christie, Indiana governor Mitch Daniels, and others who have taken on, to varying extents, the powerful government unions in their states. In a necessary effort to deal with its underfunded or flat-out broke pension funds, Rhode Island's Democratic state legislature passed and Independent governor Lincoln Chafee signed a sweeping pension overhaul. Of course, the government unions called it a "betrayal" and threatened to sue, as they did when Democratic New York governor Andrew Cuomo moved to renegotiate some state benefits and pensions.

Many cities are also drowning in debt thanks to government

unions. Former Obama chief of staff and current Chicago mayor Rahm Emanuel took on the powerful Chicago teachers' unions and laid off hundreds of city workers. The unions went bananas, but you can't get blood from a stone—and even the most hardened Chicago union thug is afraid of Rahm, especially when he's standing right in front of you, naked in the shower, angrily poking you (with God knows what) in the chest. But what the Republican and Democratic efforts to rein in the government-sector unions in Wisconsin, New Jersey, Ohio, Indiana, Rhode Island, and Chicago have shown is that where there is a political will, there is a way.

Most tellingly, when reform is carried out, it's effective. Despite the hysterical union and Democratic warnings of an imminent apocalypse, disaster has not befallen Wisconsin. To the contrary, Walker's reforms have truly begun to bring order to the state's finances. Local school districts obtained the ability to renegotiate union contracts, saving money and teachers' jobs. In many communities across the state, local officials were able to ditch the union-affiliated health insurance plans and go with less expensive competitors, in most cases saving hundreds of thousands (even millions) of dollars that could then be put back into the schools (and, as the leftists always say, it *is* all about the "children," isn't it?). As of January 2012, Walker's reforms had already saved Wisconsin's taxpayers $476 million.

Furthermore, after Walker halted the state-run dues collection, the unions' coffers began to dwindle, along with their power and monopoly. The state's budget is being brought into line, and job creation is occurring. And at long last, the Wisconsin taxpayers are being protected. Evidently, once the burly, knuckle-dragging shakedown enforcer stops showing up to rob you, most Americans don't feel they need to continue giving him money out of charity.

Because of Walker's reforms, state and local governments are forced, like private businesses, to operate efficiently. It's a concept so unheard of in the annals of government that time almost stopped and Lady Gaga almost put on sweatpants.

During the Wisconsin tumult, Obama complained of Walker's "assault" on the unions while his allied thugs pushed the protests to the edge of violence.

Walker wasn't having it. He responded, "I'm sure the President knows that most federal employees do not have collective bargaining for wages and benefits, while our plan allows it for base pay. And I'm sure the President knows that the average federal worker pays twice as much for health insurance as what we are asking for in Wisconsin. . . . Furthermore, I'm sure the President knows that we have repeatedly praised the more than 300,000 government workers who come to work every day in Wisconsin. I'm sure that President Obama simply misunderstands the issues in Wisconsin, and isn't acting like the union bosses in saying one thing and doing another."

And . . . checkmate.

━━━━

Obama's constant moves to support the unions at any cost, as well as to support hard leftists like those in Occupy Wall Street, may be smart politically. After all, unions of all stripes poured $500 million into Obama's and other Democrats' 2008 campaigns, and those Democrats in turn kept the unsustainable deals to the unions flowing. The American Federation of State, County and Municipal Employees (AFSCME), the main non-teacher government employee union in the nation, was the biggest spender in the 2010 election. Its political director gave the group a shout-out, "We're the big dog." (The original Big Dog, Bill Clinton, would like a word. . . .)

At the state level, the National Institute on Money in State Politics reported that the government-sector unions are the number one spenders in state politics. In Wisconsin, the teachers' unions are in first and third place, with trial lawyers fourth. The Democrats themselves are in second place.

Union leaders are still masters of the ground game. Obama needs their dirty resources and underhanded tactics to advance his kook agenda. That's why in May 2008, the then candidate Obama told the Teamsters that if elected president, he'd end the strict federal oversight imposed to investigate and expose corruption in the union. Citing the "drastic decline" in organized crime's influence, Obama indicated that he believed the federal role in rooting out Teamsters corruption had come to an end. He then scored the Teamsters' endorsement. And from that point on, Jimmy Hoffa and his Teamsters have had Obama's back. Meanwhile, the campaign donations rolled in like the opening scene of *Goodfellas*.

But while getting deeper into bed with the unions may be smart for Obama in terms of ideology and tactics, it is devastating for him in terms of his brand. In 2008 he positioned himself as the man of the future, and he made the Democrats the party of the future. Now, with governors such as Walker, Christie, Daniels, Kasich, and Cuomo taking on the government unions and Washington reformers like House Budget chairman Paul Ryan proposing bold new initiatives to save America from insolvency, Obama's super-glued connection to the unions makes him look like yesterday's newspaper.

At the end of World War II, union membership in the private sector was 34 percent. Today, it's 7 percent. But 71 percent of government workers are now unionized. Interestingly, only 10 percent of union-represented workers ever voted *for* unionization. At the same time, public support for unions has fallen off a cliff. In 2009, Gallup released its Work and Education Survey, which found that for the first time since the Great Depression, a majority of Americans believe that unions hurt the economy. Gallup also reported that just 48 percent of Americans approve of labor unions, even though this poll was taken during the height of the recession when union support should have been at its strongest. Furthermore, Gallup showed that 62 percent of those polled thought that unions hurt workers who *aren't* unionized. That reflects the growing public sentiment that government union workers live in a pampered world increasingly subsidized by taxpayers. Furthermore, numerous studies have substantiated the common-sense conclusion that unions kill jobs. If a union drives a company out of business, the jobs are gone. Obama's own former chief economic adviser, Larry Summers, wrote, "Another cause of long-term unemployment is unionization. High union wages that exceed the competitive market rate are likely to cause job losses in the unionized sector of the economy."

In late 2002, in a study published by the National Legal and Policy Center and the John M. Olin Institute for Employment Practice and Policy, economists Richard Vedder and Lowell Gallaway of Ohio University calculated that *labor unions have cost the American economy a whopping $50 trillion over the past fifty years alone.* The study did find that unionized labor earned wages 15 percent higher than those of nonunion workers, but it also found that *wages in general* suffered dramatically as a result of an *economy that is 30 to 40 percent smaller* than it would have been *in the absence of labor unionism.*

Despite the evidence of the enormous cost burdens the government unions place on the private sector as well as on the taxpayer, Obama and the leftists continue to support them because they all seek the same redistributive goals. Obama has championed the "stimulus," which was a massive federal bailout of government union payrolls, and card check (the hilariously named Employee Free Choice Act, which killed the worker's ability to freely choose to keep his ballot secret and which would've made unionization much easier). He also supported measures to stop union disclosure of how workers' dues are spent, and mandates that private-sector employers must post notices advising employees of their right to unionize. He backed down from an early commitment to a union-driven "buy American" provision in the "stimulus" only after the European Union and Canada threatened to retaliate and set off a trade war. He agreed to free trade agreements with Colombia, South Korea, and Panama, which had languished in the Senate, only after he secured offsets for the unions. Whenever Obama deals with labor issues, it's always government unions first, the rest of the American people. . . . wait, who are they again?

"Hope and change" have left the station without Barack Obama, but on the bright side, at least he can seek comfort in the burly arms of Richard Trumka. And he has—repeatedly. The head of the AFL-CIO, Trumka smugly bragged in February 2011 that he talked to the White House "every day" and suggested that he was actually there "two to three" times per week. Before he stepped down as the president of the Service Employees International Union in mid-2010, Andy Stern had been the most frequent visitor to the White House. Without a hint of irony, Obama had appointed him to sit on his bipartisan National Commission on Fiscal Responsibility and Reform, also known as the Simpson-Bowles deficit commission. Stern was appointed not to find spending to cut and entitlements to reform but to block any such moves in order to protect the unions. This is the same Andy Stern who wrote an op-ed on December 1, 2011, in the *Wall Street Journal* urging us to become more like the "superior" communist China and to "rethink" our "demonization of government" and "worship of the free market."

Stern's union, SEIU, also produced a "contract campaign manual" that suggests a variety of delightful tactics to be used against employers who resist unionization efforts, including how to intimidate a business financially and the art of political pressure to drive up the costs to the business. More important, the SEIU manual encourages workers to "disobey laws which are used to enforce injustice against working people." It points out helpfully, "Certain acts which might technically be illegal might be seen by the public, news media, customers, or other potential worker allies as justifiable and not something the employer should be challenging." In other words, screw the law. Perception is everything. Break the law if you have to and sell it as striking out at the injustice of "the man."

This is how the public unions have always rolled: strong-arm tactics and brute force through card check, angry mobs storming homes of business leaders, organized strikes, and leftist protests such as in Wisconsin and Occupy Wall Street. Andy Stern has said, "We watched how they voted and we know where they live."

The list of violent and inflammatory rhetoric from the hirsute Richard Trumka is long. Some of his greatest goon hits: In September 2010, Trumka praised Nancy Pelosi for taking ObamaCare and "driving it down the Republicans' throats and out their backsides." He also said, "We prefer the power of persuasion but will settle for the persuasion of power."

Right before the Occupy Wall Street protests got under way, Trumka announced that he was heading up a get-out-the-vote movement of leftists to "energize an army of tens of thousands who will return to their neighborhoods, churches, schools and voting booths to prevent a Republican takeover of Congress in November and begin *building a new permanent coalition to fight for a progressive agenda.*" (Emphasis added.)

This new Trumka project was publicized in the Marxist *People's World*, an enchanting revolutionary communist publication. Note the ultimate objective of "building a new permanent coalition." This is the endgame of their ginned-up chaos.

The fire of the Left always needs more fuel. Shortly before Occupy Wall Street hit the streets in September 2011, SEIU labor activist Stephen Lerner made it clear that the unions were going to help create and drive the protests. Speaking at the kook extravaganza, the Take Back the American Dream conference (whose star speaker was Obama's favorite commie, Tony "Van" Jones), Lerner warned that the SEIU was getting ready to "terrify" Washington and other power centers in America by mobilizing mass demonstrations, strikes, and acts of civil disobedience to "create a crisis." And so they did.

Without union muscle, the redistributionists' agenda would simply plod along. But with that muscle constantly provoking upheaval, the redistributionists have the way paved for them. One set of kooks serve as bodyguards for the others, all of them busily "fundamentally transforming" America to resemble a cross between *Reds* and *On the Waterfront*.

The country is going to Hades in a handbasket, and while many Democrats have been fleeing the scene of the accident, Obama and his minions are encouraging and embracing the chaos of high unemployment, anemic economic growth, record home foreclosures, union-led upheaval, multiple years of record-breaking spending and $1 trillion-plus deficits, and $5 trillion added to the national debt in just three years.

Size matters. And most of the American people are now convinced that the United States government is not a porn actor and that smaller is, in fact, better.

To Team Obama, however, that opinion is like the fly he killed single-handedly during an interview in the Oval Office: a minor annoyance with which he must dispense. Obama is a true believer who sacrifices as little as possible ideologically. But it's more than insects he wants to squash. He wants to pulverize our liberty. And given the robotic precision with which Obama was able to squeeze the life out of that defenseless housefly, we should all be on guard and aware of his diabolical intentions to terminate all that he's programmed to despise. Economic chaos is the fertile breeding ground on which he seeds his radical policies.

Obama knows he needs to win in 2012 to fully effectuate his most critical plans. This is why much of the destructiveness of his policies, such as the higher taxes and costs of ObamaCare and the hike in the top marginal federal income tax rate, have been designed to hit in 2013 so as not to negatively affect his reelection chances. Businesses are holding off on hiring and expanding until they know if many of these policies will stand. All sides are waiting for the outcome of 2012 to know if recovery can begin.

While normal Americans view his economic record as an abysmal failure, Obama and the kooks see it as a wild success. In a few short years, Obama has deeply embedded radical redistributionism in a nation built on individual and economic liberty. He also made certain that the tentacles of the redistributionism would be difficult, if not impossible, to unwrap. Obama and the kooks have given us their version of a "more perfect union." The country has been turned upside down, not because they *don't* know what they're doing, but because they *do*.

PART IV

DR. STRANGELEADER

Or: How I Learned to Stop Caring
and Love American Decline

GENERAL "BUCK" TURGIDSON: **Perhaps it might be better, Mr. President, if you were more concerned with the American people than with your image in the history books.**

—From *Dr. Strangelove or: How I Learned to Stop Worrying and Love the Bomb*

Our Enemies Are People Too

September 19, 2001, dawned cloudy and cool in New York. Eight days after the most lethal Islamic terrorist attack ever on U.S. soil, the city of New York remained in a stunned near-silence. People passed on the street, nodding quietly to one another and blinking back tears for loved ones lost and the pain of the survivors. Ground zero—where the tall, proud towers of the World Trade Center stood just days before, full of life, ambition, friendship, and love—smoldered with the burning, twisted wreckage of the attack. Emergency personnel made their way through the smoking steel, hoping they could rescue someone—anyone—still alive. Family members and friends posted photos of their missing loved ones. The distinct smell of deadly destruction wafted over the city. A dark cloud of grief hung over New York, as well as the two other locations where the terrorists had struck, Washington, DC, and Shanksville, Pennsylvania. The country was paralyzed by the surreal terror of the surprise attack, the nature of its execution, and the growing awareness that our national reality was now far more dangerous and uncertain. Fear, anger, dread, and mourning gripped the nation, but so did a sense of pride in the heroism shown by so many and a deep-seated faith that America would smash the enemy and emerge stronger.

On that day, an undistinguished state senator from Illinois published an article in a nondescript Chicago-area publication, the *Hyde Park Herald*. The Communist-mentored community organizer began his piece with a call for heightened airport security, more effective intelligence operations, and a "dismantling" of the "perpetrators'" organizations.

Then the Hyde Park agitator let loose with his deeply rooted anti-American kooksense:

"We must also engage, however, in the more difficult task of understanding the sources of such madness."

[Not difficult at all: it's totalitarian Islam.]

"The essence of this tragedy" [it was a personal tragedy for those who lost loved ones, but for the nation it was an act of war], "it seems to me, derives from a fundamental absence of empathy on the part of the attackers: an inability to imagine, or connect with, the humanity and suffering of others." [They were jihadists, driven by their clearly articulated faith to kill the infidel, not "empathize" with them.] "Such a failure of empathy, such numbness to the pain of a child or the desperation of a parent, is not innate; nor, history tells us, is it unique to a particular culture, religion or ethnicity. It may find expression in a particular brand of violence, and may be channeled by particular demagogues or fanatics. Most often, though, it grows out of a climate of poverty and ignorance, helplessness and despair." [As if we should have responded to the attacks by airlifting food stamps and subsidized housing to al-Qaeda. More to the point: most of the 9/11 hijackers were middle to upper middle class and highly educated, not exactly the poor, unwashed, desperate masses to whom he refers. Isn't it interesting how the leftists always see ideological threats to our system and values the exact same way? Whether it's totalitarian communism or totalitarian Islam, the Left portrays these movements as by-products of inequality and never as the militantly anti-American movements they are. Those who carried out the September 11 attacks weren't "ignorant." They were jihadists.]

Obama went on to counsel patience and warn against overreacting: "We will have to make sure, despite our rage, that any U.S. military action takes into account the lives of innocent civilians abroad. We will have to be unwavering in opposing bigotry or discrimination directed against neighbors and friends of Middle Eastern descent.

Finally, we will have to devote far more attention to the monumental task of raising the hopes and prospects of embittered children across the globe—children not just in the Middle East, but also in Africa, Asia, Latin America, Eastern Europe and within our own shores."

The United States had *just* been attacked by a barbaric and ruthless enemy, 2,977 people had been slaughtered in cold blood, and the nation was seized by grief. And Barack Hussein Obama took *that* moment to express compassion for the enemy, concern over imaginary American bigotry, a desire to socially engineer the rest of the world, and an urge to belt out that "the children are our future." He placed all responsibility for the enemy's acts upon *us* and then blamed *us* for regarding them as an enemy.

Obama's *first* instinct was not to share in the collective national suffering or to offer more than a perfunctory note of sympathy to the bereaved families or to even recognize that the attacks were acts of war. Instead, his instinct was to reach immediately for the knee-jerk anti-Americanism that's at the very heart of kookdom. It's *our* fault that there is so much injustice in the world and such hatred toward this nation. American "exceptionalism" had created big imbalances between the have nations and the have-not nations. We've been a bully, throwing our weight around the world without thought of consequence, pillaging foreign lands and tossing their people aside when they could no longer be of use to us. Western civilization overall had been guilty of being dominated by white heterosexual Judeo-Christians. America was particularly guilty because she was born into slavery and then sought to emulate the noxious imperialism of Great Britain and France. As Dinesh D'Souza points out in *The Roots of Obama's Rage*, this rabid anticolonialism informs Obama's worldview. Obama believes, as do most kooks, that we must make up for over two hundred years' worth of global rampaging through humiliating prostration, open apologies, and worldwide retrenchment. We must turn the United States from thuggish superpower into just another country, no better than any other nation, no more powerful, no more moral, no more influential. This is the mission of the kooks: the ultimate downgrade of American power.

———

The way in which the kooks seek to water down our exceptionalism is by redistributing *globally* everything that makes America great: our military and economic power, our diplomatic influence, our cultural strength—and most important, our principle of individual freedom. Obama's Declaration of Dependence would extend to our role in the world. The leftists would back the United States off from global leadership, make us increasingly dependent on other nations and multilateral institutions such as the UN, get us to lean on international law over American law and interests, and ultimately seek transnationalism, a one-world global governing regime. The kooks would see to it that America soon would become nothing special, simply another nation on the world block with about the same power and appeal as Paraguay. After all, on this great spaceship called earth, all countries, cultures, and systems of government are created equal, and constitutional republics like ours have no right to exceptionalism, either on the world stage or here at home.

In his first address as president to the United Nations in September 2009, Obama said precisely that: "In an era where our destiny is shared, power is no longer a zero-sum game. No world order that elevates one nation or group over another will succeed. That is the future America wants." No, actually that was the future *Obama and the kooks* wanted: America over, done, put a fork in her. That's why Obama's first reaction after the 9/11 attacks was so revealing. The anti-American radicalism inherent in his initial response showed the mentality he would later bring to his role as commander in chief. Most of the time, America had been wrong: arrogant, selfish, the genocidal thief who'd shoot first and ask questions later. It's no surprise that Obama spent twenty years listening to his pastor, Reverend Jeremiah Wright, slam America as a vain, unjust nation. In his sermon on the Sunday after the 9/11 attacks, Wright claimed that the United States had brought on the attacks because we had also committed terror: "We bombed Hiroshima. We bombed Nagasaki. And we nuked far more than the thousands in New York and the Pentagon and we never batted an eye. We have supported state terrorism against the Palestinians and black South Africans, and now we are indignant because the stuff we have done overseas is now brought right back to our own front yards. America's chickens are coming home to roost!" he roared.

In addition to drawing obscene moral equivalencies and disturbingly warped historical analogies, Wright was revealing the essence of kook ideology. America is the root of all evil and must be punished. Obama claimed that he wasn't sitting in Wright's pews that Sunday after 9/11, but he didn't have to be. As he had once said, "I don't think my church is actually particularly controversial."

As a senator, presidential candidate, and president, Obama had incessantly attacked President Bush on every aspect of his foreign policy. He pounded Bush for being a unilateralist cowboy, prosecuting an "unnecessary war" in Iraq, essentially abandoning the so-called good war in Afghanistan, ravaging the Constitution by establishing the terrorist facility at Guantánamo Bay, subjecting terrorists to enhanced interrogation techniques, maintaining "black sites" around the world to which terrorists might have been transferred for interrogation, instituting warrantless wiretapping and data mining to track terrorists and their financing, damaging our relationships with our allies, and needlessly antagonizing our adversaries. Bush, he suggested, was a lawbreaking renegade who had inflicted grave damage upon our international reputation.

Obama's assertions were flat-out lies. Bush built international coalitions for the military efforts in Afghanistan and Iraq. He went to the United Nations and exhausted all diplomatic avenues before ordering the military action. He went to multilateral organizations like the North Atlantic Treaty Organization (NATO) for Afghanistan, the European Union to help manage the Iranians' march toward nuclear weapons, and a coalition of five other major Asian powers to deal with North Korean aggression. He didn't do those things to dilute American power, as Obama is doing, but to assert American leadership in creating coalitions for American-led action.

The very foundation of kookology is to assign blame to others and then position yourself as the one uniquely gifted to solve the grievances you've just identified. That move also becomes your ticket to power—and to keeping it. Right on cue, Obama said that it would take years to undo all of the damage, but it could be done with the right leader who possessed an almost otherworldly ability to bring nations together and "heal the planet." Where could we find such a leader? Why, one just happened to be standing right in front of us. Imagine the luck.

During the 2008 presidential campaign, Obama made all kinds of outlandish claims, from the grand ("it was the moment when the rise of the oceans began to slow") to the grander ("we are the ones we've been waiting for"). His godlike aspirations were on particular display when he was abroad. He wouldn't have to do much of the heavy lifting of world peace because that kind of work was only required of Usual Politicians. He wasn't Usual. He was the Lamb of Chicago, walking on water and multiplying fishes and loaves to feed the masses. He could breast-feed the world and cause Chris Matthews to have to adjust his pants. A mere glance in the direction of hostile states would bring an end to conflict. He was the Magical Merlin of the World, spreading his fairy dust everywhere and watching peace bust out all over.

━━━━━

It was this kind of one-world, American reductionist gobbledygook that led to two revealing critiques from high-profile members of Obama's own party. When he was still locked in the primary fight with Hillary Clinton, she ran an ad that bitingly questioned Obama's national security experience and judgment. Known as "The 3 a.m. Phone Call" ad, it reminded us that the world is a dangerous place in which a catastrophic crisis could explode at any time. With whom would you feel more comfortable as commander in chief, reaching for the phone in the White House residence at an ungodly hour? The junior senator from New York, whose national security experience was limited to whatever knowledge she absorbed through osmosis as first lady, or the junior senator from Illinois, whose foreign policy experience was limited to visits to Epcot Center with his girls? Fast-forward to today, and this Tweedledee/Tweedledum equation of Hillary and Barry has new meaning. In many cases, it's the former junior senator from New York who is actually *making* the call at 3:00 a.m. now as secretary of state. So, as you can see, the voters actually had no real choice because these two foreign policy dopes ended up talking to each other.

Just two weeks before the 2008 presidential election, his own vice presidential pick reinforced the doubts about Obama, although from a different angle. "Mark my words," Joe Biden said. "It will not be six months before the world tests Barack Obama like they did John Kennedy. . . . We're about to elect a brilliant forty-seven-year-old senator president of the United States of America. . . . Watch, we're gonna have an international crisis, a generated crisis, to test the mettle of this guy." He was basically telling the world that when we elect this sick antelope with one eye, one horn, and one leg, he's going to get thirsty and hobble down to the riverbank to get a drink. And waiting for him there will be a giant crocodile, just barely submerged below the waterline, waiting to strike. And strike it did . . . in the form of Somali pirates, domestic terror attacks like the one at Fort Hood, and rogue regimes like Iran and Syria, which slaughtered their own people in the streets while marching toward nuclear weapons.

Hillary and Biden were pointing to a disturbing lack of national security experience and an equally important lack of steeliness to deal with the world as it was, not, as Obama and Michelle had often said in invoking Alinsky, the world as they wished it to be. Obama would do everything he could to turn the world into what he thought it should be. The "social and economic justice" he would force-feed America at home would be instituted abroad.

Obama would community-organize the world. He would be the global redistributor.

That's why Obama's first act of international diplomacy would be to log in to Facebook and send friend requests to Mahmoud Ahmadinejad of Iran, Hugo Chávez of Venezuela, Robert Mugabe of Zimbabwe, and, finally, the Winklevoss twins. All accepted his friend requests except the Winklevii.

Never mind that the world is a brutal Darwinian jungle, where only the strongest thrive and the weakest get either trampled or consumed. And never mind that cold calculations of national interest dominate; the world is not a charitable place, where do-goodism is rewarded and noble intentions are respected. To the contrary: it's a do-or-die environment, where it's far better to be feared and respected than loved.

The virtue of America has always been that in addition to our genuine do-goodism, we have projected strength and power, which we were not afraid to use to defend our and our allies' interests. As a result, we have been in the unique position of being feared and respected as well as being a true force for good. The United States has spent more blood and treasure liberating more people from tyranny and oppression than any other nation in world history. And no nation has asked for so little in return.

Leftists, however, see American power as a nefarious tool of global injustice, bursting into countries such as Vietnam and Iraq with all guns blazing, getting into bed with dark regimes such as Saudi Arabia for resources such as oil, exploiting poorer countries such as the Philippines for cheap labor and stuff, and siding with regional bullies such as Israel over the oppressed and occupied Palestinians. To the kooks, this doesn't make America exceptional. It makes her evil. The Left rejects the reality of what the world is and chooses to see only the fantasy of what they perceive that it *should* be. The kooks are much more comfortable naked in a hot tub with Hans Blix, Kofi Annan, Madeleine Albright, and current UN ambassador Susan Rice than they are at accepting the responsibilities that come with superpower status.

In order to "fundamentally transform" America, the leftists have to do internationally what they do domestically. This means realigning the global power structure such that the United States is forced down the totem pole and Obama's Declaration of Dependence is put into action internationally.

It's an approach that was reflected in a phrase by a "senior administration official" that would come to define the Obama foreign policy. In the spring of 2011, *The New Yorker* ran a deeply unsettling piece about how Obama dealt with the array of national security issues confronting him. The author, Ryan Lizza, quoted a top adviser as saying that the president's strategy was to "lead from behind." The official used those words to describe Obama's approach to fighting the war in Libya, but they had a broader application to much of the rest of Obama's foreign policy.

Lizza wrote, "It's a different definition of leadership than America is known for, and it comes from two unspoken beliefs: that the relative power of the U.S. is declining, as rivals like China rise, and that the U.S. is reviled in many parts of the world." He quoted the "senior" adviser again: "It's so at odds with the John Wayne expectation for what America is in the world, but it's necessary for shepherding us through this phase."

Evident in the comment by that "senior administration official" are several basic kook beliefs: (a) first, that America is in decline; (b) second, since the decline is inevitable, Obama's job is to manage it, not to fight it; (c) third, China is passing us on the world stage; (d) fourth, everyone loathes us, so we shouldn't do anything to make them loathe us more; and (e) fifth, by "shepherding us through this phase," they don't mean to stronger, sunny days ahead. They mean to weaker, darker days of diminished power.

The "leading from behind" approach, however, disregarded a basic truth. History shows what happens when the United States checks out of its position of global leadership: the bad guys advance, the good guys retreat, and really horrific things happen. The reality is that "leading from behind" isn't really leading at all. It's simply a clever leftist way of redistributing American power to others. Perhaps the most bizarre aspect of "leading from behind" is that Obama wanted to lead with our behinds, literally. In order to appear more humble on the world stage, he instructed all members of the State Department's diplomatic corps to bend over, grab their ankles, and face everyone ass-first. Which is ironic, since most of Obama's foreign policy is ass-backward.

Obama's foreign policy is based on the belief that because of our past "sins," we should surrender our leadership role in the world, and since other nations are taking that role from us anyway, his job of surrenderer in chief is made that much easier. Obama is operating *intentionally* as an American declinist.

We hire leaders to keep us at number one. We want any "decline" arrested and reversed, not "managed." We don't want our leaders to be wimps who just accept that America is losing it and simply move on. We want our leaders to *fight* for American dominance and greatness. To *fight* to restore America's power and influence. And to *fight* for American exceptionalism.

What we've gotten from Obama and the kooks has been not simply acquiescence to the idea of American decline but a hastening of it in real terms. They have forced America to her knees, leaving her staggering and bleeding and leaving the rest of the world to run amok. We've seen this movie before when they have downgraded America, and it doesn't have a happy ending.

Ain't Too Proud to Beg

To the kooks, America is like an ex-boyfriend who shows up at 2:00 a.m. unannounced and drunk, bursting through the door, smashing up the joint, and then leaving you alone, weeping, shaking, and on the phone to the cops. Of course, America *is* the cops, so it's unclear who would take the call. But after believing that America has busted up the global joint for decades, the kooks wanted America begging for forgiveness for perceived past injustices. In 2008, before he had even formally locked up his party's nomination for president, Obama decided he wanted to give a speech in Berlin, Germany, and at the Brandenburg Gate no less. German chancellor Angela Merkel found Obama's audacious Brandenburg Gate request "odd" and suggested that he give his speech at the Victory Column instead. In reality, an Obama speech in Germany was fitting, since Karl Marx and Friedrich Engels hailed from Deutschland.

It was there, in Berlin, months before he was even elected president, that Obama got the apology ball rolling: "I know my country has not perfected itself. At times, we've struggled to keep the promise of liberty and equality for all of our people. We've made our share of mistakes, and there are times when our actions around the world have not lived up to our best intentions."

There's the word "perfected" again. I'm not sure delivering that particular message in Germany, which started two world wars in its desire to "perfect" itself, was particularly wise. I'm sure the German people loved watching an American presidential candidate echo the sentiment of the Übermensch seeking to create a utopian state. The president of the United States—the commander in chief—explicitly and openly apologizing for America would be the most powerful symbol of the New American Humility. It would let the rest of the world know that we're now a gentle giant who's so sorry for the ruckus we've caused. We've screwed up the world and we're here to beg forgiveness. We hope you'll be kind enough to bestow it.

As soon as he entered office, Obama continued the international Apology Tour, complete with roadies and groupies.

Obama told the French that the United States had failed "to appreciate Europe's leading role in the world" and that we'd displayed "arrogance" and been "dismissive" and "derisive." I suppose the statute of limitations is up on the fact that America rebuilt Europe after Hitler destroyed it.

Obama told the Germans that "the (economic) crisis began in the U.S. I take responsibility, even if I wasn't even president at the time." This was a way of appearing to accept responsibility while really placing it elsewhere. Classic kook.

Obama appeared on Al Arabiya television and flatly declared that America "dictates" without considering "all the factors involved." He continued: "Americans are not your enemy. We sometimes make mistakes. We have not been perfect." (There's that notion of "perfecting" again.)

At the Summit of the Americas in Trinidad, he told the world that the United States had been "dictatorial" and "disengaged," and he went on to say: "But I pledge to you that we seek an equal partnership. There is no senior partner and no junior partner in our relations." Then, after listening quietly to anti-American Marxist thugs like Venezuela's Hugo Chávez and Nicaragua's Daniel Ortega bash the United

States, Obama asked all of Latin America for forgiveness for failing to carry out "sustained engagement with our neighbors." He also palled it up with Chávez, accepting a book and mini-lecture from him. "Adios, amigo!" he called to ol' Hugo, who then returned to Venezuela to land some great nuclear deals with Russia, China, and Iran. In Prague, he declared that America had "a moral responsibility to act" on arms control because we were the only nation that had ever "used a nuclear weapon."

There were some reports that he thought about also apologizing to the Japanese for dropping the atomic bomb on Hiroshima during World War II, although the White House denied it.

In Cairo, Obama legitimized Muslim grievances against the United States, vastly overstated the number of Muslims in America, hyper-exaggerated the role of Islam in American history, suggested that the war in Iraq was an unjustified act of aggression by the United States, apologized for the CIA's role in a 1953 coup in Iran, and invoked "resistance" as a euphemism for Palestinian terror.

In Turkey, Obama blamed the United States for the "strain" in "many places where the Muslim faith is practiced. Let me say this as clearly as I can: the United States is not at war with Islam." He went on to beg for Muslim absolution of America's sins.

In early 2012, after some of our military personnel in Afghanistan seized some Korans that were being used by jihadis to communicate extremist messages, another group of American personnel inadvertently burned them, setting off violent Afghan protests that killed several U.S. troops. Obama's first impulse? To convey to Afghan president Hamid Karzai his "deep regret" and "sincere apologies" for the incident. A few days later, Obama defended his apology by saying that it had helped to "calm things down." After that, even more Americans were killed.

After the successful drone strike that had killed American-born Islamic terrorist Anwar al-Awlaki in Yemen, Team Obama called the family of Samir Khan, a top al-Qaeda propagandist who was also killed in the attack. To apologize. The call went like this: "Hello, Mr. and Mrs. Khan. This is President Barry. I'm really sorry I evaporated your al-Qaeda son's body with a Hellfire missile. I've instructed the Department of Defense to send both of you an Amazon.com gift card."

In fact, Obama was so obsessed with "healing" relations with the Muslim world that he enlisted an entire government agency to help carry it out. The weird thing was that the agency he chose was the National Aeronautics and Space Agency. In early 2010, Obama announced that he was killing NASA's $100 billion "Constellation" program to return Americans to the moon. What he didn't say was that he directed NASA to use that money instead to "find ways to reach out to dominantly Muslim countries," as NASA administrator Charles Bolden put it. When asked to explain Obama's new directive, Bolden described it as outreach to "nontraditional partners," particularly nations that don't have established space programs, such as Indonesia. Under Obama, NASA's mission was no longer space exploration. Out with the romantic heroism of Neil Armstrong, Buzz Aldrin, Jim Lovell, and even the fictional Major Tony Nelson. In with the pathetic groveling of third-tier diplomats. Astronauts from Houston to Cape Canaveral were heard grumbling, "What the @$%&! just happened?"

Obama went on to bow to Saudi king Abdullah, with some suggesting that he actually bent to kiss his ring. He also bowed to the Japanese emperor, who looked more than a little perplexed by the sight of an American president prostrating himself. These acts were graphic symbols of the moral and power equivalence Obama was cultivating—as well as of the American decline he was speeding along.

Other top Obama administration officials carried out their own Apology Tours. After we scored a seat on the joke known as the UN Human Rights Council, our ambassador to the United Nations, Susan Rice, bent over backward to tell that anti-American body that "we have not been *perfect* ourselves," a statement that put us in the same category as other council members with such sterling human rights records as Cuba, China, Saudi Arabia, Russia, and Cameroon.

In China, Secretary of State Hillary Clinton said that the United States must take responsibility for being the top emitter of greenhouse gases. In Indonesia, she said that our policy of sanctions against Myanmar had failed. In the Middle East, she blurted out that the Bush policy of isolating the Iranian regime had not convinced it to relinquish its pursuit of nuclear weapons. In Mexico, she declared that it was America's big appetite for drugs that was largely driving the narcotics-related violence there. In Sweden, she asked the National Bikini Team, "How many of you have slept with my husband?"

One of her top lieutenants, Assistant Secretary of State Michael Posner, told the professional human rights violators in the Chinese government not to worry about their human rights record because ours was just as bad.

Obama touted his approach at the G-20 summit in London in April 2009: "I would like to think that with my election and the early decisions that we've made, that you're starting to see some restoration of America's standing in the world." Obama was right. They only chant "Death to America" in the Gaza Strip every *other* hour now, instead of *every* hour, like they did under George W. Bush. He later put a finer point on the one-world gobbledygook that he first advanced in his 2008 Berlin speech. During a 2010 address at West Point, Obama reemphasized his commitment to shaping a new "international order" in which he'd invest America's power and prestige in global institutions.

With apologies all around, the stage was set for the building of that new world order, in which America would relinquish world leadership to those generally anti-American "global institutions" and see to it that the traditionally solid relationships with allies and clear-eyed approaches to enemies were shattered. Big Daddy was punishing America, forcing her to sit in the corner wearing a dunce cap, while he community-organized the rest of the world to take our place.

"You Like Me! You Really Like Me!"

On October 9, 2009, the Norwegian Nobel Committee jumped the shark. It announced that it was awarding its coveted Nobel Golf

Prize to President Barack Obama for his "extraordinary efforts on the back nine." That's a prize he may have actually deserved. No, that day the Nobel Committee announced that it was bestowing the world's most prestigious award, the Nobel Peace Prize, to Obama for "his extraordinary efforts to strengthen international diplomacy and cooperation between peoples."

In other words, for not being George W. Bush.

In a spasm of politically correct white guilt, the committee did what the International Olympic Committee did not: reward Obama for being, well, Obama. Just days before the Nobel Committee let the world know that they were idiots as well as leftists, Obama jetted to Copenhagen, Denmark, to lobby the IOC to award the 2016 Olympics to Chicago. With Oprah in tow, Barry made his case and begged the IOC. Michelle referred to their participation on the taxpayer-funded European junket as a "sacrifice."

In the end, the IOC was impressed with neither Obama's "sacrifice" nor the Queen of All Media, because they awarded the Games to Rio de Janeiro instead.

Being awarded the Nobel Peace Prize, however, was, the logical result of Obama's International Apology Tour. As the *New York Times* put it in their editorial about the prize: "Countering the ill will Mr. Bush created around the world is one of Mr. Obama's great achievements in less than nine months in office. Mr. Obama's willingness to respect and work with other nations is another." Who better for the Euro-kooks to honor and the *Times* to celebrate than an American kook who was moving American decline along so nicely? They gave him the prize based on his own campaign slogan of "hope," but "hope" is neither a strategy nor an achievement. But, hey, the award has been given to Jimmy Carter, Al Gore, and Yasser Arafat over the years, so who are we to judge?

The whole episode was so bizarre that even some of Obama's most devout supporters were left wondering, "What the @$%&! just happened?" If Obama had had any respect for the prize or sense of personal decency, he would have either declined to accept it until he had accomplished something substantive *or* he would have accepted it on behalf of the United States military. Instead, he accepted it for himself and couldn't suppress a Sally-Field-at-the-Oscars faux humility: "I would be remiss if I did not acknowledge the considerable controversy that your generous decision has generated. In part, this is because I am at the beginning, and not the end, of my labors on the world stage." Other recipients had done things like founding the Red Cross, implementing the Marshall Plan after World War II, and signing the Camp David accords. But Barry's big accomplishment for world peace in 2009 was simply drawing breath.

Actually, the Nobel Committee should have taken a page from the playbook of Arizona State University, which in April 2009 decided *against* awarding Obama an honorary degree when he spoke at commencement that year. ASU spokeswoman Sharon Keeler said, "It's normally awarded to someone who has been in their field for some time. Considering that the president is at the beginning of his presidency, his body of work is just beginning." The folks at ASU should've received the Nobel Prize for Common Sense.

A year and a half later, after Obama had ordered the military surge in Afghanistan and had begun combat operations in Libya, leftist gadfly Michael Moore tweeted, "May I suggest a 50-mile evacuation zone around Obama's Nobel Peace Prize?"

Politico asked some members of the Nobel Committee if they had any regrets awarding the Peace Prize to such a Bushian warmonger. Thorbjørn Jagland, the committee's chairman, replied, "He got the prize for what he did. Not for what he did afterwards." And Geir Lundestad, the committee's secretary, replied: "The Nobel Peace Prize is no declaration of sainthood. And no American president will ever be a saint." Nice.

What the Nobel Committee liked about Barack Obama was the *idea* of Barack Obama, a young, biracial multilateralist who wasn't going to be merely the president of that horrible United States but more like a president of the world. They believed he'd make their sacred "one world" vision a reality. He'd be, in former ambassador John

Bolton's phrase, the first "post-American" president. So he got a Nobel Prize for filling the fantasy of European leftists that he'd lead them to their promised land of global redistributionism and one-world government. They hope for it still. And after their decision, there was no stopping the Obama Cult of Personality once the Man Behind the Curtain had a Nobel Peace Prize swinging from his neck.

The Kinetic Military Action Against Man-made Disasters

On May 26, 2009, Obama created a shadowy, four-person national security team known as the Global Engagement Directorate (GED), which sounded like it came straight from goofy spymaster Basil Exposition in *Austin Powers: International Man of Mystery*. In an official White House announcement, Obama bestowed the new GED with a vague mission "to drive comprehensive engagement policies that leverage diplomacy, communications, international development and assistance, and domestic engagement and outreach in pursuit of a host of national security objectives." (Imagine if President Bush had created such a sinister-sounding secretive group, reporting only to the president, with such ambiguous goals. Chris Matthews would've experienced male menopause on national television.)

The directorate set out immediately to whitewash the terminology of Islamic terror and radicalism. Under President Bush, the National Security Strategy stated: "The struggle against militant Islamic radicalism is the great ideological conflict of the early years of the 21st century." An accurate and true statement, but far too politically incorrect for Team Obama. The GED moved to sanitize the vocabulary surrounding the global war on Islamic terror, expanding the effort to soften the rhetoric first begun in the latter years of Bush's presidency. The virus of political correctness infected the way in which Obama and his fellow kooks spoke about the enemy and in how they dealt with it.

Islam? Islam? Bueller? Anyone?

On May 4, 2010, investigators made an arrest in an attempted car bombing in New York City. Faisal Shahzad, a Pakistani native–turned–naturalized U.S. citizen, was taken into custody. He was naturalized in 2009 (when Team Obama was busy scratching "Islamic terror" from the lexicon), and shortly thereafter he made a trip to Peshawar, Pakistan, a hotbed of Islamic terrorist activity and recruitment.

In the countless early stories about his arrest, not one mentioned his faith. We were left to deduce that he was a Muslim by his Pakistani ethnicity and name, although I'm sure plenty of leftists assumed someone named Faisal Shahzad could very easily be an Irish Catholic priest from Boston, a Scandinavian dairy farmer from Wisconsin, or a Pennsylvania Dutch Amish Mennonite.

This suicidal inability to call the enemy what it is comes straight from the top. Obama doubled down on Bush's late-stage wimpiness and will not go anywhere near placing the words "Islam" and "terror" together. His administration has contorted itself into all kinds of politically correct gymnastics to avoid making the connection, going so far as to term acts of terror "man-made disasters," the fight against terrorism "combating violent extremism," missions fought abroad "overseas contingency operations," and the wars themselves "kinetic military actions." When an Islamist tries to cut someone's head off, Obama calls it a "close shave."

These euphemisms for Islamic terror are dangerously counterproductive. Obama refused to speak the truth about the motivation of Army Major Nidal Malik Hasan, who referred to himself as a "soldier of Allah" and became obviously radicalized before shooting to death thirteen fellow Americans and wounding many more in the name of Islam. Nor would Obama make the Islam and terror connection with Umar Farouk Abdulmutallab, the Nigerian Muslim who tried to detonate a bomb aboard a Northwest flight and rain hundreds of bodies over Detroit on Christmas Day, 2009. Obama refused to "jump to conclusions" about what propelled them to try to kill Americans . . . although he had no problem "jumping to conclusions" about Sergeant

James Crowley of the Cambridge Police, who he declared "acted stupidly" in the arrest of Harvard professor Henry Louis Gates without knowing the full story.

In terms of pure idiocy about the Islamic threat, however, New York City mayor Michael Bloomberg's comment before Shahzad's arrest took the cake: "If I had to guess . . . this would be exactly that. Homegrown. Maybe a mentally deranged person or someone with a political agenda that doesn't like the health care bill or something." Bloomberg was kept apprised of the investigation in real time but would not acknowledge the truth. When Shahzad's identity was made public and it was clear that he was not a deranged Tea Partier, CNN then helpfully theorized that he might have acted out of frustration after having suffered the indignity of home foreclosure. CBS and the Associated Press seemed equally mystified by what may have driven Shahzad to want to blow up Times Square: "Faisal Shahzad's Motive Shrouded in Mystery," blared their headline. Of course, Shahzad's real motivation—Islamic jihad—appeared nowhere in their article. Tea Partiers were smeared as violent, crazed maniacs, but *actual* violent, crazed maniacs were getting a free pass.

Unless and until we can call this enemy and what drives them to kill what they are, we cannot and will not win this Kinetic Military Action. And yet, our leaders still choose to sugarcoat the true nature of the threat. Before Major Hasan gunned down scores of people at Fort Hood, he told anyone who would listen that as an Islamist, he hated America and was preparing to carry out an act of war against the United States. He had up to twenty e-mail communications with American-born radical cleric Anwar al-Awlaki, which drew the attention of the FBI and the Army, which later dropped the case after concluding that Hasan didn't pose a threat. Before the slaughter, he gave away his possessions, including a Koran. As he bore down on his victims, he screamed, "Allah Akbar!" Later, the administration would preposterously classify his act of jihad as "workplace violence." So, according to the Barry White House, a Muslim subversive committing the worst terror attack on American soil since 9/11 is nothing more than a parallel to the scene in the movie *Office Space* where Peter, Michael, and Samir destroy the evil computer printer that has been tormenting them at work.

When Hasan's commander in chief first appeared hours after the killings, he stunned everybody by spending the first three minutes chuckling and tossing shout-outs to his buddies in the audience. His breathtaking insensitivity at a time of national grief echoed his breathtaking insensitivity eight days after 9/11, when he argued for compassion for our enemies while only coldly acknowledging the victims.

In a particularly hilarious example of political correctness, House Democrats asked Third Way, a left-of-center think tank, and then–California representative Jane Harman to run a "terrorism-talking school" for their congressional candidates. The sessions included how to "avoid the trap of looking soft and weak" and which "strong adverbs" to use. Representative Gerry Connolly (D-VA) said that he learned to say "I'm going to fight for American interests abroad" rather than "I'm going to defend American values" because the former sounded "more assertive." I'm sure they were instructed never to use the words "Islam" and "terror" together because that's far *too* assertive.

The handling of the war by Obama and the kooks became less about protecting America from its enemies than about carrying out a public relations campaign. Obama's administration attempted to fight the war on Islamic terror according to the *Politically Correct Guide Dealing with Misguided But Fundamentally Good People Who Just Need to Be Better Understood*. After all, as he indicated in his September 19, 2001, article, our enemies are people too.

Obama couldn't wait to become president and become the White Swan to President Bush's Black Swan. All of the Bush counterterrorism policies against which Obama had long railed would be banished in a hail of executive orders: the terrorist facility at Guantánamo Bay would be closed along with third-country "black" sites to which terrorist suspects had been rendered for interrogation; enhanced interrogation techniques would be terminated; indefinite detention, warrantless wiretapping, and data mining would end; and military tribunals would be replaced by civilian criminal trials for even the most hardened terrorists. All of the "unconstitutional" Bush policies would come to a screeching halt under Obama, so the rest of the world could see that we had returned to good-guy status.

On the first full day of his presidency, Obama delivered this soft touch to the hardest of hard-core terrorists. He issued an executive order demanding the immediate closure of the terrorist detention facility at Guantánamo Bay, which he and his fellow kooks had argued was a blight on the rule of law and a terrorist recruitment bonanza. Never mind that the al-Qaeda jihadists hit on September 11, before Guantánamo even existed. Never mind that the terrorist suspects being held there are foreign enemy combatants who are not entitled to the full panoply of U.S. legal rights and privileges and that the Supreme Court had held that they could be held "indefinitely" until the end of the war. Never mind that they already had legal representation and due process through the right to federal court review. Never mind that they had three full meals a day, religious services, and state-of-the-art medical services, all under the watchful eye of the International Committee of the Red Cross. Under Obama, military tribunals, which had been in use since Revolutionary War times and held constitutional by the Supreme Court, were to be ended, with some military trials—such as that of 9/11 mastermind Khalid Sheikh Mohammed—stopped after they had already begun. Terrorist suspects held at Guantánamo would be matriculated into civilian criminal courts on U.S. soil. And with the facility closing due to Obama's executive order, there would be no choice.

Obama and the kooks decided to treat acts of war against the United States as if they were stickups at the 7-Eleven. They catapulted us back to the September 10, 2001, mind-set in which we treated international terror as a criminal justice problem, to be handled in civilian courts. The United States would prosecute even the highest-level al-Qaeda terrorists like we would Al Capone, Charles Manson, or Lindsay Lohan. We would make sure they received very public due process to show that we had reclaimed the "moral high ground" in this fight against man-made disasters.

To Obama and the kooks, this civilized approach set us apart from the enemy and demonstrated how far superior we were to them. Ironically, it had the opposite effect. Obama expected that the enemy as well as the rest of the world would view this as humility, when in fact it displayed a haughty arrogance that only inflamed anti-Americanism. The "we're better than they are and we'll show them through our judicial system" attitude did nothing but reinforce our enemies' belief that America was as arrogant and deserving of violent attack as ever. It also telegraphed to the enemy a sign of weakness that we weren't interested in going "all in" with the goal of ultimate victory, but instead showed a lack of faith in our own ability to break the enemy's resolve.

In fact, in March 2009, just two months after Obama signed the executive order to close Guantánamo, five detainees, including KSM, submitted a six-page document to their war crimes court. In it they wrote, "We fight you over defending Muslims, their land, their holy sites and their religion as a whole." The charges against them were "badges of honor, which we carry with pride." And they concluded, "We are terrorists to the bone." They also made a strange request: "Can you please bring back *That '70s Show*? The character played by Mila Kunis is very hot." They then added, "Please do not tell other terrorists that we find Jewish girl sexy."

Their beliefs, motivations, and intentions were never a mystery. They're engaged in a holy war, as they themselves describe it. This means that we are engaged in a holy war as well, whether we want to see it that way or not. The enemy is calling it like it is, while our leadership is excusing acts of war as the acts of deranged men or of people "upset with the health care bill." As the so-called twentieth 9/11 hijacker, Zacarias Moussaoui, said in open court at his trial, "I am not insane. I am al-Qaeda."

It wasn't long after Obama had ordered Holder to shutter Guantánamo Bay that Bush's Black Swan pirouetted directly into the White Swan's line of sight. It's all fun and games, idealism and romanticism during the campaign, until you become president and the crud hits the fan. That moment generally occurs when the Threat Matrix hits the Oval Office desk for the first time. Usually delivered to the president at dawn, the Threat Matrix is a phone-book-sized compendium of all the threats against the United States and our interests tracked overnight by our intelligence agencies.

The Threat Matrix is usually enough to scare straight any naive leftist tripping on kook hallucinogens. Within three months of taking office and getting a load of the Threat Matrix, Obama and Holder defended domestic spying, warrantless wiretaps, and the Patriot Act. Quite a trifecta of Bush counterterrorism goodness. It was particularly gratifying given that in 2007, then-senator Obama declared, "No more illegal wiretapping of American citizens. No more ignoring the law when it is convenient." And in 2008, the future attorney general, Eric Holder, proclaimed, "I . . . never thought that I would see that a president would act in direct defiance of federal law by authorizing warrantless NSA surveillance of American citizens." Holder just needed to wait another year and he'd see his boss do the same thing.

While Team Obama was embracing the Bush wiretapping policies, it was still stuck on stupid on what to do about Guantánamo Bay. Bringing top al-Qaeda terrorists to New York to stand trial near ground zero may have satisfied Obama's kook fantasy of showing the world that we're "better" than the terrorists who hit us on 9/11, but the policy was advanced without a plan and without a comprehensive new legal structure to deal with the detainees beyond trying them in federal courts.

Interestingly, the Obama administration continued the Bush policy of holding hundreds of enemy combatants at the larger and more secret Bagram Air Base in Afghanistan, which, because it was located in an active theater of war, was exempt from the kind of judicial review required in other locales. As it was making a very public show of wanting to close Guantánamo, Team Obama *expanded* Bagram's role as a terrorist detention center and sought to severely restrict legal avenues for those held there.

Meanwhile, nobody on Team Obama bothered to contact the mayor of New York, the New York Police Department, or the Joint

Terrorism Task Force about the wisdom of moving key al-Qaeda leaders such as KSM, Ramzi bin al-Shibh, and Abu Zubaydah to the city. Nobody on Team Obama thought it critical to secure political as well as law enforcement support for the plan. Nobody thought it important to lay the logistical groundwork for acquiring secure facilities in New York to hold these terrorists during their trials. Nobody thought about the security ramifications for the city and its residents or for the possibility that KSM and the others might turn their trials into propaganda circuses. And of course, nobody on Team Obama believed that as foreign enemy combatants, they weren't entitled to any of this.

Of course, when KSM got wind that he was movin' on up to the Big Apple, he immediately got ready for his star turn. He'd heard Sinatra croon that if you could make it in New York, you could make it anywhere. He got a contraband I HEART NY T-shirt. He demanded that Guantánamo guards refer to him as "Mr. Mohammed" and avoid eye contact. Like Prince, he changed his name to an undecipherable symbol, or the Terrorist Formerly Known as KSM. He dreamed that pretty soon he'd stroll into a New York courtroom wearing huge Paris Hilton sunglasses, carrying a rhinestone-encrusted cell phone, and tell the judge to hold while he takes a call from Ari Emanuel.

Obama and Holder didn't anticipate the fact that leftists loved to complain about Guantánamo when Bush was in office, but once they had the chance to close it, most caved. Democrats such as New York senator Charles Schumer called the plan to try top al-Qaeda terrorists in New York "wrongheaded." Public support for closing Guantánamo dropped into the 30 percent range. While many Democrats supported *in theory* the plan to close Guantánamo, they didn't want any detainees transferred to their states for trial. If they weren't going to be sent to New York, where would they go? The Supermax prison in Florence, Colorado? Democratic representative from Colorado John Salazar said no. Fort Leavenworth in Kansas? Democratic governor Mark Parkinson said no. Nobody wanted KSM in his or her backyard, envisioning their head on his sword.

Also engaged in epic "NIMBY"? Foreign countries, including the home nations of the detainees, which refused to take many of them back. Team Obama seemed genuinely shocked that these countries didn't want them. Duh! They're terrorists. A December 2010 report by the Office of the Director of National Intelligence stated that 25 percent of the detainees who've been transferred out of Guantánamo Bay return to the jihad.

Oh wait: somebody did want them. The cities of Berkeley, California, and Amherst, Massachusetts, approved resolutions to invite detainees who had been cleared of "wrongdoing" to live there. "This is one thing we can do to right some wrongs of our federal government," said Wendy Kenin, the chairwoman of Berkeley's Peace and Justice Commission (yes, there is such a thing).

Another major setback to the Obama/Holder terrorist merry-go-round occurred in the fall of 2010, when Ahmed Ghailani, a Guantánamo detainee charged in the bombings of the U.S. embassies in Kenya and Tanzania, was acquitted of all 283 terrorism charges against him and convicted on only one count of destroying government property. Sort of like the punishment you'd get if you torched a government-issued pen. If not for that one conviction, Ghailani would have walked free. The possibility that this might happen in the trials of KSM and other top 9/11 plotters put the final nail in the coffin for Obama and Holder's lunatic plan to try these terrorists in civilian courts.

In another bizarre twist, Holder had said that if any of the Guantánamo terrorists were acquitted in civilian court, he and Obama would order them held indefinitely anyway, so don't worry. What? Then what was the point of trying them in the first place? To show the world how awesome we are? To make ourselves feel better? "Not guilty!" "Yay, Inshallah!" "Not so fast, Mr. Mohammed. Please follow me back to indefinite detention." That would've had even KSM saying, "What the @$%&! just happened?"

The administration's protracted indecision on Guantánamo led the military to kill suspected terrorists on the battlefield or through drone strikes or hand off those captured to other countries for detention. They had more due process under President Bush. Special forces on the ground in Afghanistan and the judges handling the cases were clamoring for legislative clarity on detainee policy. Essentially, the

Obama/Holder detainee policy became "Crap in One Hand and Wish in the Other to See Which One Fills Up First." In the end, Obama kept Guantánamo Bay open and operational, although he hasn't ordered a single terrorist suspect sent there since he became president. He apparently finds it easier to kill them on the battlefield without due process than to have to deal with the mishegas of interrogation and detention.

In early March 2011, Obama overturned his own ban on military tribunals at Guantánamo Bay. Despite repeatedly claiming that such trials were an abomination to our system of justice, Obama and Holder acknowledged that the tribunals "are an available and important tool in combating international terrorists that fall within their jurisdiction while upholding the rule of law." The military trials of KSM and other key terrorists resumed in mid-2012. Obama was chastened and embarrassed to have to adopt yet another Bush policy, so to make himself feel better, he summoned the "Leave Britney Alone" YouTube sensation Chris Crocker to the White House, and the two of them put on guyliner, crawled under a bedsheet together, and filmed themselves crying out, "Leave Barry Alone!"

There was, however, one major policy that Obama could not abide: enhanced interrogation techniques (EITs), which, despite having been determined to be legal in 2002 and 2003 when they were used, were called "torture" by Obama and the kooks. Following the capture of top al-Qaeda operative Abu Zubaydah in Pakistan in March 2002, the CIA and the U.S. military developed interrogation techniques that were directly adapted from the training techniques used to prepare our special forces personnel to resist interrogation, such as wall standing, sleep deprivation, facial or "insult" slaps, the playing of loud music, and, until 2003, waterboarding, a form of simulated drowning.

How scary is any of this to a hardened jihadist who thinks nothing of beheading an infidel with a machete? This list of EITs sounds like a run-of-the-mill night at the Clinton White House. And yet, somehow it was all too unacceptable for Obama, Holder, and the leftists—regardless of whether or not these EITs were generating actionable intelligence that was disrupting terror plots and saving American lives. They were not, according to the leftists, "consistent with our values," so they must end.

Of course, the reason we know what constituted EITs and who was subjected to them is that in April 2009, Obama decided unilaterally to release top-secret Justice Department memoranda from the Bush administration that outlined the methods used by the agency during interrogations. It was unprecedented for the commander in chief to release such high-level secrets when the country was still at war. Obama's own CIA director, Leon Panetta, opposed the release, along with four former CIA directors who had served under both Republican and Democratic presidents. Obama went ahead with the release anyway, telling the CIA in a speech that the exposure would make us "stronger and more secure" as it showed the "power of our values, including the rule of law." I'm surprised the president didn't call up Stan Lee, the founder of Marvel Comics, and ask him if he could make an illustrated pamphlet to show the world's jihadists what we do when we catch them, and how to prepare themselves to defeat the techniques if they're caught.

This outrage led to the reemergence of the guy the Left had crucified for years as Beezelbub, former vice president Dick Cheney. Cheney doesn't come out to shoot the breeze. Cheney only emerges when Obama inflicts a particularly dangerous kind of hell on us, as he did with the release of the DOJ memos. Cheney blistered Obama and Holder for their irresponsibility and launched a formal government process to declassify and release two CIA reports on detainee interrogation, one dated July 13, 2004, and the other June 1, 2005, which Cheney said "showed the success of the effort . . . what we obtained and what we learned and how good the intelligence was."

The government finally released the CIA memos, and the memos clearly showed that the EITs had generated the majority of information we got about al-Qaeda and played a role in nearly every capture of al-Qaeda operatives since 2002. Zubaydah cracked under the pressure and then led the CIA to other high-value targets, including Ramzi bin al-Shibh. Information from bin al-Shibh then led to the capture of top-gun KSM, who in turn coughed up intelligence about a plot to attack the West Coast. "That's pretty actionable intelligence," former Bush CIA director Michael Hayden said.

In the CIA inspector general's report dated May 7, 2004, KSM was described as "probably the most prolific" of the interrogated terrorists. He "provided information that helped lead to the arrests of terrorists including Sayfullah Paracha and his son Uzair Paracha, businessmen whom Khalid Sheikh Mohammed planned to use to smuggle explosives into the United States; Saleh Almari, a sleeper operative in New York; and Majid Khan, an operative who could enter the United States easily and was tasked to research attacks (part redacted)." KSM also gave up information that led ultimately to the whereabouts of Osama bin Laden. Furthermore, the number of terrorist suspects subjected to EITs was extremely limited. In December 2007 CIA director Michael Hayden stated that "of about 100 prisoners held to date in the CIA program, the enhanced techniques were used on about 30, and waterboarding used on just three."

Three Islamic fanatics trying to kill us and we can't dribble some water up their noses? Let's be clear about the specific "torture" to which KSM and the other two were subjected: (a) threatening them with death; (b) threatening to kill their families; (c) firing off a gun in another room; (d) having one of our guys put a hood over his head and play dead so KSM would think he was next; (e) threatening KSM with a power drill; (f) playing loud heavy metal music; and my personal favorite, (g) blindfolding KSM and putting a caterpillar on him because he was afraid of insects. Poor Khalid freaked out because we put a bug on his toe.

Thanks to Obama's decision to release all of the details about our EIT program and what we will now allow (the Fred Rogers approach to interrogation found in the Army Field Manual), the enemy knows what we will do to them if they're captured and what we won't. Now they know that they won't get sleep deprived or waterboarded or a power drill by their ears or bugs on their feet. They know our hands are tied. Good luck getting any intelligence out of any captured terrorists. Oh that's right: Obama isn't capturing them, he's killing them without so much as a shout-out to the Geneva Convention.

Despite the fact that Obama's own Pentagon found "no such evidence" of abusive treatment of Guantánamo detainees in a February 2009 report, Obama and Holder decided to go to war with the Central Intelligence Agency.

In late August 2009, Obama made two incredibly dangerous and arrogant decisions. The first was the creation of the Global Engagement Directorate (GED), which put the questioning of terrorist suspects under the direct supervision of the White House rather than the CIA.

When President Richard Nixon consolidated national security decision-making in the White House, the leftists went bananas, accusing him of trying to end-run Congress. Similar charges were made against George W. Bush. And yet, it was the Obama regime that, in the fall of 2011, used the CIA's military drones to actually kill three U.S. citizens, two of whom had al-Qaeda connections. Imagine if Nixon or Bush were picking off Americans with remote-controlled airplane missiles.

Obama's shadowy GED invested him with unprecedented power over which there was no congressional oversight. It also undermined the CIA's ability to hunt, spy on, and kill our enemies.

Which brings us to his second irresponsible decision: permitting Holder to investigate CIA officers who took part in several terrorist interrogations to see if they broke the law—something that in 2007 Obama pledged to do if elected president. This opened them up to possible criminal prosecution, which, in turn, cast a chill on all CIA officers and agents in the field. Why should they aggressively pursue terrorists if they might get hauled in for prosecution? Why would smart, talented young people who want to defend their country go to the CIA if first they need to lawyer up? Pretty soon, you'll be able to go to a mall food court, walk up to a Sbarro Pizza, an Orange Julius stand, or an Auntie Anne's Pretzels, and you'll meet a bunch of ex-military personnel with master's degrees in Arabic and Farsi, waiting for Obama to leave office so they can rejoin the intelligence community.

This was a blatant and highly unethical politicization of the Justice Department, and yet, where were all of those leftists who accused Bush and Cheney of engaging in this kind of extra-constitutional behavior?

One particular leftist took on the CIA by channeling her inner Norma Desmond. On April 23, 2009, the then Speaker of the House, Nancy Pelosi, held a bizarre press conference during which she debuted a disturbing crab walk, in which she moved in and out of the room sideways. She also said that she was only briefed once—in September 2002—on the advanced interrogation methods. At the time, Pelosi was the House Minority Whip and top Democrat on the House Intelligence Committee. She said that CIA briefers told her that "the use of enhanced interrogation techniques were legal" and added that waterboarding "was not being employed." However, CIA records show that during the September 2002 briefing, Pelosi and others were given "a description of the particular enhanced interrogation techniques that had been employed" on Zubaydah, who was already being waterboarded. CIA officials said they believed agency briefers had indeed informed Pelosi that Zubaydah was undergoing waterboarding, and other members of Congress present at the 2002 briefing corroborated the CIA's version of events.

Further corroboration came from CIA logs and by former representative Porter Goss (R-FL), who was then chairman of the House Permanent Select Committee on Intelligence, later served as CIA director under President George W. Bush from 2004 until 2006, and was one of the four members of Congress briefed by the CIA in 2002.

Obama, Holder, and Pelosi lied about what they knew, when they knew it, and what the actual policy was. They blew off the fact that three former attorneys general and numerous other career Justice Department prosecutors looked at the findings of the May 2004 CIA inspector general's report as well as other evidence and issued detailed memoranda as to why "the facts did not support criminal prosecution." Holder admitted that he had ordered the investigations reopened in September 2009 without reading the memoranda. Does anybody in Washington read anything important or is it all just *Penthouse* and *Garfield*?

This would be the same attorney general who, in a May 13, 2011, hearing before the House Judiciary Committee, could not even acknowledge the existence of radical Islam.

It's not odd that Holder would show himself to be a full-blown kook unable to call the Islamic enemy by its own name. But what *was* odd is that Holder's inane political correctness about radical Islam came just eleven days after his boss had okayed a mission to blow away the world's most notorious radical Islamic terrorist.

One o'clock in the morning, Abbottabad, Pakistan. Two stealth Black Hawk helicopters land on a nondescript compound and deposit several men who enter the premises. Within a few minutes, the terrorist is dead, shot once through the chest and once through the head. As a pool of blood formed quickly around his body, a radio crackled to life: "Geronimo. Enemy killed in action." "Geronimo" was the code name for Osama bin Laden, the ultimate and elusive symbol of evil incarnate.

For years, the Left pounded President Bush for his innovative counterterrorism policies, and yet *all* were used to locate OBL and ultimately kill him. Khalid Sheikh Mohammed was captured in Pakistan and brought to a black site somewhere in Eastern Europe. There he was waterboarded and had the caterpillar placed on his toe. At some point, the EITs broke him, and he went from silence to being a Chatty Cathy. Jose Rodriguez, the head of the CIA's counterterrorism center from 2002 to 2005, said Abu Faraj al-Libbi, al-Qaeda's number three leader, started talking just one week after being subjected to the EITs. Al-Libbi was not waterboarded but KSM was, and the CIA was able to corroborate their information to come up with the nickname of bin Laden's most trusted courier, which "eventually led to the location of [bin Laden's] compound," said Rodriguez. Ultimately, we were able to listen in on a call the courier made to someone on whom we were eavesdropping under the Bush policy of warrantless wiretaps. It's ironic that Obama was celebrated for using *the exact tools and policies for which he mercilessly criticized Bush*. If Obama had any shred of class or graciousness, he would've openly thanked Bush and his team for setting up the strategic, tactical, and legal framework that made OBL's death possible. What exactly did Obama do here? Make a phone call?

Immediately after OBL's killing, the White House and its foot soldiers in the Congress and media began referring to Obama's decision as "gutsy." Thanks to consummate planning and professionalism by our *truly* gutsy Navy SEALs, the bin Laden mission was executed nearly perfectly, but the White House argued that it just as easily could've gone south. The adjective "gutsy" was used ad nauseam, as a way of equating Obama's supposed "courage" with that of the men who had actually entered the compound. Once again, it was all about Obama: his wingmen used the word "gutsy" as propaganda to tout his *political* "bravery."

Was, however, the decision by the president to okay the mission *really* "gutsy," given that our intelligence services had been piecing together key clues about bin Laden's whereabouts for nearly a year prior? If it were to ever emerge publicly that Obama knew or had a relatively good idea where bin Laden was and *didn't* act, Obama's presidency would have been over. Too many people in intelligence, the military, and the White House knew what Obama knew. If he didn't order the mission and bin Laden escaped, somebody would've leaked it and his legacy would've been destroyed. If he ordered the mission and it went badly, he could at least argue that he had tried. According to Chuck Pfarrar, a former Navy SEAL Team Six commander who wrote of the mission in his book, *SEAL Target Geronimo*, Obama was playing golf twenty minutes before the raid began so that "if this had completely gone south, he was in a position to disavow." Gutsy? Meh.

What was *truly* gutsy was *Bush's* decision to keep pressing the counterterrorism policies despite the relentless pounding he got from his critics. It would have been much easier and much more politically profitable for Bush to pack it in, shut Guantánamo, stop EITs earlier than he did, halt the warrantless wiretapping, and so on. But he knew this was not about how he looked to the *New York Times* editorial board. It was about the safety and security of the nation and prosecuting a war against an unprecedented kind of enemy. He kept the policies and took the fire for it. After 9/11, President Bush announced that we would seek out terrorist enemies of the United States wherever they are in the world and deliver justice. We now know what constitutes the Obama Doctrine. It's called the Bush Doctrine.

In the euphoria over bin Laden's elimination, however, Team Obama released far too much information about the mission and its aftermath. No one should have known the name of the courier tracked to bin Laden's compound, that retired Pakistani military officers were recruited by the CIA to watch the compound from a nearby post, which particular helicopters were used, the Afghan base from which our SEALs departed, how they evaded Pakistani radar, the number of SEALs involved in the raid, and which al-Qaeda plots we learned about from which laptops and thumb drives we seized.

Why all of the blabbing? Politics and reelection. Amazingly, Team Obama and Pentagon officials leaked highly classified details about the raid to Kathryn Bigelow, the director of *The Hurt Locker,* as she developed a film about the mission. The movie just happened to be set for release in October 2012 . . . mere weeks before the presidential election. Sony Pictures moved the release date to after the election after complaints about its possible propaganda purposes.

In its rapture to show the success of the mission, however, the administration may have compromised the next one. The first thing done by the Pakistani government—a supposed ally stung by accusations that it knew of and protected bin Laden's whereabouts—was to broadcast the name of our CIA station chief in Islamabad. This endangered his life and his and others' sensitive work in Pakistan. Thanks to Team Obama's loose lips, jihadists of all stripes now have information that can help them avoid getting smoked like bin Laden.

Most important is something Obama has done under the radar. He has *intentionally* limited the enemy to al-Qaeda and what he calls "violent extremists." By restricting the enemy simply to al-Qaeda, Obama could take out key al-Qaeda leaders such as bin Laden and al-Awlaki and lend the impression that the war on terror was drawing to a close. If bin Laden is gone and our drones are eliminating other key terrorists, then he can peddle the idea that the threat is greatly reduced and the domestic agenda can move back to center stage. But the war is not just against al-Qaeda. There are many violent and stealth Islamist groups willing to undermine or kill us. Just because 9/11 seems like a high-water mark for the jihad does *not* mean that somewhere, an anonymous new foe isn't planning something even more lethal.

Obama's self-serving limitation of the enemy to al-Qaeda makes it appear that we have no Islamic enemies beyond those particular terrorists. It also allows Obama to redefine the parameters of the war, declare victory, and retrench abroad. That's convenient for him and his break-the-bank domestic agenda, but it's untrue and dangerous. Obama saw the death of bin Laden as a good justification to withdraw from Afghanistan and in the general war on terror while turning back to his beloved domestic project.

Surgetastic!

Iraq and Afghanistan? He's just not that into them.

When Obama entered office, he made it clear that he would kick off the New American Humility by hightailing it out of Iraq and holding his nose through a surge in Afghanistan before hightailing out of there too. There would be no more John Waynes and no more Clint Eastwoods. From now on, the symbol of America would be a grown man in a soiled diaper, too afraid to confront the world, equipped with a copy of the *New York Times* in one hand and an Occupy Wall Street drum in the other.

On August 31, 2010, Obama addressed the nation about U.S. involvement in Iraq. He spoke of that week's final drawdown of combat forces as well as the Bush-negotiated status-of-forces agreement, which called for the removal of all U.S. troops by December 31, 2011. He punctuated the end of a war he had vociferously opposed from its start, a war that had included a Bush-ordered surge of more than 20,000 additional combat troops, which Obama had blasted as unnecessary, wasteful, and irresponsible. Obama continually used the war generally and the surge in particular as political daggers aimed straight at Bush and the Republican Party as well as his 2008 Democratic primary challenger, Hillary Clinton, who, while serving in the Senate, had voted to authorize the use of force in Iraq.

Many of Obama's fellow leftists attacked the war, including Senate Majority Leader Harry Reid who, while the surge was being prosecuted, proclaimed, "This war is lost." Reid's comment was classic kookology: that they are uniquely capable of real insight and discerning the "truth," in this case that the war was hopeless.

Through their incessant public criticism, Democrats like Obama and Reid—and countless other leftists—undercut President Bush and the nation's objectives in Iraq from Day One. They attacked Bush, lied about him and his motivations for going to war, and threatened him and the funding for his military and foreign policies. They did everything they could to destroy him and the war he was leading for their own political advantage. But what they didn't seem to get—or chose to ignore—is that political parties don't lose wars; countries do. Reid was willing to have the *United States* lose a war so the Republican president got the blame. The problem with that is that the enemy didn't see Republican and Democrat, it saw only the United States and an entire faction of the U.S. government inclined to let them win in Iraq. In this sense, the natural position of the Left is to aid and abet the enemy. They know that the enemy can hear them through the press. And by making statements such as Harry Reid's "The war is lost," they're acting as the enemy's getaway driver.

When the Iraqis went to the polls to vote in provincial elections just one week after Obama's inauguration, the Left was silent. There was no rejoicing that the much-maligned Bush surge had brought a measure of stability to the country or that the war itself had ushered in a decent, if not perfect, representative government. Their silence indicated just how much they wanted Reid's assertion to be true. It can be debated as to whether the price in blood and treasure that we paid to beat back a vicious, persistent insurgency and establish Iraq's democracy was worth it. But the reality is that the only functioning Arab democracy is the one built by the United States in Iraq—as long as the precipitous Obama withdrawal doesn't destroy it. Although its government is highly imperfect and fragile, Iraq has had competitive elections and, until very recently, the freest press in the region. Our efforts, and the sacrifices of countless American soldiers, sailors, airmen, and marines, created the conditions for the Iraqi people to have a shot at some form of self-governance.

The Persian and Arab peoples were watching. Their regimes were watching too. There were reports that the Iranian government was terrified that the Americans were going to take a turn to the east and overthrow it as well. At the most basic military strategic level, the bookends of Iraq and Afghanistan acted as a vise grip on Iran. Tehran was pinned in from both sides in case the Axis of Evil country decided to move beyond its borders. Regimes across the region were petrified that the democracy bug that had bitten the Iraqi people would bite their people too, and if the wave of democracy were allowed to spread—with or without direct U.S. help—the Middle East and the Muslim world would be revolutionized.

Not that "democracy" is a panacea. In the Gaza Strip, a democratic vote gave power to Hamas. But citizens in democracies eventually learn that their vote carries consequences. When Bush went into Iraq, he cracked the entire Middle East open. In the short and medium term, it led to chaos and upheaval, but in the longer term, it led to a potentially more stable Iraq and a more widespread regional demand for freedom, as seen in the earliest days of the so-called Arab "Spring."

None of this strategic nuance mattered much to Obama. The majority of Americans agreed that after seven years of war, it was time to pack it in, let the Iraqis run their own state, and bring the troops home. And so it was with great political confidence and personal self-satisfaction that Obama addressed the American people on that late-summer evening in 2010.

Obama could have focused the nation on the fact that we had won a lengthy and hard-fought war in Iraq, which gutted al-Qaeda there, neutralized the Shiite militias and their godfathers in Iran, inspired a growing rejection of sectarianism and embrace of nationalism, and created a relatively stable climate for regular elections. He didn't do that. Meanwhile, all that remained on Obama's plate was to negotiate a new status-of-forces agreement to replace the one Bush had negotiated in late 2008, which would allow a skeleton force to remain to consolidate the gains and our burgeoning alliance with the Iraqis. Take a moment the next time you hop into a BMW from Germany, a Lexus from Japan, or a Hyundai from South Korea, and remember that we still have military troops in each of those countries. The reason none of them have become failed states is that Presidents Truman and Eisenhower had the wisdom and foresight not only to help rebuild them, but to ensure a defense against future belligerence. The same was supposed to be true for Iraq.

The Iraqis wanted and expected the agreement to be renegotiated. Obama knew from Day One of his presidency that this needed to be done, as well as to provide American direction toward a centrist coalition government made up of predominantly Shiite, Sunni, and Kurdish blocs that had won nearly 70 percent of the popular vote in the 2010 elections. In a show of how little he cared about the future of Iraq, Obama farmed out the critically important task of influencing the Iraqi government to Joe Biden, who promptly screwed everything up, leaving an Iraq run by a narrow sectarian coalition in which the radical Iranian-controlled Muqtada al-Sadr faction held the balance of power.

As to the status-of-forces agreement, Obama deliberately wrecked it. The ostensible reason for the collapse of the agreement was that Baghdad refused to agree to legal immunity for U.S. forces. That, however, was just the superficial excuse. With the acquiescence of the Iraqis, our military commanders had strongly recommended keeping a 20,000-troop residual force to deter the Iranians, train the

Iraqis, and monitor our interests in the region. Obama wasn't interested in doing any of those things. He just wanted to get out, regardless of the ultimate cost of losing a vastly important strategic interest and creating a power vacuum into which Tehran quickly and effectively would step. The Iraqis were stunned by Obama's carelessness and disregard, as Sunni, Shiite, and Kurd must have turned to one another and asked, "What the @$%&! just happened?" In fact, the Iraqi government realized that it had to save the kook from his own bad decisions, so they quietly requested that a small U.S. training force stay in-country.

Obama, the man who claimed he would reject Bush's hard-power cowboyism for smart-power diplomacy showed neither smarts nor good diplomacy. As the new commander in chief, Obama had the responsibility to turn America's great sacrifice in Iraq into a long-term strategic win. Instead, he *deliberately* lost Iraq for the United States. He wanted us to ultimately fail there—for both political and strategic reasons—and he made sure it happened. He threw our hard-fought sacrifice into history's dustbin, and with it he accomplished his true goal: downgrading U.S. power in the region and the world. It turns out that Reid's declaration that "the war was lost" wasn't entirely wrong; it was probably just premature.

———

While he was selling out Iraq, Obama was also busy pulling the rug out from under our war effort in Afghanistan. Savor the irony: the antiwar president expanded the war in Afghanistan by ordering a surge of the kind he criticized scathingly in Iraq. Obama being Obama, however, he couldn't simply order an increase in troops along with a directive to achieve victory. No, Obama being Obama, he simultaneously announced the surge *and* the withdrawal, the plan to fight *and* the plan to exit, the commitment *and* the commitment phobia. He's the charming cad who says he'll call, then never does.

Long before he ran for president in 2008 and throughout that campaign, Obama cast Afghanistan as the "good war" in order to contrast it with Bush's "bad war" in Iraq. He constantly criticized the Bush administration for taking its "eye off the ball" of terrorism in Afghanistan and suggested that he would have surged troops there, where it counted, rather than in Iraq where, after all, the war was already "lost." Once he was elected president, Obama realized that he was now in a box of his own making. After three painfully long months of Hamlet-like indecision, Obama decided to surge 30,000 troops—tens of thousands of troops fewer than what the commanding generals requested—into Afghanistan, not because he wanted to but because he had to, lest his campaign word be broken and a perception grow that he was a typical kook, weak on national security.

Obama's heart, however, was never in the fight. That's why he gave only one major address about Afghanistan and never spoke about it again at any length. He sort of pretended that his surge wasn't happening. But if you're the commander in chief and you're sending our selfless men and women into expanded combat operations, you'd better believe in the mission. And you'd better fight to win, or you've got no business being commander in chief.

In October 2009, while Obama was still contemplating his navel over what to do in Afghanistan, the commanding general there had a tough time getting the president's attention. After all, he wasn't a member of the International Olympic Committee, a golf ball, or Jennifer Lopez.

Given those self-indulgent presidential distractions, General Stanley McChrystal could be forgiven for airing publicly his strategic and troop-level preferences. Appearing on *60 Minutes* and addressing a prestigious London think tank apparently were the only ways General McChrystal could get Obama's attention. It was the general as matador, waving the red silk, hoping the bull would turn and notice him.

The bull certainly noticed. After the general's disclosure that he had spoken to the commander in chief only once in the nearly hundred days he had the Afghanistan command, Obama then spoke to him twice: once by secure TeleLink and again aboard an idle Air Force One in Denmark for a twenty-five-minute discussion. So here was a four-star general who had been in uniform since 1976. A man who killed Abu Musab al-Zarqawi, the leader of al-Qaeda in Iraq. A West Point graduate with awards like the Defense Distinguished Service Medal. And President Barry gives him less time than he devotes to the average sit-down with Jay Leno.

Reports of the conversation said it involved a "candid exchange of views," which probably meant that General McChrystal reiterated his request for up to 40,000 additional troops in order to accomplish the goal of destroying al-Qaeda, turning back the Taliban, and stabilizing Afghanistan, while Obama requested more time to think.

In his London speech, General McChrystal was brutally honest about the consequences of failing to adopt the surge strategy. The country, he said, will quickly become "Chaos-istan." He summarily rejected the strategy advocated by Vice President Joe Biden to reduce troop levels and rely primarily on drone missile strikes, saying, "The short answer is no," when asked if he'd ever support it.

He also said, "Waiting does not prolong a favorable outcome. This effort will not remain winnable indefinitely, and nor will public support."

The White House was said to be "furious" with the general's public comments, with some commentators suggesting that his comments bordered on "insubordination." Obama's national security adviser, General James Jones, was more careful, saying, "Ideally, it's best for military advice to come up through the chain of command."

General McChrystal could be forgiven his impatience. Obama had ten months as president to get off the fence. He said repeatedly, including in January, March, and June 2009 (when he installed General McChrystal), that he had a "new strategy." When the general realized there wasn't a plan, he himself prepared one, which had been public for several weeks before he took to the airwaves. The only way McChrystal could have gotten to Obama sooner was if he mounted an attack on ESPN headquarters and commandeered a *SportsCenter* broadcast to present his Afghan war strategy.

Obama knew that McChrystal was onto him, so when the general gave the president the ammunition with which to destroy him, Obama used it. Just eight months after the general openly stated the troop levels he'd need in Afghanistan, *Rolling Stone* reported some impolitic criticisms McChrystal and some of his aides made about the commander in chief and a few of his top advisers. The general was summoned to Washington for a terse meeting at the White House, during which he was relieved of his command. The counterinsurgency genius behind the successful Iraq surge, General David Petraeus, was asked to take a demotion from being commander of U.S. Central Command to run the Afghanistan war in McChrystal's stead, and Petraeus agreed. Both generals must have said, "What the @$%&! just happened?"

Obama never laid out what victory in Afghanistan might look like—and his generals knew it. As he announced he was getting more in, he also announced he was getting out because, as with Iraq, that's what he wanted to do all along. According to his game plan, approximately 33,000 troops will be home from Afghanistan in time for the 2012 election. The Afghan troop withdrawal isn't in the national interest. It's in Barack Obama's interest.

On December 1, 2009, Obama gave his only comprehensive speech on Afghanistan, delivered in front of hundreds of cadets at the United States Military Academy at West Point. As he spoke, the camera panned the audience, capturing two moments that came to symbolize Obama's Afghanistan policy. One cadet was caught napping through the speech. Yes, the man once considered the Greatest Orator of All Time put strapping young warriors to sleep. Another cadet was spied reading a book while Obama spoke. It wasn't Heidi Montag's *How to Be Famous* or Suzanne Somers' *Eat Great, Lose Weight*. No, the West Point cadet was reading *Kill Bin Laden: A Delta Force Commander's Account of the Hunt for the World's Most Wanted Man*. That image said it all: the baby-faced cadet had more apparent fight in him, more passion for the cause, more urgency on behalf of his country, than the commander in chief under whom he was about to serve.

In his speech, Obama spoke not of victory but of national limitations. That wasn't exactly the quintessential American way. We know we have limitations as a nation, but we don't want to hear our president fence us in with them. The president is supposed to transcend those limitations, to get the country to go big—and win. He's supposed to be Carol Brady, not Debbie Downer. His Afghanistan speech should have stirred the soul with a sense of renewed national commitment to defeating the mass-murdering al-Qaeda and Taliban enemy and an unwavering determination of a nation at war. Instead, Obama looked like the two-bit law lecturer he is, trying to community-organize Afghanistan.

In addition to containing the good war/bad war characterization of Afghanistan and Iraq, Obama's speech was chockablock with his typical faculty-lounge dichotomies. On the one hand, he announced that it was "in our vital national interest to send an additional thirty thousand troops to Afghanistan." On the other hand, he announced an exit strategy: "After eighteen months, our troops will begin to come home." On the one hand, he was escalating the war. On the other, he was ending it. His policy was the equivalent of FDR telling Hitler and Hirohito that we were serious about defeating the whole fascism thing but we're outta there by 1944.

Obama played his cards faceup. And he set up our military to fail. Once troop withdrawals begin in earnest, he'll be able to say he gave the generals what they wanted (Petraeus, no less!) and they simply couldn't make it work. Our enemies know what the timeline is. Our allies know they can't count on us. And our troops know they're risking their lives for a mission their commander in chief has written off. They weren't allowed to win the war in a way that would have sent a clear message to the enemy.

Obama's sole "strategy" on Afghanistan was to limit the enemy to al-Qaeda, so once bin Laden and other top al-Qaeda terrorists had been killed, he could declare success and get out. Beyond that, the policy has been all confused tactics, without a grand plan to create an effective Afghan fighting force, a responsible Afghan government, or a coherent strategy to deal with Afghanistan's nuclear-armed neighbor, Pakistan. It had long been assumed by both Teams Bush and Obama that getting and keeping Pakistan on our side was the key to prevailing in Afghanistan. In fact, the opposite is true: proving our commitment to defeating the enemy in Afghanistan so they cannot return and use the country as a terrorist base would finally force Pakistan's leaders to deal with their own Taliban and terrorist presence, before they have the chance to seize power, as they almost did in 2009 when the security situation in Afghanistan was particularly bad. If Obama goes through with his withdrawal, Pakistan will face rising Islamist radicalism and the unthinkable possibility of al-Qaeda or the Haqqani terror network getting control of Pakistan's nuclear weapons. The inevitable chaos and carnage would most certainly spread into Afghanistan.

During his Afghanistan speech at West Point, Obama sounded exasperated that he had to deal with such a messy mess at all. After contemplating the age-old nature of war, Obama said, "I do not bring with me today a definitive solution to the problems of war." Well now.

Then came his familiar invocation: "But we do not have to think that human nature is perfect for us to still believe that the human condition can be perfected." Well now.

When the civilized world encounters evil, Obama believes he can formulate a sociological hypothesis for why it exists and how he can work with it.

An outrageous case in point: in very early 2012, the *Hindu* reported that Team Obama had turned to Sheikh Yusuf al-Qaradawi, the Muslim Brotherhood's leading legal authority, to mediate secret negotiations between the United States and the Taliban. Qaradawi is the most influential Sunni Islamist in the world. In 2003, he issued a fatwa calling for the killing of U.S. troops in Iraq. He calls for a world dominated by Islam and a global caliphate governed by sharia. He openly calls for jihad, suicide bombings, and the murder of civilians, and he supports Hamas and the destruction of Israel. Obama allegedly wanted this sworn enemy of the United States and Israel to help him get a deal that would install our Taliban enemies as part of a sharia state in Afghanistan. Part of the deal was to involve the release of high-level Taliban prisoners from Guantánamo

Bay in exchange for the Taliban opening a "political office" for "peace talks" in Qatar. One of the Taliban operatives on the Obama release list was Mullah Mohammed Fazi, a terrorist so fearsome that he's wanted by the UN for war crimes for the slaughter of thousands of Shiites when he served as the Taliban army chief of staff. The U.S. military has continued to detain him because it's deemed him a "high risk" for jihadist recidivism and a threat to the Afghan government. But Obama apparently thought it a swell idea to release this guy. As if that weren't bad enough, the administration also signaled that it would agree to lift UN sanctions against the Taliban and recognize it as a legitimate political party. For its part, the Taliban claimed that it would forswear violence, dump al-Qaeda, and promise to play nice with its rivals in the Karzai government. As if. Perhaps this is what Obama meant when he talked of a "more perfect union": one that got into bed with our most lethal enemies, believed their sweet nothing lies, and supported their ambitions while the American people got screwed without so much as dinner and a movie first.

The reality is that we're not going to turn Afghan president Hamid Karzai into Thomas Jefferson, although we might be able to score him a panelist gig on *Project Runway*. We're also not going to turn Afghanistan into Malibu. But what we can still achieve is an Afghan army strong enough to deal with the terrorist presence and a decent enough Afghan government that can work hand in glove with tribal leaders to keep the country stable.

And yet, as with Iraq, Obama has chosen weakness and surrender over strength and victory in Afghanistan. It's a strategy that will likely lead to deadly global convulsions. But Obama's objective in Iraq and Afghanistan is not to win and advance our interests but to wrap up what someone else started, redirect the "saved" money to his domestic projects, reduce American power and influence in the region, and use our losses there as punishing levers of humiliation against the United States.

You Say You Want a Revolution

The best day after a bad emperor is the first.

—*Tacitus, Roman historian*

In the mythology of the 2011 Arab Spring, a slap across the face set off a chain of events that changed the world. On the morning of December 17, 2010, a struggling Tunisian street vendor named Mohamed Bouazizi rolled his small cart of fruit and produce into his usual area in his hometown, Sidi Bouzid. The police arrived and began harassing him for not having the correct permit. Lacking the funds to bribe them, Bouazizi was then subjected to a humiliating beating by the local police, including a female municipal officer, Faida Hamdi, who allegedly slapped Bouazizi, spat on him, confiscated his weighing scales, and turned over his produce cart. Enraged and humiliated, Bouazizi dashed to the governor's office, only to be turned away. He then ran to a nearby gas station, got a can of gasoline, and went back to the governor's office. As he stood in the middle of midday traffic, Bouazizi shouted, "How do you expect me to earn a living?" He then doused himself and lit a match. Eighteen days after his self-immolation, he died.

Within hours of Bouazizi's altercation, protests sprang up over his treatment at the hands of the Tunisian government, first in Sidi Bouzid and then across the country. To the protesters' amazement, the army stood down and refused to fire upon them. Zine el-Abidine Ben Ali, the dictator who had kept them poor and enslaved, fled to Saudi Arabia on January 14, 2011, a mere month after Bouazizi set himself aflame. He became the first dictator to fall in the so-called Arab "Spring."

The roots of the upheaval are vast and diverse. Much of the Arab world lived under repressive regimes that allowed little or no personal freedom while their economic conditions deteriorated under rising food prices and sky-high unemployment, particularly among young people. Fed up with their regimes' inability and unwillingness to improve economic conditions and grant them even the most basic human rights, many in the Arab world discovered the courage to stand up to their governments.

It was a courage first inspired by President Bush, who advocated an aggressive "freedom agenda," about which Obama had expressed his opposition, primarily because it was applied most controversially in Iraq. But the overthrow of Saddam Hussein allowed the Iraqi people to be liberated from exactly the kind of dictator millions of Arabs protested in early 2011. The power of the Iraqi example is difficult to measure, but what isn't tough to see is the widespread desire for a greater voice.

The Arab Spring actually began over a year earlier with the Persian Spring, when a genuine revolt against tyranny began next door to Iraq, in Iran. On June 13, 2009, millions of Iranians poured into the streets, outraged over what they viewed as a fraudulent election that handed the presidency back to Mahmoud Ahmadinejad over opposition candidates Mir Hossein Mousavi and Mehdi Karroubi. Mousavi's campaign color had been green, and his supporters wore the color when they demonstrated against the regime, leading the movement to be called the Green Revolution. Protesters relied heavily on Facebook, Twitter, and other social networking sites to communicate with each other, until the government slowed them or shut them down completely. Soon, however, much of Tehran and other major cities were seas of green. The Iranian regime wasted little time cracking down. It began mass arrests of prominent reformist leaders, human rights advocates, and journalists. The Iranian government militia, the Basij, stormed the protests, deploying tear gas, breaking into houses and businesses, rounding people up and detaining them, and firing live ammunition into the crowds, killing and injuring dozens of people. As the casualties mounted and women were raped and tortured, Obama did nothing. As Iranian militias attacked students in their dorm rooms and Internet censorship spread, Obama did nothing. The mullahcracy that had been the number one state sponsor of terror for thirty years was teetering on the brink of collapse . . . and Obama did nothing.

While millions of Iranians were courageously taking their lives in their hands, they looked to the United States for support. They would have appreciated covert assistance in terms of sophisticated communication technology that would have allowed them to get around Tehran's censorship, among other things. But they would have settled for some basic moral support, a word or two from the American president in support of their aspirations for greater freedom. Instead, they got crickets and tumbleweeds from the White House. The seat reserved for the Leader of the Free World was empty.

During the 2008 campaign, Obama had promised to open negotiations with Iran "without preconditions." Several months after he became president, Obama sent good tidings to the regime at the start of the Iranian new year. He offered "the promise of a new beginning" that was "grounded in mutual respect." That came after his inaugural address announcement that he'd cozy up to enemies like Iran: "To those who cling to power through corruption and deceit and the silencing of dissent, know that you are on the wrong side of history; but that we will extend a hand if you are willing to unclench your fist." Iran greeted his "extended hand" by grabbing three American hikers on its border and holding them for two years, escalating war games, and threatening to close the Strait of Hormuz, through which over one-third of the world's oil flows.

Obama's obsession with striking a grand bargain with the Iranian regime over its nuclear weapons program was based on a single objective: he wanted to strike a historic rapprochement with Iran. If Nixon could walk through the streets of Beijing in 1972, Obama could very well walk through the streets of Tehran. Nothing would alter Obama's course of pursuing "engagement" with the Iranian terrorist dictators, not even their mass slaughter of their own people.

Obama thought that through the sheer force of his dazzling persona, he'd be able to convince the mullahs to at least pretend to want to give up the nuke dream. That, of course, was absurd on its face. Once Iran got a nuke, it would dominate the Persian Gulf, threaten Israel's very survival, and set off a regional arms race that would likely see Saudi Arabia and possibly Jordan, Egypt, and Turkey going nuclear. In fact, in early 2012 Saudi Arabia struck a deal with China to develop nuclear capability. The entire Middle East—already a white-hot tinderbox—would explode in nuclear-weapons-driven instability, but Iran would be driving the bus. They were getting tantalizingly close to their game-changing possession of a nuke just as the American president was making a yahoo out of himself with his "extended hand."

Meanwhile, negotiations over Iran's nuclear program through the United Nations and the Europeans dragged on. A lot of talking was done, mostly by everyone but the Iranians. Time and again, the Iranians talked and stalled, stalled and talked. In November 2009, Team Obama said it was willing to give Iran more time to decide whether to accept a UN-brokered deal to get Iran to move its stocks of low-enriched uranium to Russia or another country in exchange for fuel for a nuclear medicine laboratory. Iran hemmed and hawed, asking for countless amendments and more talks. The U.S. government offered all kinds of incentives, from Miley Cyrus tickets to a week of all-inclusive heaven at Sandals in Jamaica. They even offered up a chance for Ayatollah Khamenei to hang out with the stars of MTV's *16 and Pregnant*. In the end, the Iranians bailed on the deal.

Instead of dealing more realistically with a regime that had no intention of negotiating away its nuclear weapons program, Obama continued to make more accommodations, including dropping a key condition that Iran shut down its nuclear facilities during the early stages of talks. European negotiators, along with Team Obama, said they were interested in "building trust," to which the Iranians replied by again laughing themselves silly.

As those "negotiations" were going on, the Manhattan District Attorney's office unsealed a 118-count indictment accusing a Chinese national of setting up fake companies to hide his sale of millions of dollars in potential nuclear materials to Iran. And then in late July 2011, Obama's own Treasury Department accused Iranian authorities of aiding al-Qaeda in Iran, Kuwait, Qatar, and Pakistan. A few months after that, in October 2011, Obama's Justice Department busted two men with ties to Iran for allegedly plotting to blow up the Saudi and Israeli embassies in Washington and to assassinate the Saudi ambassador to the United States. This is the same Iran about which Team Obama was still "unclear" as to whether it was pursuing nuclear weapons, the same Persian Shiite country that leftists who pose as Middle East experts constantly swear would never assist an Arab Sunni terrorist network like al-Qaeda.

In November 2011, the International Atomic Energy Agency issued a definitive report saying that Iran was, in fact, actively conducting work "specific" to nuclear arms. Furthermore, the Iranian government put on a four-day "firepower show" earlier that year that showcased new missiles, developed with the help of Russian, Chinese, and North Korean technology, that have a range of 1,200 miles—putting Israel and U.S. allies, forces, and interests in the region easily within striking distance.

And still, Team Obama chased the Iranians—in Secretary of State Hillary Clinton's case, literally. At a gala dinner in Bahrain in 2010, she chased Iranian foreign minister Manouchehr Mottaki around the room, hoping to get a word with him, only to be completely blown off. Clinton told reporters on the plane ride home, "I got up to leave and he was sitting several seats down from me and . . . he saw me and he stopped and began to turn away. And I said, 'Hello, Minister!' And he just turned away." Denied! But Hillary went back for another insult. While they were both standing outside waiting for their motorcades, Clinton called out to Mottaki again, only to be met by his stony silence, like Sandra Bullock's giddy stalker character in *All About Steve*.

Obama's "extended hand" approach was, from the beginning, appeasement. After months of olive branches, bending over backward to accommodate the Iranians, lavishing them with money and other incentives, groveling at them at formal dinners and, apologizing incessantly for big, bad America, Tehran was still moving at breakneck speed to develop nuclear weapons. It got so obvious that even Obama, who had staked so much on his personal ability to get Iran off its nuclear track, had to go along with some financial sanctions. In early August 2011, ninety-two of one hundred senators sent Obama a letter demanding "crippling sanctions" on Iran's central bank, some of which the administration ultimately imposed.

Throughout the discussion of ramped-up sanctions, the Russians and the Chinese resisted them. Russia is the Costco for radical Islamic regimes, communist states, totalitarian dictatorships, and banana republics. They all go shopping there, buy big, and get great discounts. When Russian president Dmitry Medvedev visited the United States in September 2009 and indicated a possible willingness to support increased sanctions, it was described later by the Russians as Medvedev's merely being "polite" to Obama, not as a major shift in Russian policy. As Russian prime minister Vladimir Putin put it, "There is no need to frighten the Iranians."

Without truly regime-ending sanctions, Iran continues its march toward becoming a nuclear-armed terrorist state, unless either the United States or Israel takes some form of military action to foster regime change or at least set the program back, as the Israelis did by bombing Saddam Hussein's Osirak nuclear facility in 1981 and a suspect nuclear facility in Syria in 2007. Don't be surprised if Obama approves military action against Iran as we approach the presidential election in order to sow new chaos to make voters forget about his old chaos and to encourage a rallying effect. He is, after all, a Machiavellian Alinskyite. Absent direct military action or the full success of the cloak-and-dagger covert campaign against Iran's nuke program, however, Tehran will careen headlong to a "breakout" moment with its nuclear program, giving the mullahs—who deny the Holocaust; call for eliminating Israel; support al-Qaeda, Hezbollah, and Hamas; export international terror; and help to kill American soldiers in Iraq and Afghanistan—the ability to extort and commit mass murder with weapons of mass destruction.

As they worked on nukes, those multitasking Iranian leaders continued to mow down their people. When Obama did finally address the situation, he issued a vague statement to the "Supreme Leader" on the election-results controversy. The United States had been waiting for thirty years for this moment in Iran and the president makes a weak comment essentially supportive of the Supreme Leader who was killing them in the streets? The Iranian protesters must have thought, "What the @$%&! just happened?" If Obama had offered greater moral and even material support to the 2009 Iranian revolution, the ramifications may have been sweeping. If it had succeeded, it would have dealt a major blow to Islamic radicalism and terror. Iran's nuclear weapons program may have been significantly slowed or even stopped. Terrorist states such as Syria and terrorist organizations such as Hamas and Hezbollah, who lean on Iran for financial and military support, may have been weakened. There may have been a collective sigh of relief in the Sunni Arab world that the Shia mullahs were no longer a threat. In retrospect, Bush perhaps should have moved on Iran rather than Iraq, as some foreign policy observers argued at the time, but when Obama had the opening, he wouldn't move on Iran either.

In the end, the man who ran on "hope and change" simply couldn't support those things for the Iranian people.

Obama's impotence led to an even greater perception in Tehran that America was in terminal decline, and therefore there was no need for the regime to consider Obama's prostrating offers on their nuclear program or to fear U.S. threats. If the American president couldn't even muster a "go get 'em" for the Iranian people as they stared down tanks and guns, then he was a paper tiger. Iran slapped away Obama's hand each time he extended it—including blocking the "virtual" U.S. "embassy" Hillary's State Department had put online and Obama's pathetic, repeated attempts to reach out to the Supreme Leader for "talks." And the paper tiger kept cowering in a cage of its own making.

If there was any positive fallout from the Iranian people's courage in 2009, it was seen in the millions of Arabs who poured into their streets a year and a half later to demand their own change. In the initial stages of the Arab revolts, the usual rabid anti-Americanism and anti-Israeli sentiment weren't apparent. Early on, hundreds of thousands of people poured into the streets in Egypt, Tunisia, Morocco, Jordan, and Lebanon, followed by demonstrations in Syria, Libya, Yemen, Algeria, Bahrain, and even a part of Saudi Arabia.

The most consequential revolt took place in Egypt, the most populous Arab state and the most strategically important. Having seen Tunisia's longtime dictator overthrown by largely peaceful mass demonstrations, many Egyptians thought they might be able to dislodge their longtime president, Hosni Mubarak. Mubarak had come to power in 1981 following the assassination of his predecessor, Anwar el-Sadat, at the hands of the Islamists of the Muslim Brotherhood. Mubarak was rampantly corrupt, abusive, repressive, and tyrannical at home, but abroad he was a pragmatist. He continued Sadat's policy of peace with Israel, outlawed the Muslim Brotherhood and other Islamist groups, and maintained a strong alliance with the United States, which rewarded him with over $1.3 billion annually in military and other aid.

So when the crud hit the fan in Egypt on January 25, 2011, and the masses began filling the streets to protest his rule, Mubarak could have reasonably expected that the United States would either back him or stay out of the internal situation completely, as it had with Iran. Instead, Obama saw big crowds of indeterminate nature in the street of Cairo and, within eight days, told Mubarak to scram. Sitting alone, late at night, contemplating the American knife in his back, Mubarak could be heard mumbling, "What the @$%&! just happened?"

Obama, who had publicly dissed Bush's "freedom agenda" and squashed it in Iran, now attempted to co-opt it by micromanaging Egypt's revolt. With so much at stake strategically in Egypt, the United States should have been helping to move it toward a government more consistent with our values of political and economic freedom and rule of law as well as respect for those like Israel that embody those values. Instead, Obama took actions that assured a very different kind of outcome in Egypt.

Was Mubarak a dictator? No, said Biden. Yes, according to everyone else in the Obama administration. Should he bug out? Yes, and like "yesterday," according to Obama's press secretary, Robert Gibbs. Obama himself said he should consider his "legacy" and "go." But according to Obama's own special envoy to Egypt, Ambassador Frank Wisner, he should stay for the sake of stability. Not so fast, according to Secretary Clinton, who suggested that we'd be okay with Mubarak staying in office but allowing Vice President Omar Suleiman to run the show. For how long? Unnamed "senior administration officials" said elections must take place by June 2011, but Clinton said September would be fine. In the middle of a major foreign policy crisis, we didn't get a president and his team speaking with a single voice. We got a cacophony.

Our other allies in the region, from the Saudis to the Jordanians and the Israelis, watched this tangled diplomatic mess and were frantic with worry and exasperation. If Obama could so easily discard such a key, long-standing ally, might they be next? America's friendship just got seriously downgraded. And America's prestige in the Arab world skidded into the dumps. No longer feared, we were also no longer trusted or even liked.

While Team Obama was busy destroying American influence in the region, the crowds in Tahrir Square were kicking it up to the next level. Pro-Mubarak forces emerged on camelback and violent altercations broke out. Nearly a thousand people were killed and scores more injured.

Back in the West, we romanticized the revolt. In its earliest stages, there were some protesters who did truly want greater freedom, more economic opportunity, and better human rights for the Egyptian people. But were they the majority of the protesters? Was that the goal of the organizers? Is that what most Egyptians wanted? These were serious questions, which few people (least of whom the president) bothered to ask at the time. For decades, Mubarak warned that if he were to lose his grip on power, the Muslim Brotherhood and other Islamists would seize the levers of power in Egypt. Many foreign policy elites derided that as a false choice that was meant to frighten us into constant support of his regime. And yet, golly gee, it turns out that Mubarak knew Egypt better than they did.

The Egyptian protests began with a small group of organizers meeting in the Cairo apartment of one of their mothers. It included a few student leaders, Wael Ghonim, the Google executive who would mobilize social media to get people into the streets, and two representatives from . . . the Muslim Brotherhood.

The Brotherhood, or Ikhwan, was founded in Egypt in 1928 and is now the world's most important and dangerous Islamist organization. It is openly committed to the infiltration and ultimate destruction of the United States, the West, and Israel. Its motto is: "Allah is our objective; the Prophet is our Leader; the Koran is our Law; Jihad is our way; Dying in the way of Allah is our highest hope—Allahu Akbar!"

And yet, Team Obama thinks this is a group with whom we can do business. Previous contacts with the Brotherhood had occurred outside U.S. policy, egged on mainly by leftists in the State Department, intelligence communities, and Team Obama. As part of his vaunted policy of "engagement" with our enemies, Obama opened formal contacts with the Brotherhood and sought out its Palestinian terror branch, Hamas. The previous policy of non-engagement with the Brotherhood was meant to prevent a legitimizing of its stealth jihadist agenda and designating its leaders as mainstream. But Team Obama moved to do exactly that.

James Clapper, Obama's director of national intelligence, testified to Congress that he wasn't much worried about the Muslim Brotherhood because it was a moderate, "largely secular" organization with "no overarching agenda." His wildly incorrect assessment of the Brotherhood came just weeks after ABC News' Diane Sawyer had to inform him of the arrests of twelve terrorism suspects in London, about which Clapper had no clue.

Several months before Clapper's comments, the Muslim Brotherhood's Supreme Guide, Mohammed al-Badi, called for waging jihad against the United States: "Arab and Muslim regimes are betraying their people by failing to confront the Muslims' real enemies, not only Israel but *also the United States. Waging jihad against both of these infidels is a commandment of Allah that cannot be disregarded.*" (Emphasis added.) So much for "renouncing violence." So much for not targeting the United States. Al-Badi, like the Iranian mullahs, went on to say that America was in irreversible decline and therefore ripe for jihad. In fact, the Brotherhood has always supported the use of violence when it would advance Islamism; it only tactically renounced violence against the Egyptian government because it knew Mubarak would have come down on them like a brick house and because they were advancing the Islamist agenda through the system anyway.

Shortly after Mubarak exited, the Brotherhood brought back to Egypt from exile its foremost jurist, Sheikh Yusuf al-Qaradawi. His return was announced at a massive post-Mubarak rally, at which Ghonim, the young Google guy who had helped to set the revolution in motion, was thanked and promptly escorted off the stage. (This is the same Qaradawi to whom Obama reportedly turned to "mediate" negotiations with the Afghan Taliban. Leave it to Obama to bring together those two crazy kids, the Muslim Brothers and the Taliban!)

The young people and democrats who had propelled the early days of the Egyptian revolt were cast out, like the useful idiots they were, and the Brotherhood immediately set out to forge an alliance with the ruling military regime. The Muslim Brothers had waited eighty years for this moment in Egypt. They're not about to blow it.

In the eyes of Obama, Mubarak was a horrible dictator who had to go, but the Muslim Brotherhood is a reasonable bunch of chaps who are just misunderstood. Under President Bush, all brands of Islamists were considered threats. Under Obama, we're killing some of them and getting into bed with others. It shows the Islamic enemy—whether it's al-Qaeda, the Muslim Brotherhood, or any other group—that we are unserious about waging the broader war against Islamism in all its forms.

On Super Bowl Sunday in February 2011, Fox News' Bill O'Reilly sat down with Obama in the White House for a pregame interview. He asked Obama point-blank if the Muslim Brotherhood was a threat to the United States. "I think that the Muslim Brotherhood is one faction in Egypt," Obama replied. "They don't have majority support in Egypt. But they are well organized and there are strains of their ideology that are anti-U.S."

Saying that the Muslim Brotherhood has "anti-U.S." elements is like saying al-Qaeda has "anti-U.S." elements. We have long been clear that al-Qaeda, the Taliban, Hamas, and Hezbollah are the enemy. We've been less clear as to whether the Brotherhood is the enemy. According to their own statements and beliefs, the Muslim Brothers are sworn enemies of the United States and our allies. But Obama's reluctance to identify them as a threat speaks volumes.

First, if he answered that the Brotherhood is indeed an enemy of the United States, he'd then be obliged to take them on here by getting tougher on the Council on American Islamic Relations (CAIR), the Islamic Society of North America (ISNA), the Muslim Students Association (MSA), and other organizations frequently referred to as Muslim Brotherhood "front" or "associated" groups. He'd also have to confront his pro-terror pals like Rashid Khalidi and Bill Ayers. And he'd have to take on the Islamists in Egypt and elsewhere. He is unwilling to do those things. And second, by refusing to identify the Brotherhood as a threat, he revealed his position on Islamism, which is to let it set up shop anywhere it likes.

The only way to defeat an enemy is by first being honest about who they are and their intentions and then to be relentless and, if necessary, ruthless in battling them.

Obama not only refuses to call the Brotherhood an enemy of the United States, but he's moved toward proactively embracing them as a potential partner. Did Obama *want* the Muslim Brotherhood to control Egypt all along? Is that why he rushed to toss Mubarak under the bus? Did Obama also see the University of Maryland's WorldPublicOpinion.org poll of Egyptian Muslims conducted between late 2006 and early 2007 that showed that 67 percent of those interviewed wanted "to unify all Islamic countries into a single Islamic state or Caliphate" and that a whopping 74 percent of those polled wanted "a strict application of sharia law in every Islamic country"? Did he also see a more recent 2011 Pew Research Center poll that showed that 62 percent of respondents in Egypt wanted sharia and 50 percent said that it was "very important" for religious parties to be part of any future government? Did Obama know that if the secular regime of

Mubarak collapsed, the vast majority of Egyptians would choose an Islamist replacement and sharia? Obama knew that the Muslim Brotherhood was the most organized and well-funded political organization in Egypt, and therefore he knew that it was the group most likely to ascend to power if elections were held quickly. Rather than push for a delay in the elections to give more secular groups time to establish themselves as legitimate opponents to the Brotherhood, Obama demanded speedy polling and a "full transfer to a civilian government" to those best positioned to take it over: the Islamists.

Given the Egyptian people's feelings about Islamism and sharia, it should have shocked no one that the Muslim Brotherhood did, in fact, prevail in the first parliamentary elections since Mubarak's ouster—particularly after the Islamists won big in the two first Arab Spring elections, in Tunisia and Morocco. The Islamists have been very clever in cloaking their true affiliations and intentions. In Tunisia, they called themselves the Revival Party. In Morocco, they were the Justice and Development Party. And in Egypt, the Muslim Brotherhood christened itself the Freedom and Justice Party. The even more openly extreme Salafists called themselves the Light Party. Of course, no one in the White House or in the West at large considered what the Islamists *meant* by "revival," "freedom," and "justice." They meant justice under sharia and the freedom to follow sharia, certainly not our conceptions of "freedom" and "justice."

By the end of polling in early 2012, it was clear that the Islamists had walked away with Egypt: 70 percent of the vote went to the Brothers and the Salafists, giving them full majority control of parliament.

The results of the first post-Mubarak elections likely *did* shock Jimmy Carter, who had earlier said, "I think the Muslim Brotherhood is not anything to be afraid of in the upcoming political situation and the evolution I see as most likely. They will be subsumed in the overwhelming demonstration of desire for freedom and true democracy." Right again, Jimmy!

Here's the extent of Carter's myopia: the only shining achievement in his sorry record as president is the Camp David accords formalizing the peace between Israel and Egypt. And yet, over thirty years later, he's cheering on an Islamist mob committed to destroying that peace and, along with it, his legacy.

Even before the elections that cemented the Brotherhood's hold on power, the Egyptian military began wooing some of Israel's and our biggest enemies. The glorious new government set out to empower Iran and its regional clients, including terrorist groups Hamas and Hezbollah. In February 2011, two Iranian warships were permitted by the "New Egypt" to sail through the Suez Canal into the Mediterranean Sea for the first time since Iran's 1979 Islamic Revolution. They were en route to participate in war games with their ally, Syria. Iran appointed an ambassador to Egypt in April 2011 for the first time in three decades; Egypt's new foreign minister reopened the Rafah crossing into Gaza, allowing the freer flow of weapons and militants there; and Egypt's new intelligence chief chose to visit Syria on his first foreign trip. The "New Egypt" also allowed the repeated bombing of the major oil pipeline into Israel while it considered whether to abrogate the Camp David accords. In one massive Brotherhood rally at Cairo's most prestigious mosque right before the elections in November 2011, thousands of Egyptians vowed to "one day kill all Jews."

———

Now that the Islamists are going pedal to the metal in Egypt, they'll make sure the new Egyptian constitution is Islamist, overwhelm the military's listless attempt to blunt the Islamists' influence, increasingly threaten the Coptic Christians, and shift away from the United States and Israel and toward Iran. All in the Islamists' day's work.

Most ominously, Obama's actions suggest that he *preferred and sought* the rise of the Islamists. After the Brotherhood secured power, Team Obama okayed $1.5 billion in aid to Egypt. Obama was also fine with the Brotherhood and other Islamists positioning themselves to take over in Syria, Libya, and elsewhere. Mubarak's Egypt was no flower bed of freedom, but the successor regime is even less committed to human rights and openly hostile to our interests. Mission accomplished, Mr. President. Pandora's box had been opened, and all across the Muslim world the mobs on the Arab street were seeking armed revolution in the name of Islam.

———

The successful overthrow of Mubarak emboldened the Syrian people to attempt to dispose of their own brutally oppressive regime, headed by Bashar al-Assad, the former ophthalmologist and son of the previous dictator. Thousands of people poured into the streets of Damascus and other cities, but unlike in Egypt and Tunisia, where the armies largely stood down, Syrian security forces cracked down with extreme violence, as they had in Iran. Over the many months of upheaval, thousands of people have been killed and scores more injured by the Syrian regime, which is propped up by its brother-in-terrorist arms, Iran.

Although Obama had helped to shove longtime ally Mubarak from power, when an actual enemy of the United States was under pressure from within, Obama invoked the same response he gave during the 2009 Iranian revolt. He summoned some weak outrage over the slaughter and then announced that Assad had "lost legitimacy." Hillary Clinton, like Obama, resisted the call to publicly demand the removal of Assad. In fact, months earlier, she had indicated that the administration had big hopes for him: "Many of the members of Congress of both parties who have gone to Syria in recent months have said they believe he's a reformer."

Say what? Assad had always run the same vicious police state as his father, the mass-murdering Hafez al-Assad. And yet, Hillary and Obama believed that the younger Assad was moments away from becoming a committed democratic reformer and human rights champion. That's probably why Clinton exploded with frustration when someone dared to ask her why Team Obama wasn't demanding Assad's exit. "It's not going to be any news if the United States says, 'Assad needs to go.' Okay, fine. What's next?" she asked.

Neither she nor Obama wondered "what's next" in Egypt before they called for Mubarak's ouster—and we got the Muslim Brotherhood. If her point was that in Egypt our words carried more weight because Mubarak had been an ally but would carry none with an enemy such as Syria, then she and Obama once again dismissed the importance of a moral declaration on the part of the United States. As usual, Team Obama went to the United Nations for a typically tooth-less resolution condemning the violence, expressing "grave concern," and levying some weak sanctions on the regime. It was as if he had taken his response to the Iranian regime's mass murder and read from a Xeroxed copy. Months into the slaughter, Obama and Clinton ulti-mately did call for Assad to pack up his "lost legitimacy" and "step down," and by early 2012 they were whispering about an international "militarization" of Syria—perhaps because by that point, the Muslim Brotherhood and other Islamists were better prepared to ascend. Assad, of course, ignored the White House. Meanwhile, his thugs stormed our embassy in Damascus; the U.S. ambassador, whom Obama had re-posted in an ill-conceived attempt at "engagement," was ultimately forced to flee. Team Obama's response? To request compensation from Damascus for the property damage to the embassy. This is what happens when you put liberals in charge of foreign policy.

So pathetic was Obama's response to the Syrian slaughter that even the grossly corrupt Arab League moved more aggressively against the regime, suspending Syria's membership and levying stronger sanctions. In January 2012, the most direct denunciation of Assad came from, of all people, French president Nicolas Sarkozy, who called publicly for Assad to step down. Meanwhile, as with Iran and Egypt, Obama's policy toward Syria was strategically and morally bankrupt—and that wasn't by accident.

———

There is, after all, one thing that all of Obama's responses to the Arab revolts have in common: he has supported the revolutions that will ultimately turn previously secular states into Islamist ones. He has supported those who are either defending Islamist regimes (in Iran) or those who seek to establish them (in Egypt, Syria, Tunisia, Libya, Turkey, and Yemen). He has refused to stand by more secular allies (Mubarak, Yemen's Saleh, Libya's Gadhafi, who had his more secular moments) while reaching out to Islamists, particularly of the Brotherhood.

It's either a wild coincidence that Obama has sided with the forces of Islamism, or it's by design. If large swaths of the Middle East fall to the Islamists, many observers will ask, "Who lost Egypt, etc.?" But if Obama's *intention* were to encourage the Islamists' ascent, he won't view it as a loss at all. In fact, he'll view the Islamist revolutions as the expression of what he *meant* by "democracy" in the Muslim world.

It's not up to America, you see, to choose governments for the rest of the world or even to try to influence pro-American outcomes. The United States is simply a passive observer, a facilitator at best, declining in power anyway. If much of the Muslim world chooses Islamists, then the United States would respect that choice and work with them. Under Obama, moral equivalence between allies and bad guys rules the day, and the bad guys are the preferred choice of the American president. The kooks are community-organizing the Muslim world, and what better way to do that than by working side by side with the ultimate community organizers of the Muslim Brotherhood?

Springtime for Moammar and Libya

> **I don't oppose all wars. . . . What I am opposed to is a dumb war. What I am opposed to is a rash war.**
>
> —*Illinois state senator Barack Obama*
> *speaking on Iraq, October 2, 2002*

On that autumn day in 2002, Barack Obama stood before an antiwar rally in Chicago and said that Saddam Hussein's extreme brutality wasn't enough to justify removing him from power using military force.

"I also know," he said, "that Saddam poses no imminent and direct threat to the United States, or to his neighbors, that the Iraqi economy is in shambles, that the Iraqi military is a fraction of its former strength, and that in concert with the international community he can be contained until, in the way of all petty dictators, he falls away into the dustbin of history."

Instead of deposing Saddam by force, he said, we should "fight" for democratic reforms in nations such as Saudi Arabia and Egypt (right on track!), tougher international nuclear safeguards (welcome to the nuclear club, Iran!), and energy independence (yes to Solyndra and other green jobs boondoggles but no to the private-sector Keystone XL pipeline!). "Those are the battles that we need to fight," he said. "Those are the battles that we willingly join—the battles against ignorance and intolerance, corruption and greed. Poverty and despair." Note the shades of the "social justice" speech he gave just days after the September 11, 2001, attacks.

What a difference a few years and actually being president make.

For four decades, Libyan dictator Moammar Gadhafi was the Michael Jackson of the Middle East. Gadhafi often wore elaborate military uniforms, complete with decorative epaulets, favored an elite bodyguard unit made up strictly of women, sported dark shades even at night, slept in oxygenated tents, and had his plastic surgeon on speed dial. He moonwalked across the region, luxuriating in his own bizarre rituals and cult of weird personality.

Gadhafi had been a charter member of the original swingin' Rat Pack of Terrorists, which included the Chairman of the Board Yasser Arafat (you know, if you can make it in Ramallah, you can make it anywhere). In the 1980s Libyan agents bombed the La Belle nightclub in West Berlin and blew up Pan Am flight 103 over Lockerbie, Scotland, killing 270 people, most of whom were Americans. Gadhafi supported various international terrorists, including the Palestinian Liberation Organization (PLO), Carlos the Jackal and the Revolutionary Armed Forces of Colombia (FARC), and the Black September movement, which carried out the massacre of Israeli athletes at the 1972 Summer Olympics in Munich, and who gave safe harbor to the convicted terrorist of Pan Am 103, Abdelbaset al-Megrahi. But President Reagan's punishing retaliatory attacks chastened Gadhafi, who never again attacked us.

Following the 2003 invasion of Iraq, Gadhafi was so worried that he was going to be the next target of U.S.-led regime change that he reached out to Washington to resolve outstanding issues between his government and the United States. President George W. Bush's team brokered a deal with Gadhafi in which he abandoned his advanced weapons programs, including his nascent nuclear program, and began providing the Bush and Obama administrations with critical intelligence about the Islamists and terrorists operating within Libya and in the region. Libya is overrun with Islamists who seek to destroy America and the West; on a per capita basis, more Libyans joined the jihad against the United States in Iraq than Islamists from any other nation. Ultimately, the State Department took Libya off the U.S. list of state sponsors of terror because Gadhafi had become "an increasingly valuable partner against terrorism."

Gadhafi warmly engaged Bush secretary of state Condoleezza Rice and even displayed a crush on her. Gadhafi had called Obama his "Muslim brother." Both administrations had embraced him, his regime, and his willingness to help root out Islamist enemies of America. We had even provided foreign aid to him and sent taxpayer-funded contributions to charities managed by some of Gadhafi's sons. Libya is a major oil producer, but while Europe relies on Libyan oil, the United States does not. There were no vital American interests at stake in Libya, unlike in Iraq. But Gadhafi rightly considered himself a partner of the United States. We were at peace with his government. Imagine, then, his surprise when suddenly American bombs were falling on him.

Like Mubarak before him, Gadhafi must have thought, "What the @$%&! just happened?"

How did we go from an intelligence-sharing partnership with Gadhafi to prosecuting a "dumb" war against him in a matter of days? The Arab "Spring" had come to Libya, but not in the same magnitude that it had settled upon its neighboring countries. There were some limited demonstrations, but nothing like the mass protests that had occurred in Egypt. Gadhafi had mobilized some security forces, but there was no real need. And yet, the president who had derided Bush's policy of preemptive war launched his *own* preemptive war with neither significant U.S. interests at stake nor real violence being committed by the regime in question.

The ideological framework for Obama's "dumb" war came from one of his top foreign policy advisers, Samantha Power, whose concept of "responsibility to protect" was embraced by Obama and NATO as the rationale for military intervention in Libya. Obama spoke of the need to respond to humanitarian crisis: "When the entire international community almost unanimously says that there is a potential humanitarian crisis *about to take place* . . . that a leader has turned his military on his own people, we can't simply stand by with empty words. We have to take some sort of action." (Emphasis added.)

In other words, preemption. In 2006, Bush's doctrine of preemption stated: "We do not rule out the use of force before attacks occur. . . . We cannot afford to stand idly by. . . . This is the principle and logic of pre-emption." In 2010, Obama reworded it: "While the use of force is sometimes necessary, we will exhaust other options before war whenever we can . . . when force is necessary we will continue to do so in a way that reflects our values and strengthens our legitimacy."

That last tortured phrase meant that Obama would do what Bush did and seek the blessing of the UN, NATO, the Arab League, or whatever other international institution before acting. And like Bush, Obama reserved the right to act alone if necessary. So: same policy, more gobbledygook to make it look like Obama was more "enlightened" than Bush.

"Responding to humanitarian crises" can come in many forms: economic, diplomatic, and so on. It doesn't necessarily have to involve military action. But that's the route Obama chose to take in Libya. Libya is a rough-and-tumble tribal society in which the removal of Gadhafi won't stop the internal brutality. And furthermore, Obama chose *not* to intervene when tyrannies in Iran, Syria, China, Russia, and elsewhere slaughtered and repressed their people. Going into Libya was about accelerating a regime change there that would bring about "democracy," which would, in turn, result in an Islamist government.

And so, without warning, Gadhafi, like Mubarak, went from being a valued partner of the United States to an enemy who had to be overthrown. Unlike Bush, who sought and received congressional authorization for the war efforts in Iraq and Afghanistan, Obama went to war in Libya without getting that authorization. Perhaps "leading from behind" is just an excuse to avoid getting congressional support. Obama leaned only on the Arab League's okay and a United Nations Security Council resolution that called for a no-fly zone to protect civilians. It did not call for war against Libya or regime change, and yet Obama saw to it that both were carried out. Despite assuring that there would be "no boots on the ground," Obama sent in covert intelligence operatives to help the "rebels," who, with our help, took up arms against Gadhafi.

Who were these Libyan "rebels"? They weren't exactly a band of Mother Teresas, roaming Libya desperately trying to protect civilians. While there may have been some authentic democratic reformers among them, they included a large and varied mix of Islamists and violent jihadists. Among their commanders were al-Qaeda operatives, including at least one who had been held at Guantánamo Bay, and others who had recruited terrorists to fight Americans in Iraq. As the United States and NATO were targeting Gadhafi and his henchmen, our "rebels" were rounding up black Africans and lynching and beheading many of them. When they started advancing with the help of NATO firepower, they seized thousands of weapons such as shoulder-launched missiles and missile launchers and funneled many of them to their Islamist comrades in al-Qaeda and Hamas in Gaza.

In a March 2011 interview with NBC, Obama was asked about his "strategy." He replied, "We may not be applying the same tools in each country, in every case."

How about applying some of those tools to places that are actually strategically important to the United States? Say, Iran, Syria, Bahrain, Yemen? Obama was basically saying, "My only goal is to destroy American power and buck up our enemies. So: I may intervene. I may

not. Some terror states I like; some I don't. Some civilian protests I
like; some I don't. Some days, I'm for regime change; some days I'm
not. Some places, I'll stop genocide; some places I won't. Some days,
I eat Froot Loops; other days I eat Count Chocula."

When asked if he was considering arming Libyan rebels—about
whom we knew little beyond their ties to al-Qaeda or the Muslim
Brotherhood—Obama said: "I'm not ruling it out. But I'm also not
ruling it in."

At the start of military operations against Libya, Obama told members of Congress that any U.S. military involvement would last "days
not weeks." As days stretched into weeks and weeks into months,
administration lawyers began to issue warnings that Obama's prosecution of the war was violating the constitutionally dubious 1973 War
Powers Resolution, which limits the commander in chief to a ninety-
day commitment to a military action before requiring him to come to
Congress for further authorization. Obama turned to a fellow kook,
State Department counsel Harold Koh, who conveniently argued that
invading Libya, dropping bombs all over it, and trying to take out its
leader didn't amount to "hostilities," so Obama the Nobel Peace Prize
winner was free to pound Libya and try to kill Gadhafi for as long as
he wanted. And so it came to pass that the man Reagan had called
the "mad dog of the Middle East" met his end at the hands of a pack
of mad dogs far more rabid than he.

Under Obama, Gadhafi didn't get much due process. No Saddam
Hussein–like trial by his countrymen. No stint at Guantánamo Bay,
complete with ACLU lawyers and Geneva Convention protections.
That kind of legalese was for loser rule-of-law guys like Bush.

Before Gadhafi's body was cold, the leader of the Libyan Transitional National Council, Mustafa Abdul Jalil, proclaimed that sharia
would be the "basic source" of Libyan law. Lenders were immediately
banned from collecting interest on loans and multiple wives were instantly legal for men. Here again, Obama threw over a U.S. partner in
favor of anti-American forces who pushed toward an Islamic state. To
Obama, there were no foes of the United States, just friends waiting
to be made. He would let every nation know, whether they wished

America well or ill, that he would pay any price, bear any burden, meet any hardship, support any friend, and oppose any foe . . . to assure the survival of polygamy in Libya.

The Gadhafi dictatorship was hardly a basketful of puppies. But his unsavory regime had turned its back on supporting terror, was cooperating with the United States against Islamists, and was reaching out to the West economically and politically. For that help, he was overthrown by a U.S.-led military operation, dragged through the streets, and assassinated. Lesson to the Iranian ayatollahs: don't give up your nukes and try to be friends with the U.S. or you guys could end up on a freezing cold slab of stainless steel in a random meat locker.

If Obama had a *victory* strategy, he certainly didn't articulate one. Instead he singled out Gadhafi as ripe for overthrow, but only because the "world" was clamoring for it. He hid behind the Arab League and the UN to authorize the use of force in Libya. When Syria and Yemen blew up, he essentially justified not intervening in those places by saying, "Gosh, golly. I'd really love to help y'all, but the UN/NATO/Arab League/Congress/American people just won't let me!"

Is there an Obama strategic doctrine, or is it an ad hoc mess? Is America's foreign policy being done on the fly, or is it all part of a deliberate grand strategy to reduce our influence in the world and encourage the world's dark forces to advance? The Libyan operation was sold as a mission on behalf of human rights of an aggrieved people. It ended with a U.S. partner murdered by a wild-eyed Islamist mob, the rise of al-Qaeda and other terrorist and militia groups, and an emerging violently anti-American Islamist regime. If that's what Obama had intended all along, then his motives for the Libyan war were sinister. If it wasn't what he intended, then his policy has been an abject failure, with U.S. interests far more threatened than they had been before.

The answer may be found in what was flying over Benghazi within days of Gadhafi's death: the al-Qaeda flag.

For all of Obama's Muslim "outreach," for all of his attempts at "engagement" with our enemies and his bailing on suddenly inconvenient allies, for all of his talk about "remaking" relations with that part of the globe, he has laid an egg. A May 2011 Pew Research Center poll found that America's favorability rating across the Arab world has *dropped* precipitously under Obama and so has his personal favorability rating to 10 percent or less. In Egypt, just 5 percent viewed the United States favorably and only 3 percent agreed with Obama's policies. Similar bottom-of-the-barrel numbers were reported from Turkey to Pakistan. The results also showed that the United States was more popular in the Muslim world under President Bush than it is under President Obama.

Obama promised to change the world's perceptions of us through a radical shift in policy and the force of his magical persona. Obama thought he'd just flash his megawatt smile, pass out apologies like Halloween candy, give a speech in Cairo, enlist NASA, and voilà! The Muslim world would "heart" us. After all, his middle name was Hussein. What wasn't to love? A lot, apparently. Not only did the vast majority of Muslims around the world dislike Obama personally, but their disapproval of American foreign policy hit unprecedented levels. All of that bowing and scraping earned him gongs, not applause. And it decimated American prestige, power, and respect beyond anything previously imaginable.

The revolts that occurred across the Middle East gave us a providential opportunity to encourage real freedom in the region and reduce the threats of Islamist jihad. Instead, our strategically incomprehensible and morally vacuous policies have led much of the Middle East to exchange one form of fascism for another. Election victories simply embolden the Islamists to move faster and more aggressively to advance their agenda. As we've seen in Iran, Islamic theocracy breeds savage oppression, deep corruption, and terrorism. And yet, that's where the bulk of the Middle East is heading, primarily because Obama's version of a "freedom agenda" resembled more of an "Islamist free-for-all agenda." If millions of people in the Middle East and North Africa end up consigned to the perpetual darkness of Islamist rule, it will be

Obama who will go down in the history books as the man "who lost the Middle East." On purpose.

Better Red Than Dead I: Reset? Nyet!

In early March 2009, Secretary of State Hillary Clinton boarded her jet to Moscow with a small surprise packed in her luggage. She couldn't wait to arrive and present it to her host, Russian foreign minister Sergei Lavrov. What awaited Lavrov was one of Obama's olive branches. Actually, it wasn't a real olive branch. It was a large, red, plastic button like the kind you hit on *Jeopardy!* when you're ready to answer in the form of a question. During the 2008 campaign, Obama had criticized the Bush administration for damaging relations with the Russians through "provocative" acts such as promising our Eastern European allies a missile defense shield and criticizing Russia for its invasion of democratic Georgia. Obama promised that he'd work to restore relations with Russia through his ready incentives offensive. Bush had used sticks; Obama would use carrots. How could the Russians not want to give up their national interests and fall madly in love with Obama the way so many others had already done? Obama promised to hit the reset button in order to restart our bilateral relationship.

And so, somebody in the State Department—perhaps Hillary herself—came up with the button gimmick. With dramatic flair, she presented the plastic button to Lavrov. Stamped on top was the Russian word for "reset." Or so she thought. "We worked hard to get the right Russian word. Do you think we got it?" Hillary asked eagerly. Lavrov took one look at the button and smiled broadly, suppressing a major eye-roll. "You got it wrong," he replied. He then told the U.S. Secretary of Hope and Change that the Russian translation of the word wasn't "reset," but "overcharge." Hillary laughed nervously and said, "We won't let you do that to us." Lavrov simply nodded, probably wondering how the United States had gone from Thomas Jefferson to this pantsuited fool. Lavrov would've been more satisfied with a T-shirt that had an arrow pointing in Hillary's direction that said I'M WITH DUMMY.

The leftists were determined to make the U.S.-Russia relationship more Oprah and Gayle and less Kim and Paris. In order to move away from the Bush-era hostility and woo Moscow into being our BFF, Obama settled on the idea of a "reset," which essentially meant giving away the store to the Russkies. He didn't stop at simply "overcharging" the Russians; he let them take every advantage. Obama fell over himself to shower the Russians with unprecedented concessions in order to show them that we could be friends instead of frenemies or outright enemies.

This kook approach ignored several things. First, the cold war didn't end when the Soviet Union collapsed. It simply changed form. The Russians remain as competitive with the United States over the global chessboard as ever, but the competition is more indirect, more economic than military, more stealthy and, in some ways, more dangerous. The only reprieve we got from this grand game of strategy was the eight years Boris Yeltsin was president and hammered on vodka all the time.

Second, Russia has its own national interests and ideology that are diametrically opposed to ours, and no matter how much schmoozing we do, that reality can never be changed. Warm personal relationships between leaders can soften relations at the margins but they never override clear-eyed pursuits of interests. Conflicts stemming from differences in national interests can be managed but not eliminated.

And third, Obama's "I Heart Russia" approach ignored the fact that Russia had become far more authoritarian under Putin/Medvedev; had journalists, lawyers, and others killed who dared to speak about rampant corruption and oppression; was seeking to reassert control within the former Soviet Union; and was intervening in the Middle East on the side of bad guys like Iran and Syria, including providing crucial assistance to their nuclear programs.

Instead of confronting Russia on these issues, Team Obama sought to reward it for its bad behavior. The "reset" policy signaled one thing to Russia: the United States is in strategic retreat. That meant that they could go to town with their fellow villains around the world and the United States wouldn't lift a finger to stop them. If the American president believed in restricting U.S. power, who were the Russians to stop him?

The first casualty of the "reset" was America's close friends in Eastern Europe. During the fifty years of the cold war, the United States provided an unequivocal beacon of moral, political, and ideological support for the tens of millions of people trapped behind the Iron Curtain. U.S. policy was to seek the liberation of the "captive nations" by all available means, from materially supporting dissident movements such as Solidarity in Poland to broadcasting Radio Free Europe across the Soviet bloc. Everyone behind the Iron Curtain knew that the United States stood for freedom and that it was doing everything it could realistically do to support them. When liberation arrived with the fall of the Soviet empire in 1989 and in the years that followed, those nations enjoyed special relationships with the United States that involved political, economic, military, and moral backing as the young democracies found the Russian bear breathing down their necks. But they always knew that the United States would stand behind them, confront Russia when necessary, and defend their interests, which were, after all, American interests.

That is, until Obama became president. He would set aside inconvenient facts such as Russia's support for the Iranian and Syrian nuclear programs, not to mention Hugo Chávez's nuclear ambitions in Venezuela. He would overlook Russia's intimidation of its neighbors. He would ignore Russia's extortion over oil supplies to countries like Ukraine and Poland. Russian weapons proliferation to rogues around the world? Not a problem. There would be no more bullying from the United States. No more old-school cold war games. No more distrust.

In the fall of 2009, Obama made his first major anti-American move vis-à-vis the Russians. He announced that as a gesture of goodwill, he was canceling the Bush administration's plans to deploy a missile defense shield in Eastern Europe. The missile system—which would have been comprised of ten ballistic missile interceptors in Poland

and a radar center in the Czech Republic—was sold as a defense system against long-range Iranian missiles that would be able to reach deep inside Eastern Europe. But to the Russians, it was treated as a provocation that essentially would render useless their ballistic missile capability. Russian president Medvedev had threatened to station tactical missiles on Poland's border if the United States went ahead. Bush, however, was committed to protecting our close friends in Eastern Europe, arguing to the Russians that the plan was defensive and not offensive in nature and that they should also be worried about the Iranian nuclear and missile threat. Not Obama. No missile defense for you! Instead, he announced a new, vastly scaled back and sea-based deterrent that wasn't nearly as comprehensive as the Bush plan. It left our Eastern European allies bitterly disappointed. Former Polish president and Solidarity hero Lech Walesa said, "It's not that we need the shield, but it's about the way we're treated here."

Once the Russians knew they could roll Obama, they then did so routinely. Part of Obama's motivation in dropping missile defense was to gain greater cooperation from Moscow in dealing with Tehran's nuclear program. After Obama's announcement, senior Russian officials said explicitly that no assistance would be forthcoming. When tougher sanctions came up soon after Obama threw Eastern Europe down the stairs, the Russians were said to be "very reserved," which was diplo-speak for "go fly a kite." From that point on, whenever new sanctions on Iran came up at the United Nations, the Russians balked. When missile defense cooperation between the two countries came up, the Russians were "noncommittal." And on the new U.S. sea-based missile defense system (the one for which we chucked the land-based one in Eastern Europe), the Russians oppose *that* because it "could pose an even stronger security threat to Moscow." This is generally what appeasement produces.

In a classic Obama maneuver designed to make him appear tough, he called Medvedev and said that he knew the real cause of the Chernobyl nuclear meltdown. Barry said he had secret video footage of why it happened and accused the Russians of storing radioactive alien technology that they had brought back from the moon. A stunned Medvedev said through his translator, "Mr. President, that was not real. That was the plot of *Transformers: Dark of the Moon*."

Just when the Russians couldn't believe their good fortune in getting everything they wanted on Eastern Europe without having to give anything in return, they got another dazzling gift from Obama in early 2010: a promise to never use nuclear weapons. Fully embracing the most far left position since the advent of the Bomb, Obama prohibited the use of these weapons, except in the narrowest of circumstances. According to the *New York Times*: "For the first time, the United States is explicitly committing not to use nuclear weapons against non-nuclear states that are in compliance with the Nuclear Nonproliferation Treaty, even if they attacked the United States with biological or chemical weapons or launched a crippling cyberattack."

Let those words sink in. Your commander in chief told the world that he will not defend you or the nation with nuclear weapons *even if* we are attacked with a massive anthrax or poison gas attack that has people dying in the streets in the most horrific ways. *He will not defend you. He will not even threaten to defend you.*

He said he believes those threats could be "deterred," but he also carved out exemptions for Iran and North Korea because they have either renounced the Non-Proliferation Treaty (North Korea) or blown it off (Iran)—as if they had *ever* held to the commitments on a piece of paper. (Hmm . . . Iran and North Korea. Two of the original three members of the "axis of evil." See: Bush Was Right, Volume 38, 674.)

The single most frightening thing Obama said about the new policy was this: "I don't think countries around the world are interested in testing our credibility when it comes to these issues."

Testing our credibility is the *only* thing our enemies are interested in. Enemies poke and prod us, and when we bend, ignore, or appease them, they believe we are weak. When we fail that credibility test, they then step up their aggression. Witness: Pearl Harbor, the entire history of the cold war, and September 11. To his "no first use" policy, Obama added another longtime kook pipe dream: a "world without nuclear weapons." In order to get the ball rolling, he decided the United States would develop no new nuclear weapons while he was president. His own first Defense secretary, Robert Gates, and many Democrats argued for allowing the development of new ones and the modernization of our current arsenal. Obama refused.

———

Speaking of nukes, ever wonder how many nuclear weapons we have? Wonder no more. It's 5,113! For the first time in U.S. history, an American president revealed the precise size of our nuclear arsenal. And he followed up that outrage with another: on December 31, 2011, Obama issued a signing statement attached to the fiscal year 2012 defense authorization bill. In it, he indicated a willingness to share top-secret U.S. missile defense secrets with Russia. We spent decades, trillions of dollars, and countless lives to defeat the Russkies. Now Obama is just handing them our greatest national security secrets without asking for so much as a Mentos in exchange.

And he didn't just disclose the particulars of *our* nuclear arsenal. Why, our allies should be in on the fun too, so Obama also disclosed top-secret intelligence about the *British* nuclear arsenal to the Russians, cavalierly disregarding our ally's pleas to keep the information secret. Peace out, GB!

———

Obama then set out to complete the U.S.-Russia Strategic Arms Reduction Treaty, a cold war–era relic that forced us to cut nuclear weapons as Obama pushed for their total elimination. The New START treaty cut our nuclear arsenal by 30 percent, hamstrung our missile defense and the Prompt Global Strike system (intercontinental ballistic missiles with conventional warheads), ignored tactical nuclear weapons (which are most available and vulnerable to terrorist acquisition), exempted Russian rail-based ICBMs, and failed to demand ironclad verification of Russian compliance. God-awful deal for us, great deal for Russia, so of course Obama heralded it as a landmark treaty. Most senators unfortunately agreed and ratified it just days before Christmas 2010.

The Russian response? The Kremlin stepped up its stonewalling on Iranian and Syrian sanctions, didn't resume compliance with another cold war–era treaty, the Conventional Armed Forces in Europe (CFE) agreement, and threatened to target U.S. missile defense sites in Europe with their offensive missiles unless Obama dropped *all* missile defense plans. They also threatened to withdraw from the New START treaty completely if Obama didn't accede to their demands. In December 2011, even Hillary Clinton grew exasperated with the Russian intransigence and blurted out the *Bush* argument for missile defense in Europe: "This is not directed at Russia, it is not about Russia. It is frankly about Iran and other state or non-state actors who are seeking to develop threatening missile technology," she said.

The Russians weren't having it: Putin accused the United States of allegedly stoking protests against his party, United Russia, after a suspect parliamentary election win in late 2011, and a top Russian general warned of a new "arms race." Obama gave the Russians a yard with the New START treaty and they took a mile. Personally, Obama went further. In March 2012, he was caught on mic telling Medvedev to tell Putin to wait until after November for more give-away-the-store deals: "After my election," he whispered to Dmitry, "I have more flexibility." He also gave the Russians his Social Security number, the PIN to his ATM card, the spot where he hides the extra key to the White House (under the flowerpot), and the name of his wife's ob-gyn.

If only Obama were, in the words of Ahmadinejad, an "amateur" and "inexperienced." His pattern of helping our worst enemies and dissing our allies suggests far more dangerous and sinister motives. His policies reflected his view that American power is a problem in the world, not a solution. He has sought to reduce it at every turn, from signing bad treaties with Russia that severely constrain our ability to defend ourselves to disclosing the particulars of our nuclear weapons to banning the development of new nuclear weapons. American power is something to be limited and ultimately reduced to inconsequentiality. And American retreat is to be carried out with all deliberate speed.

Better Red Than Dead II: Hu's on First

On a frigid day in mid-February 2010, a quiet, unassuming man slipped into the White House. Wearing simple robes and slippers, hands clasped before him, he humbly prepared to meet the Leader of the Free World. He was supposed to have had this meeting months before but was told at the time that Obama had a scheduling conflict. With that dis, Obama became the first president since 1991 to ice the Dalai Lama.

Obama sacrificed His Holiness—a gentle, spiritual man who has done nothing but peacefully champion the rights of the Tibetan people held under the jackboot of the Chinese communists—because Obama wanted to schmooze the Chinese to keep buying our debt to float his record deficit spending and to get them to cooperate on tougher sanctions on Iran. Obama refused to share a cup of tea with the Dalai Lama, at least until he had the chance to meet with the Chinese first.

This was a major reversal for Obama who, during the 2008 campaign, called on Bush to boycott the opening ceremonies at the Beijing Olympics over the violent Chinese suppression of peaceful demonstrations in Tibet. Bush, by the way, gave the Dalai Lama the Congressional Gold Medal in 2007. When Obama blew off His Holiness, there wasn't a peep of protest from human rights groups, leftists who say they fight for human rights, or Richard Gere.

After His Holiness finally did get his meeting with Obama, he was escorted out a side door of the White House, past towering piles of smelly garbage. As he walked by the filth, Joe Biden emerged from the trash heap and said, "Hey, Mr. Lama! I loved it when you were reincarnated as Brad Pitt in *Seven Years in Tibet*." The Chinese commies must have gotten a hearty chuckle at the sight of their nemesis negotiating his way past bags of empty pizza boxes, used paper towels, and what looked like an old bedspread.

The Russians saw Obama's anti-Americanism when he caved on the European missile defense shield, the Iranians saw it when he kept throwing olive branches at them, and the rest of the world saw it when they got repeated apologies for American power and action. The message they all got was that this president could be rolled with his own anti-Americanism and that sometimes he'll even preemptively surrender, as he did with the Dalai Lama.

In mid-April 2010, Obama attended the Nuclear Security Summit in Washington, DC. As he approached Hu Jintao, the Chinese president and the general secretary of the Chinese Communist Party, he did the Obama Move. He bowed. The bow to Hu came after a string of previous Obama bows: to the Saudi king, the Japanese emperor, and (my favorite) the mayor of Tampa, Florida. Other lesser-known bows included to Stevie Wonder, Andrea Bocelli, Big Bird, Triumph the Insult Comic Dog, and King Friday XIII from *Mister Rogers' Neighborhood*. I guess Obama has a thing for bowing to questionable dignitaries and puppets. He bows so much, Barry should just walk around life in a constant bow. Could you imagine him delivering a State of the Union address bent forward, ass in the air? For his grand finale, he could turn around and once again lead from behind.

Hu looked completely baffled and slightly amused at the sight of the president of the United States and supposed champion of freedom bowing before him. Of course, he read it as American impotence while Obama thought he was signaling a new humility that would quickly translate into cooperation.

Not so fast. The Chinese proceeded to join the Russians in opposing every major attempt we and the Europeans made at the United Nations to sanction Iran over its nuclear program. Without fanfare, Hu blew Obama off. In fact, before the Chinese leader left Washington, a reporter asked him what he had told Obama regarding Iran's nuclear program. Jintao turned slowly to the journalist and answered, "I said, 'Mr. President: F@&% HU!'"

In the spring of 1993, I traveled with my then boss, President Nixon, to China. Seeing Asia for the first time with the man who had changed the face of that region—and indeed the world—was extraordinary. As we took a boat ride around the outskirts of Shanghai, Nixon gazed with astonishment at the hundreds of high-rises and endless construction projects. He gestured toward the Chinese landscape of ambition and said, "None of this would have been possible without our opening in 1972."

Over the past few decades, China has gone from being an important but secondary concern for the United States to being an important and primary one. When Nixon made his triumphant touchdown in Beijing in 1972, there was only one thing that brought the United States and China together: the growing strategic power of the Soviet Union and its threat to the global balance of power.

Today, the relationship is much more complex and nuanced. China's stunningly rapid economic rise and its growing military assertiveness have made it more of a competitor than a strategic partner. There is a debate raging within China between those who argue for a "peaceful rise" and those who believe China should lay claim to superpower status and directly challenge the United States. As the two sides battle it out in China, they are united on one goal: to surpass America as the number one economy in the world. In mid-2011, the International Monetary Fund asserted that China will accomplish that by 2016. As the communists' version of managed capitalism spurs China's rise, Beijing believes that America is in irreversible decline thanks to its extreme debt and profligate ways. Every time top Chinese officials have met with Obama, Secretary of State Clinton, Treasury Secretary Geithner, or other U.S. officials, they have never missed an opportunity to scold them over our spending and debt levels and the dangers of inflation. And they're right.

The Chinese are hardly angels, however. They keep their currency undervalued, which has sent the U.S. trade deficit with China skyrocketing and hurt American jobs. China also doles out subsidies to state industries and encourages the theft of intellectual property, both of which also give Chinese goods hugely unfair advantages.

Whenever Obama, Clinton, or Geithner complains about these economic maneuvers, Hu listens politely, makes a note to discuss them with his politburo, and then heads back to Beijing to continue business as usual. Economic tricks and shady moves have produced explosive economic growth. The Chinese aren't about to abandon them just because Obama flashes his toothy grin, Hillary promises a schmoozefest with Bill, or Geithner offers a free tax-avoidance tutorial.

For the Chinese, one of their major concerns is the value of their holdings of U.S. assets. Our largest foreign creditor, they hold over $1 trillion of our debt. If they were to stop buying our debt or sold off significant amounts of it, we'd be screwed. They're worried about potential losses from a rapid sell-off in Treasuries, so they've been looking for Team Obama to reassure them that U.S. debt remains safe. The Chinese received lip service from the administration about the security of our debt, even as they've watched Obama pile on over $5 trillion more of it.

As they worry about the safety of their U.S. assets, the Chinese also know that holding so much of our debt gives them enormous leverage over us. As one high-ranking Chinese military official put it in late 2010, it's about "economic warfare." Our debt has gotten so astronomical that in fairly short order, the interest alone that we will be paying to Beijing will fund the entire People's Liberation Army. So get this: we borrow money from the Chinese to finance our debt, then pay them back with interest, which they then use to fund their ever increasingly aggressive military. Never before has a major power funded the rise of its successor.

Meanwhile, as China's economic strength has grown, so has its strategic power and willingness to flex it. China has become increasingly assertive in the South China, East China, and Yellow Seas, where the U.S. fleet operates. It has also issued claims of sovereignty over disputed areas, provoking serious conflicts, including with our close ally Japan over fish-rich islands. It has let its client state, North Korea, run wild, attacking our ally South Korea twice since 2009 in armed conflicts that resulted in the deaths of dozens of South Korean soldiers and civilians.

Furthermore, China has been engaged in a military buildup not entirely unlike the Soviet one that had Deng Xiaoping so panicked in

1972. Today, Beijing is building new aircraft carriers to dominate the Pacific as well as global waters. China has been dispatching ships to harass offshore oil and gas explorations conducted by Vietnam and the Philippines while claiming vast swaths of mineral- and resource-rich areas for itself. It is developing a new ballistic missile capability. In 2011, it tested a new stealth fighter jet. China continues to proliferate nuclear weapons, technology, and expertise to villains such as Iran, Syria, Venezuela, North Korea, and Pakistan. And it spearheads crippling cyber attacks aimed at our military and commercial interests.

———

At the same time, Obama set out to accelerate American decline through unilateral disarmament. From the outset, he intended to slash defense spending, even while the nation is still at war. In January 2012, he announced a major military "restructuring," a euphemism for "evisceration." Defense Secretary Leon Panetta looked like he was passing a gallstone when he announced Obama's plan to slash defense spending by $489 billion over ten years, including cutting troop levels by half a million men and women, canceling about fifty major weapons programs, and bagging the five-decades-old policy of maintaining the ability to fight two wars in different theaters at once.

Obama's defense cuts were an eager jump start on the automatic sequestration of Pentagon funding that's set to kick in in January 2013 thanks to the super committee's failure to agree on spending cuts. That called for the automatic reduction of the defense budget by $650 billion over ten years. Further defense cuts would leave us dangerously vulnerable. Obama went on to announce plans to cut our nuclear arsenal by 80 percent (far beyond the reductions required in New START), leaving us with fewer operational warheads than China.

Defense analysts warn that if the deeper cuts are allowed to occur, the Marine Corps will shrink to its smallest force in fifty years, the Army will be reduced to pre-9/11 levels, the Air Force will have two-thirds fewer fighters and bombers than in 1990, and the Navy may lose one or two aircraft-carrier battle groups and have its overall fleet down to pre–World War *One* levels. Missile defense plans are likely to be delayed, making our allies and us more vulnerable to the growing ballistic missile threat. And Panetta told Congress that big defense cuts would mean troop reductions, costing up to 1.5 million jobs and adding 1 percentage point to the already astronomical unemployment rate.

In the words of Panetta, "The Department of Defense will face devastating, automatic, across-the-board cuts that will tear a seam in the nation's defense." And yet, Obama fought hard to get *this precise outcome*.

Obama *wants* the defense cuts. He *wants* the military decimated. He *wants* us more vulnerable. After all, less money for the Pentagon means more money for his domestic projects. He only rushes to cut things vital to our survival. A hollowed-out military also fits his bigger agenda: if we can't project power, we can't continue to be a superpower.

Our allies in the region see the major U.S. defense *cuts* at the same time they see the Chinese *increasing* their military budget by 10 percent or more each year for the last twenty years. Japan, South Korea, Vietnam, Taiwan, and others are pacing the floorboards as they desperately seek our reassurance about continuing U.S. protection. Obama's answer to the increased Chinese naval bullying was to send Hillary Clinton out to wave around the UN Law of the Sea Treaty (LOST), which so imperils U.S. sovereignty that the Senate won't ratify it.

At an Asia-Pacific Economic Cooperation (APEC) summit in late 2011, Obama toughened his stance a bit, citing a "slight improvement" in the value of the Chinese yuan but claiming it wasn't nearly enough. He also scolded China to behave more responsibly in addressing strategic and trade challenges. "Now they've grown up," he said, "and so they're going to have to help manage this process in a responsible way."

No they don't. In fact, the Chinese—whose culture is millennia old—took particular umbrage over Big Daddy's use of the phrase "grown up." "The U.S. intends to solve economic problems by exerting political pressure on China. Such a mission is hollow and ultimately doomed to failure," the state-run *Global Times* said in an editorial that also accused the United States of "over-confidence." They continued, "Maybe the U.S. should learn to accept the reality of a multi-polar world and change its mentality."

The global community organizer isn't playing well in China, where they have repeatedly told Big Daddy to take a hike. China knows that Obama is stuck between a Barack and a hard place: when Obama tried a unilateral move in response to China's currency manipulation and slapped a steep 35 percent tariff on Chinese tires in 2009, the Chinese remained unmoved; more severe tariffs would certainly spark a devastating trade war and are therefore unlikely. The Chinese also know that multilateral moves through institutions such as the World Trade Organization are slow and also unlikely.

Furthermore, the Chinese know that they've got essentially a free hand on human rights as long as Obama is in office. In 2009, Hillary Clinton turned her back on victims of Chinese oppression when she gave a speech that suggested we'd look the other way on human rights as long as we could deal productively on economic and strategic issues. The Chinese subsequently ramped up their policy of jailing, torturing, and killing democracy advocates, ethnic minorities, and Catholics, among others. By early 2011, Clinton had backed off from her "see no evil" position. Obama, however, has utterly failed to take on the Chinese on the issue. I was in the room in Beijing in 1993 when President Nixon blasted the Communist leadership on human rights. Their only counterargument was a lame point about the need to control over one billion people. Nixon wasn't having it, and neither should Obama. Human rights are the one area in which we actually do have some leverage with the Chinese, and yet Obama has been an AWOL moral warrior.

The shadow boxing occurring between Washington and Beijing has been carefully managed by both sides, but with the economic, diplomatic, and military competition ratcheting up, we face the increasing danger of direct conflict. China isn't about to stop spreading its wings simply because Big Daddy has lectured them to act like "grown-ups." Who's on first? Hu's on first on many issues, and he knows it. If this next century is going to be a Pacific century, we ought to have a president who makes sure that it's an American Pacific century and not a Chinese Pacific one. Ultimately, we may be on a collision course with China, and Obama may have to make a tough call: direct confrontation or appeasement. Appeasement is his natural comfort zone, and the Chinese know it.

Señor Alinsky on the Border with a Corona and Chaos

Welcome to Cinco de Cuatro!

> —Barack Obama to the Mexican ambassador to the
> United States, Arturo Sarukhan, attempting to mark
> Cinco de Mayo on May 4, not May 5, 2009

Midmorning, March 27, 2010: Rancher Robert Krentz was working on his property. He had taken his all-terrain vehicle out to tend to fences and water lines on the 34,000-acre cattle ranch in southern Arizona that had been in his family since 1907. Krentz was known as a good soul, someone who would always assist people in need, including the hundreds of illegal aliens who would break into the country via his property. He'd often take care of those who were sick or exhausted and provide water to them because, as he told PBS, "that's just my nature."

That particular morning, Krentz radioed his brother to say that he had come upon an illegal alien and was going to offer him assistance. Krentz was supposed to meet his brother at noon, and when he didn't show up, the brother called police, who launched a search of the rugged desert terrain.

Twelve hours later, a state police helicopter found Krentz slumped over in his vehicle, the engine running and the lights on. He had been shot to death. His dog lay next to him, critically wounded by another bullet. Days later, the dog's ashes were spread about the ranch along with Krentz's.

Tracker dogs followed the tracks of the killer back into Mexico, fifteen miles to the south.

Late night, December 14, 2010: U.S. border agent and former marine Brian Terry was on duty with several fellow border agents. Using thermal binoculars, they monitored the remote desert area of Peck Canyon, a notorious drug-smuggling corridor north of the Arizona-Mexico border. At about 11:15 p.m., the agents noticed movement. One of the agents determined that at least two of the five illegal aliens were carrying rifles. A grand jury indictment later indicated that the five illegals were armed with at least two AK-47 semi-automatic assault rifles and were "hunting" border agents like prey, with the intent to "intentionally and forcibly assault" them. The indictment said that at least two of the illegals carried their rifles "at the ready position" and were "patrolling the area in single-file formation."

The agents identified themselves in Spanish as police officers and ordered the illegals to drop their weapons. When the illegals refused, two agents used their shotguns to fire "less than lethal" beanbags at them. One of the illegals then opened fire, shooting Terry in the back. Two of Terry's fellow agents returned fire, hitting Manuel Osorio-Arellanes, who later admitted that all five of them were armed to the teeth. The four other drug smugglers fled the scene.

Terry fell to the ground immediately, bleeding profusely from his punctured aorta. "I'm hit," he cried. "I can't feel my legs. I think I'm paralyzed." He died within minutes.

Two AK-47 assault rifles found at the scene came from the Obama administration's Fast and Furious gunwalking operation.

———

Either the United States is a nation of laws, as the Founders intended, or we're a banana republic. Either rule of law and the respect for it prevails, or we're a nation of capricious, politically driven decisions that puts the ambitions of men over the sovereignty of the country.

Diluting American power and sovereignty is what Obama's border and immigration policy is all about: flood the zone, and watch America the exceptional melt away. If Obama's goals are realized, America will look more like the United States of Yugoslavia. And we know well how that hellhole turned out. Oh, that's right; it doesn't exist anymore. Barry's goal is to turn America into a Balkanized polyglot mess, devoid of a national creed or purpose.

When Jimmy Buffett sang about Mexico, it was a much more idyllic place than it is today. Over the past several years, drug cartel and illegal immigrant violence along our southern border has exploded. According to the Mexican government's own estimate, over 47,000 people have been killed in drug-related violence since President Felipe Calderón launched a military offensive against the cartels in late 2006. Mexican smugglers have become far more aggressive on the U.S. side of the border, as many of the major drug cartels now use former Mexican soldiers, police, and other law enforcement personnel to protect drug kingpins and their henchmen headed into the United States. Many drug lords have targeted U.S. Border Patrol agents and state and local police, offering bounties of up to $50,000 per killing. The cartel brutality has created a state of near–civil war in Mexico, with the military mobilized to support law enforcement in combating the mass killings, beheadings, and kidnappings of judges, journalists, elected officials, noncorrupt law enforcement officials, and civilians. That violent upheaval, coupled with the endless flow of hundreds of thousands of illegal aliens across our unenforced border each year, has created a war zone from San Diego to the Gulf of Mexico.

In early September 2010, Secretary Clinton acknowledged the obvious, saying that the drug cartels operating in Mexico, in Central America, and at the border were beginning to look like an "insurgency," and that Mexico was "looking more and more like Colombia looked twenty years ago, where the narco-traffickers control certain parts of the country."

Within twenty-four hours, Obama slapped her down. He told the Spanish-language magazine *La Opinion*, "Mexico is a vast and progressive democracy, with a growing economy, and as a result you cannot compare what is happening in Mexico with what happened in Colombia 20 years ago." Upon hearing this very public dis by her boss—a man she nearly beat for the Democratic nomination—Hillary said, "What the @$%&! just happened?"

The *real* reason Obama slammed Hillary's argument? If it were allowed to stand, then Obama would have to actually do something to enforce the southern border. Obama doesn't take much action to secure the border because he *needs* the chaos it engenders.

The more illegals trespassing into the United States, the better: more votes for him and his party, more drain on essential services such as schools, hospitals, and police, leading to demands for ever-bigger government and the spending to support it, and more diluting of American power and exceptionalism. The chaos of a wide-open border hits all redistributionist goals in one efficient swoop. *Muchas gracias*, Señor Alinsky!

Indeed, illegal immigration creates two distinct forms of chaos craved by the kooks: economic and criminal. According to a 2011 study by the Federation for American Immigration Reform (FAIR), illegal immigration now costs federal, state, and local taxpayers about $113 billion per year. Approximately 75 percent of that cost is borne by the states. You and your family paid $1,117 in taxes in 2011 to support illegal aliens. Fifty-one percent of Mexican immigrant households use one major welfare program, such as food stamps, Medicaid, school lunches, the Women, Infants and Children Program, and subsidized public housing, and 28 percent use more than one. The cost to educate the children of illegals? Fifty-two billion dollars.

The crime statistics involving illegal aliens—although notoriously difficult to measure—show an even darker side to the problem. The illegal population is roughly 12 million, although it's nearly impossible to get an accurate count. Of those, 57 percent are estimated to come from Mexico and 24 percent come from other parts of Latin America. The rest are from other parts of the world. While all commit the crime of entering the country illegally, once here most do not go on to commit other crimes. But those who do cause significant harm to America in terms of violence and the costs of criminal prosecution and incarceration. According to the Pew Hispanic Center, 40 percent of all sentenced federal offenders were Latinos, and of those, 72 percent were not U.S. citizens. The Department of Homeland Security estimates that there are about 225,000 noncitizens in the nation's jails, while the Federal Bureau of Prisons reports that 26.4 percent of inmates in federal prisons are noncitizens. The estimated cost to incarcerate them is about $2 billion just in federal prisons alone.

The unenforced border also invites international terrorism. The 9/11 Commission Report warned that "the challenge for national security in an age of terrorism is to prevent the very few people who may pose overwhelming risks from entering or remaining in the United States undetected."

Terrorist suspects with known ties to Hamas and Hezbollah have been arrested after crossing the border; many of these suspects have been known to work with the most violent Latin American gangs, including Mara Salvatrucha (MS-13) and Los Zetas (which was implicated in the 2011 arrest of two men tied to the Iranian government in a terror plot to have been carried out on U.S. soil). According to the Department of Homeland Security, in 2010 alone, 663 people arrested along the southern border were from countries designated as "special interest" for their support and export of terrorism, including Afghanistan, Libya, Pakistan, Somalia, and Yemen, and four other countries that have been designated by the State Department as state sponsors of terror—Cuba, Iran, Syria, and Sudan. We're strip-searching Gramps at the airport while half the Taliban strolls into Nogales.

Nothing generates the kind of sustained economic, criminal, and national security chaos as widespread and unchecked illegal immigration, which is the most basic reason it's embraced by the kooks. When confronted with its human and economic costs, the leftists invoke their patented emotional arguments: Who among us wants children of illegals to starve or to go without medical care or an education?

After all, it's not their fault they were brought to this country illegally. As for their parents, well, they're just here looking for work and their home countries are basket cases, so can you really blame them for coming here? This is why we need a path to citizenship, amnesty of different kinds, and the Development, Relief and Education of Alien Minors Act (DREAM Act), which would offer permanent legal status to illegals, up to age thirty-five, who arrived here before age sixteen, if they have no criminal record and completed either two years of college or service in the military. In fact, when Congress rejected the DREAM Act in mid-2011, Obama issued an implicit executive order for Immigration and Customs Enforcement (ICE) agents, lawyers, and others to exercise "prosecutorial discretion" for these illegals.

Show "compassion," they say. We can't help it if America is so awesome that they want to come here, and as for that border, well, you know, it's so long and stuff that we really can't enforce it even if we wanted to. This is the kook attitude that has gotten us to the point where the illegal immigration chaos on the border and around the nation has cost us all in lives and treasure. As with the terrorism issue, the leftists frame illegal immigration as a problem with *America* as the root cause, and because only *they* understand that root cause, they're best suited to lead us. It's a setup to seize ever more power.

In late April 2010, one state had had enough. Arizona, which bears the biggest brunt of the violent crimes, drug trafficking, kidnapping, vandalism, trespassing, and harassment associated with illegal immigration, got a new law on its books. Passed by the legislature and signed by Governor Jan Brewer, SB 1070 prohibited the harboring of illegal aliens and made it a state crime for an illegal to commit certain federal immigration crimes. Its most controversial provision required a police officer to verify a person's immigration status with the federal government when, in the course of a traffic stop or other legitimate contact, the officer came to a "reasonable suspicion" that that person was here illegally.

The law was concurrent with the federal immigration laws, didn't violate or trump federal law, and was only needed because the federal government was either unwilling or unable to enforce federal law. Since 1976, the U.S. Supreme Court has recognized that states may act on immigration as long as those laws don't run up against federal laws and as long as Congress hasn't explicitly forbidden those state laws. Even the U.S. Court of Appeals for the Ninth Circuit—the most kook appellate court in the nation—upheld Arizona's 2007 law making it illegal to knowingly employ illegal aliens. SB 1070 fit the criterion for being legal and ethical.

Predictably, however, the leftists went berserk. The American Civil Liberties Union and the Mexican American Legal Defense and Education Fund, among other far-left groups, called it unconstitutional; others screamed that it was "bigoted," "racist," and "un-American"; and Alinskyites organized protests and handed out Mexican flags. Isn't it interesting how if your state decides to pass a law legalizing same-sex marriage, the Left loves it, but if that same state wants to crack down on illegal alien lawbreakers, then it's evil? To the Left, states should have some rights but not others. To the Left, states such as New York, Vermont, and Massachusetts are all considered forward-looking gay paradises . . . but Arizona is run by a modern-day Eva Braun named Jan Brewer who's turning it into a fascist superstate. Funny, I thought they liked fascism. Just remember, if you're a state pushing for Harry and Dick to get married, that's okay. But passing a law to deport an illegal alien drunk driver? You've got issues.

The president—whose job it is to protect the border and defend the sovereignty of the nation—then weighed in on the law, calling it "misguided." He ordered the Justice Department to examine it to determine its constitutionality. Attorney General Eric Holder took a look, all right—at his boss's agenda and his own leftist politics—and decided to sue Arizona over the law, which Holder later admitted he hadn't read before filing suit, despite the fact that the law itself was just a few pages long. (Does anyone in this administration ever read *any* legislation before they either criticize it or sign it into law?)

The law was supported by Arizona's police associations, 70 percent of Arizonans, and over 60 percent of all Americans. But Obama,

Holder, and the kooks whined that it would create a police state that would violate the "civil liberties" of illegal aliens. Obama and Holder cited the problem of having a "patchwork of immigration laws" across the nation. And yet, none of the state laws ran afoul of the federal laws, and there wouldn't be a need for the state laws if Obama, Holder, and crew did their jobs in enforcing the federal laws in the first place.

But Team Obama was more concerned about protecting the "rights" of illegal aliens—potential Democratic voters—than it was about protecting the American citizens in Arizona, which is why Holder sued it as well as Utah, Alabama, and South Carolina, which passed similar laws. (A lower court blocked key parts of the Arizona law, leading the state to ask the Supreme Court to consider the case. In its brief to the Court, Arizona warned of "extraordinary confrontations between the federal government and other states" over illegal immigration.) The president of the United States believes that American states— *American citizens*—are greater lawbreakers than the illegal aliens subjecting them to invasion and threat every day. This is what law enforcement means to the nation's chief law enforcement officer.

In a *Clockwork Orange* display of perverse absurdity, Obama cheered on Mexican president Felipe Calderón as they stood together in the Rose Garden and Calderón ripped Arizona for wanting to protect itself from his country's murderers, drug dealers, and thugs. One week before Calderón arrived in Washington, he blasted the Arizona law as "criminalizing immigration," which he said "opens the door to intolerance, hate and discrimination." With Calderón standing next to him, Obama chimed in, "In the United States of America, no law-abiding person—be they an American citizen, a legal immigrant, or a visitor or tourist from Mexico—should ever be subject to suspicion simply because of what they look like." The spectacle of the president of the United States joining a foreign head of state to bash one of our own states put Obama's anti-Americanism in bold relief. He wasn't defending the United States in the face of foreign criticism. There was no "evil empire" moment. He didn't rally to our sides. He rallied to the sides of the lawbreakers. Afterward, Obama told Calderón that he had recently seen the film *The Treasure of the Sierra Madre*, and that if the Mexican president and his group of bandits needed any more help ripping off America, he would definitely assist them.

Obama has pushed "comprehensive immigration reform," which is code for amnesty, and a few other new laws he won't enforce. He's actually pushing for a massive new voter base, which is why he's always pandering to such radical open-borders, pro-amnesty groups as the National Council of La Raza. In fact, in early 2012, Obama chose a former senior vice president of La Raza, Cecilia Muñoz, to head his Domestic Policy Council. Nothing says "kissing Latino butt" like putting a La Raza honcho in charge of U.S. domestic policy.

Early on, the Obama administration had increased some deportations of violent criminal aliens, but by late 2011 it had put the brakes on deportations. It also couldn't find the time to deport Barry's uncle Onyango Obama and aunt Zeituni Onyango, both in the United States illegally and, in Aunt Zeituni's case, on the taxpayer dole. She claimed that the "system" took advantage of her and proclaimed, "If I come as an immigrant, you have the obligation to make me a citizen." I see where Obama gets his kookocity. Uncle Onyango was arrested for driving under the influence in Massachusetts, but was released and went back to work in a liquor store. Obama's idea of family values.

Obama has invited in more illegals by reducing the National Guard troop presence on the southern border from 1,200 to fewer than 300. And he has enacted backdoor amnesty by end-running Congress on the DREAM Act, issuing new ICE memoranda that radically changed deportation policies, creating a shadowy new interagency working group to dismiss pending deportation cases, and moving to grant work authorization to some illegals. He has also refused to stop sanctuary cities from impeding federal law enforcement and looked the other way as states such as New York, Massachusetts, and Illinois have stopped participating in the Department of Homeland Security illegal immigrant information program, Secure Communities. He has essentially ended worksite enforcement operation except for auditing I-9 employment eligibility forms and has not included E-Verify in any of his "jobs" plans.

Because Obama and the kooks require chaos, they're always looking for ways to create more tumult. What better way to capitalize on the violent bedlam on the southern border than by introducing *more* chaos by running guns across it?

When Team Obama came into office in early 2009, they came upon a legitimate program already in place called Project Gunrunner, which was designed to track the flow of guns. Project Gunrunner took place in Arizona, when Janet Napolitano, now the Department of Homeland Security secretary, was governor. Project Gunrunner spawned another operation called Operation Wide Receiver, which was designed to trace illegal firearms in Mexico. Wide Receiver was tightly managed, with all illegal firearms transactions done under close monitoring, and it was limited, involving only about 500 guns, most of which had fail-safe radio tracking devices. Most important, Wide Receiver was conducted with the full knowledge and buy-in of the Mexican government.

Team Obama saw Operation Gunrunner and the smaller Operation Wide Receiver begging to be used for leftist purposes. Obama often expressed the view that "more than 90 percent of the guns recovered in Mexico come from the United States, many from gun shops that line our border." That's a two-for-one kookism: it's anti-gun *and* anti-American! Too bad for the kooks that it's not true. Only about 17 percent of the guns in Mexico come from the United States. But if Team Obama were going to design their own gunrunning operation, they'd do it with one goal in mind: to ramp up the flow of guns, and when the guns were linked to murder and mayhem, they'd have an urgent excuse to crack down on law-abiding gun owners in the United States.

This wasn't incompetence. It was intentional. As CBS News' Sharyl Attkisson reported in December 2011, documents showed that the Bureau of Alcohol, Tobacco, Firearms and Explosives (ATF) discussed *creating and using* Fast and Furious to press for *new and stricter rules on gun sales*. "ATF officials didn't intend to publicly disclose their own role in letting Mexican cartels obtain the weapons," Attkisson reported, "but emails show they discussed using the sales, including sales encouraged by ATF, to justify a new gun regulation." We know the true kook purpose of Fast and Furious thanks to intrepid reporting by Attkisson, Fox News' William LaJuenesse and some others, who pursued the story despite gangsta threats from White House crisis manager Eric Schultz, who even "screamed at" Attkisson for being "unfair and biased by pursuing" the story. Obama and his acolytes were so used to having the media protect, defend, and advance them that when a reporter actually did his or her job, they lashed out in a torrent of intimidation.

In mid-2009, the administration midwifed a gunwalking program so out of control that hundreds of people now lay dead, including border agent Brian Terry and customs enforcement agent Jaime Zapata. Fast and Furious was a sinister operation that blended antigun politics with willful negligence to arm brutal Mexican drug lords and their henchmen. The plan was to get arms dealers to make illegal gun sales to "straw buyers," who were tasked to transfer the weapons to illegals, drug runners, and other criminals. In theory, the "straw buyers" were supposed to lead them to the drug cartels against whom they could move legally. In practice, it led to murder and mayhem, as expected.

Thousands of guns were permitted to walk, ATF lost track of most of them, and they disappeared into the Bermuda Triangle of Mexico's violent gangs. The dramatic prosecutions of major drug kingpins of which Holder dreamed never materialized; charges were brought against about twenty people, none of them significant cartel players. Meanwhile, the guns began showing up at savage crime scenes on both sides of the border, including in Arizona at the murder scenes of Agents Terry and Zapata. Of course, the most basic ATF mission is to *not lose track of guns*.

When the story blew wide open, Team Obama tried to point to Operation Wide Receiver in order to once again blame Bush and suggest that both programs were the same. In fact, unlike Team Bush, Team Obama never bothered to inform the Mexican government of the gunwalking, approved the transfer of thousands—not hundreds—of guns, lied to lower-level ATF agents about the policy, and let the entire operation spin out of control.

Predictably, no one among Team Obama knew nothin' about no stinkin' guns. The president claimed *he* didn't know that thousands of guns were walking across the Mexican border, even though he is commander in chief. Despite the fact that some of his top deputies knew about Fast and Furious, including Assistant Attorney General Lanny Breuer and former deputy attorney general David Ogden, Attorney General Eric Holder claimed *he* didn't know, even though his department oversaw the program. Secretary of State Hillary Clinton claimed *she* didn't know, even though the operation occurred over an international border. Secretary of Homeland Security Janet Napolitano claimed *she* didn't know, even though the matter involved international criminal activity and came out of the program she oversaw as governor. Moe, Larry, and Curly in Obama's cabinet have zero idea about the guns that killed border agent Brian Terry. Yet Eric, Hillary, and Janet all frequently get behind policies that affect every aspect of our personal liberties. I guess everything is sophisticated and nuanced until an American hero is killed by an American gun in the hands of a Mexican outlaw.

Congressional investigations unearthed memoranda that indicated that, contrary to Holder's previous testimony that he had first learned of Fast and Furious in early 2011, he'd actually been briefed on it far earlier. He testified that he didn't see the relevant memos because, after all, he had his hands full with suing U.S. states over immigration and letting the 2008 Black Panthers voter intimidation scandal slide. The chairman of the House Committee on Oversight and Government Reform, Darrell Issa, was so infuriated with his continuous stonewalling and refusal to release requested documents that Issa had to issue a slew of subpoenas to get them. And in the ultimate insult, when asked if he had spoken with or apologized to the family of slain agent Terry, Holder replied, "No." Then he released to the media a copy of the letter he had sent to the family—before they had received it. He then abruptly ordered sealed court records containing the grim details of how Mexican drug smugglers killed Terry with a Fast and

Furious firearm. So much for the "most transparent" administration in history.

As the scandal grew, Team Obama attempted damage control. It moved key players around as if they were deck chairs on the *Titanic*. The acting head of the ATF, Kenneth Melson, was transferred into a made-up position at DOJ with the fanciful title, "Senior Adviser on Forensic Science in the Office of Legal Policy." Others deeply involved with Fast and Furious were moved out of their positions or promoted. The only resignation was by U.S. Attorney Dennis Burke in Phoenix, who attempted to smear an ATF whistle-blower and then denied Agent Terry's family crime victim status in a court case brought against the lowlife who bought the guns used in Terry's murder.

A government-run program to illegally transfer thousands of guns to violent Mexican drug gangs? What could go wrong? It was the epitome of leftist thinking: if they could get the program to go awry just enough, not only would they have a ready-made reason to crack down on legal U.S. guns but they could also jump to blame the United States for its appetite for drugs and guns. It's our fault, you see, that we're a nation of druggies that creates so much demand for the Mexican drug lords. It's our fault that we've got this stupid Second Amendment with the right to bear arms. It's our fault that so many illegals want to come here to work and live, and therefore the burden is on us to make them feel at home. And if you disagree, you're a heartless jerk.

The illegal alien invasion squares nicely with the kooks' objective of removing American greatness, which is why Obama and Holder sued some of our own states and never apologized for the violent mayhem of Fast and Furious. In fact, the gunwalking operation continues exactly as planned, with Holder predicting that "for years to come, guns lost during this operation will continue to show up at crime scenes on both sides of the border." Kook mission accomplished.

We usually assume that our leadership is on the side of the rule of law and law enforcement. But as Obama reminded La Raza: "The

Democrats and your president are with *you*. . . . Remember who it is we need to move to change the laws."

Obama's active encouragement of the illegal invasion is community organizing at its best. It's also a genius application of Alinsky's revolutionary strategy: stoke chaos to pave the way for your radical agenda. To the leftists, the *American* people need to be browbeaten, sued, abused, and attacked by their own government in service of their greater goal of "fundamentally transforming" the nation. And if you don't like it, here comes a Mexican drug lord with a Fast and Furious gun we gave him to convince you of the error of your ways.

Bonfire of the Olive Branches

Obama seems to believe that diplomacy is a zero-sum game: that is, as you seek improved relations with your adversaries, you must sucker-punch your friends. No American president has blown off long-standing and loyal allies with as much speed and fervor as Obama has slammed into Israel, Egypt, Great Britain, France, Germany, Honduras, Iraq, Japan, and South Korea, prompting them all to think, "What the @$%&! just happened?"

When he first entered the White House, Obama dissed our greatest allies, the British, by returning a bust of Winston Churchill, the savior of Western civilization. The bust was a gift from the British government, but Obama needed to make room for all of those photos of Michelle showing off her buff arms, so something had to go. He also disrespected the British by giving the then prime minister, Gordon Brown, DVDs that he was unable to watch on European players, and to Her Majesty the Queen, he gave an iPod. As she turned it on for the first time, eagerly anticipating the latest Flo Rida single, the British sovereign had her ears assaulted by endless Obama lectures on the virtues of wind farms. She was further stunned to discover that Obama had forgotten to erase a bunch of things from it, like Reverend Wright's sermons, the Jane Fonda workout, a video clip of Fredo Corleone screaming in *The Godfather: Part II*, and a ton of Barbra Streisand songs.

He insulted the French by arriving in Paris only to turn down a dinner invitation from French president Nicolas Sarkozy. He further offended the French by sending a letter to the French president—Jacques Chirac—when Sarkozy was the actual president of France at the time, and he held a town hall meeting while there but didn't call on a single French citizen. *Mon Dieu!*

He dinged the Germans by canceling his scheduled appearance in Germany on November 9, 2009, to mark the twentieth anniversary of the fall of the Berlin Wall. The collapse of the wall is one of the greatest triumphs of liberty over tyranny in the history of mankind, but Obama couldn't be bothered. He had other stuff to do. Like play golf. Smoke. Chat up J. Lo. Shoot hoops.

He dissed our South Korean allies by refusing to deal aggressively with their—and our—North Korean enemy on its nuclear program, its widespread proliferation, its attack on a South Korean ship that killed forty-six South Korean citizens, and its military assault on the South that resulted in several deaths. The message South Korea and another great U.S. ally, Japan, took from this? You're on your own. Good luck with that whole North Korean nightmare thingy. Oh, and that Chinese colossus thingy too.

Obama blew off the pro-American, pro-Israel Kurds in northern Iraq who, once they heard about his decision to withdraw completely from Iraq, sent their leader, Kurdistan president Massoud Barzani, to Tehran to seek protection from the Iranian government.

Obama has sold out Honduras, which was desperately trying to prevent a socialist takeover by an anti-American authoritarian whom Hillary Clinton's State Department thought was a swell fellow to support. This thrilled the Cuban dictators Fidel and Raúl Castro and South American strongmen such as Venezuelan president Hugo Chávez and Bolivian president Evo Morales. Their fight for socialism was made so much easier with the United States not just out of the way but actively championing their cause. *Muchas gracias*, American gringos!

In the most egregious example of the Obama ally blow-off, he took our special friendship with Israel—our historically close friend, our most reliable strategic partner in the Middle East, and a nation with which we share democratic and free market principles—and he drop-kicked it. Schooled on the Israeli-Palestinian conflict from the terrorist sympathizer and Columbia University professor Rashid Khalidi, Obama came to office with the view that Israel is an occupying force of lands historically, legally, and morally Palestinian and that Israel bullies its way around the region, exaggerating the threats it faces and holding the so-called peace process hostage with outrageous demands. It's no wonder that once he became president, he reoriented our policy away from a staunch alliance with Israel and toward one far more sympathetic to Palestinian demands. When he was campaigning in 2008, then–Senator Obama blurted out, "There is a strain within the pro-Israel community that says unless you adopt an unwavering pro-Likud approach to Israel that you're anti-Israel." If Obama's GOP rival, Senator McCain, had said that, the leftist press would have raked him over the coals for its outrageousness as well as its inaccuracy. When Obama referred to Likud, the party had been out of power for two years, replaced by the centrists of Kadima and led by Prime Minister Ehud Olmert, who had been discussing a major territorial compromise. Furthermore, it was under Likud governments that Israel had carried out its biggest territorial withdrawals from Sinai and Gaza. But to Obama, Likud and frankly every Israeli government was seen as uncompromising and hostile to peace.

A few months after entering office, Obama told American Jewish leaders that essentially he had had enough of the close U.S.-Israeli relationship. Referring to the Bush years, he said, "For eight years there was no light between the United States and Israel, and nothing got accomplished." It was during those "nothing" years that Likud prime minister Ariel Sharon removed thousands of Israelis from Gaza and the northern part of the West Bank and enforced the withdrawal with the Israeli Defense Forces. Sharon was so committed to a two-state solution that he resigned from Likud to form a new party to try to see it through.

After arrogantly scolding both Israeli and U.S. Jewish leaders about their selfish ways, Obama turned his attention to the "international community." Speaking before the virulently anti-American, anti-Israeli United Nations General Assembly in September 2009, Obama told his audience that "America does not accept the legitimacy of continued Israeli settlements." The UN crowd went wild. Obama had been repeatedly warned by Middle East experts that the demand that Israel halt settlement construction would be disastrous, but he went ahead anyway. Palestinian leader Mahmoud Abbas then ran with it, making a settlement freeze a precondition for negotiations, knowing he was backed by the American president. Since Israel agreed to only limited construction stoppages, the result was the longest period without direct talks between the parties in over seventeen years.

Abbas later said that he felt betrayed by Obama, who, feeling the pressure from American Jewish leaders and congressional Democrats, essentially backed away from the settlement demand and left Abbas twisting in the wind. Abbas said, "We both went up the tree. After that, he came down with a ladder and he removed the ladder and said to me, jump. Three times he did it." If you're going to sell out a close American ally, at least do it in a way that doesn't also tick off the adversary you're trying to help.

In the spring of 2010, Vice President Joe Biden visited Israel. While he was there, a local Jerusalem office announced plans for new settlement construction in a part of the city. Biden left Israel in a huff and Obama began a full-frontal assault on the Jewish state. Secretary of State Hillary Clinton dressed down Prime Minister Benjamin Netanyahu in a forty-five-minute phone call during which she blamed him for "harming the bilateral relationship." When she was done berating him, she ordered the Israeli ambassador to the State Department and had him flogged in much the same way. The administration canceled their Middle East envoy's scheduled trip to Israel, and it joined a European Union condemnation of Israel. Members of Team Obama fanned out on television and radio to call Israel's planned housing construction an "insult" and an "affront." Apparently, everyone in this world is allowed to build houses except Jews. Hamas can build houses in Gaza, and Hezbollah can build houses in Lebanon. But if you're a Jew? No house for you. Did Obama really believe he could tell a country that it couldn't build houses in its own capital city? I guess so. Or perhaps he was just mad that his fellow anti-Israel kook, Jimmy Carter, wasn't asked to help build the houses with Habitat for Humanity.

The ease and rapidity with which they could summon all of this sound and fury against Israel was striking, and yet they couldn't manage one word of condemnation for the Palestinians who, just minutes after Biden had left the West Bank, honored Dalal Mughrabi, a Palestinian terrorist responsible for an attack that had killed thirty-eight people, including children and an American. The response from the administration? Crickets and tumbleweeds. Within two weeks, Netanyahu had arrived in Washington to try to smooth things over but was left cooling his heels at the White House by Obama, who not only ditched Bibi mid-meeting to have dinner with his family, but who also denied him a photo-op, a joint statement, and even an honorable exit. He forced Netanyahu to leave through a side door, perhaps to commune with the Dalai Lama who had been shoved out the same trash-strewn exit.

Obama's anti-Israeli moves escalated. In late May 2010, a flotilla sponsored by the Islamist forces in Turkey set sail with the stated mission of busting the Israeli-Egyptian blockade of terrorist-run Gaza and to distribute "humanitarian" aid to Palestinians living there. Israel was allowing all kinds of humanitarian and other assistance into Gaza, had invited the flotilla organizers to transport the aid through land crossings but was refused, and Gaza had its own government, Hamas, which was supposed to be providing for its people. But none of that mattered to the flotilla organizers, who included American radicals such as Bill Ayers and Jodie Evans, the leader of the leftist organization CODEPINK, who colluded with Hamas to arrange the operation. Another American kook who was involved in the Free Gaza movement was former Democratic congresswoman Cynthia McKinney, also known as "Much Ado About a Hairdo." She has repeatedly joined with Muslim radicals in attempting to overrun the Israeli blockade. At one point, she was even caught and held in an Israeli detention facility. Unfortunately for us, the Israelis couldn't stand her either and deported her back to the United States.

On May 31, the ships were intercepted by Israeli speedboats and helicopters, from which Israeli commandos arrived to force the ships to dock in the Israeli port of Ashdod for inspection. The commandos were brutally attacked aboard one of the ships by what a United Nations report later described as a "hard-core group" armed with iron bars and knives. Ten Israeli commandos were wounded in the attack, and nine of the Gaza-bound militants were killed.

This had been a deliberate act of provocation, designed to instigate a violent confrontation in order to bring global condemnation of Israel, and yet Israel responded by easing its blockade of Gaza, freeing the flotilla militants, and returning the ships. What did Israel get for its magnanimity? Israel got the Turkish government breaking off diplomatic relations with Jerusalem, rupturing one of Israel's closest strategic partnerships in the Muslim world. And it got the American president offering no backup to its ally; instead, in the perverse anti-Israel world of Obama, he actually pressured the *Israeli* government to apologize to Turkey for defending itself.

In late May 2011, with the Arab world in turmoil, Israel's partnership with Egypt threatened, and Israel's enemies in Iran, Hezbollah, Hamas, and the Muslim Brotherhood emboldened, Obama slammed into the Jewish state with a brazen demand that it return to its indefensible pre-1967 cease-fire lines with land swaps. At one of its greatest moments of vulnerability, Israel heard the person who should have been its greatest friend and defender publicly negotiate away its security position yet again.

In early September 2011, the Arab "Spring" came knocking on the door of the Israeli embassy in Cairo, Egypt. A mob of thousands, many of whom were tied to the Muslim Brotherhood, swarmed around the embassy. In short order, they took a battering ram to the concrete security wall, breached it, and then ransacked the embassy, smashing furniture and tossing confidential documents from the windows to the streets below. Israeli embassy staff found safety in a steel-doored safe room, but were ultimately whisked to safety by Egyptian commandos.

Defense Secretary Leon Panetta assured the Israelis that the United States would provide protection for the embassy personnel, but Obama's only public reaction was a written statement expressing his "grave concern."

A few months later, Obama sent out Defense Secretary Leon Panetta to yell at the Israelis to "get to the damn table" and negotiate with the Palestinians. Panetta also scolded Israeli officials about their supposed eagerness to launch a full-fledged war against Iran's nukes. Obama then wheeled out Secretary of State Hillary Clinton to blast Israel over what she called "anti-democratic" legislation proposed by Israel's religious right regarding the media, charities, and the courts. Team Obama refused to "meddle" in Iranian and Syrian internal affairs while those regimes were slaughtering their people and refused to criticize the Muslim world generally for its systematic oppression, but it had no problem "meddling" in internal Israeli controversies.

Several months later, Obama attended the G-20 meeting in France and was caught by a hot microphone denigrating Netanyahu to French president Nicolas Sarkozy. Sarkozy said, "I cannot bear Netanyahu. He's a liar," to which Obama replied, "You're fed up with him? I've got to deal with him every day!" Sarkozy subsequently apologized to Netanyahu. Obama did not.

Obama made it clear that under his leadership, America was through kissing Israeli butt. He didn't demand meaningful concessions from the Palestinians in terms of demanding that they recognize Israel's right to exist, quit terrorism, give up the so-called right of return, which would dilute the Jewish state out of existence, and negotiate in good faith over the final status of Jerusalem. Obama paid sporadic lip service to those things, but he never pushed the Palestinians to carry them out. The burden was always placed on the Israelis to negotiate more, self-reflect more, give up more.

Perhaps this is why, in September 2011, the Palestinians ignored Obama's entreaties to refrain from seeking statehood through the United Nations and did it anyway. They knew that under Obama, Israel would get the security guarantee of the United States but not much more, even as the United States was rushing to elevate its

Islamist enemies and pressuring Israel not to defend itself against the existential threat posed by a nuclear Iran. This is somewhat worse than getting your Churchill bust thrown back at you, but it's reflective of the same anti-ally attitude.

But if you're an enemy of the United States, belly right up to the bar! Let's canoodle, Iran! Let's nuzzle, Russia! How about an aperitif, North Korea? Take a load off and enjoy a state dinner, China! What up, Hugo Chávez!

You can't treat allies like this and expect them to stay allies for long. But if the overarching Obama objective has been to weaken America's place in the world in order to create a new world order in which the bad guys are elevated by our own hand, then he has succeeded. The actions of the president have clearly shown that he's more comfortable consorting with our enemies than bunking with our friends.

In July 2010, President Obama sat down with the *Washington Post* investigative reporter Bob Woodward, who was writing a book about Obama's national security and foreign policies. During their talk and as quoted in *Obama's Wars*, the president uttered four incredibly revealing things.

Woodward reported that Obama and his team were bombarded by warnings of terrorist attacks on the homeland and were scrambling to find ways to prevent them. When asked by Woodward about it, Obama replied, "We can absorb a terror attack. We'll do everything we can to prevent it, but even a 9/11, even the biggest attack ever . . . we absorbed it and we are stronger."

Consider his language: "we can absorb a terror attack." It's cold, sterile, robotic. It's Michael Dukakis's answer when he was asked what he'd do if his wife were raped and murdered. "We can absorb it." It's detached and programmatic. It's not emotional and raw and real, which is what we would expect a president's response to be in the post-9/11 era. Just like his September 19, 2001, article, Obama's answer to Woodward was foreign, alien, inhuman. What if Obama had used that phrase after Congresswoman Gabrielle Giffords was shot? He wouldn't have dared. And yet he can very calmly rationalize something worse happening to all of the American people.

The second revealing moment came in an October 26, 2009, conversation between Obama, Defense Secretary Robert Gates, and Secretary of State Hillary Clinton about the possible troop surge in Afghanistan. "This needs to be a plan about how we're going to hand it off and get out of Afghanistan," Obama said, according to Woodward. "I'm not doing ten years. I'm not doing long-term nation building. I am not spending a trillion dollars."

Suddenly the Keynesian freak was concerned about spending $1 trillion. Also note his Big Daddy tone with Gates and Clinton: you will do this because I said so! Obama was obsessed with pulling all of our troops out of Iraq and as many as logistically possible out of Afghanistan for three reasons: (a) he doesn't believe that the United States should be projecting its power around the world; (b) to launch meaningful U.S. military retrenchment; and (c) to redirect that $1 trillion (and more) into his domestic adventure. Again, the weakening of the military is a critical part of that project, so it's a kook two-fer.

In his interview with Woodward, Obama made a third telling comment. When asked about the possibility of nuclear terror in the United States, Obama called it "a potential game changer." He continued, "When I go down the list of things I have to worry about all the time, that is at the top, because that's one where you can't afford any mistakes."

If a nuclear attack on the homeland by Islamic terrorists is the highest worry on his list, then why is he so coldly academic about it? Perhaps because he's a cold academic. He stated that we "could absorb" a terror attack and, in reference to a nuclear attack in particular, referred to it as a "*potential* game changer." To Obama, a mushroom cloud over Manhattan is just a "*potential* game changer." Maybe an *actual* game changer, maybe not. Depends on the size of the nuke or if it were detonated by Iran or al-Qaeda or a terrorist lone wolf or how many fallout victims there were or whether Obama had intended to take Michelle on a date night in New York that day and the damn radiation ruined their plans. No American president should ever be referring to a nuclear terror attack on U.S. soil as a "*potential* game changer," as if he'd have to have Valerie Jarrett run a focus group first to figure out how to respond. It would be a true game changer of such magnitude that the future of the world would be put on a completely different trajectory.

The fourth revealing Obama moment: after he informed the military brass of his decision to ignore their request for 40,000 additional troops for Afghanistan and go with 30,000 in just a brief escalation, the commanders continued to push for more troops. Obama snapped, "Why do we keep having these meetings?"

Woodward then quotes Obama as scolding the chairman of the Joint Chiefs of Staff, Admiral Michael Mullen, Gates, and Clinton: "In 2010, we will not be having a conversation about how to do more. I will not want to hear, 'We're doing fine, Mr. President, but we'd be better if we just do more.' We're not going to be having a conversation about how to change [the mission] . . . unless we're talking about how to draw down faster than anticipated in 2011."

This was Obama as Super Big Daddy. It was his way or the highway, the nation's security be damned. According to Woodward, General David Petraeus, who had engineered the successful surge in Iraq, interpreted Obama's decision as a personal repudiation. Petraeus had argued for continuing a "protect the Afghan people" counterinsurgency approach, but Obama insisted on a far narrower and shorter-term plan because he wanted out of there. And Obama's own "responsibility to protect" approach had yet to kick in; it was good enough for the Libyans but not, apparently, for the Afghanis.

These four exchanges tell us a few things about the commander in chief. They tell us that to him, the American people are a blob he's forced to protect instead of millions of individuals with lives, families, and beating hearts. They tell us that "no drama Obama" has drama happening all around him, much of it self-created. They tell us that he's a petty man who's a terrible manager and a reckless commander of the armed forces. And they tell us that he's a stone cold kook.

American superpower exists to keep the world's most malevolent forces at bay, but when we're considered a pushover, the bad guys act up and it never ends well. The inevitable result will be a collapse of order and violent chaos, in which the forces of evil march forward—unless they are stopped by force applied by the good guys. But when the world's biggest and most powerful good guy checks out, it's curtains for peace and stability.

In Obama's hands, American decline isn't just a few statistics on a piece of paper. It's a steep, irreversible, and very real plummet to weakness and irrelevance—and Obama is taking us there fast with his own foot on the $4-per-gallon gas.

By turning us from America the Exceptional into America the Ho-Hum, Obama has ushered us into the years of living dangerously.

PART V

AMERICA, UNLEASHED

DOROTHY: Oh, will you help me? Can you help me?

GLINDA: You don't need to be helped any longer. You've always had the power to go back to Kansas.

DOROTHY: I have?

SCARECROW: Then why didn't you tell her before?

GLINDA: Because she wouldn't have believed me. She had to learn it for herself.

—*The Wizard of Oz*

America Lost?

"You are an American, yes?" The burly New York City cabdriver looked at me through the rearview mirror as he asked the question, his voice saturated with a heavy Eastern European accent.

"Yes, I am," I replied.

"Tell me: what are you doing?"

About a year into Barack Obama's presidency, I climbed into this man's cab for a short trip across Manhattan. Engaging city taxi drivers can go one of two ways: it can either be an enjoyable, interesting experience or it can end in a torrent of profanity in multiple languages. This particular cabdriver was friendly and gregarious, particularly when I asked him about the source of his accent.

"The Bronx," he replied. "Oh, you mean where I am *from*?" He paused for a moment and then said, "I was born in Bulgaria. But I am an *American*." And then this big, strapping man grew emotional as he told me his story: "I am an American by choice. And you'll forgive me, but I think those of us who are Americans by choice rather than by birth have a different view. Many Americans, you do not appreciate your freedom. You have always had it. You don't know anything else. I have lived under communism. I have been beaten and put in jail. I have heard the knock of the secret police in the middle of the night. I have had neighbors disappear. I have had the government open my mail and listen in to my phone. I have gone days eating only potatoes because the store shelves were bare. There was no medicine, no good doctors."

He told me that his family fled Bulgaria to escape the tyranny and brutality of Communist rule and came to the United States to seek the very promise of America: freedom. That's when he asked me, "Tell me: what are you doing? Why are you letting America be destroyed?"

His voice quaked with despair and frustration as he railed against what he called "enslaving debt," "communist medicine," and "a jack-boot government." As he stopped at my destination, this refugee from communist hell turned around, threw his arm over the seat, and looked directly at me. "Please don't let this happen to America. It's creeping in here, and it's creeping in fast. We came to America to get *away* from socialism. If it comes here, where will we go? Where will *any* of us go? There's no other hope anywhere else. You're letting your freedoms be taken from you, and you don't even see it. Or you see it but you don't care, which is the worst kind of treason."

Treason. The word stung me. By allowing the insidious tyranny of the ever-growing state, were we actively betraying our country? Were we all essentially traitors to America for permitting our own government to seize our freedoms and move us into debilitating dependency with our own lazy acquiescence? Were we complicit in our own destruction? Were we guilty of citizen malpractice?

That grizzled New York City cabdriver pointed to an enduring truth about America: that it is still seen by billions of people around the world as—in Abraham Lincoln's words—"the last best hope of earth." But he also warned that the country was in grave danger of slipping beneath the waves, pulling that last best hope of humanity into the perpetual darkness of state domination, economic collectivism, and human misery. Would we allow our current government to cripple us and atrophy American power? Or would we heed the words of Thomas Paine: "It is the duty of the patriot to protect their country from its government."

America. The name itself is lyrical, carrying dulcet notes of promise and optimism. America the place is spectacular. But America the *idea* is what has animated a way of life based not on government coercion but on the freedom of the individual, limited and constrained government, economic opportunity, personal generosity, tolerance and responsibility, community, faith, and human dignity. In their wisdom, the Founding Fathers crafted the philosophy first and then built a nation—a nation that kindled blazing liberty, endless aspiration, and fierce independence. No other country on earth had ever tried such an enterprise. They knew the exceptional nature of the system they were bequeathing as well as its fragility. On the final day of deliberation at the Constitutional Convention in 1787, Benjamin Franklin descended the steps of Independence Hall. A woman approached him to ask what kind of government they had given us. "A Republic," he replied, "if you can keep it."

That was, perhaps, the first warning that the American system would require constant care if it were to remain exceptional. The Founders admonished the American people to remain vigilant because threats to liberty come in many forms. They may appear as international threats or as "emergency" responses to domestic crises. They may appear as seemingly innocuous appeals for "modernizing" or "updating" the Constitution. They may come in the polished package of a professed "savior," or as a philosophy that promises to deliver a "more perfect union." All threats to liberty must be turned back before they have the chance to take root and metastasize. As Patrick Henry put it, "Liberty, the greatest of all earthly blessings—give us that precious jewel, and you may take every thing else! Guard with jealous attention the public liberty. Suspect every one who approaches that jewel."

One hundred years after the Constitution became the law of the land, Alexander Tyler, a Scottish history professor at the University of Edinburgh, described the fall of ancient Athens with a succinct and accurate summary of how and why democracies decline. "A democracy will continue to exist up until the time that voters discover that they can vote themselves generous gifts from the public treasury," he wrote. "From that moment on, the majority always votes for the candidates who promise the most benefits from the public treasury, with the result that every democracy will finally collapse over loose fiscal policy, (which is) always followed by a dictatorship. The average age of the world's greatest civilizations from the beginning of history, has been about 200 years. During those 200 years, these nations always progressed through the following sequence:

"From bondage to spiritual faith;

"From spiritual faith to great courage;

"From courage to liberty;

"From liberty to abundance;

"From abundance to complacency;

"From complacency to apathy;

"From apathy to dependence;

"From dependence back into bondage."

We are now in the final phase. How did we get here?

What the @$%&! just happened?

The particular horror is that we are allowing the theft of freedom to be done *to* us by our own government. While we luxuriate in abundance, complacency, and apathy—many of us knowing nothing else—Obama and the kooks are maneuvering us quickly into bondage. Once we are truly bound, the relationship between the individual and the government will be changed irrevocably: the individual will have dwindling and ultimately meaningless "freedoms" and the people will be led toward European-style dependence; we will be an enslaved mob. This is why what Tyler wrote is so important. If people believe they can vote themselves a raise, they will. And once that mentality finds its way into the middle class, then America as the land of the free will be history.

Over the past few decades, the kooks have succeeded in uprooting many of the foundations of liberty built by the Founders and replacing them with an expanding nanny state over which they have near-complete control.

The state is in your paycheck, taking upwards of 50 percent of it for its endless demands. The state tells you what medical treatments you can and cannot have. The state tells you what you can and cannot eat, drink, and God forbid if you want to be merry. The state tells you how many calories are in that Big Mac. The state tells you whether or not you can build or renovate your supposedly "private" property, and, if it agrees to let you do what you'd like, makes you abide by infinite regulations and pay extravagant fees for the privilege. The state tells you how to heat, air condition, and illuminate your property. The state tells you that you may buy this toy for your child, but not that one. The state tells you that you cannot have plastic bags for your groceries and the paper ones will cost you. The state is in your car and gas tank, imposing fuel mileage standards and huge gasoline taxes. The state is on your telephone lines, taxing your landlines, cell phones, and text messages. The state is on the Internet, taxing your online purchases and monitoring some of your Web usage. The state is in every business you patronize with taxes, rules, regulations, and fees. The state tells you that you can smoke, just not over here, over there, and certainly not over there. The state tells you to hate Fox News and love MSNBC. The state tells you to hate pickup trucks and love the Chevy Volt. The state tells you to hate your mom and dad and to go instead with two dads named Barry and Joe. You literally cannot breathe in America without the government monitoring you. The kooks have plunged this nation into an Orwellian nightmare in which they pull the strings and you must dance at their command. The state is the ultimate buzz kill.

With every new state control, the leftists choke off more of your freedom and then leverage it into more power for their government Leviathan. They are turning America into a rotted-out, condemned building, a broken shell of something that was once great and majestic, where the riffraff of society occupy each abandoned level. There are street gangs and union thugs on Level 1, needle users and community organizers on Level 2, Democrats and MSNBC analysts on Level 3, and up on the rooftop of Level 4 is Paul Krugman, screaming into the sky about the evils of capitalism while dropping bowling balls on fancy cars driving by. This collage of mayhem is the next exciting role-playing game, *Final Fantasy: The Obama Years*.

At the same time, the kooks have downgraded American power internationally through apologias, retrenchment, an increasingly gutted military, the active cultivation of our enemies, and the willful disregard of our allies. In their hands, America has been cut off at the knees, left broken and limping, a second-rate power largely incapable—and undeserving—of projecting influence in the world without a multilateral orgy of approval.

The leftists' grand design is centered on one basic premise: redistribute American power. Redistribute our wealth, economic energy, political strength, military power, cultural appeal, constitutional genius, and exceptional ingenuity both at home and abroad. Redistribute the elements of our greatness. Dilute our power in order to destroy it. They have executed their plan with precision and cold efficiency, particularly once they discovered their perfect agent in a mysterious stranger from the shores of Indonesia, the beaches of Hawaii, and the precincts of Chicago.

The allure of kookdom is its false promise of an easier life. At its core, it's about the state coaxing—or forcing—you to transfer responsibility to the state. This is part of what made communism and socialism so appealing in theory: the nanny state would care for all of your cradle-to-grave needs. Don't worry about a thing. The state's got you covered, from your education and health care to your transportation, home, and job to how and when you kick the bucket. As the kooks adapted the redistributionist welfare state to make it go down smoother in America, they refined their sales job. As they assumed more and more responsibilities for you, they told you that they were clearing a path for a less burdensome life. It was a seduction to which many Americans succumbed—and continue to succumb.

In fact, the opposite is true: when the state seizes more power and responsibility, your independence and freedom are degraded. And rather than liberation from responsibility, you face a burden of dependence—yours and everyone else's—that grows heavier by the day. It's a devil's bargain, and the devil is running the show.

The Founders saw things differently. They rejected the idea of an omnipotent state taking on an endless buffet of responsibilities. Instead, they saw the inseparability of freedom and responsibility. They made clear that if you want the unprecedented freedoms of America, you must accept the outcomes of your own decisions. That's why they built America upon the simple and profound premise that freedom and responsibility rest not with the state but with the individual. And they expected us to fight for what they had created: a unique system of self-governance based on individuals responsible enough to manage their own—and the nation's—liberty, power, and affairs. Are we still up to that challenge?

Enter the Happy Warrior.

The Happy Warrior believes in two essential truths: first, that America *can* be saved, and second, that it is *worth* saving. We need a nation of Happy Warriors—focused on those two truths and the tough reality that the threats to our survival are all around us—to perform the rescue operation.

What is a Happy Warrior and how do we become a nation of them? There are ten essential keys to the Happy Warrior, all of which require hard work, dedication, and attitudinal changes. But if we understand and undertake them, the journey to renew America will be spectacularly rewarding.

First, we must recognize that the Happy Warrior is above all a *warrior*. We must realize that we are in a war. We're in an ideological war, an economic war, a political war, a cultural war, and a war abroad for our superpower primacy. When Reagan became president, he knew we were in brutal economic and international wars for America. When Margaret Thatcher became prime minister, she knew Great Britain was deep in those wars as well. Once we recognize that we're in the war, then we must be prepared to fight it. That means understanding that the other side is going to hit back ruthlessly and relentlessly, and that we've got to persevere despite the attacks and hit back too, as difficult as that may be. So the first step for the Happy Warrior is to realize that we face a very real danger and that there's no getting out of the war without fighting it.

Second, we must win these wars before they escalate into bigger cataclysms. We've got to be smart and self-aware enough to learn from our history, avoid repeating it, and letting things deteriorate until a devastating war is upon us, as with the Civil War, World War II, and September 11, 2001. We must adopt a warrior attitude *now*, before it's truly too late, and be prepared to be strong, confident, and unwavering as we fight it.

Third, we must recognize that any war requires pain and sacrifice. The Happy Warrior's choice—and *only* choice—is to face those uncomfortable things now or face much greater pain later.

Fourth, in most cases, we are at war with *ourselves*—the tendency to go wobbly, seek the easy way out, relinquish responsibility to the nanny state, fall into the waiting arms of the kooks promising the path of least resistance. We must fight these impulses in *ourselves* in order to form the *national* strength to fight these wars.

Fifth, the Happy Warrior fights to hold the other side responsible for its actions. The kooks fight to transfer responsibility and power away from the individual to the state. They argue that *we* are the ones who have to change and adapt to *their* freedom-crushing template. We reject that perversion of the American ideal.

Sixth, the Happy Warrior is fully comfortable that the underpinning of freedom is, in fact, individual responsibility. The kooks try to sell, hypnotize, and addict us to the idea that they will assume responsibility for us without requiring us to relinquish our freedoms. We know that we've got to turn back that Big Lie and take responsibility for fighting for American interests, at home and abroad. The Happy Warrior is responsible for himself and believes that everybody else is responsible for themselves. If we all fought determinedly for that belief, the state would naturally shrink as we the people won more of our own power back.

Seventh, the Happy Warrior believes in the inherent goodness of man. We believe that the state should get out of the way not just so we can prosper, but so we can share that prosperity unencumbered by the state. The Left's philosophy of "social justice" requires the state to *compel* "charity" in order to "spread the wealth around." And yet, without government compulsion, the American people are the most charitable on earth. Most other countries give about 1 percent or less of their national wealth to charity. The United States doubles that. While we recognize that there is a proper role for government to discharge its constitutional duties and provide a reasonable social safety net, we also recognize that the kooks have so expanded government in the false name of "compassion" that we now have a nearly unrecognizable America.

Eighth, the Happy Warrior doesn't believe that America is zero-sum, that success in one place must be punished to elevate the less successful somewhere else. The depraved premise of the kooks is that the rich got their wealth by "taking" it from the poor. In fact, approximately 80 percent of all millionaires are the first generation in their family to be rich. They didn't inherit their wealth, à la Paris Hilton. They earned it through hard work and sacrifice. Unlike the professional victimhood hustlers of the Left, the Happy Warrior believes that economic expansion creates real growth. We don't believe in expanding the *money supply* in order to create the *illusion* of growth in order to redistribute all over the place. We believe in restraining government so individuals can do their thing and prosper.

Ninth, an effective Happy Warrior is a disciplined one. As long as our directives are consistent with the founding principles of constitutionally limited government, fiscal responsibility, and properly regulated free markets, we must focus on the fight for them until America has been restored.

And finally, the Happy Warrior is, in fact, happy. We take on our mission joyfully, certain that traditional American values are worthy of a passionate defense and that American power is not something to be ashamed of but celebrated. The attitudinal shift away from Howard Beale outrage to Reagan/Thatcher exuberance will animate the fight with our natural optimism. The best way to temper the inevitable pain of the battle is to carry it out with good cheer, confident in our mission, its integrity, and success.

What made previous Happy Warriors such as Reagan and Thatcher particularly strong leaders was their vision of individual freedom and national power, their charismatic articulation of it, and their ability to persuade their people that their policy path was the right way to go. Today we need people who are proud to make an unequivocal, unapologetic, and full-throated case for America. We need people willing to make the *moral case* for the free market and American superpower. We need people willing to reject outright the kooks' contention that redistributionism is a moral system of "economic justice" and argue for how and why capitalism empowers the individual and creates a steady expansion of prosperity and opportunity. We need people willing to make the *moral case* for a strong U.S. presence in the world, keeping the bad guys at bay and advancing the causes of freedom and peace. We need people willing to tell the truth about the kooks' lies that redistributionism at home and wobbliness abroad ensure greater global "justice" and "equality." And absent leaders who will make these arguments, we must take it upon ourselves to make the moral case for America. We have our work cut out for us, because the class warrior and defeatist punks aren't just going to step aside.

———

Obama once likened his brief time in the private sector to being "a spy behind enemy lines." In mid-December 2011, Obama gave a major economic speech in Osawatomie, Kansas, that revealed just how much he still believed economic freedom is the "enemy." Why would the president of the United States choose that particular location to once again lecture America on the injustices of capitalism? Teddy Roosevelt launched modern progressivism in a speech there in 1910, making it something of a sacred mecca for leftists. In fact, the radical anti-American group the Weather Underground—yes, the Bill Ayers and Bernardine Dohrn Weather Underground—named their publication *Osawatomie*. The summer 1975 edition of *Osawatomie* was a delightful paean to the Vietnamese communist Ho Chi Minh, with a cover illustration of the mass murderer saying, "The American invaders will be defeated." I'm sure that in the summer of 1975, pubescent Barry was feeling the changes in his body. He was fourteen years old, and like all boys going through puberty, he liked to spend time alone in his bedroom. The difference between him and the other boys, however, was that Barry wouldn't vanish into his room with a pilfered copy of *Playboy*. Instead, he'd lock the door behind him with a copy of *Osawatomie*.

In his Osawatomie speech, given nearly three years into his tenure, Obama proved yet again that he is committed to his domestic demolition project, regardless of the economic pain or even his own reelection. Class warfare, wealth redistribution, unprecedented spending, record-breaking deficits and debt, socialized medicine, higher taxes, oppressive state regulations . . . they are all working for the greater end. The wrecking ball he let swing is smashing through every part of the economy, exactly as planned.

"Now, just as there was in Teddy Roosevelt's time, there is a certain crowd in Washington who, for the last few decades, have said, let's respond to this economic challenge with the same old tune," he intoned. "'The market will take care of everything,' they tell us. Now, it's a simple theory," he continued. "And we have to admit, it's one that speaks to our rugged individualism and our healthy skepticism of too much government. That's in America's DNA. And that theory fits well on a bumper sticker. But here's the problem: It doesn't work. It has never worked."

Obama was really saying that economic freedom doesn't work. Economic decisions cannot be left to individuals, who are too selfish, greedy, and reckless to make them. They must be consolidated in the hands of the state, which can more evenly "spread the wealth around" to ensure equality of outcomes rather than equality of opportunity.

Obama is America's chief misery merchant, and his job is to guarantee that all joy is sucked completely from the American people. He knows that a joyless people is a desperate people, and thus he must maintain an atmosphere of stagnation where upward mobility is impossible. He is constantly positioning himself as the great defender of the middle class, but much of what he has done has been geared toward destroying it: engaging in record government spending, exploding deficits, inflating the currency and devaluing the dollar, raising taxes, and burdening businesses with ever-increasing costs and regulations. While he hits the highest earners, his real target is the middle class, which is less able to manage the leftist economic assault. His ultimate goal is to so *weaken* the middle class that it becomes utterly dependent on government as well. This is at the core of Obama's Declaration of Dependence.

"I believe that this country succeeds when everyone gets a fair shot, when everyone does their fair share, when everyone plays by the same rules," he said in Osawatomie. He hasn't changed his thinking or his policies one iota. He keeps telling us who he is. Do we believe him now?

First, consider *Obama the Liar*:

On the "stimulus," Obama told us that it would keep unemployment at or under 8 percent. Nearly $1 trillion later, unemployment sailed over 10 percent and then settled into the 9 percent range, and when the rate dropped, it was largely because people stopped looking for work, not because they found jobs. Obama calls that improvement.

On spending, Obama told us he'd institute "pay-as-you-go budgeting" because he wanted to reduce spending levels. Instead, he produced multiple budgets over $3.5 trillion each—all rejected by Congress—and proposed endless spending proposals. He also refused to actually cut spending in any meaningful way, except in national defense.

Also on spending, Obama told us that he'd "go through our federal budget—page by page, line by line—eliminating those programs we don't need, and insisting that those we do, operate in a sensible, cost-effective way." He hasn't done either.

On the deficit, Obama told us that he'd cut it in half by the end of his first term. Instead, he more than tripled it, producing years' worth of record $1 trillion–plus deficits.

On the debt, Obama told us he'd slow its growth. Instead, he's piled on a record $5 trillion in three years, more than any other president ever. As a senator in 2006, he called raising the debt ceiling "a failure of leadership." As president, he requested and got four mega-increases in the debt ceiling in less than three years. He's on pace to borrow more than $6.2 trillion in just one term, which is more debt than was accumulated by all U.S. presidents from Washington through Clinton combined.

On ObamaCare, Obama told us it would help to improve the economy, lower costs, deliver greater accessibility, and if we "liked our current plan," we could "keep it." Instead, ObamaCare brought job creation to a screeching halt, prices are already skyrocketing before the bulk of it has even been enacted, rationing has kicked in, many Americans have discovered that they won't be able to keep their plans, and the Supreme Court has been forced to decide its very constitutionality.

On "green energy," Obama told us to expect a green jobs revolution (backed by taxpayer money). Instead, we ended up paying tens of billions of dollars in subsidies to "clean energy" companies only to have them supply a measly 2.4 percent of the nation's power, that is, when they didn't go belly-up.

On traditional sources of energy, Obama told us that he wanted to reduce our dependence on foreign sources of oil and gas. Instead, he called for hiking taxes on domestic oil and gas production, halted offshore drilling and exploration and then made them more difficult, and blocked the private-sector construction of the Keystone XL pipeline.

On ethics, Obama told us that he'd lead the "most transparent administration in history" and a new era of "accountability." Instead, Team Obama has stonewalled every investigation from Solyndra to the New Black Panther Party voter intimidation case to his own murky background to Fast and Furious. He has also blamed the bad economy on everything but his own policies. And he has depended heavily on his vast network of "czars," through whom he *really* exercises power.

On presidential signing statements, Obama told us he wouldn't engage in the practice "as a way of doing an end-run around Congress." As of early 2012, he had put his name to nineteen signing statements, on issues from dispersing "stimulus" money to negotiating with foreign governments to detaining Americans, a new power he claimed he didn't think he'd ever use. But you never know.

On lobbying, Obama told us there would be no lobbyists in his administration and no lobbyist money going to his campaign. Instead, he has happily welcomed both with open arms.

Obama promised a thriving economy and a united country. We have gotten neither.

About that promised thriving economy . . . consider *The Obama Reign of Economic Terror*:

Chronic unemployment worse than what it was during the Great Depression.

The longest stretch of sky-high unemployment since the Depression.

The worst jobs record of any president in the modern age.

The lowest labor participation rate since the early 1980s.

An unprecedented number of underemployed people.

Plummeting real median income; since June 2009, the income of Americans has fallen by over 6.5 percent.

Black unemployment at its highest level in nearly thirty years, with black youth unemployment reaching a staggering 50 percent.

The lowest number of youth, ages sixteen to nineteen, employed since 1948.

The steepest drop in the American standard of living in over fifty years.

A rate of economic growth only slightly higher than the decade of the Great Depression.

As percentages of GDP, federal spending, the budget deficit, and the national debt at their highest levels since World War II.

U.S. credit downgraded for the first time in history.

The misery index at its highest level and consumer confidence at its lowest level in more than three decades.

A housing crisis worse than the one that occurred during the Great Depression, with median home values declining every month Obama has been in office.

Over seven thousand new regulations, rules, and guidelines issued.

Creeping inflation, particularly in the goods Americans use every day: food and fuel.

A record increase of Americans living in poverty, including record numbers of children.

A record number of people—48 million—on food stamps.

The largest number of people—just under 50 million—since the early 1990s without health insurance.

The highest level of government dependency on one or more federal benefit programs in American history.

To Obama, this isn't a record of failure. It's a record of extraordinary success. It was all designed and executed to near perfection by Obama and the kooks, who had to uproot the existing economic system in order to replace it with their redistributive one. They knew it would be painful, messy, and jarring; they just didn't care.

Because Obama and his fellow kooks believe that the *American* system is unjust, unfair, and evil, they set out to replace it with their own enlightened, twenty-first-century leftist revolution. As old-school commies like Castro and the Chinese moved toward more capitalist systems, the kooks believe we should meet them halfway. So they set out to install their brand of leftism through shrewd political force in order to so weaken America domestically and internationally that the changes would be irreversible.

Meanwhile, Obama attempted to obfuscate his agenda's failures by blaming *us* for not getting with the leftist program. At a 2011 San Francisco fund-raiser, he sighed that "we have lost our ambition, our imagination, and our willingness to do the things that built the Golden Gate Bridge and the Hoover Dam." A few weeks later, he lamented that we had gotten "a little soft." And then shortly after that, while attending the Asia-Pacific summit, he complained to world leaders that Americans had gotten "lazy" in attracting foreign investment.

To the contemptuous Obama, we're just a bunch of rubes who don't get the brilliance that is his vision. When Michelle said during the 2008 campaign, "Barack Obama will require you to work," what she—what they—meant was that they'd require us to work under *their* rules and toward *their* goals. George W. Bush once said, "Either you are with us, or you are with the terrorists." But if Obama has ever thought anything similar, it would most likely sound like, "Either you are with us, or you are with the capitalists."

Like any self-respecting authoritarian, Obama also hated having to deal with the coequal branches of government and dissenting points of view. His exasperation burst out in his repeated slams of the Supreme Court, and in his July 2011 comments to La Raza: "Believe me, right now, dealing with Congress . . . the idea of doing things on my own is very tempting." But he had already been circumventing the legislative process and violating the spirit of the law for years. When a growth-killing Internet regulation proposal failed to pass Congress, Obama's Federal Communications Commission announced that it was going to regulate the Web anyway, defying a federal court ruling. The Obama/Holder Justice Department also unilaterally decided that it would no longer enforce federal laws against marijuana use and the Defense of Marriage Act. All hail an unaccountable and undemocratic bureaucratic welfare state, and never mind that pesky Constitution.

In one of his most flagrant floutings of the rule of law, Obama made four recess appointments in early 2012 when the Senate was not in recess. It was a blatant violation of the constitutional separation of powers, a trampling of Congress's constitutional authority, and a dangerous concentration of executive power. But to be fair to Obama, he was under the impression that a recess appointment took place after lunch but before language arts class.

The system is not "broken," as Obama likes to complain; it's exactly as the Founders intended, made up of checks and balances to restrain his most radical impulses. Or at least it was until he got his kook hands on it. He doesn't care that when a branch of government gets out of control, we've got lawful options, such as elections and impeachment. Why should Obama respect the existing processes when he can overhaul the whole shebang to his specifications?

━━━━━

Amid all of the wreckage, however, there is a silver lining that marks the beginning of our own "fundamental transformation" of America: the Obama economy is finally shattering the myth of the Left. The monumental success of American capitalism had prevented leftism from being exposed as a fraudulent ideology designed to kill off prosperity at every turn. Until now. The wealth redistribution ideology is collapsing, swamped by its own internal contradictions and disastrous consequences. If Keynesianism truly worked, the unprecedented spending blowouts of the Obama-Pelosi-Reid era would have had the U.S. economy now at Herculean strength. Instead, we have years of economic basket-case-ism. The romanticism of the Left is over. But the kooks cannot possibly look in the mirror and find the fault within themselves, because doing so would mean the end of leftism, the end of their cottage industry of victimhood and dependency, the end of their calamitous agenda. They cannot abide this kind of ignominious end, so they continue their lies and playing Blame Roulette. But the curtain has been pulled back on them. And their emperor has been shown to have no clothes. I might also add that the skinny socialist emperor could really use a sandwich. I can see his rib cage. Then again, maybe he plans to don some angel wings and try out for the Victoria's Secret Fashion Show.

Given what the @$%&! has just happened, three particularly prescient past warnings stand out. The first, from Benjamin Franklin: "Make yourselves sheep and the wolves will eat you."

The second, from a generation after America's founding. On June 1, 1837, Massachusetts senator Daniel Webster said, "There is no nation on earth powerful enough to accomplish our overthrow. Our destruction, should it come at all, will be from another quarter. From the inattention of the people to the concerns of their government, from their carelessness and negligence. I must confess that I do apprehend some danger. I fear that they may place too implicit a confidence in their public servants and fail properly to scrutinize their conduct; that in this way they may be made the dupes of designing men and become the instruments of their own undoing."

And the third warning came a little over a hundred years later. On June 25, 1940, former president Herbert Hoover took the stage at the Republican National Convention in Philadelphia and warned of the cataclysmic convulsions of statism that had rent apart Europe:

In every single case before the rise of dictatorships there had been a period dominated by economic planners. Each of these nations had an era under starry-eyed men who believed that they could plan and force the economic life of the people. They believed that was the way to correct abuse or to meet emergencies in systems of free enterprise. They exalted the state as the solvent of all economic problems.

These men thought they were liberals. But they also thought they could have economic dictatorship by bureaucracy and at the same time preserve free speech, orderly justice and free government. They were the spiritual fathers of the New Deal.

These men were not Communists or Fascists but they mixed these ideas into free systems. It is true that Communists and Fascists were round about. They formed popular fronts and gave the applause.

These so-called liberals shifted the relation of government to free enterprise from that of umpire to controller. Directly or indirectly they politically controlled credit, prices, production of industry, farmer and labor. They devalued, pump-primed and inflated. They controlled private enterprise by government competition, by regulation and by taxes. They met every failure with demands for more and more power of control. And they employed that handmaiden of power, named "Gimme a Billion, Quick!"

These leaders ignored the fact that the driving power of free economic life is the initiative and enterprise of men. . . .

Initiative slackened, production in industry slowed down. Then came chronic unemployment and frantic government spending in an effort to support the unemployed. Government debts mounted. And finally government credit was undermined. Out of the miseries of the people there grew pressure groups—business, labor, farmers—

demanding relief or special privilege. Class hate poisoned co-operation.

Does this sound unfamiliar to you? It was all these confusions that rang down the curtain upon liberty.

Sadly, President Hoover, it's all too familiar.

Our own "carelessness and negligence" led to Obama's rise, making us the "dupes" of this particular "designing man." If we are to reverse the damage he has done and save the nation from his redistributionist abuse, we are going to need far more than a simple change in leadership in 2012 and beyond, as necessary as that is. We are going to need a "fundamental transformation" of our own: a transformation of our thinking, our expectations, and our understanding of what America is and what it should—must—be. In this fight for freedom, we're gonna need a bigger boat.

But along with moral and practical outrage, we need to inspire hope. The faux "we're the ones we've been waiting for" hope Obama peddled in 2008 dissipated fast because he sold hope in *himself*, rather than in America *itself*.

Our brand of hope has always been based not on men but on an enduring truth: that government exists to protect and defend us from threats foreign and domestic and to ensure that everyone has the opportunity to compete—and that *we*, not the state, are responsible for the consequences.

It's a hope found in our symbolic power as a beacon of liberty and in our real power as a superpower able and willing to defend ourselves, our interests, and the forces of freedom around the world.

It's a hope echoed in the Bulgarian cabdriver's plea to me: don't let what has made and kept you exceptional slip away.

About a week before the presidential election in 1980, Ronald Reagan and Jimmy Carter held their final debate. In his closing statement, Reagan looked directly at the American people and asked a few deceptively simple questions:

"Are you better off now than you were four years ago? Is it easier for you to go and buy things in the stores than it was four years ago? Is there more or less unemployment in the country than there was four years ago? Is America as respected throughout the world as it was?"

Reagan was the consummate Happy Warrior. He spoke softly, but he carried a big stick. He tapped into the sentiment held by most Americans who, after years of being trapped under big-government deadweight, yearned to breathe free again. And here we are, thirty years later, faced with the same questions. Only Barack Obama and the kooks aren't your father's Democrats. They are a wrecking crew who've learned not to repeat the timidity and compromise of your father's Democrats.

That's why the challenge for us is much more difficult than it was in 1980. The problems are bigger, the economic disaster more catastrophic, the debt so much bigger, government so much more monstrous, and American influence more weakened. We need to seize the moral and practical outrage we felt in 1980 and cube it because this time, the very essence of America is at stake.

That's why we need to once again become a nation of Happy Warriors, armed with a positive battle cry of renewal, a set of policies, and a relentless optimism that will sustain us even through the harshest kook pushback and the dislocation of unraveling decades of their corrosive policies and entrenched redistributionist mentality.

Is America lost? Not yet, but the hour is late, and with each passing moment we get closer to the tipping point. If we are to find America again, we need to rediscover our inner Happy Warriors and get on with it.

Captain America vs. Robin Hood

Yes we can!

—*Barack Obama to the American people, 2008*

Yes we can, but . . .

—*Barack Obama to Jon Stewart, 2010*

A funny thing happened to Barack Obama and the leftists on their way to "fundamentally transforming" the nation: many Americans stood athwart history and yelled, "Stop!"

The Americans who make up the Tea Party take their job as sentinels for the nation seriously. If their leaders were going to rape the people, pillage the Treasury, and bankrupt the nation, they would respond with peaceful resistance. And so they did: Americans of all stripes began to organize regular Tea Party protests around the country. Town hall meetings held by members of Congress, usually sleepy affairs, became raucous events during which the people demanded answers about the abuses of power to which they were being subjected. Many of those Democrats, who had gleefully embraced the bust-a-gut spending and the redistributionist nightmare of ObamaCare, recoiled in genuine shock at the response of the people. Some of them refused to face the very people who pay their salaries. Some opted for quick press releases, while others attempted "virtual town halls." But all were cowering in fear, hiding under their desks, wearing soiled Pampers with pacifiers in their mouths.

Republicans, however, were put on notice too. The Tea Party did not originally grow out of opposition to the agenda of Obama and the Democrats. It first grew out of a failure of the establishment *Republicans* to stand for constitutionally limited government, fiscal responsibility, and free markets. If the GOP had always stood strong for those principles, there would have been no need for a Tea Party. The Tea Party originated to put a spine back into the Republican Party, to get it to return to constitutional truths. Every time establishment Republicans get defeated, as did Gerald Ford in 1976, George H. W. Bush in 1992, and John McCain in 2008, conservatism always finds a way to come roaring back and give the tired old GOP a course correction.

The Tea Party has establishment Republicans worried, of course, because they fear the end of the big spending gravy train, traditional "I'll scratch your back if you scratch mine" style of negotiation, and the upset of their comfortable status quo. It has already succeeded in replacing establishment Republicans such as Kentucky's Trey Grayson and Pennsylvania's Arlen Specter with principled conservatives Rand Paul and Pat Toomey.

But above all, the Tea Party strikes real, deep, profound fear in the hearts of the kooks. Without wealth redistribution and economic control, they are nothing.

The irony is luscious: Obama and the kooks came to Washington to "fundamentally transform" things, and while they did, they also gave rise to an even more powerful force that changed things in the polar opposite way. The Tea Party forced not only a pullback of the Left's objectives but a realignment of the way taxpayer money was treated. Gone were the days of the Ted Kennedy three-martini deal-making lunch and the cavalierly spent trillions that went along with them. Gone too was the famous Ted Kennedy/Chris Dodd Waitress Sandwich that always accompanied said three-martini deal-making lunch. Instead, at least some greater awareness of fiscal responsibility and spending restraint took their place.

Fool us once, shame on you. Fool us twice, shame on us. As Obama's kook march pressed on, more and more Americans began forming a line of resistance. We put the "but" into "yes we can, but . . ."

We are witnessing the great final battle between the statist, wealth-distributing, central-economic-planning ideology of Barack Obama versus the dynamic, free market, individual liberty, limited government philosophy of traditional America. It's a battle between the kooks and the rest of us. It's a battle between Robin Hood and Captain America. Which side will win?

The path back to America must, of course, begin with replacing Obama as president. The country's foundational principles cannot withstand his relentless assault for much longer. If he and his team are allowed another term, they will, in the words of Obama himself, "finish the job." By that, he means finishing off the country. Whatever he will not be able to get through the standard legislative process, he will effect through executive fiat. And without the worry of reelection, there will be no stopping him.

So Job One must be to "de-kookify" our leadership. After "de-kookification," we must move to salvage the nation from decline and decay.

Where do we begin? The world is a complicated place, rife with complex problems to which there are no easy solutions. Usually, there are also big trade-offs in any course of action, in which certain principles and goals have to be sacrificed in service to others. What follows is not meant to be a comprehensive, detailed, or exhaustive set of policy prescriptions. Instead, it's a general look at how to begin to restore America. As John Milton wrote in *Paradise Lost*, "Long is the way and hard, that out of Hell leads up to light." We mustn't let the difficulty of the task discourage or deter us. The kooks have been 100 percent committed to their project, and we must be 100 percent committed to our restorative one. We must gird Captain America with every possible tool to use in his battle against the kooks' demented Robin Hood.

America at Home. As we survey the domestic damage of the past few years, we've got to recognize that the first step is to prevent more harm from being done. That means taking the keys of the kingdom away from the skinny socialist and his toxic band of radicals.

Next, we must counter class warfare with a prosperity vision for America. We must adopt commonsense economic solutions that will put the U.S. economy back on its traditional rocket path. This is the strength of America. It is the source of our greatness. My Bulgarian cabdriver gets it. The American people get it. Billy Idol gets it. Obama and the kooks get it; they just wage war on it.

No great nation can remain so if its people are burdened with shouldering the irresponsibilities of the state. As Thomas Jefferson put it in his First Inaugural Address in 1801, "[A] wise and frugal government . . . shall restrain men from injuring one another, shall leave them otherwise free to regulate their own pursuits of industry and improvement, and shall not take from the mouth of labor the bread it has earned. This is the sum of good government."

In order to restore the nation, we must remove the sources of economic destruction and uncertainty and replace them with policies that will inspire certainty, confidence, and optimism. This will require a multilayered attack on the Obama agenda and institutional inertia while simultaneously advancing pro-growth, deregulatory, and limited government policies. In other words, doing the exact opposite of what Obama has done and using a blueprint similar to what President Reagan used to spur the tremendous economic recovery of the mid-1980s. Reagan's emphasis was on *economic liberty*, and that's the way forward today, just as it was thirty years ago.

Out of the gate, we should demand from our leaders a fundamental attitude adjustment on spending. By adding to the deficit, the feds are stopping businesses from borrowing to create jobs and blocking consumers from getting the capital they need. Treasury debt is up by about 40 percent over the past few years while commercial and consumer debt is down by roughly 20 percent. There's very little movement in the broader economy largely because the government is monopolizing the loan window. The entire economy is tied in to the spending levels of Washington.

We can no longer tolerate a federal government that refuses to restrain even the *growth* of government, never mind refusing to actually *cut* it. We need a fundamental change in the budget's engineering, something Representative Paul Ryan began to propose with the Republicans' 2012 and 2013 budgets. Ryan, the chief conservative green-eyeshade guy, has been hip-deep in budget matters for years. His ideas represent a clear path forward to fiscal sanity and ultimately the economic health of the nation. Implementing even parts of his plan may be exceedingly difficult, but it has already accomplished two critical things: (a) It has gotten our leadership and the public focused on the reality that we cannot go on spending and amassing debt at these levels. And (b) it recognizes that we're in an economic war—and its solutions embody the principles of the Happy Warrior. His program may or may not be the endgame, but it—like Obama's blown-off bipartisan deficit reduction commission—truthfully acknowledges the seriousness of the economic battle and the weapons and will we're going to need to fight it.

To start, we must aim to shrink spending by trillions of dollars over the next ten years. Ryan's budget calls for $6.2 trillion in savings. Other plans offer similar spending reduction targets. We've got to reduce the percentage of debt to GDP and adjust the spending trajectory to bring down the debt. Ryan's plan brings spending below 20 percent of GDP. Other recommendations go even further, aiming to push federal spending down to 18 percent. Getting federal spending down to those levels would reduce deficits by about $4.4 to $5 trillion. In the context of a national debt speeding toward $17 trillion, it's not a cure-all, but it's a start.

Several key reforms must be carried out to bring spending down. Spending on domestic government agencies should be kept at or below 2008 levels and frozen for five years, while unnecessary and redundant departments and bureaucracies should be eliminated entirely. EPA, I'm looking at you. If the government wants to study the mating habits of the North American egret, then they should get a private organization to fund it. Taxpayers don't exist to pay for bird sex. In addition, permanently banning earmarks; getting rid of Fannie Mae, Freddie Mac, and other tax dollar–sucking government-sponsored enterprises; and eliminating "green" and farm subsidies such as ethanol would also cut federal outlays significantly. Numerous subsidies also should be terminated or reformed, the federal workforce cut through slashed budgets and attrition, and wasteful spending at the Pentagon eliminated rather than hitting Defense through the Obama cuts and the pell-mell reductions coming in 2013, thanks to the Super Committee mega-choke.

We're in such a deep debt hole that if Ryan's reform plans were put in place and kept "as is" (which never happens in Washington over any duration), it would still take us twenty-eight years to balance the budget. Senator Rob Portman, who served on the Super Committee, has suggested a "dollar-for-dollar rule" as a permanent debt-limit policy. He argues that if we match debt increases with spending cuts, we could cut over $5 trillion over the next decade and balance the budget without raising tax rates. Representative Connie Mack has advanced the "Mack-Penny" plan, which would cut federal spending by 1 percent each year over the next six years, cap spending at 18 percent of GDP by 2018, and reduce overall spending by $7.5 trillion over the next decade. The Ryan, Portman, and Mack plans are serious proposals that deserve serious attention. We can debate their individual merits, but we can't stall deep spending cuts for much longer.

To spur economic growth, consequential tax reform is a critical companion element to spending cuts. Reform that would simplify the tax code and infuse it with pro-growth incentives would increase competitiveness and fire up job creation, consumer spending, and investment and other economic activity. Ryan suggested two rates: 25 percent and 10 percent. Steve Forbes has argued for years for a flat tax, in which all existing tax rates would be junked and replaced with a flat, across-the-board 17 percent rate and expanded exemptions for individuals and children so that a family of four would pay no income taxes on the first $36,000 of income. Furthermore, there would be no tax on Social Security, pensions, or personal savings, and his plan would zero out capital gains. Newt Gingrich proposed an optional 15 percent flat tax, and Herman Cain championed a 9 percent individual federal income tax rate, a 9 percent corporate tax rate, and a 9 percent national consumption tax. A flat federal income tax has the virtues of being simple and equitable; everyone would have to pay something, giving everyone a stake and a responsibility. Nations that currently have a flat tax include numerous former Soviet bloc states such as Hungary, the Czech Republic, Lithuania, Georgia, and my cabdriver's place of birth, Bulgaria. Iraq has also instituted a flat tax.

Other tax reform advocates have suggested scrapping all federal taxes on personal and corporate income and replacing them with a Fair Tax, which would be a national consumption tax on all retail sales that would provide rebates to poorer Americans to offset its regressive nature. Various concerns about revenue neutrality (but not about spending!), the development of underground economies, and general workability come up in discussions about a flat or fair tax, but they deserve real attention.

More traditional approaches to tax reform involve lowering the top individual and corporate rates from 35 percent to about 25 percent or below. The Simpson-Bowles deficit commission recommended reducing and flattening individual income tax rates to 8 percent, 14 percent, and a top rate of about 24 percent depending on how many and which tax breaks were eliminated. Another bipartisan deficit commission, Rivlin-Domenici, advised reducing tax rates to 15 and 27 percent. Simpson-Bowles recommended cutting the corporate tax rate to 26 percent and Rivlin-Domenici suggested a corporate rate of 27 percent in exchange for jettisoning multitudes of corporate subsidies and tax breaks. Obama and most Democrats wouldn't hear of it. Their mission is to soak the rich and hit their enemies, and that doesn't involve cutting tax rates on them. That's why we must insist on it, for the health of the economy as well as the body politic.

Of course, the Machiavellian Obama may pretend to move toward adopting some of the Simpson-Bowles recommendations before the 2012 election to appear newly "fiscally responsible." If he does, be aware of the charade. As his long record of profligacy shows, he has no intention of seeing through major fiscal reforms. Tax increases of any kind would damage an already fragile economy by taking more money out of what's left of the private economy. Besides, we hope that Republicans have finally learned their lesson about agreeing to Democrats' tax increases in exchange for promised spending cuts. In 1982 President Reagan agreed to a budget deal in which the Democrats promised to cut $3 in spending for every $1 in tax hikes. They lied. The tax hikes arrived but the cuts never did. George H. W. Bush was duped in similar fashion when he agreed to tax increases in exchange for spending cuts, which of course never materialized. Most Republicans have finally tired of sprinting eagerly toward the spending-cut football while Lucy the Democrats constantly pull it away.

We need a flatter and broader tax base, which would force everyone to pay something to the federal government rather than exempt about half from paying anything at all. With everyone having at least some skin in the game, everyone would then have a stake in how their money is spent. Demands for accountability would rise, as would revenues. We also need *permanent* tax cuts and incentives, not gimmicky temporary ones that fail to stimulate growth because they do nothing to reduce uncertainty. The kooks' goal is to institutionalize their new spending levels of 25 percent of GDP, which will then require ratcheting up tax rates forever. We cannot allow that spending level to become the "new normal." Most reform advocates—and most of the American people—agree that the current labyrinthine tax code discourages the working, saving, investing, risk taking, and hiring necessary for growth and prosperity. Tax reform along any of the proposed lines would also raise revenues not by raising tax rates but by stimulating growth, jobs, and greater wealth creation.

Structural reform of the big-budget monsters of Medicare, Medicaid, and Social Security is also necessary to save those programs from complete collapse. Those who oppose major reforms of these programs argue that they would be imperiled by exposure to major cuts and the whims of the market. And yet, if nothing is done, the programs will buckle under the weight of their own unsustainability. All significant entitlement reform proposals take pains to ensure that those at or near retirement age would be grandfathered in to the existing programs and benefits. There must, however, be responsible changes for future program recipients. Ryan suggested replacing the giant, opaque, and fraud-ridden slush fund of Medicare with the same kind of health care plan enjoyed by members of Congress. Later gaining the bipartisan support of Democratic senator Ron Wyden, Ryan built reform around the concept of a "premium support" system where seniors, with federal financial help, could choose from a menu of private plans, each offering Medicare-equivalent benefits and with providers competing for their business. In a premium-support model, Medicare would make payments to the plan chosen by the patient, subsidizing its costs while giving the beneficiary more freedom to make decisions over his own health. Furthermore, the Ryan-Wyden plan would still offer the traditional fee-for-service option and provide more help for lower-income Americans and those who are sicker and at higher risk for getting ill. Medicaid would be converted into a block-grant program to the states, in a way similar to the Clinton-GOP welfare reforms of the 1990s. This would allow the states to design a better range of options for their residents and increase the program's efficiency. Ryan proposed similar reforms to the food stamp program in order to eliminate the perverse incentives that reward states for adding to their rolls. These proposals have provoked the ire of the leftists and others who refuse to acknowledge the dangers of the status quo. But we mustn't get lost in the fog of political passions: these plans offer at least a meaningful starting point for reform, without which Medicare and Medicaid are going to end up in the emergency room, unable to be resuscitated.

On Social Security, Obama's deficit reduction commission made important recommendations to ensure its future solvency: gradually raising the retirement age and slowing the growth of benefits, new formulations of cost-of-living adjustment (COLA) calculations, and raising the payroll tax (something the Republicans did not embrace). The Democrats flat-out lie when they say that such reforms are designed to destroy Social Security. To the contrary: a truly radical conservative plan would eliminate Social Security (as well as Medicare and Medicaid) altogether. That's not what Ryan, the GOP, and the bipartisan Simpson-Bowles commission are suggesting. They are proposing practicable ways to get Social Security to sustainability so that it may continue for generations of seniors. The year 2011 was the first time the program paid out more than it took in, and with the repeated raiding of the "trust fund" for other spending and payroll tax holidays and the huge number of baby boomers now retiring, there's no way that Social Security can withstand the strain without critical reforms.

When Standard & Poor's downgraded the U.S. credit rating, it said that unless and until we pair entitlement reform with pro-growth policies in a coherent long-term plan to deal with our debt, our economy will continue to slide. And forget about ever seeing that AAA credit rating again.

No spending and deficit reform would be complete without addressing the Mother of All Entitlements, ObamaCare. We must pull the plug on that fiscal time bomb before it detonates. Until the entire law can be repealed, eliminating budgeting for ObamaCare is needed immediately in order to prevent it from squeezing the life out of our health care system like a hungry python. This would include eliminating budgeting for its unsustainable expansion of Medicaid and the new rationing board in charge of Medicare.

As critical as repealing ObamaCare is, however, reverting to the status quo ante isn't acceptable either. The health care system needed reform; it didn't need nationalization. Unless real market-based reform is undertaken, health care costs will consume 100 percent of our GDP within the next two decades, leaving no money for defense, Social Security, or anything else. ObamaCare will accelerate costs, not drive them down.

Market and patient-based health care reform proposals aim to truly lower costs by increasing competitiveness: allowing insurance to be sold across state lines, permitting insurance portability from job to job, enacting significant tort reform to lower malpractice costs, and empowering individuals by allowing them to control their own costs with personal health-savings accounts and other means. Real reform would also eliminate oppressive government mandates such as issue guarantee and other directives that force insurance companies to guarantee coverage and offer similar pricing to every person and family. Ryan's plan in particular would change the way the tax code treats health insurance. Employer-based coverage isn't taxed on par with wages, so the government encourages companies to offer coverage rather than provide higher wages and let employees buy their own insurance. When the value of the coverage goes up, so does the tax break to the company, resulting in inflationary incentives. Real reform would take the tax break and turn it into a tax credit for those who get their coverage from their employers as well as those who purchase it themselves. If you wanted to buy insurance that costs more than the credit, you'd pay the difference. The logical result would be that people would buy less expensive coverage and would be more likely to pay for regular medical expenses out-of-pocket, thus driving prices down. Individuals would have more control over their coverage, rather than having to rely on an employer, and because people wouldn't have to switch insurance as often, the preexisting-conditions issue would eventually diminish.

Any serious addressing of the spending and debt crisis should also involve a revision of the debt limit law. Because spending is so out of control, we're hitting the artificial debt-ceiling limits faster than ever. Soon, interest on the debt alone will destroy our economy. As economic writer Stephen Meister has proposed, instead of constantly raising the debt limit, we should be talking about changing the law so that rather than stopping future *borrowing* once the limit is reached, the law would ban future *spending* in excess of receipts—until the limit is raised. By changing the debt limit law to incorporate incentives to curb spending, even temporarily, the skyrocketing debt would at least be brought somewhat under control.

Others have argued for a balanced-budget amendment (BBA) to the Constitution as a way of forcing future Congresses to live within the country's fiscal means. Unless it's coupled with an enforceable spending cap of 18 to 20 percent of GDP and real entitlement reform, however, a BBA wouldn't be sufficient. Let's say that the government takes in $17 trillion one year through sky-high taxes. It could spend all $17 trillion and still call the budget balanced. Spending restraints and structural entitlement reform must be married to a BBA if it's to have any chance of enforcing fiscal responsibility. A BBA is necessary and those who support it have their hearts in the right place, but we need to ensure that the kooks and other big spenders don't rip that heart out and stomp all over it.

A lesson of history: in 1974, Congress, infuriated by President Nixon's relentless attempts to control spending, passed the ridiculously titled Congressional Budget and Impoundment Control Act, which actually did the exact opposite. The law blew out the president's ability to impound congressional spending and empowered Congress to go as hogwild on spending as possible. Federal spending exploded, helped by new "baseline" budgeting rules that automatically increase spending year over year.

Some, including Ryan, have indicated a desire to try to fix that destructive law rather than attempt a constitutional amendment. If it could be amended to toss baseline budgeting, restore presidential impoundment power, and require two-thirds majority to okay tax increases, the runaway train of spending and debt could be addressed now, without having to wait for a constitutional amendment.

Changing *what* the government spends is tough enough. Changing *how* government spends requires a full attitudinal adjustment. Without solid enforcement mechanisms, future Congresses would not be bound by the new rules, deals could be broken, and the spending and entitlement reforms could fall by the wayside. The irreversible and enforceable spending caps in the Ryan budget would ensure that Washington will only spend and tax what it needs to fill its constitutional duties. If we don't take real steps to cut spending and reform how government works, America will collapse beneath the weight of its own debt. The welfare state is over, from California to Greece. Now we have to make hard decisions to avert disaster. If those issues are dealt with in a comprehensive, serious, and urgent manner, job creation and economic growth will follow. In order to lift the cloud of uncertainty, government in all its forms must be brought under control. That includes rolling back Team Obama's job-killing Dodd-Frank financial regulation and oppressive EPA mandates.

It also means finally getting serious about developing our domestic sources of energy. Since the oil shocks of the early 1970s, we've had president after president pledge to pursue true energy independence. We're not even close, despite sitting atop more oil, gas, and coal resources than any other nation on earth. Permitting construction of the Keystone expansion was such a no-brainer in terms of jobs, energy independence, and private-sector investment that of course Obama torpedoed it. It should, however, be one of the first things on the next president's agenda. In addition, we must press for increased offshore and onshore drilling and exploration, including in the Arctic National Wildlife Refuge and the Bakken oil shale formation, and a resumption of timely permitting. Hydropower and nuclear energy should also be expanded, and the hog-wild dispersion of tens of billions of dollars in taxpayer subsidies to "green energy" boondoggles must stop: compete in the marketplace on your own, and either prosper or fold.

Hydraulic fracturing or hydrofracking, in which pressurized fluids are used to create fractures on rock formations to release natural gas or petroleum, should also be granted widespread approval. In states such as Pennsylvania where fracking is allowed, tens of thousands of jobs have been created around the industry, which has been found to be environmentally safe. One bill that's sure to receive a veto from Obama is H.R. 765, also known as the Go Frack Yourself Energy Bill of 2012. Put forth by House Republicans, it calls for natural gas exploration in some of America's most remote and dangerous terrain . . . like the scalp of Joe Biden, the rolling turkey-gobbler chins of Michael Moore, the armpits of Barbara Boxer, and the lunar surface of Al Gore's hairy back.

Also putting the government kibosh on economic growth: public-sector unions that maintain a stranglehold on the taxpayer in every state in the union. If the nation's fiscal crisis is to be resolved, we need more heroic Scott Walkers and John Kasiches and fewer give-away-the-store Jerry Browns. We need to elect and stand by leaders at the federal and state levels who will take on the entrenched interests, bust up the incestuous relationship between the government unions and the Democrats, and protect the taxpayer.

As this great nation has doled out its economic sovereignty, it's also voluntarily ceded its physical sovereignty. It is not in the national interest to have a never-ending swarm of illegal aliens pouring into the country unchecked. It is not in the national interest to have our security compromised by a porous border that permits drug cartels and international terrorists to waltz in. It is not in the national interest to have diseases once thought to have been eradicated come walking across our southern border. No foreigner has an inherent right to arrive in the United States to live without first going through the legal channels the American people, through their government, have approved. If you disregard those laws, then you simply have no right to come and stay. But instead of properly enforcing that basic supposition, we've made illegal aliens a protected group, and we've put up with sanctuary cities, limited deportations and workplace enforcement, and an essentially open border.

We've also put up with a failure to demand assimilation and the adoption of the American culture. Today, immigrant populations, both legal and illegal, have been allowed to siphon themselves off from American culture, often resulting in mini-nations within the larger one. They have been aided and abetted by the leftists, who have encouraged foreigners to remain foreign, have supplied them with grievances against America, and have tried to make America conform to them instead of the other way around. The basics of the kook playbook—grievance identification and multicultural celebration— are now applied routinely in our schools and universities. The result has been an America that is divided against itself.

Many Democrats and Republicans have argued for "a path to citizenship" for illegals already in country that includes proposals from making illegals go to the back of the line for legalization to outright amnesty. None of those plans are necessary, however, when we already have a "path to citizenship" called *legal* immigration. If you would like to come to the United States to live and work, we're happy to have you, but you must have enough respect for our nation that you will respect its most fundamental laws of entry. Legal immigration takes a long time and isn't cheap. But it *should* be difficult to get into the greatest republic on earth. And those who navigate that legal path become truly proud Americans, ennobling them *and* the country they've chosen.

In order to deal with the illegal alien invasion, a few steps should be taken immediately. The border must be enforced with more border patrol agents and National Guard units. High-tech security fences should be installed. Worksite enforcement should be ramped up. Employers should be required to prove worker citizenship. Immigration data should be readily available to other federal agencies and to the states. Visa compliance efforts should be improved so illegals cannot overstay their visas and fall through the cracks. Violent criminals and ideologues should be expelled and blocked from further entry, as France, Australia, and Switzerland have done. English should be made the official language, and photo identification should be required at every polling place in America before anyone is permitted to vote (despite Attorney General Eric Holder's efforts to block it). And the states should be permitted to pass their own laws concurrent to federal laws so they may be able to enforce the nation's immigration laws if the feds will not or cannot do it.

Remember: the Happy Warrior is fighting two wars: a domestic war for freedom and a foreign one for survival. They are interlocking pieces of the same national challenge. Just as we mustn't tire of the struggle at home, we mustn't grow weary of the external fight to reestablish American power and influence abroad.

America and the World. The world is a complex web of vexing problems, complicated issues, terrifying dangers, and unsavory trade-offs. As with our domestic challenges, there are no easy answers. There are simply policies that have a better chance of serving America's interests than others. When the United States happily embraces and unabashedly exercises its strong, leading role, our interests are better served than when we abdicate that role and allow our friends to flail and enemies to advance. Given our economic constraints, projecting U.S. power will be more difficult. And given the complexities of the issues, there are no paths to guaranteed national security; there are only potentially more effective ones.

A superpower cannot remain so if it willfully cedes its claim to global exceptionalism. "Leading from behind" must be discarded on the pile of other strategies that have hobbled the United States. American primacy must be restored if we are to avoid a global cataclysm sparked by our continuing weakness, both real and perceived. As President Nixon once put it, "There is no substitute for American power."

The first priority should be to recognize the five elements of kookdom that have so weakened American influence.

First, one-worldism. This is the kooks' belief that no nation is superior to any other, that we're all equally responsible for other nations and peoples, and that a one-world system of governance and economics is morally superior to a system of sovereign states. They also believe that this is the only way to submerge U.S. power once and for all.

Second, redistributionism. This is the kook principle that elements of American greatness should be redistributed around the world to clear a smooth path to one-worldism.

Third, international social "justice." This is the logical extension of the first two points as they chase global "equality" and "justice."

Fourth, zero-sum calculus. This is the kook presupposition that if you are deprived of something, then someone else took it from you. And if you have it, then you must be forced to give it up to someone who's lacking it. When carried out on a worldwide scale, its objective is to stop the growth of the wealthier nations by redirecting their assets to poorer ones.

And fifth is the belief that America is the root of much of the injustice, inequality, and turmoil in the world and therefore should pay for its sins by mortgaging its claim on global dominance. Most of the Obama foreign policy can be explained by these interrelated leftist beliefs. Just as they do domestically, the kooks step in to assume responsibility for all other actors, regardless of how anti-American they are. We have seen repeatedly from Team Obama an assumption of responsibility for the bad behavior of Iran, the Muslim Brotherhood, Syria, the Palestinians, the Taliban, North Korea, Russia, China, Venezuela, and others. They have made the United States assume the burden of responsibility for the conflicts rather than demand responsibility from the other parties. And that has led to a devastating moral equivalence among the United States and other nations and groups and an undermining of our global exceptionalism.

We've got to "de-kookify" our national security.

The Happy Warrior's approach first requires the reestablishment of a central organizing principle for American foreign policy that's based on U.S. strength and values rather than defeatism and decline. Our security depends on the hard power of a healthy, growing economy and a formidable defense. But it also depends on nurturing democracy, human rights, and liberalization around the world. When we stand firmly for those things, our hard power is infused with moral clarity. Support—moral, diplomatic, political, economic, and, if appropriate, military—should be given to those crying out for greater freedom. Those facing down brutal regimes and terrorists should know that the United States stands with them. American values must once again be made clear and actionable.

The second major priority must be to shore up our military strength. The planned over $1 trillion in defense cuts over the next ten years, from Obama's announced cuts to the additional ones set to automatically kick in in January 2013, should be stopped. No responsible commander in chief should be willing to allow our defenses to be gutted to such an extent that we will be left irretrievably crippled, unable to defend ourselves, our interests, and our allies, and incapable of projecting power where it's needed. The Pentagon is not immune from wasteful spending. Smart cuts would involve targeting the significant overspending and waste throughout the Defense Department. As former secretary of the Navy John Lehman has pointed out, we won World War II with fewer than 100,000 civilian defense bureaucrats. Today there are over 750,000. As with the rest of government, the Pentagon has grown bloated. Let's cut back the unnecessary spending and preserve the sinews of our strength. A strong national security policy begins with a fearsome U.S. military that no enemy of America would be tempted to challenge. In the fierce budget battles ahead, one thing must be made clear: none of the domestic priorities will matter if we're all dead.

Next, diplomacy is critical and should be utilized effectively to support rather than weaken our interests. Under Obama, our relations with some of our closest allies have frayed. Our special relationships with Great Britain, Canada, and Israel need particular care. Building trust again may be difficult after Obama's breaches, but we ought to make clear that the United States will no longer betray them in ways big and small. The missile defense shield once set for Eastern Europe should be revisited, and the United States should move ahead with other missile defense planning. We should be prepared for Russian unhappiness on this point, but we should also be prepared to do what is in America's interests. Furthermore, NATO ought to be reassured that the United States is back to play a leading role, both militarily and diplomatically—and not "from behind."

Israel should once again have the full diplomatic confidence and military support of the United States as it navigates its increasingly dangerous neighborhood. Israel's enemies should understand that acts of aggression against the Jewish state will not be excused by the United States. There can't be any sunlight between us, particularly on the issues of Iran's nuclear weapons program and the rise of Islamists across the Middle East. This raises the key question of preemption: if Israel is hit, will we retaliate on its behalf? When nuclear weapons are involved, we've got to act *before* acts of aggression can take place. America's policy remains deliberately vague on that question. Furthermore, on the Israeli-Palestinian conflict, the United States should stop buying into the Arab propaganda that the crisis controls much else in the Middle East. It does not. The next president should act immediately to move the U.S. embassy from Tel Aviv to the capital city of Jerusalem. In 2009, Obama postponed the move, despite the fact that this relocation policy is based on a law that was passed by Congress in 1995. We must also stop funding the Palestinian Authority until it not only quits inciting terror but affirmatively sells the idea of peace based on an acknowledgment of the Jewish state's right to exist. Until this point is reached, any notion of a "peace process" is fraudulent.

The goal of Hamas is the destruction of Israel in stages. For the United States to press Israel to make any kind of a "deal" with the Hamas-Fatah gang would be strategically irresponsible and morally reprehensible. Furthermore, the United States should quit negotiating away Israel's position in public and facilitate private talks only if they are in Israel's interest. More than ever, Israel needs the backing of the United States through weapons sales, trade, and diplomatic and moral support. This might include a U.S.-run program with Domino's Pizza and the Mossad, the Israeli covert ops organization, to deliver large pizzas covered in bacon, ham, and pepperoni to every member of Hamas.

Our relationship with the Iraqi government also requires serious attention. Obama's decision to withdraw precipitously all U.S. troops at the end of 2011 has imperiled our hard-won gains. Prime Minister Nouri al-Maliki has engaged increasingly in authoritarian abuses, from mass arrests to crackdowns on free speech, and we are now far less able to guide his government toward greater liberalization and pro-Western policies. We should focus on repairing that relationship and, if possible, consider reintroducing a modest military force if the Iraqis so desire to ensure that the gains we've achieved are not lost in a hail of Islamist violence and Iranian-bred chaos.

Furthermore, enemies of the United States should understand that the days of no-strings-attached olive branches are over. If they want to genuinely extend their hands in peace, we will prudently consider their overtures. If, however, they continue belligerent actions and marches toward weapons of mass destruction, we will not merely offer up empty threats. We will say what we mean, mean what we say, and follow through if necessary.

Arguably the gravest immediate threat to the United States and the world is a Khomeinist Iran armed with nuclear weapons. America will have zero credibility if, after years of warning about the "unacceptability" of an Iranian nuclear weapon, Tehran goes nuclear. Traditional containment and doctrines of "mutual assured destruction" may not work against the fanatical and apocalyptic Islamic regime the way they did against the secular and rational Soviet communists. Iran must understand that if it continues its pursuit of a nuclear weapon, the United States may hit it with an array of countermeasures, from slapping on truly strangling sanctions to placing a naval blockade against Iran in the Persian Gulf to engaging in ramped-up covert sabotage of its nuclear and other infrastructure to an outright military attack on its suspected nuclear installations. Any action may provoke Iranian retaliation, as Tehran has previously threatened to strike Israel and the United States at home and abroad and block oil exports through the Strait of Hormuz. We've got to be prepared for whatever the Iranian response may be and persevere with our own aggressive approach. We are in a war. The choice may very well be a tough military confrontation now or a much more brutal and widespread cataclysm later. In order to avoid having Iran plunge us into a nuclear hell, we've got to be ready to act soon, since, according to the IAEA's final 2011 report on Iran's nuclear progress, Tehran is moving at a fast clip.

Some foreign policy elites have warned that if we or the Israelis strike Iran's nuclear weapons facilities, the Iranian people would rally to the regime. A 2007 "guerrilla poll" of Iranians appeared to support that contention: 90 percent of Iranians polled said they'd "fight back against the attackers," while just 5 percent said they'd "welcome" such an attack. After the bloody 2009 regime crackdown, however, the Iranian people changed their minds. In an August 2010 poll of the same group of Iranians, only 9 percent said they'd "fight back," while a stunning 62 percent said they'd "welcome" an attack "*if* it results in toppling the regime."

Regime change in Tehran must be the goal of any U.S. policy. The majority of the Iranian people are with us, but they need to know that we are with them. Many Iranian dissidents complain that our Voice of America/Radio Farsi sounds like it's run by the regime, while Israel's Radio Farsi actually broadcasts messages of freedom and interviews with dissidents. Obama had no problem pushing out our allies Mubarak and Gadhafi. We should have even less of a problem helping to push out our mortal enemies in Tehran.

Russian and Chinese obstruction of anti-regime measures at the UN Security Council is a huge problem, as is their (and others') continuing nuclear assistance to Iran. There are no easy ways around their intransigence. The best practicable option for the United States is to work with like-minded parties, such as the Europeans and Israelis, to try to buckle the Iranian nuclear program and, if necessary, to act unilaterally against the threat. Too often, we have bluffed, only to have Iran call our bluff and continue working on the bomb (knowing there would be no U.S.-led action). This is an exceedingly difficult problem; if it were easy, previous presidents would have dealt with it already. Any policy choice involves huge trade-offs, and the consequences could range from the unpleasant to the devastating. But it's got to be faced squarely—and soon—before we're forced to deal with a bigger convulsion down the road.

We should also make clear to Moscow and Beijing that the United States is unwavering in its support of our allies in Europe and in Asia, and that any attempt to intimidate them by extortion or force will be met with a vigorous response. The ill-conceived "reset" with Russia is long over, as Moscow reverts to greater authoritarianism and steps up its direct challenges to the United States over missile defense, Iran, and our debt. We should signal that we're no longer going to bend over backward to prove to Moscow that we're a steady partner; instead, the burden will be on Russia to prove to the United States that *it's* a willing and trustworthy partner.

China is a direct competitor of the United States. Our challenge will be to try to manage the competition while keeping it from deteriorating into militant hostility. We'll be walking a very fine line: previous attempts to lean on China with regard to its currency manipulation and other unfair trade practices have produced few results. One of the most effective ways to deal with a rising Beijing will be to bring down our debt so that China will have less economic leverage over us in the coming decades. The United States should also be more active in the Pacific by carrying out more frequent naval exercises and giving greater care to our diplomatic and economic relationships with Japan, South Korea, Taiwan, Singapore, Australia, the Philippines, Vietnam, Cambodia, and Thailand. Each of those bilateral relationships is critically important to our regional security, and each nation has its own complex set of concerns. Obama began an important reorientation of our foreign policy toward Asia. The next administration should follow it up with even deeper strategic partnerships with our regional friends.

North Korea remains the problem child of Asia, and, after a leadership succession in 2012, it's even more unpredictable. It should be made clear to Kim Jong-un that the policy of the United States will no longer be to try to bribe his regime to halt its nuclear weapons program, only to have it take our money to sell nukes to rogues such as Iran, Syria, and Burma. While we've wasted years gassing around in the Six-Party Talks with North and South Korea, China, Russia, and Japan, Pyongyang has developed and tested nuclear weapons and honed its ballistic missile program. The days of rewarding their bad behavior have got to end. We should use whatever influence we may have with Beijing to lean on its client. That may prove difficult, as it has been in the past, but given that sanctions have shown limited utility, China is the most accessible diplomatic route we've got. Furthermore, we should make clear that we've had enough of the North's attacks on our ally in the South and if its regional bullying continues, the United States is prepared to respond in a variety of ways. Those options may range from increasing diplomatic and economic pressure to military action. The deceased North Korean dictator Kim Jong Il loved wearing women's clothes, specifically high-heeled shoes. I wonder if his son does too. If so, then perhaps a way to lure the regime away from its militant ways is to load up a fleet of B-52 bombers with crates of Jimmy Choos and Manolo Blahniks and carpet-bomb the entire country.

In the broader Middle East, a new Iron Curtain is now falling, thanks largely to Obama's pro-Islamist foreign policy. Here too we are in a war, whether we want to see it or not. The Islamists now dominating the Middle East should understand that the United States will not play footsie with jihadists in any form, whether they are the violent jihadists of al-Qaeda or the stealth jihadists of the Muslim Brotherhood and other groups. There must be no negotiation with self-professed enemies of the United States that actively and openly seek our destruction. The United States should try to minimize the damage to our security from their rise in places like Egypt, Libya, Syria, Yemen, Tunisia, and Morocco by supporting and encouraging genuinely pro-American and pro-Western factions in these nations to at least try to blunt the carefully calibrated but determined Islamism of the new governments. U.S. aid to nations dominated by the Brotherhood and other enemies of the United States should end altogether. In the case of Egypt, if the peace treaty with Israel is abrogated, the United States must immediately end assistance, consider transferring it to Israel, and make sure our ally knows that we will back it with every resource. We should also try to correctly identify secular, pro-Western elements (as we failed to do with the Libyan and Syrian "rebels") and support them much the way we supported Solidarity and other pro-Western forces behind the old European Iron Curtain.

Elsewhere around the neighborhood, we need to deal straightforwardly with several nations playing their own double games. Our relationship with nuclear-armed Pakistan is particularly fraught; we need its assistance in fighting al-Qaeda, the Taliban, the Haqqani terror network and other extremists in the region, and it enjoys our military and financial aid. The powerful Pakistani security service, the Inter-Services Intelligence (ISI), is shot through with Islamists who continue to threaten the regime. If they were to gain control of Islamabad's nuclear weapons, the world would immediately be a far more dangerous place. (It was under President Bill Clinton that Pakistan developed and tested nuclear weapons in direct violation of the Non-Proliferation Treaty. Let's hope Obama isn't Captain of the Dumb-Ship to the point where Iran is now able to hoodwink another Democrat and develop a nuke.)

We cannot continue to allow Pakistan to encourage militants to smuggle weapons into Afghanistan to kill U.S. soldiers and to allow al-Qaeda, the Taliban, and members of the Haqqani network to cross the Afghan-Pakistan border to give aid and comfort to our enemies. Since September 11, 2001, we have given Pakistan $20 billion in aid. The Enhanced Partnership with Pakistan Act of 2009 committed $7.5 billion to Islamabad over five years, but it conditioned the dough on Pakistan's behavior. We need to make clear to Pakistan that if it continues to support terrorism, spread nuclear technology to rogue regimes, and lie to us about all of it, we will eliminate U.S. aid, halt intelligence cooperation, continue drone air strikes in country, and possibly declare Pakistan a state sponsor of terror and impose sanctions. Because Pakistan is so central strategically to our efforts to combat extremism in the region, any of these actions would involve a complex balancing act. But Pakistan must believe that our threats are not empty and that we have every intention of carrying them out. Furthermore, Islamabad should understand that if the United States moved on any of these policies, it would not be able to retaliate effectively and that the United States would seek to develop a strategy for Afghanistan that would not be dependent on Pakistan's assistance. If, however, Pakistan ends its support for terrorism, helps us battle terrorist networks, and stops its aid to our enemies in Afghanistan, we should be prepared to increase our economic, military, and political aid. A productive relationship with a stable Islamabad is far preferable to a hostile one, but we cannot continue rewarding bad behavior. As with any deal with the devil, our relationship with Pakistan involves deep trade-offs. Our job is to walk carefully the line between working with the devil and letting him run roughshod over us.

Interestingly, Obama made a strategically critical decision to strengthen the U.S. relationship with India, Pakistan's great rival. An economic powerhouse and functioning democracy, India shares many of our geopolitical and economic interests. If we continue to nurture our relationship with India properly, it could serve as a valuable counterweight to growing Chinese power. If neglected by the United States, however, India could seek shelter in alliances with Beijing, Moscow, and elsewhere. Furthermore, India has a substantial Muslim population, borders Pakistan, and is dealing with the threat of Islamic terror, providing another area of bilateral cooperation. India's regional dominance and shared values make it a valued partner for the United States—and the next president should work to develop further the Washington–New Delhi relationship.

Afghanistan presents another complicated challenge. As Kabul hosts U.S. troops, it's also cozying up to our enemies in neighboring Pakistan and Iran. Our relationship needs extra care, as Afghanistan might easily slip back into the grip of extremism and terror, aimed at its own people as well as at the United States. Obama's cynical policy of negotiating with the Taliban in order to expedite a full U.S. withdrawal is the ultimate in getting into bed with the devil. Soon enough, the devil devours you. There are no meaningful, peace-seeking negotiations to be had with entities for whom "peace" is achieved when you are either subjugated or dead. Whatever continued assistance we offer to the Karzai government should be made more conditional on anticorruption reform, political liberalization, and, as with Pakistan, the degree of helpfulness the government provides to us. If our commanders request it, the next president should try to maintain a significant enough presence to give our military efforts there more time to succeed. That may be a tough political sell, given the war's length, budgetary constraints, and an inflamed region, but if the full Obama withdrawal is allowed to proceed, Afghanistan—like Iraq—may soon collapse into a hotbed of terror and oppression once again. And we may end up facing a far more dangerous and expensive threat.

Traditional allies Saudi Arabia and Turkey have also been engaged in duplicity, with Riyadh long supporting both terrorism and our efforts to fight it, and Ankara growing increasingly Islamist, cuddling up to Iran, and acting to turn Syria into a client state. The Saudis were particularly miffed over Obama's rapid and dispassionate disposal of Egypt's Hosni Mubarak, a close friend of the Saudi regime. King Abdullah reportedly had at least one contentious telephone call with Obama over his handling of the Arab Spring there, and the relationship has been strained ever since. The Saudis are not saints, particularly in their support for terrorism and their leading role in OPEC (Organization of the Petroleum Exporting Countries) price extortion, but they have been critical players in terms of ensuring the global oil supply and serving as a counterweight to Iran. Tehran's march toward a nuclear weapon and its escalating belligerence have created broad agreement among Israel, the Gulf states, and the West that Iran poses a dangerous threat that must be dealt with aggressively.

Meanwhile, we should also very carefully seek to encourage reform there and in neighboring Bahrain. Those regimes seem more airtight, but no government is completely immune from upheaval. As we saw in Egypt, if more moderate parties cannot organize, governments could face internal pressures both organic and stoked by outside powers such as Iran. We shouldn't expect the home of Mecca and Medina to become a secular, tolerant, democratic lover of human rights. But we should try to influence Riyadh into taking on incremental changes to preempt a possible cracking of its brittle regime. If Saudi Arabia were destabilized, the region would be thrown into unprecedented turmoil and the global economy would be shaken to the core.

In Ankara, democratically elected Turkish prime minister Recep Tayyip Erdoğan has moved his country away from its previously secular and Western orientation and toward Islamism and America's enemies. Europe is partly responsible, as it has rejected the Turks' requests for membership in the European Union for more than a decade. If Europe says no to Turkey, and America says no to Turkey, then perhaps one day soon, it will be Iran or Russia eating a Turkey sandwich. The United States should be doing what it can in terms of diplomatic, political, and economic incentives to move Turkey back to a pro-Western stance. "Who lost Turkey?" might be as devastating a question as "Who lost Egypt?"

And in Tripoli, because of Obama and the Europeans' failure to guide Libya's revolution, the Islamists are running wild and may turn that nation into a base for al-Qaeda and other terrorists—a base much closer to Europe and the United States than was Afghanistan. It may not be too late to try to move Libya to a more pro-Western orientation. If Gadhafi were able to see the virtues of working with the United States, his successors may as well, but the United States must move fast to get in there before the militants become completely entrenched.

In dealing with terrorism more broadly, Team Obama has seen the virtues of using sophisticated drones to locate, identify, and take out terrorist suspects around the world—until it allowed the biggest state sponsor of terror, Iran, to get its hands on one. Once Tehran was assumed to have passed off the drone technology to Moscow, Beijing, and who knows who else, our stealth technology was rendered more vulnerable. Former vice president Dick Cheney reported that he heard that Obama was presented with three options to either recover or destroy the drone before the Iranians could take possession of it. Cheney said Obama rejected all three. Permitting Tehran to get the drone was the quintessential example of Obama redistributing American power to the world. Take one of our most high-tech defenses and give it to a sworn enemy? Why not? America's greatness belongs to everyone!

Nuclear proliferation also remains a major problem, with the nuclear pipeline constantly flowing among Russia, China, North Korea, Iran, Pakistan, Syria, and Venezuela, among other rogue nations. The sensitive job of identifying and securing nuclear materials and enforcing international protocols against their transfer ought to be of the highest priority for the next administration.

Furthermore, Obama chose to kill high-level al-Qaeda terrorists rather than deal with the legal hassles of interrogation and detention, but he has opted to keep open the detainee facilities at both Guantánamo Bay and Bagram, Afghanistan. Capturing terrorist suspects and subjecting them to aggressive interrogation can yield valuable intelligence that disrupts terrorist attacks and saves American lives—as it has over the past ten years. In some cases, killing them may be the right choice; in others, capturing and interrogating them may be wiser. We desperately need a coherent legal framework and detainee policy going forward. We need something beyond Barack Obama and Eric Holder sitting a bunch of al-Qaeda terrorists in a circle and playing Duck, Duck, Goose to decide who goes where.

There are many other areas of the world that are crying out for greater U.S. attention, such as Latin America, which continues to be roiled by leftists, drug cartels, migration issues, and the growing influence of China there, and Africa, which continues to struggle with the AIDS epidemic, rampant corruption, grinding poverty, and spreading Islamism. Since we're broke, we're severely constrained in terms of what we can do in those regions, but we should use diplomatic and political levers to try to guide greater pro-democratic, pro-market outcomes that will eventually help to alleviate some of their seemingly intractable problems.

The United States also needs to put the United Nations back in its proper place. While the body has its uses, particularly with some refugee missions, it is a scandal-plagued viper's pit of tyrant love and rampant anti-Americanism and anti-Semitism. It's also hyper-resistant to any kind of reform that would bring greater effectiveness, greater transparency, greater accountability, and less moral relativism. While the United States should remain in the UN, we should make clear that we will use the body when possible but we will not be used *by* it. International organizations will have our leadership and participation, but only when it serves our interests.

The days of a servile, apologetic, groveling, and weak America need to come to a close. And a new day of strong, vibrant, unapologetic, muscular American global leadership must dawn. In this new world, enemies will once again respect and fear us, allies will trust us, and those who want to challenge us will think twice. Good-bye, kook foreign policy; hello to the Happy Warrior approach.

The Battle Cry of the Happy Warrior

Hard pressed on my right. My center is yielding. Impossible to maneuver. Situation excellent. I attack.

—*Marshal Ferdinand Foch, France, 1914*

In 1977, Margaret Thatcher, then the leader of the opposition in Great Britain, delivered a major speech to the Zurich Economic Society. By then, it was clear to almost everyone that under the "old" Labour government, Britain was weak, flailing, lost, crushed by deadening statism. The country was broke and held hostage by its powerful unions, which used paralyzing strikes to extort huge demands. Garbage piled up on every corner, courtesy of striking sanitation workers. Dead bodies rotted in the open air, thanks to striking gravediggers. Inefficient state-run industries and suffocating regulations had turned the once-great empire into a socialist Third World backwater. The moment was ripe for a strong leader who refused to resign herself and her nation to such a fate. The moment was ripe for someone to reverse the economic stagnation caused by the corrosive effects of socialism and to tell the truth about what reversing national decline would require. The moment was ripe for an alternative based on pro-growth capitalism, individual freedom, and moral leadership. The moment was right for Margaret Thatcher, Happy Warrior.

"Where the state is too powerful," she said, "efficiency suffers and morality is threatened. Britain in the last two or three years provides a case study of why collectivism will not work. It shows that 'progressive' theory was not progressive. On the contrary, it proved retrograde in practice. That is a lesson that democrats all over the world should heed."

Thatcher didn't shrink from making the brutally honest case against socialism: "In the end," she had thundered, "the real case against socialism is not its economic inefficiency, though on all sides there is evidence of that. Much more fundamental is its basic immorality."

Ah, a leader who was unafraid to make the moral case for the free market! A leader who rejected declinism with every fiber of her being and who made it her life's work to reverse it by cutting taxes, restraining spending, privatizing industries, deregulating, reining in inflation, subduing the unions, and flexing British military muscle. The dislocation was severe and the political opposition intense; at its lowest, her job approval sank to 23 percent. She was, however, ultimately vindicated by a long, sustained cycle of economic growth and national optimism. In the end, she had defied the critics, cowards, thugs, and defeatists to do what they had deemed impossible: she had restored Britain's greatness.

In her Zurich speech, Thatcher also did something as critical as laying out a policy program. She hit a powerfully sunny note: "Yet I face the future with optimism. Our ills are creating their own antibodies. Just as success generates problems, so failure breeds the will to fight back and the body politic strives to restore itself."

Thatcher struck a chord that made her and her political soul mate, President Reagan, extremely effective reformers. They believed in their nations. They believed in their people. And they believed in the regenerative dynamism of liberty. In times of crisis, we have always created our own antibodies for survival, mending, and a return to full health. This is why Obama will fail when it comes to his single biggest goal. He wanted to be a transformational president, but instead he has been merely a transitional one because he always refused to take into account the larger view of how his short-term disruptions to the American dream would be judged by history once they'd been completely undone in the ensuing years, which is almost a certainty.

The great American comeback begins with each of us. It's up to us to make the "what the @$%&! just happened?" moment an anomaly in American history, a brief aberration that did a lot of damage but is fixable with the right leadership and policies. The circumstances of today's American crisis are different from those faced by Reagan and Thatcher, but the basic challenge is largely the same: to reverse corrosive leftism and its attendant decline. We need to take this "what the @$%&! just happened" moment and turn it into a question on *Jeopardy!* under the category "Weird American Acid Trips."

But we've got to move fast. Time is not on our side as the tentacles of kookdom wrap themselves around our governing institutions, private sector, and every other aspect of our lives. After an unmistakable electoral repudiation of Obama, his leftist agenda, and those who pushed it, the next key to unleashing America is to get the rest of us to uproot the toxic and ravenous nanny state, replace it with the limited government, economically free model, and do the hard work of rallying the public to the comeback. None of this will be easy, and success is not guaranteed. The problems are immense, the entitlement culture is entrenched, and the kooks will not go down without a NatGeo Serengeti-style fight. But America still possesses huge strengths economically, politically, militarily, culturally, and constitutionally.

Most significant, it has *us*. At every major turning point—the founding, the Civil War, the Great Depression, World War II, the civil rights struggle, the malaise of the late 1970s—we have produced leaders who were prepared for the fight to restore the nation. But it was the American people who led the charge. We have always known that we don't have to settle for anything less than the Founders' ideal and that we don't have to put up with con men and other sundry kooks as they butcher the Constitution. This time is no different. Team Obama and his wingmen moved with all deliberate speed, and so must we.

Most important, we must do it as Happy Warriors, infusing the ferocity of the mission with an optimistic, joyful love of America. Nattering nabobs of negativity don't score big in battles over the future. Reagan and Thatcher succeeded largely because their messages were correct on policy and positive in attitude. We need to summon courage and selflessness. We need to tell the truth about what's happened and what's required—of all of us—to get us back on the rails. If we want America restored to AAA status *in every way*, we're going to have to do it ourselves. Disaster may be all around us but, like Marshal Foch, we say, "Situation excellent." And we attack.

This is our battle cry, Happy Warriors. It's time to get back to the idea of Big America (as opposed to Big-Government America): high growth economically, powerful militarily, strong politically, dynamic culturally, and adventurous from sea to space. It's time to reclaim American Exceptionalism—without exception.

The path toward national salvation will be arduous and long, but we must undertake it lest we truly do lose our exceptional country to the malign forces of redistributionism and degradation. On the day that exceptionalism was codified in the Declaration of Independence, the Liberty Bell rang out. A witness to history said, "It rang like it meant something." This nation of reinvigorated Happy Warriors must do the hard work to get that Liberty Bell ringing like it means something again. We are, after all, *the* nation of renewal, opportunity, and reinvention.

At the end of *The Wizard of Oz*, Dorothy is told by Glinda the Good Witch that the power to go home was within her all along. And so it is with us. The ability to "fundamentally restore" America to its timeless principles has been with us all along. And like Dorothy, we had to learn that for ourselves. If we summon our true Happy Warrior spirit, grit, and determination, we can make America *America* again. We can go home again, and at the same time, America—our birthright, our heritage, our home—will return to us.

ACKNOWLEDGMENTS

Over dinner one night in June 2011, I mentioned to a close friend that I was thinking about writing a new book but was still unclear as to its focus. Our attention then turned to the crushing of our individual freedoms at the hands of Barack Obama. As we listed example after example of the kooks' madness, we realized that their extremist agenda had led to not just tangible damage to the economy, the body politic, and the Constitution but to the nation's very psyche. "What the @$%&! just happened?" I sighed. We then both exclaimed, "*That's the title!*" So my first thanks go to my wonderful friend Bettina Zilkha for inspiring me to undertake this project.

Throughout this process, I benefited from the support and encouragement of many others. I extend my deep gratitude to Adam Bellow, editorial director at Broadside Books, and HarperCollins senior vice president Jonathan Burnham, who enthusiastically championed this book from the start, to Kathryn Whitenight, who supervised the manuscript expertly, and to Jessica Gavora, whose first-rate editorial advice kept the work focused, lean, and flowing. Thanks also to my agent, Mel Berger, at William Morris Endeavor, for cheerfully nudging me—more than once—to keep going.

Several great friends also took part of this journey with me. For their hilarious contributions and for *always* making me laugh, big thanks to A. J. Rice and Matthew Fox. Their talents are unmatched. For superb research support, my gratitude to Briana Pashcow, and for her help in verifying her great-grandfather's quotes, my thanks to Margaret Hoover and the dedicated folks at the Herbert Hoover Presidential Library and Museum. And for their incomparable wizardry with hair and makeup, I thank Michelle Frazzetta and Ashana Morgan for my cover look—and for their invaluable friendship.

Of course, no writing project would be complete without sundry technical nightmares. My heartfelt thanks to John Yoo, who rescued me from an ancient Word program, multiple computer viruses, and one paralyzing crash, and to the two Mikes, who kept me writing through Hurricane Irene's weeklong blackout by powering my laptop from their truck. Couldn't have done it without you guys. Literally.

I am particularly thankful to my remarkable family—my mom, Patricia, and my sister, Jocelyn, and brother-in-law, Alan—for their boundless love and support.

My deepest and enduring gratitude goes to Bill, from whom I received indispensable ideas and inspiration for this project and from whom I receive extraordinary wisdom, joy, encouragement, generosity, friendship, and love every day.

And finally, I will always hold a special place in my heart for President Richard Nixon, who gave me the most incredible opportunity to learn from a master. He was an exceptional mentor, friend, and patriot, who showed me again and again that an American life is a uniquely blessed one—and why it's so worth defending.

INDEX

ABOUT THE AUTHOR

Monica Crowley is a political and foreign affairs analyst for the Fox News Channel, and hosts the nationally syndicated radio program *The Monica Crowley Show*. She has also been a regular panelist on *The McLaughlin Group*. She served as foreign policy assistant to former president Richard Nixon from 1990 until his death in 1994, and wrote two bestsellers about her experiences: *Nixon Off the Record* and *Nixon in Winter*. She has also written for the *New Yorker*, the *Wall Street Journal*, the *Los Angeles Times*, *Newsweek*, and the *New York Post*. She holds two master's degrees and a doctorate from Columbia University.

www.MonicaMemo.com

Twitter: @MonicaCrowley